MAKING OUR MEDIA

Global Initiatives
Toward a Democratic Public Sphere

VOLUME I
Creating New Communication Spaces

edited by

Clemencia Rodríguez
The University of Oklahoma

Dorothy Kidd
University of San Francisco

Laura Stein
The University of Texas at Austin

HAMPTON PRESS, INC.
CRESSKILL, NJ 07626

Library of Congress Cataloging-in-Publication Data

Making our media : global initiatives toward a democratic public sphere / Clemencia Rodríguez, Dorothy Kidd, Laura Stein [editors].
    p. cm.
 Includes bibliographical references and index.
 ISBN 978-1-57273-792-1 (hardbound) -- ISBN 978-1-57273-793-8 (paperbound)
 1. Local mass media. 2. Mass media--Social aspects. 3. Mass media--Political aspects. 4. Digital media--Political aspects. 5. Information society. 6. Information technology--Social aspects. 7. Communication, International--Social aspects. I. Rodríguez, Clemencia. II. Kidd, Dorothy. III. Stein, Laura.
 P96.L62M35 2009
  302.23--dc22
                                    2009018270

Hampton Press, Inc.
23 Broadway
Cresskill, NJ 07626

CONTENTS

SECTION III
EXAMINING INTERNAL STRUCTURES, DYNAMICS AND FORMS

SECTION IV
OUR MEDIA AND THE STATE

LIST OF FIGURES

ACRONYMS

ABC Australian Broadcasting Corporation
AWFT African Women Filmmaker's Trust (Zimbabwe)
AID Alternative for India Development
AIR All India Radio
AMARC World Association of Community Radio
APC Association of Progressive Communicators
AREDMAG Asociación Red de Emisoras Comunitarias del Magdalena Medio (Colombia)

BBC British Broadcasting Corporation

CASET Cassette Production Facility (South Africa)
CDS Center for Digital Storytelling - US
CMAQ Centre des media alternatifs du Québec
CINEP Centro de Investigacíon y Educacíon Popular)

DDS Deccan Development Society (India)

ELN Ejéricto de Liberacíon Nacional (Colombia)
EZLN Zapatista Army of National Liberation (Mexico)

GAD gender and development

ICT Information and communications technology
IMC Indymedia Center
IMF International Monetary Fund
ICASA Independent Communications Authority of South Africa
INI National Indigenist Institute (Mexico)
ICTV Indigenous Community Television (Australia)
IDASA Institute for Democracy in South Africa
ILO International Labour Organisation
ITU International Telecommunications Union
IRC Internet Relay Chat

KMVS Kutch Mahila Vikas Sanghatan (India)

MIR Movement of Revolutionary Left (Chile)

NGO non-governmental organization
NAFTA North American Free Trade Agreement
NCRF National Community Radio Forum (South Africa)
NEMBC National Ethnic and Multicultural Broadcasters' Council (Australia)
NWICO New World Information and Communication Order

PAN National Action Party (Mexico)
PIRG Public Interest Research Group (North America)

SAP Structural adjustment program

UN United Nations
UP Unidad Popular (Chile)

WID women in development
WIPO World Intellectual Property Organization
WB World Bank

ZANU Zimbabwe African National Union
ZAPU Zimbabwe African People's Union

VOLUME I
Introduction

Dorothy Kidd

Clemencia Rodríguez

These two volumes, *Making Our Media: Global Initiatives Toward a Democratic Public Sphere*, emerged from the transnational network called OURMedia/Nuestros Medios (www.ourmedianet.org). Initiated in 2001 by long-time researchers Clemencia Rodríguez, Nick Couldry, and John Downing, the global network fosters an ongoing dialogue about what has variously been called *alternative, radical, alterative, autonomous, tactical, participatory, community, and citizens'* media (terms that we discuss below). OURMedia provides a meeting space to exchange, support, and strengthen these more inclusive and participatory media and to collaborate on larger efforts to democratize national and global media systems.

OURMedia reflects an important conjuncture. Grassroots media have grown from a set of small and isolated experiments to a complex of networks of participatory communications that are integral to local, national, and transnational projects of social change, as well as to campaigns to transform all aspects of information and communications systems. At the same time, there has been a burst of new research and publications from activists, academics, and policy advocates, which put alternative, community, and citizens' media at the center of their enquiry.

The structure of the two volumes reflects this complex praxis, between the construction of new communications models and spaces, the reform of existing media systems, and the creation of new research and theory. The first volume, *Creating New Communications Spaces*, features analyses of locally directed and managed radio, video, independent media centers (IMCs), and other web-based news

1

services from grassroots activists and academics from Chile, Colombia, Mexico, South Africa, Zimbabwe, India, Japan, Australia, the United States, Canada, Wales, and England. Anchoring their work in earlier studies of alternative and community media, and international development communications, this newer generation of researchers add interdisciplinary perspectives, often complicating earlier analyses with more nuanced and disjunctive accounts, to explain the rapidly changing nature of grassroots and citizens' communications. Their focus is on the democratization of the internal organization and production practices of grassroots media and the subsequent impact of these media on democratizing society.

The second volume, *National and Global Movements for Democratic Communication* addresses larger campaigns to reform the media. Authors from Korea, Peru, Chile, Brazil, Argentina, Austria, Germany, and the United States examine national and transnational campaigns to involve citizens and grassroots movements in the democratization of information and communications policy and to extend social justice using communications media. The overriding goal of both volumes is to appraise some of the emergent designs these projects and campaigns provide for people around the world whose goal is the reconstruction of our media systems for the benefit of all.

Stepping back from the very concrete appraisals of local projects, this volume introduction provides some historical and theoretical context. We begin by revisiting some of the watershed historical moments in the global mediascape of the last 30 years, drawing the connection between the growing power and reach of giant global commercially dominated media networks and the emergence of grassroots communications networks based on the direction and capacities of social justice groups. Book-ending this period, we begin with the call for a New World Information and Communication Order (NWICO) led by the nonaligned countries of the global south and end our review with a discussion of the communications dimensions of the global justice movement.

If the defeat of NWICO paralleled a hiatus in alternative and radical participatory media theory, the scope and scale of communications and media practice of the latter movement has led to a burst of new research from scholars, activists, and advocates. This most recent wave of scholarship, some of which is represented here, is notable for two reasons. First, rather than another set of new overreaching theories or disconnected case studies, the contributors adapt from an overlapping set of multidisciplinary and multiregional theoretical and analytical frames, providing a much needed contrapuntal conversation for this newly emerging field. Secondly, reflecting the composition of OURMedia itself, the contributors bridge the worlds of social movement activism, nongovernmental organization, and the university. The nexus of all three research approaches is a pragmatic investigation: what is working and not working, under what conditions and for whom, in the quotidian process of remaking communications practices and institutions for social transformation.

INTERSECTIONS

We trace the roots of OURMedia to the 1970s and the movement for a New World Information and Communication Order (NWICO) for three reasons. It was the first truly international forum to consider perspectives and evidence from a wide-ranging remit; many of the analyses of the structural inequities of global information and media systems, as well as their political and cultural ramifications, still seem prescient. Secondly, the NWICO movement underscored the importance of grassroots and alternative media in the democratization of communications and of societies. Finally, the contest over NWICO signaled the beginning of the current era of neoliberal globalization.

NWICO emerged in the 1970s when a coalition of national governments of the poorer countries of the south began to flex their new voting power at the United Nations (U.N.) to redress the structural inequities of the colonial system from which they were emerging (Carlsson, 2005: 197). In 1974, a group of 77 nations (G77) called for a New International Economic Order (NIEO) to reverse their structural dependency on the first-world powers and establish a fairer system of world trade and aid (Chakravartty & Sarikakis, 2006: 31). During the same period, they also began to call, with UNESCO, for a new international information order, which later became NWICO (31). After over a decade of extensive research, discussion, and debate, UNESCO published *One World, Many Voices*, or the MacBride Commission Report, named after the Chair, Sean MacBride (International Commission for the Study of Communication Problems, 1980).

The Commission condemned the North-South inequities in media and information systems, which, they argued, had been designed to serve the interests of the Western military powers and transnational corporations. They underscored the "constraints imposed by commercialization, pressures from advertisers and concentration of media ownership" (Thussu, 2000: 46). The resultant asymmetry in news and information flows had a serious negative "impact on national identity, cultural integrity and political and economic sovereignty," a critique shared by both poorer countries and richer ones such as France, Finland, and Canada (Ó Siochrú, Girard, & Mahan, 2002: 77). Perhaps the most innovative recommendation was the recognition they gave to the potential of radical, community, and trade union media to act as a counterbalance to the top-down information generation of communication monopolies, with their openness to horizontal communication among a multiplicity of participants (46).

The MacBride Report represented a greater international consensus on a common framework, justification, and set of remedies than ever before or since (Ó Siochrú, Girard, & Mahan, 2002: 78). However, the window of political opportunity for the NWICO movement, and for the wider movement for global economic and political equity, was short-lived. The U.S. and U.K. Governments, supported by the corporate commercial media, fiercely disagreed with the Report, arguing that any measures to limit media corporations or journalists amounted to state censorship. Unable to sway the other national representatives, in 1983, the U.S. Government withdrew from UNESCO, followed soon after by the U.K. and Singapore Governments.

Weakened by the loss of a quarter of its budget, and stymied by internal and external dissension, UNESCO never again supported any direct confrontation with the United States. Operationally it continued to support a redress of the skewed communications flows by building capacity in poorer countries via local radio, video, and Internet projects and news agencies; and training and exchanges for journalists and researchers (Ó Siochrú, Girard, & Mahan, 2002: 79-80). However, in the late 1990s, when UNESCO again convened discussions about international governance issues with 140 countries in the U.N. World Commission on Culture and Development, they were careful to delete or weaken any controversial recommendations (81).

The NWICO Movement was also constrained by its own lack of vision and internal inconsistencies. The movement's credibility suffered as many national leaders, who called for the democratization of multilateral institutions on the world stage, brutally repressed movements for economic and cultural rights at home and enabled local political and corporate elites to dominate communication. In retrospect, perhaps their greatest limitation was their strategy; their challenge to the neocolonial powers was based on shoring up weaker national governments in the interstate system (Chakravartty & Sarikakis, 2006: 32). The main lesson of NWICO, according to Ó Siochrú, Girard, and Mahan, was that "the way forward would have to be through the democratization of media and communications, rather than through state- or industry-led efforts" (2002: 79). This strategic shift, in which civil society took the leading role in developing alternative media projects and models of communications, defines the groups and movements in both volumes.

THE NEW MEDIASCAPES

The NWICO debate took place on the cusp of a seismic shift in global political governance, in which communications played a major role. During the late 1970s, many Western governments began to adopt market-based regulatory frameworks. The Reagan and Thatcher administrations were the most vociferous advocates of what is now called neoliberalism, or the Washington agenda (Hesmondhalgh, 2007: 86). In 1983, when the U.S. Government exited the multilateral politicized fora of the U.N. and UNESCO, they argued that they needed instead to ensure the global competitiveness of their own capitalist industries, including the information and media industries, which are so critical to the U.S. economy.[1] Domestically, the U.S. Government called for the unfettering of these industries through the privatization of public communication systems and the removal of rules governing the ownership structure and behavior of media corporations (Ó Siochrú, Girard, & Mahan, 2002: 27). Internationally, the U.S. Government lobbied for the promotion of their own information and entertainment industries, combining calls for corporate property rights, liberalization of trade rules, and the harmonization of telecommunications regulatory policy (Calabrese, 2004: 5) at the World Trade Organization (WTO), the World Bank (WB), the International Telecommunications Union (ITU), and the World Intellectual Property Organization (WIPO), with bilateral (free) trade agreements with weaker countries.

National governments around the world followed suit, privatizing or severely cutting back public broadcasting and telecommunications systems and dropping most values of universality and public service within infrastructure planning and content review, as well as access to telecommunications and production resources (Miège, 2004: 189). A decade of what is more accurately called 're-regulation' substantially changed the balance of forces. National governments were by no means eclipsed; rather media and other corporations secured prominent positions in the framing of laws and policies to the detriment of citizens everywhere, as well as to smaller media and cultural production companies and national governments.

After an unprecedented wave of mergers and acquisitions of old and new media industries, a handful of giant U.S., Japanese, and European transnational conglomerates emerged as the principal owners of a complex interdependent global system. Much of the production of music, film, news, and information services was outsourced to regional corporations, or more flexible clusters of smaller creative companies. Nevertheless, the decentralization of production did not change the overall patterns of hyper-market-driven and industrially produced media (Miège, 2004: 89). The core Northern industries continued to provide the templates for production and to control global sales and advertising markets, optimizing strategic alliances on specific projects to produce the constantly changing content demanded by a multiple of audiences around the world (Hesmondhalgh, 2007: 176).

The result was a significant realignment of the media and information ecology. There was a decisive shift, as James Deane notes, from "government control to private (and to a much less extent, community) ownership and control of media" (2005:179). The upsurge of commercial and community radio, and also of information and communications technologies (ICTs) offering much more dynamic interactive content, initially benefited many regions and populations (Deane, 2005: 180-181). However, the imbalance in global news and cultural programming, first cited by the MacBride Report, continues; most news perspectives are still framed by Northern-based news providers (185), and Hollywood images still dominate the majority of the world's screens. In addition, the initial upsurge of local media outlets quickly shrank as competition intensified, with the result that content is shaped much more by the "demands of advertisers and sponsors" who tend to target young, male, affluent consumers in urban centers the world over (Deane, 2005: 182). Reporting, discussion, and deliberation of local and regional public issues, particularly of poverty and social injustice, education, and healthcare are increasingly left out (183). The majority of the world, and especially those marginalized in rural areas and by poverty, literacy, patriarchal, racial, and caste oppression, are largely excluded from basic media access, let alone the interactive and participatory possibilities of expression and dialogue.

THE THIRD SECTOR

If the shift to neoliberalism drastically skewed global communication, it also created conditions of radical possibility (Uzelman, 2002: 77-80). Media activists have appropriated some of the technologies first designed by corporate and military apparatuses and reshaped them to meet local information and communication needs around the world. As the MacBride Report promised, they also provided living examples of new forms of democratic communication. Although marginal in many respects, their emerging design patterns turn the neoliberal blueprint of communications on its head and its architecture inside out.

If the commercial media is tilted towards a Northern axis of U.S. English-language production centers in Hollywood and New York, Latin America has been the epicenter for much participatory communications activity, as the high number of contributions to these two volumes attest. Jesús Martin-Barbero points out that Latin American scholars were key drafters of the original NWICO proposal, drawing on the region's experiences of national policy work and alternative communications (Communication Initiative, 1999). Many of the projects documented in this volume were inspired by Latin American examples, such as the Bolivian miners' radio, whose 60-year run modeled local participation and governance, as well as courage in the face of military and government repression. Since then, the lessons of Latin American *radio popular* have become even more important, as radio has become the world's most significant medium, especially for marginalized groups in both rural and metropolitan areas.

This emphasis on the deep involvement of marginalized communities is integral to community radio and the other media projects described in this volume. It is distinct from the user-generation of Web 2.0, which, while still in development, has already revealed a dangerous tilt towards an intense level of surveillance and data-mining of participants by corporate brands (Chester, 2006). Instead, the meaning and practice of participation presented here is more extensive, based in collective design, decision making, creative interchange and governance, at all stages of the production and circulation of meaning, up to and including the ownership and self-government of the media outlet.

In addition to providing some of the earliest models for local projects, Latin Americans were leaders in creating alternative kinds of global networks. Working together with Canadian, U.S., and European media activists in the 1980s, they built networks of video and community radio producers. Beginning in 1987,

Latin American video producers met annually to share information on production, distribution, training, and technology, as well as national and regional communications policies, inspiring similar meetings in other regions (Ambrosi, 1991: 17). After meetings in Canada and Latin America, community radio producers formed the World Association of Community Radio (AMARC, by its French acronym). Unlike the commercial media networks, based on central hubs, AMARC is a network of networks, linking 3,000 projects in 106 countries, including a wide variety of stations and content combines.[2] Rather than a market-based industrial network, replicating a small number of advertising or sponsor-driven production routines and programming genres, AMARC recognizes a diversity of forms, including 'community radio,' 'rural radio,' 'participatory radio,' 'free radio,' 'alternative radio,' 'radio popular,' 'educational radio' and 'indigenous radio.'

The Latin American contribution of NWICO, *radio popular*, and alternative media networks arose partly out of necessity. For example, during the 1980s, when Latin America suffered severely from the combined ravages of structural adjustment programs (SAPs) imposed by the World Bank and IMF, and of war, social movements turned to local and national alternative media to circulate information and debate, as Bresnahan documents in this volume. Recognizing how the SAPs and other neoliberal policies were decided at the global level, Latin American and other communicators formed a computer-linked network of NGOs and other organizations involved in human and environmental rights, the rights of labor, and women's rights. This network eventually became the Association of Progressive Communicators (APC) (Murphy, 2002).

This convergence of networks of social movements and communications was amplified on January 1, 1994, when the Zapatista National Liberation Army emerged from the Lacandón jungle to protest the signing of the North American Free Trade Agreement (NAFTA) (Martinez-Torres, 2001). A guerilla movement unlike any of its Latin American predecessors, the Zapatistas promoted an inclusive strategy that was not focused on taking state power (Martinez-Torres, 2001: 348). Much like the Mapuche communicators in Chile, whom Salazar documents, the Zapatistas "gave indigenousness new importance, even while reinventing its meaning" (348). Their playful use of images, sounds, and narratives consciously appealed to the participation of the poor and middle classes of Mexico. Via face-to-face *encuentros*, publications, and the Internet, they also circulated their experiences and analyses to allies around the world (Russell, 2001: 359-360). The combination of creative and tactical uses of communications, emphasizing local and direct self-representation, contrasted with the relentless and anonymous messages of corporate globalization and became a source of inspiration for media activists from around the world (Herndon, 2003).

In 1999, this new conceptualization of globally networked participatory communications took another leap forward, when 80,000 antiglobal capitalism activists convened in Seattle to resist the neoliberal mandates of the World Trade Organization (WTO) (Kidd, 2004: 334). A coalition of social justice organizers, media activists, and open-source computer designers drew from the experience of the Zapatistas, other tactical media,[3] and their own experience in alternative media projects of micro and community radio, independent video, and computer networks to create the first Independent Media Center (IMC) (Halleck, 2002) Their highly collaborative planning and production process and their goal of disseminating news as widely as possible to activists around the world quickly became a global network of exchange, articulation, and consensus building about alternatives to corporate globalization (Downing, 2003; Kidd, 2003b). The IMC has been an influential pioneer of many collaborative news production practices, and we include several evaluations in this volume (Brooten & Hadl, Royce & Martin, Skinner et al., Anderson).

THE EMERGING FIELD

In the last decade there has been a resurgence of research and writing about alternative media, in large part spurred by a critical mass of projects around the world and the recognition of their role in processes of social change. In contrast to the homogenization of content and standardization of program genres and modes of production, marketing, and audience research of the dominant commercial and state-owned media, the grassroots media sector is characterized by heterogeneity, multiple modes of genre, address, and a plethora of production models. Trying to keep up with the politics, aesthetics, technologies, and communication philosophies of these newer media projects, researchers and advocates have begun a search for different analytical, theoretical, and methodological proposals to investigate them.[4]

The two volumes of *Making Our Media* reflect this growth in the scope and scale of communications projects and of the research. The authors develop more nuanced, critical assessments of the projects, and re-assess earlier conceptualizations and definitions of the interrelated processes of communications, democratization, and social change. The work also reflects a deepening of the field, as several of the projects bridge approaches to research drawn from the university academy, the policy or advocacy realm, with media production and social justice practice. None of these theoretical or methodological developments are uniform or without tension, as we describe below.

OVERVIEW OF THE VOLUME

Making Our Media: Volume One is divided into four sections with introductory essays providing the context for key themes and issues. The first section, *Pushing Theoretical Boundaries* deals, as Nick Couldry writes in his introduction, with questions of definitions. "What do we call what we study?" and "What aspects of the practice do we give the greatest priority?" This second generation of researchers draws from the literature of the field, either deepening the theorization with the richness of particular places, peoples, and media, or creating new syntheses with the adaptation of theory from other disciplines or research practices. Critiquing earlier conceptualizations of 'community' radio, Tanja Bosch instead examines Bush Radio in South Africa through the lens of Deleuze and Guattari's notion of the rhizome, an underground grasslike tuber with multiple entry points and routes. Her mapping of the station's multiple, fluid, and disjunctive patterns of impact on producers, other media, and audiences inaugurates more complex ways to think of evaluation than the usual—and not very helpful—audience analyses.

Juan Francisco Salazar documents the media of the Mapuche people in Chile, which has been historically excluded from the dominant commercial media and national government policy frameworks and from the alternative or citizens' media of nonindigenous groups. Building his argument from the work of several theorists, including Foucault, Nancy Fraser, Rafael Roncagliolo, Guillermo de la Peña, and Clemencia Rodríguez, Salazar argues that Mapuche media create new insurrectionary imaginaries as part of a fluid counter-public sphere, intervening in public discussions of land, resources and communications within Mapuche communities, the Chilean and Argentinean nation states, and among the wider indigenous movement throughout Latin America.

Chris Anderson compares three online participatory journalism sites: Wikipedia, the Northwest Voice in Bakersfield, California, and U.K. Indymedia. He reviews how these new practices of citizens' journalism are changing notions of reporting, objectivity, and the nature of democratic participation. He is less sanguine about whether citizens' journalism will result in any substantial institutional change in journalism, or larger political and economic structures of society, absent strong connections with off-line geographic communities and/or larger political movements.

The second section, *Communication for Social Change Projects*, reviews participatory communications projects with just those dimensions. The three studies examine media based in poor, rural communities in Zimbabwe, India, and Colombia respectively, and within larger projects of social change. Working within the legacy of development communications, they utilize global feminist and other kinds of scholarship to analyze the collective processes of reconstructing local knowledges and histories, analyzing common problems, and empowering themselves and their communities. They also all deal with the value of popular participatory media in promoting dialogue among highly conflicted populations, divided by the legacies of violence from civil war, caste, class and gender oppression.

The third section is especially concerned with interrogating questions of process. As Ellie Rennie suggests in her section introduction, the guiding thread to these projects based in the richer countries is "Why can't it work better?" The research team of Meadows, Forde, Ewart, and Foxwell examine the relationship between producers and audiences in the rapidly growing Australian community radio sector, which has stepped up to provide basic communications spaces for communities defined by locale and/or cultural identification, encouraging dialogue between diverse publics and ultimately affecting the larger public sphere.

The other three chapters in this section deal with the global Indymedia network (IMC). Since beginning in Seattle in 1999, the IMC Network has grown to over 150 sites, replicated by activists covering social justice issues around the world. The IMC pioneered many of the technologies and softwares that are now part of the user-generated menu of Web 2.0, starting with a networked system that allows anyone with access to the Web to upload multimedia content. However, the real innovation of the IMC was its DNA of participatory democracy, which informed every aspect of the Network, from the consensus-based forms of decision making of each autonomous local site, special production team, and technical crew.

This rapid growth was not without growing pains, many of which are dissected in the three chapters in this section. In the face of criticism and waning activities in the Canadian IMCs, the research team of Skinner, Uzelman, Langlois, and Dubois examined three different city sites to assess the viability of the IMCs as sites of resistance to dominant forms of media and political power. Lisa Brooten and Gabriele Hadl interviewed participants from several different sites and analyzed website content and internal newslists to assess the status of gender dynamics in content production, governance, and conflict resolution. Janet Jones and Martin Royston interrogated power relations within the U.K. IMC. Applying Habermas' conception of the ideal public sphere, they tested the goals of consensus-based democratic participation in content generation and governance with the realities of existing on- and offline social and technological elites and computer protocols. As of 2007 and this writing, it remains to be seen how the IMC Network will respond to these internal challenges and to the rapid growth of other models of participant-driven news networks.

As John Downing points out in his Introduction to the last section, *Our Media and the State*, these accounts of indigenous community radio in Mexico, alternative media in Chile, and Welsh digital storytelling within the BBC deal with the "everyday low-intensity contestation of established power." Government media systems have sometimes supported the cultural expression of ordinary people, partly because it is a safer alternative than the extension of political power. Jennifer Kidd asks whether the BBC is less interested in popular expression than in incorporation, and Castells Talens describes how some Mexican indigenous stations received more support during the height of the Zapatista movement in the 1990s, when government leaders preferred their 'multiculturalist' emphasis to the political threat of the Zapatistas. As a contrasting case, Bresnahan reveals both the unexpected openings provided by the Catholic Church in Chile during the Pinochet period and the unexpected closings during the so-called period of democratization, when the imposition of neoliberal communications policies marginalized and/or eliminated some forms of alternative media.

METHODS

The research optics and language of this volume reveal some of the tensions of the multisectoral alliance that is OURMedia. Most authors are not solely interested in these topics as academic research, but combine roles as producers/participants, participant/researchers, or researcher/advocates. Clemencia Rodríguez describes a stance common to many of the contributors, in which "academic research should be *at the service of* praxis" (398) with the knowledge produced usable by the projects themselves.

The process of 'collective construction of knowledge,' common to earlier feminist and participatory action research approaches, has been enriched with inventive mixes of qualitative methods. Several employ participatory and ethnographic observation and in-depth interviews. Many contributors also provided more opportunities for collaboration and reflection from participants via video documentaries (Salazar, Matewa), radio programs (Bosch), Internet wikis (Brooten and Hadl), memory workshops (Rodríguez), and virtual ethnographies (Royston and Martin). These approaches were supplemented with institutional policy research, textual analysis (Salazar, Bresnahan, Brooten and Hadl, Bosch), and audience research using focus groups (Pavarala and Malik) and quantitative surveys (Meadows et al.). As a result, the voices, experiences,, and perspectives of the participants are much more in the foreground, and several of the chapters incorporate a multiperspectival narrative form.

Most of the chapters also met the criticism, often dealt to social change communications research, of 'silo' thinking, or being too inward, or singularly focused. Instead, they took a variety of comparative approaches. Several studies are national in scope, including Pavarala and Malik, Castells Talens, Skinner et al., and Meadows et al.; and Matewa and Rodriguez compared projects in subnational regions. Anderson compared three different kinds of participatory journalism sites, and Salazar assessed different kinds of Mapuche media. Brooten and Hadl, Pavarala and Malik, and Matewa all employ gender lenses across several projects. The comparative approaches all effectively act to reveal important dimensions and dynamics across each set of practices.

NAMING

Terminology, as Nick Couldry discusses in his Introduction to Section 1, is another of the key dimensions of this field of research. The terms are multiple, as a recent study by Ferron outlines.[5] This wide variety is in part due to the truly global scope of the field, and the very different historical and political paradigms in which these media and the research about them have developed. The relentless focus on naming is perhaps also indicative of the relative isolation and underdevelopment of the field and the multitude of alternative visions and practices it has to cover.

This volume contributes to this process of defining the field, providing a critique of three of the foundational terms, 'development communications,' 'community media,' and 'alternative media,' and suggesting new formulations in light of new experiences and new analyses. Bosch, Matewa, Pavarala and Malik, and Rodríguez are uniformly critical of the early notions of 'development communications' emanating from UNESCO and other international development agencies. Bosch notes the persuasion bias inherited from Western models of 'propaganda' and Matewa, and Pavarala and Malik critique the lack of foregrounding of women as active agents of change. All revise earlier definitions of 'participatory communications,' and argue instead for more collective decision making of all stakeholders in order to ensure the inclusive and interactive nature of the production process. In addition, Bosch, Pavarala and Malik argue for ownership of media by participants.

Tanja Bosch also interrogates the notion of 'community,' a foundational concept of her own Bush Radio in South Africa, and of the Australian, Mexican, and Indian community radio projects described elsewhere in the volume. Drawing from feminist and poststructural critics, she cautions against the invocation of 'community,' which can reinforce static identities and exclusionary boundaries, a nostalgic return to a nonexistent past, or acceptance of a permanent lower status in relation to state or commercial media. She utilizes Deleuze and Guattari's idea of the rhizome to theorize about the multiple and more contingent connections between people, ideas, and culture that constitute Bush Radio and many other grassroots radio stations.

'Alternative media' is also unpacked. Several authors use the term to distinguish between media produced by collectives and communities for purposes of social change and media driven by state or corporate interests. However, most of the authors find the term limiting, and either use it in combination with other terms or introduce new ones. Juan Salazar uses 'alterative media,' coined by Peruvian scholar Rafael Roncagliolo, to highlight the power of these media to alter the social world. Skinner, Uzelman, Langlois, and Dubois argue that 'alternative' media only concentrate on the outcomes of counter-information or counter-discourses within mainstream media, to the detriment of formative processes of making media. Instead, they proffer the term 'autonomous media' to signify radical changes in the content produced and in the use of more participatory and dialogic processes of production (Uzelman, 2002: 85).

Many of the volume contributors follow Clemencia Rodríguez (2001), who argued that 'alternative media' implies a reactive relationship with dominant media and a corresponding acceptance of a lesser status. Coining 'citizens' media,' she redirected the analysis away from the comparison with mass, commercial media, to focus instead on the cultural and social power processes triggered when local communities appropriate ICTs. Several of the contributors (Castells Talens, Meadows et al., Salazar, Bosch) adopt 'citizens' media' to describe the complex internal and external dynamics of local social and political communications.

More recently, the term 'citizens' media' itself has been perceived as problematic. On one hand—and although as defined by Rodríguez the term is far from liberal understandings of citizenship—the term cannot escape its connotation of inclusion and exclusion based on the legal status of the citizen, a status that is systematically denied to millions because of their nationality, work and health status, or sexual orientation. On the other hand, as recently articulated by Thomas (2007), citizenship as defined by liberal democratic theory—as a birthright and not in Rodríguez' definition as everyday political action—cannot be easily dismissed "for in its implementation lies security for millions of people" (37) in the global South.

More important than reaching a consensual definition is the process of naming in which important issues and relationships are highlighted and clarified by academics, producers, activists, and artists. Ultimately this sharing of issues, questions, goals, and meanings help establish the parameters and contours of the field.

THEORETICAL FRAMEWORKS

In an earlier two-volume collection about radical media, Armand Mattelart wrote about the challenges of documentation:

> [T]his slow, collective and spontaneous accumulation of everything a social group did ... is scattered with long public silences, blanks in the soundtrack. Periods of advance and periods of withdrawal ... the difficulty of formalizing experiences of struggle, to reflect together on what has happened to the group, sometimes because of the impossibility of doing so, other times because of a latent desire for amnesia as a defense mechanism against failures and errors.... (Mattelart & Siegelaub, 1983: 18-19)

This volume, with its cross-regional scope, is beginning to fill in some of the 'blanks in the soundtracks' of earlier grassroots media history. Although the contributors draw insights across disciplines of communications, social movements, technology studies, women's and indigenous studies, among others, they employ enough similarity in their frameworks to further a common conversation. Rather than designing representative samples allowing for generalizable conclusions, the chapters in this volume take a more anthropological approach. Based on thick descriptions and ethnographic evidence of subtle changes in media use, culture, and power, the volume's authors theorize key elements, processes, structures, and relationships. Although this knowledge is not easily transferred to other media initiatives with very different contexts, it does provide more sophisticated theoretical and analytical understandings of community and alternative media. It is our hope that these pioneering theoretical perspectives provide new lenses with which to review other alternative and community media projects.

Many of the authors pivot their analysis around the concept of the 'public sphere,' if albeit, two updated versions. Following Nancy Fraser (1992), they describe the interconnection of plural sets of spheres, distinguished between dominant and counter-public spheres, in which marginalized groups develop their own communications spaces to articulate social and political needs and formulate positions and remedies. Individuals operate as members of multiple and overlapping spheres. For example, Pavarala and Malik's account of grass-roots women radio producers in rural India shows the fluid interchange of different subject positions and discourses as they circle outwards from membership in rural women's circles, dalit families, and rural villages, to present a multiple of subtle challenges to patriarchy, casteism, and local and national political elites.

Several contributors also draw on John Downey and Natalie Fenton (2003), who in line with Habermas' more recent writings argue that the contemporary era combines conditions of global dominance of multimedia conglomerates with the growth of decentralized, localized forms of citizen-responsive media and of media used by NGOs or civil society (188). Civil society groups may be able to exploit periodic crises for the enhancement of political mobilization and participation, or they may be more subject to fragmentation and polarization (189).

Both ends of this continuum are described in the volume. In Australia, the number of community radio stations has surpassed those of commercial radio. If this growth is partly due to the mobilization of what Meadows et al. call 'communities of interest,' it has also resulted from the evacuation of commercial and state media from rural areas and from the provision of communications services for indigenous peoples and 'multicultural' groups, due to market-friendly policy decisions. In contrast, in Chile, the market liberalism policies of the *Concertación* government led to a greater decline of alternative media than under the more repressive state controls of the Pinochet regime. In the more competitive market climate, left-oriented media were explicitly refused funding by both commercial and state advertisers. Moreover, in some cases, legalization hindered rather than helped many of the activist community radio stations, which were turned down for licenses. The Mexican experience of state-supported indigenous radio further complicates the picture. The neoliberal policies of decentralization and austerity led to an increase in the number of radio stations, as well as cuts in resources and paid staff. However, as Castells Talens explains, some indigenous communities were able to broker more power when decentralization increased their relative remove from the power elite in the capital city of Mexico, and simultaneously, the successful mobilization of the Zapatista movement increased the overall currency of indigenous languages and traditional knowledges.

Both studies of indigenous media highlight another debate within the public sphere and social movement literature. Is the goal of these communications projects, and of the larger campaigns for social change of which they are a part, more to do with cultural struggles related to "the recognition of the distinctive perspectives of ethnic, national, religious, and sexual minorities" or political claims for a "more just distribution of resources and wealth" (Fraser, 2005: 445)? Salazar's and Castells Talens' accounts challenge this false binary (Phillips, 2003), as they demonstrate the interconnection of recognition and redistribution struggles and of the related dimensions of 'representation' and 'rights' (Sreberny, 2005). The negotiation of Mexican indigenous peoples for recognition of 'indigenous self-expression' and for the rights and redistribution inherent in expressions of 'indigenous nationalism' (301) are both political and cultural. In Chile, the Mapuche media constructed new cultural imaginaries for Mapuche counterpublics and also created spaces in the dominant public sphere for political claims for resources and the consolidation of the Mapuche historical territories.

The volume does not provide any definitive answers to these larger questions of the relationship between alternative media, counter- and dominant public spheres, representation, and social change. However, the documentation of very particular contexts, across medium, genre, and time, provides comparative details about the ways that these media do contribute to a 'multiplication of forces' to further social change (Downey & Fenton, 2003: 194).

INTERNAL DEMOCRACY

The contributors to this volume are also especially interested in questions of internal democracy within media. They draw on a combination of traditions, whose links between media structure, process, product, and social change long predate the 'discovery' of audience participation and collaboration of Web 2.0. Several of the studies build on alternative media literature, which highlighted the "emancipatory possibilities of organizational and technological innovation in the media" (Hesmondhalgh, 2000: 18). Others develop feminist critiques of structures, which limit women in "access to resources and in the development of collective, consensus-based and nonhierarchical organizational structures" (Brooten & Hadl, this volume, p. 207). Still others draw from the turn to participatory communications within international development and its attention to human-centered and not media-centered processes, "channeled through the collective decision-making of all stakeholders" (Bosch, this volume).

The contributors highlight the questions these new media pose to the structure, process, and content of state-run and corporate commercial media. In particular, the emphasis on the direct representation of multiple voices and locales challenges the point-to-mass media hierarchy. The centering of counter-publics contrasts with the mainstream media's marginalization of these populations and perspectives. Their participatory media routines, which combine modes of address, present very different kinds of truth telling than the mainstream news routine of 'two points of view' representing the dominant political and corporate authorities.

If a recurrent theme is that the circulation of these new messages contest the dominant discourses and should be seen as political acts (Bosch, this volume), these analyses go much further than those of previous alternative media accounts. Uzelman writes that current practices not only separate themselves "from the logics of command and accumulation" of commercial and state media (in Skinner, this volume, p. 186), but also from the single-minded attention precursor groups gave to producing counter-information. In a parallel argument, Rodríguez underscores how the attention to process and form marks a turning point away from the reactiveness of earlier left media practices.

Most celebrated among these ground-breaking participatory practices have been the open news wires of the IMC, which in 1999 first allowed contributors from anywhere within access of an Internet site to post text, audio, or video content.[6] However, the volume also provides details about the participatory practices of precursor media such as community radio and video. What is now called 'crowd sourcing,' for example, is a core activity of many groups, who as Pavarala and Malik, and Matewa describe, systematically draw programming content from local community organizations and generate popular dramatic plots and casts from audiences of rural poor.

However, if the contributors describe many 'best practices,' they are also bracingly reflexive about the difficulties of operationalizing internal media democracy. The projects are often inherently precarious, caught between the power of the state to nullify their operations or put them out of existence and smothering competition in the marketplace. The nagging questions of how counter-publics, expressly committed to democratization, resolve power differences based on class and cultural power, race/ethnicity, and gender is taken up in many different ways. Several contributors undertake microscopic examinations in order to unveil subtle processes by which the new participatory practices and the technologies themselves can reify power hierarchies, inclusions and exclusions, centers and peripheries. They remind us that even the most celebrated uses of ICTs—such as Indymedia, for example—need to be scrutinized and updated so that dynamics of oppression, silencing, and exclusion do not creep in and settle.

They also challenge some of the most hard-held liberal notions of 'information as power.' For example, Brooten and Hadl note that the idealization of 'free expression' in the IMC is not necessarily liberatory, if used to mask continuing forms of social dominance such as sexism and patriarchy. In southern India, a staff member wonders whether community radio can ever resolve the real problems for the rural poor, noting that empowerment is often limited to those most closely involved, with the most marginalized unable to participate because of their obligation to work long hours elsewhere.

The volume stands in stark contrast to the latest round of techno-utopianism of Web 2.0, with its lack of attention to the realities of global inequalities of power and structure. In his review of three on-line participatory journalism sites, Chris Anderson asks whether the new sites lead to 'concrete radical change . . .'

within journalism or the 'larger political and economic structures,' or whether they instead promote 'hyperlocal,' nonradical approaches, which are easily reincorporated by the commercial media against which they were rebelling.

Overall, the volume assembles a set of dynamic pictures of the ongoing practices of participatory communications. The analysis, with its deep roots in specific contexts, extends well beyond the idealization of individual 'expression' for wealthy young, consumers in urban technological hot spots, to instead probe how participatory communications is and is not working for a cross-section of the world's majorities. These projects are not only a breeding ground for new kinds of social justice–oriented content, but prefigure new modes and genres of more inclusive production. As Juan Francisco Salazar suggests, these mediated communications processes are "imperfect media" (2004), sometimes used, and sometimes abused, in the larger processes of social, cultural and political change. Continuous research and evaluation of these practical experiments will help to redirect their action towards the elusive horizon of social justice for all.

NOTES

1. This was by no means the first time the U.S. Government had supported the global expansion of U.S. media; in the 1920s, the U.S. State Department worked with Hollywood to guarantee global market dominance (Trumpbour, 2002).
2. AMARC facilitates organizational links between individual stations, among regions, and globally as well as via a women's network, the Pulsar news syndication service, and other regular content-oriented campaigns.
3. Korean and Filipino media activists also participated in the demonstrations in Seattle (Kidd, 2004: 333). During the financial crisis in 1997, South Korean labor and other social movement activists simultaneously broadcast their demonstrations against the International Monetary Fund (IMF) in several cities and opened the first web-based interactive news service, Jinbonet. Their work followed several other important tactical media campaigns against authoritarian states. In 1989, the year the Berlin Wall came down, prodemocracy activists in Czechoslovakia transferred foreign news coverage of their antigovernment demonstrations to videotape and circulated them as widely as possible (Jones, 1994: 147); and activists in Hong Kong used fax machines to "send messages of support along with uncensored news from the outside world" to those demonstrating in Tienanmen Square (Jones, 1994: 152). In 1992, the Thai activists of the 'cellular phone revolution' used both faxes and cell phones to demonstrate against the corrupt and autocratic military regime (153). Attempting to avoid harassment and government censorship during the break-up of the former Yugoslavia, the radio producers of B 92 in Belgrade, Serbia established a web link in 1996 with XS4ALL in Amsterdam. This allowed them to continue sending out information via email news bulletins or a Real Audio stream (Markovic, 2000).
4. Published almost simultaneously, the works of John Downing, with Tamara Villareal Ford, Gèneve Gil and Laura Stein (2001), Gumucio-Dagrón (2001b), Clemencia Rodríguez (2001) and Chris Atton (2002) explored and applied theoretical frameworks

that ranged from Adorno, Mártin Barbero, and Freire (Downing), to Foucault, Williams, Bakhtin, Spivak (Atton) and Mouffe and McClure (Rodríguez). See also works on community media, including Nick Jankowski and Ole Prehn's edited volume (2002), Andrés Geerts, Victor Van Oeyen and Claudia Villamayor's study of community radio in Latin America (2004), the transnational works of Kevin Howley (2005); and Ellie Rennie (2006). In addition, see the edited collections of Laura Stein, Bernadette Barker-Plummer and Dorothy Kidd (1999), Kidd and Barker-Plummer (2001), Nick Couldry and James Curran (2003), Andy Opel and Donnalyn Pompper (2003), and Chris Atton and Nick Couldry (2003). For perspectives on radical alternative media, see Dee Dee Halleck (2002), Dorothy Kidd's work on the IMC (2003a, 2003b, 2004), Mitzi Waltz (2005) and Andrea Langlois and Frédéric Dubois' edited volume (2005). For scholarship about indigenous media, see Morris and Meadows (2001), Molnar and Meadows (2001), Donald Browne (2005), Lorna Roth (2005), Faye Ginsburg (2002), Juan Francisco Salazar (2007, 2004, 2003, 2002), and Rodríguez and El-Gazi (2007).

5. Recently Ferron (2007) inventoried the following terms: alternative (Atton, 1999, 2002), radical (Downing et al., 2001), citizens' (Rodríguez, 2001), marginal (Trejo, 1980; Zapata, 1989), participatory (Alfaro Moreno, 2004), counter-information (Cassigoli, 1989), parallel (Chadaigne, 2002), community (Fuller, 2001; Gumucio-Dagrón, 2001a; Van Oeyen, 2003), underground (Lewis, 2000), popular (Van Oeyen, 2003), libres (Cazenave, 1984), dissident (Streitmatter, 2001), resistant (Switzer & Adhikari, 2000) pirate (http://en.wikipedia.org/wiki/Pirate_radio"en.wikipedia.org/wiki/Pirate_radio), clandestine (Soley & Nichols, 1987), autonomous (Langlois & Dubois, 2005), young (David, 2003), and micro-médias (Rio Donoso, 1996).

6. See the growing literature of Atton (2002), Couldry and Curran (2003), Downing (2003), Halleck (2002), Herndon (2003), Kidd (2003a, 2003b, 2004), Uzelman (2002), Waltz (2005).

REFERENCES

Alfaro Moreno, R. M. (2004). Culturas populares y comunicación participativa: En la ruta de las redefiniciones. *Comunicación, 126,* 13-19.

AMARC (2007). Radio voices without frontiers. Retrieved March 25, 2007, from http://rvsf.amarc.org/index.php?p=allaudios&l=EN.

Ambrosi, A. (1991). Introduction: Alternative communication and development alternatives. In N. Thede & A. Ambrosi (Eds.), *Video: The changing world* (pp. 1–19). Montreal/New York: Black Rose Books.

Atton, C. (1999). A reassessment of the alternative press. *Media, Culture and Society, 21*(1), 51-76.

Atton, C. (2002). *Alternative media.* London: Sage.

Atton, C., & Couldry, N. (Eds.). (2003) *Media, Culture & Society, 25*(5).

Browne, D. R. (2005). *Ethnic minorities, Electronic media and the public sphere: A comparative approach.* Cresskill, NJ: Hampton Press.

Calabrese, A. (2004). Toward a political economy of culture. In A. Calabrese & C. Sparks (Eds.), *Toward a political economy of culture: Capitalism and communication in the twenty-first century* (pp. 1-12). Lanham, MD: Rowman & Littlefield.

Carlsson, U. (2005). From NWICO to global governance of the information society. In O. Hemer & T. Tufte (Eds.), *Media and global Change: Rethinking communication for development* (pp. 193-214). Suecia: Nordicom.

Cassigoli, A. (1989). Sobre la contrainformación y los así llamados medios alternativos. In M. Simpson Grinberg (Ed.), *Comunicación alternativa y cambio social. 1. América Latina* (pp. 63-71). México: Premia Editora.

Cazanave, F. (1984). *Les radios libres.* Paris: Presses Universitaires de France.

Chadaigne, P. J. (2002). *La communication alternative: La presse parallèle en France desannées 60 à la fin des années 90.* Paris: PhD Dissertation, Université Paris II-Panthéon Assas.

Chakravartty, P., & Sarikakis, K. (2006). *Media policy and globalization.* Edinburgh: Edinburgh University Press.

Chester, J. (2006). Google, YouTube and you. *The Nation.* Retrieved May 1, 2007, from http://www. thenation.com/doc/20061030/chester. Posted online on October 16, 2006. .

Communication Initiative. (1999). Interview with Dr. Jesús Martin-Barbero. Retrieved May 5, 2007, from <comminit.com/interviews/int1998-99/interviews-22.html>.

Couldry, N., & Curran, J. (Eds.). (2003). *Contesting media power: Alternative media in a networked world.* Lanham, MD: Rowman & Littlefield.

David, V. (2003). Presse jeune: Des démangeaisons dans la plume! *L'infométropole, 120,* 18-19.

Deane, J. (2005). Media, democracy and the public sphere. In O. Hemer & T. Tufte (Eds.), *Media and global change: Rethinking communication for development* (pp.177-192). Göteborg, Sweden: Nordic Information Centre for Media and Communication Research.

Downey J., & Fenton, N. (2003). New media, counter publicity and the public sphere. *New Media & Society, 5*(2), 185–202.

Downing, J. D. H. (2003). The IMC movement beyond 'the West.' In A. Opel & D. Pompper (Eds), *Representing resistance: Media, civil disobedience and the global justice movement* (pp. 241-258). Westport, CT: Praeger.

Downing, J.D.H. with Ford, T. V., Gil, G., & Stein, L. (2001). *Radical media: Rebellious communication and social movements.* London: Sage.

Ferron, B. (2007). Les médias alternatifs: Entre luttes de définition et luttes de (dé-)légitimation. *Les enjeux de l'information et de la communication,* numéro spécial 8e colloque Brésil-France. Available at http://w3.u-grenoble3.fr/les_enjeux/2006-supplement/Ferron/index.php

Fraser, N. (1992). Rethinking the public sphere: A contribution to the critique of actually existing democracy. In C. Calhoun (Ed.), *Habermas and the public sphere* (pp. 109-142). Cambridge: MIT Press.

Fraser, N. (2005). Toward a nonculturalist sociology of culture: On class and status in globalizing capitalism. In F. Jacobs & N. Hanrahan (Eds.), *The Blackwell companion to the sociology of culture* (pp. 444-459). Malden, MA: Blackwell.

Fuller, L. K. (2001). Community media: International perspectives. Aboriginal/indigenous experiences, Current case studies, Virtual community visions. Paper presented at the OURMedia I Conference, Washington DC: Our Media, Not Theirs I. Retrieved May 1, 2007, from <http://www.ourmedianet.org/om2001/ica2001.html>.

Geertz, A., Van Oeyen, V., & Villamayor, C. (2004). *La práctica inspira. La radio popular y comunitaria frente al nuevo siglo.* Quito: ALER.

Ginsburg, F. (2002). Screen memories: Resignifying the traditional in indigenous media. In F. Ginsburg, L. Abu-Lughod, & B. Larkin (Eds.), *Media worlds: Anthropology on new terrain* (pp. 39-57). Berkeley: University of California Press.

Gumucio-Dagrón, A. (2001a). Call me impure: Myths and paradigms of participatory communication. Paper presented at the OURMedia III Conference, Barranquilla, Colombia. Retrieved May 1, 2007, from www.ourmedianet.org/papers/om2001/Gumucio.om2001.pdf.

Gumucio-Dagrón, A. (2001b). *Making waves. Participatory communication for social change.* New York: Rockefeller Foundation.

Halleck, D. (2002). *Hand-held visions: The impossible possibilities of community media.* New York: Fordham University Press.

Herndon, S. (2003). On Indymedia Seattle. Paper presented at the III Conference of OURMedia, Barranquilla, Colombia. Retrieved May 1, 2007, from <http://www.our-medianet.org/papers/om2003/Herndron_OM3.rtf>.

Hesmondhalgh, D. (2000). Alternative media, alternative texts? Rethinking democratization in the cultural industries. In J. Curran (Ed.), *Media organisations in society* (pp. 107-126). London: Arnold.

Hesmondhalgh, D. (2007) *The cultural industries* (2nd ed.). London: Sage.

Howley, K. (2005). *Community media: People, places, and communication technologies.* Cambridge: Cambridge University Press.

International Commission for the Study of Communication Problems. (1980). *Many voices, one world: The MacBride Report.* Paris: UNESCO.

Jankowski, N., & Prehn, O. (Eds). (2002). *Community media in the information age: Perspectives and prospects.* Cresskill, NJ: Hampton Press.

Jones, A. (1994). Wired world: Communications technology, governance and the democratic uprising. In E. Comor (Ed.), *The global political economy of communication* (pp. 145-164). New York: St. Martin's Press.

Kidd, D., & Barker-Plummer, B. (Eds.). (2001). Social justice movements and the Internet. *Peace Review, 13,* 3.

Kidd, D. (2003a). The independent media center: A new model. *Media Development 4.* Retrieved June 11, 2007, from <http://www.wacc.org.uk/wacc/publications/media_development/archive/2003_4/the_independent_media_center_a_new_model>.

Kidd, D. (2003b). Indymedia.org: A new communications commons. In M. McGaughey & M. Ayers (Eds.), *Cyberactivism: On-line activism in theory and practice* (pp. 47-69). New York: Routledge.

Kidd, D. (2004). From carnival to commons: The global IMC network. In E. Yuen, G. Katsiaficas, & D. Burton-Rose (Eds.), *Confronting capitalism: Dispatches from a global movement* (pp. 330-340). New York: Soft Skull Press.

Langlois, A., & Dubois, F. (Eds.). (2005). *Autonomous media: Activating resistance and dissent.* Montreal: Cumulus Press.

Lewis, J. (2000). The underground press in America (1964-1968): Outlining an alternative, the envisioning of an underground. *Journal of Communication Inquiry, 24*(4), 379-400.

Markovic, S. (2000). Internet censorship case study: Radio B92 and OpenNet. The Association for Progressive Communications: European Civil Society Internet Rights Project. Retrieved November 12, 2008, from http://europe.rights.apc.org/cases/b92.html

Martinez-Torres, M. E. (2001). Civil society, the Internet, and the Zapatistas. *Peace Review. A Transnational Quarterly: Social Justice Movements and the Internet, 13*(3), 347-355.

Mattelart, A., & Siegelaub, S. (Eds.). (1983). *Communication and class struggle: Liberation socialism.* New York: International General.

Miège, B. (2004) Capitalism and communication: A new era of society or the accentuation of long-term tendencies. In A. Calabrese & C. Sparks (Eds.), *Toward a political economy of culture: Capitalism and communication in the twenty-first century* (pp. 83-94). Lanham, MD: Rowman & Littlefield,

Molnar, H., & Meadows, M. (2001). *Songlines to satellites: Indigenous communication in Australia, the South Pacific and Canada.* Leichhardt: Pluto Press.

Morris, C., & Meadows, M. (2001). *Into the new millennium: Indigenous media in Australia.* Final Report. Brisbane: Griffith University.

Murphy, B. (2002). A critical history of the Internet. In G. Elmer (Ed.), *Critical perspectives on the internet* (pp. 27-45). Lanham, MD: Rowman & Littlefield.

Opel, A., & Pompper, D. (Eds). (2003). *Representing resistance: Media, civil disobedience, and the global justice movement.* Westport, CT: Praeger.

Ó Siochrú, S., & Girard, B. with A. Mahan. (2002). *Global media governance: A beginner's guide.* Lanham, MD: Rowman & Littlefield.

Phillips, A. (2003). Recognition and the struggle for political voice. In B. Hodson (Ed.), *Recognition struggles and social movements* (pp. 263-273). Cambridge: Cambridge University Press.

Rennie, E. (2006). *Community media: A global introduction.* Boulder, CO: Rowman & Littlefield.

Rio Donoso (Del), L. (1996). *Les micro-médias imprimés. Recherches sur la micropress pendant la résistance chilienne. 1973-1989.* Introduction. PhD Dissertation, Université de la Sorbonne Nouvelle-Paris III, Institut des Hautes Etudes de l'Amérique Latine.

Rodríguez, C. (2001). *Fissures in the mediascape. An international study of citizens' media.* Cresskill, NJ: Hampton Press.

Rodríguez, C., & El-Gazi, J. (2007). The poetics of indigenous radio in Colombia. *Media, Culture, and Society, 29*(3), 449-468.

Roth, L. (2005). *Something new in the air: The story of first peoples television broadcasting in Canada.* Montreal: McGill-Queen's University Press.

Russell, A. (2001). The Zapatistas and computer-mediated peace. *Peace Review, 13*(3), 357-364.

Salazar, J. F. (2002) Activismo indígena en América Latina: Estrategias para una construcción cultural de tecnologías de información y comunicación. *Journal of Iberian and Latin American Studies, 8*(2), 61-79.

Salazar, J. F. (2003). Articulating an activist imaginary: Internet as counter public sphere in the Mapuche movement, 1997-2000. *Media International Australia Incorporating Culture and Policy, 107,* 19-30.

Salazar, J. F. (2004). *Imperfect media: The poetics of indigenous media in Chile.* Unpublished doctoral dissertation, University of Western Sydney, Australia.

Salazar, J. F. (2007). Indigenous peoples and the cultural constructions of information and communication technology in Latin America. In L. E. Dyson, M. Hendriks, & S. Grant (Eds.), *Indigenous people and information technology* (pp. 14-26). Hershey, PA: Idea Book Publishing.

Siriyuvasak, U. (2005). People's media and communication rights in Indonesia and the Philippines. *Inter-Asia Cultural Studies, 6*(2), 245-263.

Soley, L. C., & Nichols, J. S. (1978). *Clandestine radio broadcasting: A study of revolutionary and counterrevolutionary electronic communication.* Westport: CT: Praeger.

Sreberny, A. (2005) Globalization, communication, democratization: Toward gender equality. In R. A. Hackett & Y. Zhao (Eds.), *Democratizing global media: One world, many struggles* (pp. 245-268). Boulder, CO: Rowman & Littlefield.

Stein, L., Kidd, D., & Barker-Plummer, B. (Eds.) (1999). *Peace Review: Media and Democratic Action. 11*, 1.

Streitmatter, R. (2001). *Voices of revolution. The dissident press in America.* New York: Columbia University Press.

Switzer, L., & Adhikari, M. (Eds.). (2000). *South Africa's resistance press. Alternative voices in the last generation under apartheid.* Athens: Ohio University Center For International Studies.

Thomas, P. (2007). The Right to Information movement and community radio in India. Observations on the theory and practice of participatory communication. *Communication for Development and Social Change, 1*(1), 33-47.

Thussu, D. K. (2000). *International communication: Continuity and change.* London: Arnold.

Trejo, R. (1980). *La prensa marginal* (2nd ed.). México DF: El Caballito.

Trumpbour, J. (2002). *Selling Hollywood to the world: U.S. and European struggles for mastery of the global film industry, 1920-1950.* Cambridge: Cambridge University Press.

Uzelman, S. (2002). *Catalyzing participatory communication: Independent media centre and the politics of direct action.* Unpublished masters thesis, Simon Fraser University, Burnaby, Canada.

Van Oeyen, V. (2003). Los desafíos de la Radio Popular y Comunitaria en América Latina. Barranquilla: OurMedia III. Retrieved September 9, 2007, from <http://www.ourmedianet.org/ papers/om2003/VanOeyen_OM3.pdf>.

Waltz, M. (2005). *Alternative and activist media.* Edinburgh: Edinburgh University Press.

Zapata, M. (1989). Testimonios: El combate de la radios marginales. In M. Simpson Grinberg (Ed.), *Comunicación alternativa y cambio social. 1. América Latina* (pp. 353-351). México: La Red de Jonas, Premia Editora.

SECTION I
Pushing Theoretical Boundaries

INTRODUCTION TO SECTION I

Nick Couldry

It is worth remembering how we got here. At the end of the 1990s the study of media production outside the mainstream appeared to be a specialist pursuit of a few well-meaning scholars, themselves operating on the margins of mainstream media research. If there was a common agenda to this research, it was invisible to those defining the priorities for media studies who saw such research as the semi-utopian dreamings of those still entangled in the aftermath of a failed left politics-driven project. Nick Garnham's 1999 book *Emancipation, the Media and Modernity*, so innovative in other ways, only repeated the old orthodoxy in this respect (1999: 68; *cf* Garnham, 1990).

By 2005, almost everything had changed, and this book and this section's essays are an embodiment of that change. First, and most importantly, the idea that a radical left perspective is something of 'the past' *itself* now appears quaint, as the hegemony of neoliberal discourse is increasingly challenged through political action and practical organization across the world (for example, in Seattle, Buenos Aires, and Paris) and through the resources of global online networks. Second, the proliferation of media outputs in the digital media age—including, for example, the growth of citizen journalism (whatever one might think of its actual radical credentials)—makes increasingly outdated the earlier insistence that only media institutions that reach mass audiences are worth studying: there is simply no scholarly reason to believe that now, even if we accept (which we shouldn't) that there was a good reason to accept this in the past. Third, the late 1990s and early 2000s have seen a major growth in accessible scholarship on media beyond the mainstream, *both* in traditional media *and* in online forms (e.g., Atton, 2002, 2004; Browne, 2005; Downing, 2001; Rodríguez, 2001). Of course work that pays attention to such media is also likely to resist any automatic claims that the only place to look for exciting developments is where the myths of technological 'progress' tell us to look; it is just as indefensible to ignore the continued presence and relevance of traditional media (whether on their own terms or in alliance with online resources) as it is to ignore the huge potential of what Chris Atton (2004) has called the 'alternative Internet.' In this new situation there is an abundance of research being produced across the world on nonmainstream media, and there are increasing opportunities to read this work comparatively (for example, Couldry & Curran, 2003) in a way that throws up key differences and sharpens our sense of underlying questions.

There is, in other words, an emerging *field* of 'alternative media' research with a geographically very wide range of contributors and an undoubted relevance to the contested and unstable state of global politics that no longer needs to fear the invisibility or marginality to which earlier orthodoxies tried to assigned its predecessors. Alternative media research is firmly established on the new map of media research. The three sharply contrasting chapters in this section are clear evidence of this and the research ferment it signals.

We must however immediately put the term 'alternative media' in scare quotes, because the terminology we use for what we study has emerged as one of the key questions contested in this newly established field. In fact there are two questions that over the past five or six years have come to seem increasingly central to our debates, even as the scope of research has expanded. The *first* question is: What do we call what we study? This is just a blunt way of asking: What are the descriptive features to which we give the greatest priority in a field where, as it were suddenly (but, as just pointed out, this is an illusion), we are confronted with a huge range of media practices to research operating on many scales? The *second* and related question is: What aspects of this practice do we give the greatest priority to investigating? Both questions underlie at various points the detailed discussions of the chapters in this section.

Taking these in more detail, the first question is harder than it seems. It is hardly surprising that different authors have emerged with different priorities as they tried to get the subject of nonmainstream media onto the media studies map: Such definitional questions are just the type of thing you would expect to get resolved in the early years of an emerging field. But there is more at stake here than this suggests. For one thing, although the broadly left political sympathies of those working in this field can probably be assumed, it is another matter to insist, for example, that the subject matter of the field is *defined* by a radical political, social, or cultural agenda, as John Downing (1984) famously did in his account of 'radical media.' The counter-argument is that media outside the mainstream that don't fit that definition—for example white racist media or religious media that operate with a different definition of 'radicalism'—may also need to be studied just as urgently (Atton, 2004). This question potentially becomes quite complex when wildly different visions of economics and politics compete with each other for hegemony, as in contemporary Latin America—for example, Hugo Chavez's Venezuela.[1] If, however, we remove any reference to radical content from our definition of what we study (so 'alternative media' becomes, simply, any "media produced outside mainstream media institutions and networks," Atton & Couldry, 2003: 579), there are new counter-arguments: Doesn't this remove a major feature that *motivates* people to enter this research field in the first place? Worse, in an age when in some respects the resources for producing media are being decentralized, particularly online, what substance is left to the term 'alternative'—or as Peter Dahlgren put it provocatively, "can you have online media that are alternative?"—if we limit the term 'alternative' media to this *non*-politicized sense?[2]

At present this question of definition remains unresolved. It clearly might be resolved in different ways, for example by clarifying what we think alternative media is 'alternative' to—perhaps to a particular concentrated distribution of symbolic power (Couldry, 2002)—or by adjusting our definition of what is political in the media we study (see Rodríguez, 2001). The following essays take up different positions, as we will shortly see.

Meanwhile, the second question is less resolved and perhaps even less debated. Is our priority still, as it previously was, to understand better the production practices that underlie 'alternative media'? Or is it now just as important, particularly in a world where there are so many different 'alternative' media outputs, to

study their audiences (Downing, 2003)—not of course to reinstall the old orthodoxy, that only media with 'big' audiences matter, but rather to understand better
how particular media contribute to everyday practice, and not just that of the
producers themselves? And what about the study of the texts of alternative
media, and particularly the *intertextual* universes that the proliferation of alternative media online now generate? In part these are questions to be sorted out within media research, but they intersect with the larger disciplinary question of
whether alternative media research should be seen primarily as the analysis of
social movements or the analysis of processes of mediation. Once again, the chapters in this section take up interestingly different positions.

    Juan Francisco Salazar's chapter also considers community media in a time
of major political transformation: the media of the Mapuche people of Chile and
Argentina following the fall of the Pinochet dictatorship. Once again, a particular
historical setting challenges theoretical generalization; in this case, the theory
under challenge is the concept of the 'public sphere.' As Salazar points out, the
notion of anything like a unitary public sphere is meaningless in a state that seeks
directly or manages inadvertently to make large communities and their media
'absolutely invisible.' Under such harsh conditions, the process of mediation is
vital to sustaining both counter-public spheres (in Nancy Fraser's term) and the
very existence of the suppressed nations that they embody. Mapuche media are,
Salazar argues, not just alternative to a particular distribution of symbolic
resources, but '*alterative*'; that is, they constitute in themselves a redefinition and
transformation of national and cultural participation. As one videomaker quoted
by Salazar puts it: "I make [films] to change the situation of the Mapuche . . . [to]
see the Mapuche reality change." Drawing effectively on anthropological
research, Salazar brings out the contribution of a wide range of media to this
process, including the online networks that connect otherwise scattered audiences and communities. In this way Salazar enriches our understanding of
approaches to nonmainstream media that foreground their political and civic
dimensions.

    Chris Anderson's chapter by contrast shows how much can also be gained by
foregrounding the aspects of nonmainstream media that specifically contest particular structures of media production, especially news production. Anderson
considers three contrasting examples of 'grassroots journalism' online—U.K.
Indymedia, Wikinews, and The Northwest Voice (an online version of a local
newspaper in Northern California)—from a theoretical perspective influenced
by the sociology of journalism and Bourdieu's field theory. Here we see the non-
political definition of 'alternative media' being put to work in an interesting way
to understand a range of cases that only partly intersect with what is politically or
socially radical. Paradoxically, however, minimally political examples like The
Northwest Voice may help us see how the media process, and its field of participants, are being transformed by digitization (links here both to Bosch's and
Salazar's chapters). Anderson argues that we need to acknowledge multiple
notions of 'politics' salient on different scales, including the local 'making do' that

The Northwest Voice in its online, citizen-sourced version represents. He also offers a useful critique of the journalistic and political dead-end offered by Wikipedia's insistence on 'objectivity' from its contributors in conditions of production that are wholly divorced from any community or activist networks.

Tanja Bosch's chapter addresses directly the uncertainties about what exactly are the processes we should study in what particular media practitioners do. Starting from a critical review of the debate about definitions (question one above), Bosch insists that new concepts are needed to understand alternative media's contribution to 'community dynamics' on the ground. Bosch's case study of community station Bush Radio in Cape Town, South Africa, is based on extensive fieldwork, much of it as a radio producer. Insisting on the continued importance of radio as the most pervasive medium in poor, especially rural, communities, Bosch acknowledges the theoretical complexities of the term 'community' and argues that Deleuze and Guattari's concept of 'rhizomatic' structures offers a useful mid-range concept for grasping the open-ended ways in which community radio constructs 'community' from highly heterogeneous elements: varied media forms, diverse audiences, and fast-changing social and political circumstances in the post-Apartheid South Africa. Her insights into Bush Radio's long battles with regulators and its intersections with political action are illuminating, as is her broader account of how, over time and through multiple routes, Bush Radio has developed a practice of denaturalizing media power and dismantling mythical boundaries around the media process.

In three sharply contrasting ways, then, the chapters in this section illustrate the many routes along which the competing definitions, concepts, and empirical priorities mapped out earlier are being developed by researchers around the world. Indirectly, they confirm what a vital space the field of researching 'our media' has become.

NOTES

1. For an interesting Swedish study, which with deliberate paradox raises the question of whether Radio Free Europe's practices during the Cold War can in any sense be seen as 'alternative media', see Andersson (2004).
2. Comment at an international workshop on 'Media Civic Agency and Democracy,' Södertörn University College, Stockholm, May 18 2006.

REFERENCES

Andersson, L. (2004). US-governed radical media: Radio Free Europe in Eastern Europe. *Mediestudier vid Södertörns högsola* (Huddinge, Sweden), 1.
Atton, C. (2002). *Alternative media.* London: Sage.

Atton, C. (2004). *An alternative internet.* London: Sage.

Atton, C., & Couldry, N. (2003). Introduction to special issue of *Media Culture & Society, 25*(5), 579-586.

Browne, D. (2005). *Ethnic minorities, electronic media and the public sphere: A comparative study.* Cresskill, NJ: Hampton Press.

Couldry, N. (2002). Mediation and alternative media, or relocating the centre of media and communication studies. *Media International Australia, 103,* 24-31.

Couldry, N., & Curran J. (Eds.). (2003). *Contesting media power: Alternative media in a networked world.* Lanham, MD: Rowman & Littlefield.

Downing, J. D. H. (1984). *Radical media.* Boston: South End Press.

Downing, J. D. H. (2003). Audiences and readers of alternative media: The absent lure of the virtually unknown. *Media Culture & Society, 25*(5), 625-646.

Downing, J. D. H., with Ford, T. V., Gil, G., & Stein, L. (2001). *Radical media: Rebellious communication and social movements.* London: Sage.

Garnham, N. (1990). *Capitalism and communication.* London: Sage.

Garnham, N. (1999). *Emancipation, the media and modernity.* Oxford: Oxford University Press.

Rodríguez, C. (2001). *Fissures in the mediascape. An international study of citizens' media.* Cresskill, NJ: Hampton Press.

MAKING CULTURE VISIBLE
The Mediated Construction of a Mapuche Nation in Chile

Juan Francisco Salazar

The material presented in this chapter is the result of several years of participatory multisited research carried out with Mapuche organizations in Chile, such as Lulul Mawidha and Jvfken Mapu in Santiago, and to a lesser extent Mapuexpress in Temuco. The driving research question was to identify mechanisms through which Mapuche community media products and processes serve as vehicles for putting into practice alternative understandings of ethnic citizenship. The core methods employed are grounded in practice-based research, primarily through the production of a documentary video titled *From Land To Screen* (2004), which I produced in collaboration with Jeannette Paillan, executive director of Lulul Mawidha. Practice-based research is defined as "the use of research-inspired principles, designs and information-gathering techniques within existing forms of practice to answer questions that emerge from practice in ways that inform practice" (Epstein, 2001: 17). In this way, the main purpose of the research was to understand and advocate (nationally and internationally) for the potential of Mapuche alternative media being produced by several Mapuche social media collectives. The research was conducted mainly between 2002 and 2004, with systematic and exhaustive review of online documentation prior to (2000-2002), during, and after (2004-2006) the main research stage (production of the documentary film). In-depth interviews with Mapuche media makers were conducted in the winters 2002, 2003, and 2004.

Indigenous media is a field of research and practice that has received coveted attention in many countries as an important cultural resource, a critical area of political activism, and a fertile field of theorization in studies of media and culture. This chapter looks at the emergence of indigenous Mapuche media in Chile, concentrating on the poetics of media practice, or the ways in which Mapuche media makers, policy advocates, and communication analysts are articulating digital media to make culture *visible* in a wider national public sphere.

It is worth mentioning that Indigenous media production remains significantly overlooked in Chilean media and cultural studies. It has yet to be appropriately integrated in public media policy—as demonstrated by the lack of reference to indigenous media in recent audiovisual media policy reform—and has been considerably excluded from current communication and media research. There has been little theoretical debate about the implications of indigenous media on the public domain, other citizen-oriented media practices, or community media at large, which in Chile has played such a pivotal role, particularly during the pro-democracy movement against the military regime during the 1980s. As could be expected, indigenous media is absolutely invisible in corporate media architectures and mainstream media, either print-based or broadcasting. Indigenous media productions remain absent from mainstream screens and circuits, where an indigenous imaginary continues to be largely constructed by the dominant Chilean society.

The materialization of Mapuche communication practices in the last fifteen years finds its roots in historical contradictions and grounds itself in the context of redemocratization that has followed sixteen years of military rule in the country (1973-1990). It also occurs simultaneously with strong processes of ethnic resurgence flourishing across Latin America, especially after 1992. In what has been described as a new pan-American movement of Indigenous re-emergence in Latin America (Bengoa, 2000), Mapuche media are firmly established in local social solidarities and have had a remarkable impact within local communities. Today they also play an important part in challenging both national state policy/law as well as corporate commercial media discourses and practices. They are an important element of new civil society media formations, and, more importantly, Mapuche media practices open up new discursive avenues from which to challenge the enclosures of the public sphere in what is arguably a counter-public sphere at a small scale, following Downey and Fenton's (2003) consideration of counter-public spheres as "politics that seeks to challenge the dominant public sphere rather than simply be independent from it" (Downey & Fenton, 2003: 193).

In a context of cultural and political effervescence, this incipient yet fervent development of indigenous communications in Chile has had an arrested development that can be best characterized as a strong, yet often disperse movement towards the conception of an oppositional public sphere from where to contest the indifference and coercion of corporate commercial media, the inefficacy of current legal and cultural policy frameworks to promote indigenous participation in the cultural industries, and the lack of appropriate bridges between indigenous communication rights advocacy and other citizen-oriented media practices. In many cases, *making culture visible* becomes a process of strategic reversal, from where indigenous media makers are able to challenge long-standing cultural stereotypes and create novel forms of healing historical disruptions in traditional knowledge, social memory, and cultural identity.

MAPUCHE MEDIA AS CITIZENS' MEDIA IN COUNTER-PUBLIC SPHERES OF ACTION

According to the latest population census carried out nationally in 2002, the Indigenous population in Chile accounts for roughly three-quarters of a million people, distributed in eight distinctive ethnic groups. The Mapuche people, with a population of 604,349 (INE, 2003), are not only the most numerous indigenous nation in Chile, but also one of the largest ethnic groups in all of Latin America, with an important number (another 200,000 people) living in the south-west of Argentina. The ancestral Mapuche country covered an extensive territory from the south-central valleys of Chile, across the Andes mountains all the way to the Atlantic coast. Between 1860 and 1890, this territory was forcefully and violently incorporated into the Chilean and Argentinean states, and millions of hectares of collective indigenous land were expropriated. Of the total Mapuche population living in Chile today, three quarters reside in urban areas—around 150,000 Mapuche people in the capital Santiago alone—whereas nearly half is located in what has been recently conceptualized by several Mapuche intellectuals and activists as the *Wallmapu*, or the ancestral Mapuche territory in the south of the country (Ancan & Calfio 2002; Cayuqueo & Painemal, 2003).

Mapuche organizations played a pivotal role during the last years of military rule and the transition to democracy by supporting the opposition coalition that defeated the Pinochet regime in 1988. The first democratically elected government of Patricio Aylwin was able to introduce the new Indigenous Act of 1993. Minor constitutional reforms were also introduced in 1994 during the government of Eduardo Frei, which recognize the existence and importance of 'ethnic groups' in the constituency of the country. Several analyses concur in that today this tacit agreement between the coalition of democratic parties (in government since 1990) and the major Mapuche organizations is broken. Despite the fact that three successive *Concertación* governments have returned thousands of hectares of indigenous land confiscated during the years of military repression, Mapuche intellectuals, historians, and social scientists have increasingly articulated an oppositional discourse, citing the Chilean government's failure to ratify several international laws pertaining to the protection of indigenous resources and heritage. These claims actually demonstrate that the Indigenous Law of 1993 has rapidly become dated in many respects, and its monolithic nature has not captured the dynamic cultural change happening in the country—for example, the fact that 75% of the indigenous population lives in heavily populated urban areas.

Like most Indigenous and tribal cultures worldwide, Mapuche people also wrestle against the vast challenge posed by increasing media globalization and the infiltration of their cultures through a range of technologies of information and communication that until now they have rarely controlled or owned. Media products are not isolated phenomena, but rather are situated in specific historical conditions and embedded in multimedial and intertextual frameworks of reference. In a contemporary media scene characterized by technological convergence, global flows in interconnected cultural economies, by textual networks and intensive patterns of media use, indigenous users and makers of media can no longer be regarded as passive recipients of messages, in isolation from the production and cultural construction of technology. On the contrary, it is extremely important to highlight the many cases that show the creative role of media production and consumption in the everyday lives of indigenous peoples.

Over the past two decades a wide range of literature has made it possible to document the ways 'ethnic minority' groups have been embracing, appropriating, and using an array of communication/information technologies, including film, video, radio, and new digital media (Browne, 1996; Ginsburg, 1991, 1995, 1999, 2000, 2002; Gumucio-Dagrón, 2001; Molnar & Meadows, 2001; Prins, 1997; Riggins, 1992; Roth, 2000; Turner, 1991, 2002). These media have been creatively appropriated as viable options for *making culture visible* (Wortham, 2002) in different local and global social spaces. Importantly in most cases is the fact that these media have been conceived as ways of contesting the imposition of dominant cultural practices and elaborating or reformulating their own. In this regard it is crucial to also mention recent work being conducted on new social movements as counter publics (Asen & Brower, 2001; Downing, 2001; Fraser, 1993; Rodríguez, 2001; Warner, 2002) that stress the ability of social formations—historically not considered as being part of the public sphere—to actually exist and function outside the scapes of the dominant public, acting primarily and foremost as sites of "critical oppositional force" (Palczewski, 2001). In this regard, any examination of indigenous media in Latin America must certainly look at how indigenous organizations are challenging both the "practice and terms of citizenship in Latin America's new democracies" (Yashar, 1998: 23). Unfortunately, little work that looks at the implications of indigenous media production has been conducted in Chile. There are no audience or reception studies pertaining to indigenous cultural consumption of mass media, nor any study of the political and legal restraints posed by inadequate public media policy.

The notion of counter hegemony is relevant to understand how community media, video collectives, and particularly Internet activism (including free software movements and peer to peer networking) have opened up opportunities for indigenous peoples to form what Nancy Fraser (1993) has termed *counter-public spheres* of action. Fraser's influential work is critical, as it frames theoretically the way in which Mapuche media challenge the notion of an open, accessible and inclusive public sphere. Fraser's critique points to the fact that in reality, the bourgeois public sphere as defined earlier by Jurgen Habermas (1989) is actually based on exclusions (of women, workers, immigrants, sexual and ethnic 'minorities') from the public domain. What we see today is a series of competing publics, where the boundaries between the private and public are much more hazy and blurred.[1]

In this sense, I consider the appropriation or indigenization of media technologies in light of what Michel Foucault terms the "insurrection of subjugated knowledges" (Foucault, 1980: 81). Foucault argued that the primary role of the new historian was to politically assist in the insurrection of those knowledges that are permanently being disqualified by the prevailing regimes of thought for not being scientific, logical, or rational. Looking at the way in which it has developed since 1990, Mapuche media practices may be clearly articulated as a cultural project opposed to the centralizing forces of dominant structures of institutional power, where subjugated Mapuche visions of their history, present, and future rise up to the forefront of public debate.

On yet another level, Mapuche media may be constructed not only as alternative to the mainstream, but may also be understood in relation to the notion of *alterative* media proposed by Rafael Roncagliolo (1991). Roncagliolo's conceptualization of *alterative* media differs from more general approaches to alternative media in the fact that it stresses the proactive engagement with media for social change, and not a mere alternative running in parallel to mainstream corporate communication infrastructures. It looks at the transformative power of media. This view is also related to Clemencia Rodríguez' proposal of *citizens' media*, which is helpful to understand, for example, the way several Mapuche sectors in Chile appropriate media as a way to perform their ethnic citizenship within a state that recognizes their existence as native or aboriginal people, but fails to recognize any form of indigenous citizenship and/or nationality. Therefore, any participation at a national level in line with Habermas' notion of public sphere would be impossible for indigenous people, mostly because they are not allowed to participate as 'ethnic citizens' because they are not recognized as such, and national citizenship is a critical imperative for taking part in a given public sphere. The Chilean constitution only recognizes the existence of ethnic groups within a unitary national state.

The concept of 'ethnic citizenship' has been formulated by Mexican anthropologist Guillermo de la Peña (1995), who has revisited Renato Rosaldo's (1985, 1994) notion of cultural citizenship in his analysis of cultural assimilation in the United States. Hence, the notion of ethnic citizenship is used here to refer to the processes of political and social participation in which indigenous people are able to partake in the public sphere not only as Chilean, Bolivian, or Mexican citizens, but also as Mapuche, Aymara, or Zapotecas. Redefining cultural participation in Latin America today means acknowledging an indigenous counter-public sphere, which as an arena of oppositional consciousness, locates agency in indigenous peoples, and allows for different and multiple forms of representation to exist simultaneously. What Mapuche media makers are today contesting is the opportunity for participating in a democratic public sphere as Mapuche, and not necessarily as Chileans.

Therefore in order to examine the ways indigenous people in Chile are embracing media as social practices, I focus on the development of Mapuche media as a particular process of cultural objectification, based on a reconceptualization of the Mapuche idea of Nation; the *Wallmapu*. Media technologies of objectification such as video or the Internet perform strategically as a reversal and displacement of shifting public policies or dominant techniques of representation in order to construct new practices for making culture visible. For Mapuche organizations and "territorial identities,"[2] *Mapuche imaginary* is not just a lyrical mental faculty for fantasizing an ancestral past. On the contrary, it refers to the challenge of constructing an ancestral future within a realm of images, representations, and ideas of self-determination and autonomy. It is only the current phase of a war of images that resists oblivion. Neither of these postdictatorship laws provides specific definitions of cultural diversity in the culture and creative industries and are lacking in deploying an appropriate media ecology that considers autonomous indigenous communications.[3] Moreover, indigenous media have been remarkably disregarded in recent public policy directed at consolidating the new "audiovisual institutionality" (Aliaga, 2000) being driven by the Chilean state.

The lack of specific prescriptions for state-supported indigenous media is partly explained by the fact that the Chilean media environment is among the least pluralist in the region. Due primarily to an excessive level of economic and ideological property concentration (Palacios, 2002), what is also striking is a general lack of appropriate regulation on this issue (Sunkel & Geoffroy, 2001). However, as will be discussed in more detail in the following sections, Mapuche media have begun creating the first fissures in this mediascape (*cf* Rodríguez, 2001).

FROM LAND TO SCREEN

In examining the processes by which the Chilean public and media sphere have created a historical field of inclusions and exclusions, the new public social space formed by Mapuche organizations working on communications, video activists, and online networks is increasingly becoming a counter public sphere at a small scale. Mapuche communities, both rural but particularly urban, are at the center of a very particular historical moment in which they are confronted by ideals of nation building. Media makers are an integral part of this moment, holding the responsibility to assist in the articulation (imagination) of renewed Mapuche social formations at the public, national level.

The possibilities for 'Making Our Media' have become a tour de force for several Mapuche professionals working in the field. A new mediated Mapuche imaginary, constructed from within the Mapuche, as shown by videos such as Jeanette Paillan's *Wallmapu*, or the newspaper *Azkintuwe*, or the writings of José Ancan (1994, 2003), draws attention to the ways in which Mapuche cultural resistance and desire for a better society are projected onto technologies capable of delivering a potential realm of completeness (see Figure 1.1). More importantly, the appropriation of technologies of imagination and information is a self-conscious process of political action. As Mapuche filmmaker Jeannette Paillan has expressed: "I do not make films only to show what is going on here ... I make them to change the situation of the Mapuche ... I prefer to make less videos and see the Mapuche reality change" (Jeannette Paillan, personal communication, July 2003).

But perhaps the most important impact of an emergent indigenous public opinion is that the people, who have been historically interpellated by dominant discourses, now have their own. This new Mapuche activist imaginary expressed through communications media has been constructed as a source of political assets and values, not only at the base level of internal mobilization and solidarity, but also in terms of transnational communication and cross-cultural communication. The Mapuche diaspora around the world is very significant, due to the particular situation of several hundred Mapuche individuals—including political activists, peasants, and professionals—who were exiled by the military regime in the 1970s. As I have discussed elsewhere (Salazar, 2003), the development of a Mapuche 'activist imaginary' via the Internet, has renewed a 'resource of hope,' in Faye Ginsburg's words, "bringing about fresh issues about citizenship and the shape of public spheres within the frame and terms of a traditional discourse on polity and civil society" (Ginsburg, 2000: 39).

These transformations need to be conceptualized as grounded on social movements for indigenous empowerment, cultural autonomy, and claims to land, which in the Chilean case arise primarily from a circle of educated Mapuche intellectuals from big urban centers like Temuco, Concepción, or Santiago or activist organizations in rural areas like Lumaco, Arauco, and Malleco. In any case, they set up the precise political framework to understand the current situation of indigenous radio, the emergence of indigenous video and the Internet, as well as a wider revitalization of indigenous cultural politics in general, characterized in a wave of Mapuche poetry, video art, music, and traditional arts and crafts.

All of these cases demonstrate that in recent years there has been a robust increase in Mapuche media, all of which make allusion to a Mapuche 'nation', the *Wallmapu*, that spreads across the south of Chile and Argentina. This territory of about 150,000 square kilometers is conceived in different regions divided between the Gulumapu (in Chile's south) and the Puelmapu (in Argentina's south-west).

Among the current wave of Mapuche intellectuals, Jose Ancan has become a key figure as a prominent Mapuche thinker. Art theorist, scholar, and activist, founder of the Liwen Mapuche Research Group based in Temuco in the early 1990s, Ancan is one of the most determined voices advocating for a much more

FIGURE 1.1. Filmmaker Jeannete Paillan at work with displaced Pewenche communities in Alto Bio-bio region, July 2003.

radical perspective on autonomy, one that involves re-building what he calls the "Mapuche country." He talks about an "ineludible construction of a legitimate and self-conscious *fin de siècle* utopia: the return and repopulation of the historical Mapuche country; *the Wallmapu*" (Ancan & Calfio, 2002: 3; my translation and emphasis). Interestingly, Ancan's conceptualization of the Wallmapu has a historical foundation in the semi-autonomous Mapuche territory in existence 120 years ago, but more importantly it incorporates a conceptual and discursive 'country' to be reconquered. Ancan goes beyond the common distinction between rural and urban Mapuche to establish a distinction between the Mapuche population living in the historical Mapuche country (the Wallmapu), which accounts for roughly 40% of the Mapuche population (INE, 2003), and those Mapuche living outside this 'country', which Ancan has called *sujetos de la diáspora*, or diasporic subjects (Ancan & Calfio, 2002: 6). Ancan is at the forefront of a strong, yet not always popular, political undercurrent at the core of the Mapuche movement that is pushing for the constitution of an autonomous Mapuche nation, with territorial independence on the basis of a sovereign Mapuche parliament. This view is not shared by everyone within the Mapuche movement (Foerster 1999; Foerster & Vergara 2001; Mariman 1998) and marks the more extreme nationalist positions set in motion only in the last decade, amid what Calbucura calls the "painful uprooting of the Chilean political class" (Calbucura, 2001).

The question of Mapuche ethnic nationalism frames one of the most important Mapuche radio programs, *Wixage Anay!*, broadcasting on FM Radio Tierra, from Santiago. The program may be traced back to when Jvken Mapu Documentation Centre, which emerged in early 1993 as a collective of Mapuche social communicators decided to occupy spaces in the Chilean mediasphere (Elias Paillan, personal communication, 2002). Founded by Clara Antinao, Fresia Paillal, Jose Paillal, and Ramon Curivil, with funding from a Christian congregation, the collective began broadcasting the first program on *Radio Nacional* in June 1993, only months after the passing of the Indigenous Act.

Wixage Anay! has been important in the formation of an ethnic consciousness within Mapuche listeners in the marginal suburbs of Santiago. The program promotes itself as a space for cultural and political debate and supports mobilizations for the cause of the Mapuche communities in the south of the country, currently at the centre of the land struggle. It has become an important venue for urban Mapuche living in the peripheries of Santiago to become participating citizens who can partake—often in their own language—in the events that directly affect them, in the neighborhoods, in the rural communities in the south, in the Mapuche country at large. *Wixage Anay!* is perhaps the longest running Mapuche radio program in the country, probably the most listened to, and recently celebrated eleven years of service in June 2004. It runs in both Spanish and Mapudungun and should be regarded as a crucial medium in the construction of an incipient Mapuche 'audience'. Despite ongoing financial problems the program keeps running to 'amplify' the voice of the urban Mapuche and provides one of the few spaces where the informative agenda of the Chilean media is examined from a Mapuche perspective (Mariqueo, 2003).

Azkintuwe newspaper is also a key example of this attempt to construct a sense of nation, in this case more specifically related to the appropriation and use of mass print-based media. Put together by Pedro Cayuqueo and other young Mapuche activists and journalists from Temuco, the newspaper was launched in late 2003 in both print and online versions. The first point that stands out from this publication is the editors' emphasis on its 'nationality'. Its principal aim is to reconstruct "that old *utopia* of the Mapuche country" (Cayuqueo & Painemal, 2003) in what may be a direct reference to Ancan's position on what Hernandez calls "incomplete citizenship" (Hernandez, 2003). This declaration of principles on the first issue guides the editorial views of the newspaper. With a printed circulation spanning most of southern Chile and Argentina, including Santiago, the paper covers relevant issues in both countries. *"From the Wallmapu, to the Wallmapu"* is the motto of a venture that demonstrates a serious and solid attempt to build a Mapuche idea of nationhood that transcends the geographical boundaries imposed by the Chilean and Argentinean states in the past century. As a printed newspaper and online news service, *Azkintuwe* is a continuation of the editors' previous experience in Kolectivo Lientur, a group of 'counter-information' created in Temuco in 1999. It is one among many other online news and advocacy portals recently developed in different places of the 'Wallmapu', but perhaps the only one with an aspiration to address a Mapuche audience.[4] For Cayuqueo, the aim is also to construct a Mapuche audience or readership that feels represented as a *Nation*, not just as an ethnic group (Pedro Cayuqueo, editorial, *Azkintuwe* No. 1, October 2003). Printed Mapuche media do not have a long history, and not many have had the endeavor to decidedly work towards the building of a new Mapuche imaginary that services the Mapuche people as a nation within an ancestral territory, as *Azkintuwe* is ready to do, directly contravening the political Constitution of the country and current attempts to reform it.

In a similar way to *Wixage Anay, Azkintuwe* also acts as an important critique to mainstream Chilean investigative print journalism and may increasingly become an important element of political intervention in the national mediaspheres by placing a Mapuche 'national' discourse on the public domain, for everyone to access. It offers parallel discursive arenas where Mapuche organizations, both in and outside the Wallmapu, circulate counter-discourses, allowing them to formulate oppositional interpretations of their own cultural histories and futures. Because the newspaper works as a bilingual document, language (Mapuzungun) becomes an active instrument generating an oppositional forum where Mapuche people can voice ideas in their own language.

What is extremely important to consider is that most Mapuche media cross-feed information, therefore generating a cohesive discourse that may be found on the web sites, on the radio programs, and also on video productions and documentaries. Like print-based media, the role of video in the Mapuche movement has been quite marginal in terms of numbers of productions, but has been fervently embraced as a tool of documentation and media activism. In comparison to other countries, indigenous video in Chile was—with a few exceptions—a relative newcomer until the late 1990s. If prominent indigenous videos were already being produced in the early 1980s in other Latin American countries, such as Mexico and Brazil, Mapuche video starts off as recently as 1994, primarily through the work of José Ancan and Jeannette Paillan, both working in Santiago at the time.

When looking at the origins of Mapuche video, José Ancan is a key figure because he paves the way for the building of Mapuche video practice with an article published in 1994, which in a sense opens the discursive field of Mapuche video practice. In this article, Ancan also tackles the problems and potentialities of audiovisual media in cultural recovery and survival. Moreover, he discusses the need for a cultural construction of video media as a way of appropriating the technology in such a way that Mapuche people could not only contest images of the broader society, but also, and more importantly, look at themselves in the mirror of history. In the same year, Ancan also shot his first video, *Wiñometun Ni Mapu* (Return to the Land), which may be regarded as the first directed by an indigenous person in Chile. The idea of the return to the Mapuche country is a motif in much of Ancan's work, not only on video but also in literary and cultural criticism.

From there on, Jeannette Paillan's work has always revolved around the conflict between the Chilean state, the Mapuche nation, and the corporate interests in the area. Her first fully produced video, the 27-minute documentary *Punalka:*

The Spirit of the Bio-Bio, was shot in 1994 after two years working with Pehuenche communities in the Bio-Bio region, south of Santiago. It is however in her latest documentary, *Wallmapu*, that Paillan attempted to rethink Mapuche identity as a self-conscious contestation to official history. The film also works as a call to the visualization of a historically rooted national consciousness and attempts to simultaneously uncover a Mapuche counter-history and counter-memory. *Wallmapu* is to date the strongest Mapuche televisual text to tangle video media as a space of negotiation within broader domains of difference within Chilean society. The notion of the *Wallmapu* becomes in Paillan's work a clear metaphor for locating a Mapuche identity, where the Mapuche struggle is consistently tied to the social solidarities in which it is grounded. The video not only documents and visualizes a history according to the Mapuche—or a certain sector within the Mapuche *intelligentsia*—but more importantly, works as a (media/tion) practice of imagining a Mapuche nation not just within the Chilean nation, but more likely, adjacent to it. *Wallmapu* is a text that therefore acts as a kind of "televisual practice of location" (Wortham, 2002), providing a sense of place rooted in a different imaginary—an "activist imaginary" (Marcus 1995, 1996). On another level, Paillan's video is also a product, a technological artifact, and an object. Here the individual agency of the media maker becomes a practice of cultural objectification, whereby there is a process of reflection that involves the representation of the filmmakers' own collective (urban Mapuche) and individual identity (woman, video maker) on video media.[5] *Wallmapu* is in this sense the most ambitious of all of Paillan's films, as it looks at reframing the Mapuche conflict in the media, envisioning strategies of political autonomy, and more importantly, visualizing and representing a political project of Mapuche nationhood. Paillan's film was awarded an award for best historical documentation at the 2003 Human Rights Film Festival of Buenos Aires. It was also awarded the same prize at the seventh version of the Indigenous Film and Video Festival of Indigenous Peoples held in Santiago in June 2004.[6]

This political project of rearticulating the Mapuche nation can also be seen in the last example in question—the impressive array of Mapuche organizations and individuals in Chile and abroad, who have constructed a remarkable digital network of websites and online communication. These organizations have vehemently embraced the Internet as a viable tactic for building a counter-hegemonic discourse that has started to impact in the national public sphere. These instances stand out as notable cases of radical indigenous media practices, which I argue can be seen as a strong yet incipient indigenous (Mapuche) public sphere. In general, the Mapuche online network is a locus without a center and without vertical control with the potential to host a "free and influential public space, a sphere of social action not separate but fully linked to and a protagonist in conflicts and antagonisms" (Carlini, 1996: 21, cited in Bentivegna, 2002: 59).

It seems for a moment that there is a noteworthy leap from oral to digital forms of communication without a strong phase of electronic (radio and video) communications. This may be explained by the fact that the dynamics of

Mapuche Internet media have been so productive and fruitful, especially when compared to the lack of opportunities in televisual media. For example, and unlike broadcasting, Internet has facilitated the building of an online community to support the Mapuche struggle and redefine its position within the national imaginary. Today, the intricate network of Mapuche online activism supposes a potential mediasphere that is being constructed from the small rural towns in the south of Chile, to the big cities of Temuco and Santiago, as well as hubs in Brighton, U.K., Amsterdam, Paris, and Uppsala in Sweden.

In this sense, Mapuche communities and organizations have had a 'counter-public' as their social basis for resistance for quite some time now, even before the building of the first websites in 1996. Most importantly, an autonomous dissident voice has definitely been possible through the Internet. Today, there are at least 25 distinctive Mapuche websites, some hosted in Chile, many others in countries such as Sweden, the Netherlands, the United Kingdom, France, Germany, Belgium, and Spain. Most of these sites have been used as vehicles of expression for processes of "rebellious communication" (Downing, 2001) and mobilization originating at the community level. The existence of a Mapuche identity in the Internet proves that the notion of cyberspace is not always "a place apart from off-line life ... [where] participants are abstracted and distanced from local and embodied social relations" (Miller & Slater, 2000). On the contrary, the reinvention of a Mapuche identity in cyberspace is grounded in the social solidarities and the cultural materialities of the everyday. The Mapuche information network is an effort to create alliances in order to impede the neutralization by the Chilean media and mainstream public opinion of an independent, autonomous, often counter discourse emerging from community and other forms of social organization struggling to fight against their victimization.

In general terms, the Mapuche websites have contributed to observe the legacy of the military dictatorship in the national media architecture, even after 15 years of successive democratic governments. Examples of this are the neoliberal policies affecting indigenous peoples and the environment, and the infliction of the antiterrorist law of 1979 on Mapuche peasants and activists. The Mapuche websites have been also crucial in showing images of police abuse, the action of paramilitary groups, and the militarization of rural communities in the south. They have proven to be efficient forms for denouncing irregularities affecting rural Mapuche communities, such as the fact, for example, that 70% of waste deposits in the Araucania Region in southern Chile are located on Mapuche land. They have raised fresh claims over the control, production, and circulation of images and the ownership of media and communications outlets, as was put forward at the First National Encounter of Mapuche Communicators of the Wallmapu in October 2004.

One such organization is *Mapuexpress*, a Mapuche communication rights advocacy group based in Temuco, southern Chile. Through an effective online news and current affairs service they have become in their five years of existence a solid space for enriching the Chilean public and media sphere. They have played a pivotal role in exposing the conservative and oligarchical nature of the Chilean media, which have in fact been instrumental in supporting the state and private interests in recent conflicts in the south of the country. *Mapuexpress* has effectively exposed the hidden family links between government and opposition, the legacies of the Pinochet regime in the media, as well as several cases of discrimination, abuse of civil rights, and lack of appropriate governance schemes for the regulation of indigenous knowledge and its dissemination. Developed in 1999 by Alfredo Seguel and *Konapewman*, a collective of young Mapuche activists from Temuco, *Mapuexpress* is presented on the web as a regularly updated political information service directly out of Mapuche territory, the Wallmapu. The website is sponsored by the *Mapuche Folil* foundation in the Netherlands and contains an impressive list of articles and online publications as well as a Mapuche online library. The extensive use of photographs used in this website is a strong argument against the enclosing of information by the Chilean big media and has had an important impact on the construction of an activist imagination. These enclosures refer to the way in which images are pigeonholed, manipulated, and circulated within certain boundaries, whereas the Mapuche websites allow civil society to access information and 'see' the events from a Mapuche perspective.

CONCLUSIONS

In the past decade, and despite little interest from academics, the state, or nongovernmental organizations in Chile, Mapuche activists have been able to develop an alternative and more comprehensive public arena through which members of different urban collectives and communal organizations have been able to start talking back to Chilean society across divisions of cultural difference. In the Mapuche case it remains to be seen how the emergence of an "informally mobilized body of nongovernmental discursive opinion could serve as a counterweight to the state," as has been the case with the Zapatista communities in Mexico, for example (Ford & Gil in Downing, 2001). Nevertheless, it is a fact that by "using the inscription of their screen memories in media," as Ginsburg (2002) argues, Mapuche media makers have been able to 'talk back' to structures of power and state. Moreover, the new information and communication technologies have been critical tools to enter the context of an 'international' community, or as some would argue, an 'information society,' without having to have the Chilean state as a valid mediating interlocutor.

As has been demonstrated throughout the chapter, a well informed, internationally supported Mapuche public domain already exists. It is also somewhat possible to argue that this Mapuche sphere has opened a fissure in the Chilean mediascape (*cf* Clemencia Rodríguez, 2001) that has set up an unavoidable challenge to the "regimes of truth" imposed by national and commercial media and has given rise to fierce disputes in Congress, where right wing senators have actively called to proscribe the Mapuche media outlets that support the

Mapuche movement and ongoing uprising. What the examples described show is nothing less than the political resonance of a new Indigenous counter-public sphere (Stephenson, 2000). Similarly to the Zapatista case in Mexico (see, for example, Downing, 2001), the Mapuche informational counter-publicity is having a strong impact on both the public sphere in Chile, where demands, repression, and militarization of indigenous lands get reported on national television, and also on transnational public spheres and circuits such as the United Nations, European progressive newspapers and human rights groups.

Because, as some authors argue, the capacity of social groups in Chile to act upon the public stage has diminished since peaking in the early 1990s (de la Maza, 2004), Mapuche media provide a new space of debate and horizontal flow of information. It has not only allowed for the embodiment of an idea of nationhood—the Wallmapu or Mapuche country—but has also proven that few normative frameworks exist in Chile to favor the growth, consolidation, and influence of an active civil society. If nongovernmental organizations were critical in the mid 1980s to mid 1990s in setting much of the social agenda, today the landscape is covered with organizations that do not have real power in public affairs. The cohesion of the Mapuche media may serve as an important model of community citizens' media.

At the core of the debate is the fact that different sectors within the Mapuche movement, especially the more radical organizations pushing for self-determination and political autonomy, see 'citizenship' not only as a legal status but also as a form of identification. As Chantal Mouffe puts it, "a type of political identity: something to be constructed, not empirically given" (Mouffe, 1992b: 231, cited in Rodríguez, 2001). Citizens have to enact their citizenship on a day-to-day basis through their participation in everyday political practices, and in this sense the Internet may be conceived as a new form of 'citizens' media' for the Mapuche movement. And this is what the new Mapuche political subjects are demanding.

The Mapuche movement is currently at an important historical crossroads. It is as fractured as it has ever been. Many achievements have been accomplished in terms of land rights and access to media. Nevertheless, the road ahead is even tougher and demands the collective effort of a series of actors working together to assist in the much needed and long overdue indigenous communications program. Although the *Concertación* governments have attempted to repair historical injuries in the relations between the state and Mapuche people,[7] it is no less true that the repression of the indigenous movement has been unacceptable. The relentless demand for the democratization of public spaces may be found across all Mapuche media practices. What is lacking still at a national level is the design of consensual policies and actions that correspond to concrete means of reduction of the social phenomenon of information exclusion in the country. A truly democratic audiovisual normative, unlike the one recently approved by the Chilean congress, should also include regulations about minimum amounts of airtime for indigenous content and encourage the formulation of new national editorial policies for the creation of special publishing houses focusing on indigenous issues or managed by indigenous organizations. This is particularly important given the relevance of Mapuche literature in recent years and the large number of Mapuche poets generating strong and creative work. Perhaps underlying this entire complex scenario is the particular need for equitable and high-quality education, one that promotes multiculturalism and cultural diversity and becomes relevant to the country's diverse citizens.

NOTES

1. For a critical consideration of Habermas' conception see Downey & Fenton, 2003.
2. This concept has been increasingly in use by several Mapuche to refer to the social organization of cultural identities based on the ancestral territory of the Wallmapu.
3. It is critical to point out here that Chile remains the only Latin American country that has still not ratified Convention 169 of the International Labor Organization (ILO) on Indigenous and Tribal Peoples, despite repeated pledges to the Working Group on Indigenous Peoples of the United Nations.
4. Other recent examples include *El Kimvn*, a printed local newspaper in Neuquen, Argentina, and *Wajmapu*, an email bulletin service also originating in Neuquen. A group of students has created Mapurbe, a local newspaper for urban *Mapuche* in the city of Bariloche, Argentina. In Chile, apart from the more established Mapuche online media, a series of local newspapers has also been developed, such as *El Toki* by the Asociación Ñancucheo in Lumaco as well as *Rakiduam* by the Asociación Poyenhue from Villarrica. A special Mapuche informational bulletin was also created in Boyeco, in the outskirts of Temuco where Mapuche families have been seriously affected by the crisis of waste deposits in the area.
5. Erica Wortham (2002) has explored similar issues in her research of indigenous televisual media practices in Mexico as social practices of narration and location.
6. Interestingly, all the promotional material of the festival made it clear the festival was being held in Wallmapu, not necessarily Chile.
7. For example by returning over 350,000 hectares of land to the communities, creating a Commission of Truth and New Treatment, developing the *Orígenes* Program, and funding indigenous productive development and social programs.

REFERENCES

Aliaga, I. (2000). *Industria audiovisual en chile: Antecedentes, políticas públicas, datos y cifras* [Audiovisual industry in Chile: Antecedents, public policies, data and figures]. Ministry of Education Document, Chile.

Ancán, J. (1994). La imagen en el espejo. Hacia el audiovisual mapuche [The image in the mirror. Toward a Mapuche audiovisual]. *Lengua y Literatura Mapuche, 6*, 18-24.

Ancán, J. (2003). Prólogo [Prologue]. In I. Hernández, *Autonomía o ciudadanía incompleta: El Pueblo Mapuche en Chile y Argentina* [Autonomy and incomplete citizenship: The Mapuche people in Chile and Argentina]. Santiago: CEPAL.

Ancán J., & Calfio, M. (2002). Retorno al país mapuche: Reflexiones sobre una utopía por construir [Return to the Mapuche country: Reflections about an utopia to be constructed]. *Ñuke Mapuförlaget* Working Paper Series 6.

Asen, R., & Brower, D. (2001). *Counterpublics and the state.* Albany: State University of New York Press.

Bengoa, J. (2000). *La emergencia indígena en América Latina* [Indigenous emergence in Latin America]. Santiago: Fondo de Cultura Económica.

Bentivegna, S. (2002). Politics and new media. In L. Lievrouw & S. Livingstone (Eds.), *Handbook of new media: Social shaping and consequences of ICT* (pp. 50-60). London: Sage.

Browne, D. (1996). *Electronic media and indigenous peoples: A voice of our own?* Ames: Iowa State University Press.

Calbucura, J. (2001). La cuestión indígena y el dilema del doloroso desarraigo de la clase política chilena [The indigenous question and the dilemma of painful exile of Chile's political class]. *Rocinante* No.30. Retrieved July 26, 2007, from http://www.mapuche.info/mapuint/Calbucura010400.htm.

Cayuqueo P., & Painemal, W. (2003, October). Hacia un imaginario de nación [Toward a nation imaginary]. *Azkintuwe* Monthly Newspaper, pp. 12-14.

de la Maza, G. (2004). Modernization *a la chilena*: Integration and exclusion. *ReVista, Harvard Review of Latin America,* 29-31.

de la Peña, G. (1995). La ciudadanía étnica y la reconstrucción de los indios en el México contemporáneo [Ethnic citizenship and indigenous reconstruction in contemporary Mexico]. *Revista Internacional de Filosofía Política, 6,* 116-140.

Downey J., & Fenton, N. (2003). New media, counter publicity and the public sphere. *New Media & Society, 5*(2), 185–202.

Downing, J. D. H., with Ford, T. V., Gil, G., & Stein, L. (2001). *Radical media: Rebellious communication and social movements.* London: Sage.

Epstein, I. (2001). *Clinical data mining in practice-based research: Social work in hospital settings.* New York: Haworth Social Work Practice Press.

Foerster, R. (1999). Movimiento étnico o etnonacional Mapuche? [Ethnic or ethno-national Mapuche movement?]. *Revista de Crítica Cultural, 18,* 52-58.

Foerster, R., & Vergara, J.I. (2001). Algunas transformaciones de la política mapuche en la década de los noventa [Several transformations in Mapuche politics during the nineties]. *Anales de la Universidad de Chile.* Serie VI.

Ford, T. V., & Gil, G. (2001). Radical Internet use. In J. D. H. Downing et al. (Eds.), *Radical media: Rebellious communication and social movement* (pp. 201-234). Newbury Park, CA: Sage.

Foucault, M. (1980). *Power/knowledge.* Brighton: Harvester.

Fraser, N. (1993). Rethinking the public sphere: A contribution to the critique of actually existing democracy. In B. Robbins (Ed.), *The phantom public sphere* (pp. 1-32). Minneapolis: University of Minnesota Press.

Ginsburg, F. (1991). Indigenous media: Faustian contract or global village? *Cultural Anthropology, 6*(1), 92-112.

Ginsburg, F. (1995). Production values: Indigenous media and the rhetoric of self-determination. In D. Battaglia (Ed.), *The rhetoric of self making* (pp. 121-138). Berkeley: University of California Press.

Ginsburg, F. (1999). Shooting back: From ethnographic film to indigenous production/ethnography of media. In T. Miller & R. Stam (Eds.), *A companion to film theory* (pp. 295-322). Malden: Blackwell Publishers.

Ginsburg, F. (2000). Resources of hope. In C. Smith & G. K. Ward (Eds.), *Indigenous cultures in an interconnected world* (pp. 27-47). Sydney: Allen & Unwin.

Ginsburg, F. (2002). Screen memories: Resignifying the traditional in Indigenous media. In F. Ginsburg, L. Abu-Lughod, & B. Larkin (Eds.), *Media worlds: Anthropology on new terrain* (pp. 39-57). Berkeley: University of California Press.

Gobierno de Chile. (1992). Ley del Consejo Nacional de Televisión [Law of the National Television Council]. No.19.131.

Gobierno de Chile. (1993). Ley Indigena [Indigenous law]. No.19.253.

Gobierno de Chile. (2004). Ley de Fomento y Promoción del Cine y el Audiovisual [Law of film and audiovisual promotion]. No.19.981.

Gumucio-Dagrón, A. (2001). *Haciendo olas: Comunicación participativa para el Cambio social* [Making waves. Participatory communication for social change]. New York: Rockefeller Foundation.

Habermas. J. (1989[1962]). *Structural transformation of the public sphere.* Cambridge: Polity Press.

Hernández, I. (2003). *Autonomía o ciudadanía incompleta: El pueblo Mapuche en Chile y Argentina* [Autonomy or incomplete citizenship: The Mapuche people in Chile and Argentina]. Santiago: CEPAL.

Instituto Nacional de Estadísticas (INE). (2003). *Censo Nacional* [National Census].

Marcus, G. (1995). Ethnography in/of the world system: The emergence of multi-sited ethnography. *Annual Review of Anthropology, 24,* 95-117.

Marcus, G. (1996). Introduction. In G. Marcus (Ed.). *Connected: engagements with media* (Late Editions, 3, pp. 1-18). Chicago: University of Chicago Press.

Mariman, J. (1998). *Transición democrática en Chile: Nuevo ciclo reinvicativo mapuche?* [Democratic transition in Chile: New vindicating cycle for the Mapuche?]. Temuco, Chile: Centro de Estudios y Documentacion Mapuche.

Mariqueo, R. (2003). *The Mapuche and the Chilean media.* Online document. Mapuche International Link. Retrieved February 11, 2007, from www.mapuche-nation.org.

Miller, D., & Slater, D. (2000). *The internet: An ethnographic approach.* London: Sage.

Molnar, H., & Meadows, M. (2001). *Songlines to satellites: Indigenous communications in Australia, the South Pacific and Canada.* Annandale, Sydney: Pluto Press.

Paillan, E. Personal communication. Santiago, July 9, 2002; Santiago, July 10, 2003; Temuco, July 22, 2003.

Paillan, J. Personal communication. Santiago, June 24, 2002; El Huachi, July 5, 2002; Santiago, July 28, 2003; Santiago, July 1, 2004; Santiago, January 2005.

Palacios, R. (2002). Concentración oligopólica de la industria cultural en Chile: Escenario global y nacional [Oligopolic concentration of Chile's cultural industry: Global and national scenario]. *Revista Latina de Comunicación Social.* La Laguna (Tenerife) Year 5 Number 52. Retrieved February 11, 2007, from www.ull.es/publicaciones/latina/2002palaciosoctubre5206.htm

Palczewski, C. (2001). Cyber-movements, new social movements, and counter-publics. In D. Brower & R. Asen (Eds.), *Counter-publics and the state* (pp 161-186). Albany: SUNY Press.

Prins, H. (1997). The paradox of primitivism: Native rights and the problem of imagery in cultural survival films. *Visual Anthropology, 9,* 243-266.

Riggins, S.H. (1992). *Ethnic minority media: An international perspective.* London: Sage.

Rodríguez, C. (2001). *Fissures in the mediascape. An international study of citizens' media.* Cresskill, NJ: Hampton Press.

Roncagliolo, R. (1991). The growth of the audio-visual imagescape in Latin America. In N. Thede & A. Ambrosi (Eds.), *Video the changing world* (pp. 22-30). Montréal: Black Rose Books.

Rosaldo, R. (1985). Chicano studies, 1970-1984. *Annual Review of Anthropology, 14,* 405-427.

Rosaldo, R. (1994). Cultural citizenship and educational democracy. *Cultural Anthropology, 9*(3), 402-411.

Roth, L. (2000). Bypassing of border and building of bridges: Steps in the construction of the Aboriginal Peoples Television Network in Canada. *Gazette, 62*(3–4), 251–269.

Salazar, J.F. (2003). Articulating an activist imaginary: Internet as counter public sphere in the Mapuche movement, 1997-2000. *Media International Australia, 107,* 19-30.

Seguel, A. (2002). Personal communication. Temuco, July 12.

Stephenson, M. (2000). The impact of an Indigenous counter-public sphere on the practice of democracy. *Taller de Historia Oral Andina in Bolivia.* Working Paper, No. 279.

Sunkel, G., & Geoffroy, E. (2001, February). Concentración económica e ideológica en los medios de comunicación: Peculiaridades del caso chileno [Economic and ideological media concentration: The peculiarities of the Chilean case]. *Revista Rocinante,* no. 28.

Turner, T. (1991). The social dynamics and personal politics of video making in an indigenous community. *Visual Anthropology Review, 7,* 68-76.

Turner, T. (2002). Representation, politics, and cultural imagination in Indigenous video: General points and Kayapo examples. In F. Ginsburg, L. Abu-Lughod, & B. Larkin (Eds.), *Media worlds: Anthropology on new terrain* (pp. 39-57). Berkeley: University of California Press.

Warner, M. (2002). *Publics and counter-publics.* New York: Zone Books.

Wortham, E. (2002). Narratives of location: Televisual media and the production of Indigenous identities in Mexico. Unpublished Ph.D. dissertation. New York University, USA.

Yashar, D. J. (1998). Contesting citizenship: Indigenous movements and democracy in Latin America. *Comparative Politics, 31*(1), 23–42.

ANALYZING GRASSROOTS JOURNALISM ON THE WEB

Reporting and the Participatory Practice of Online News Gathering

2

Christopher Anderson

Over the past six years, beginning with the 1999 protests against the World Trade Organization in Seattle and accelerated by dramatic global developments during the first term of George W. Bush, technological and social advances in the world of online journalism have spurred many analysts to argue that "we are witnessing journalism's transformation from a 20th-century mass media structure to something profoundly more grassroots and democratic" (Gillmor, 2004: xii). Many observers have discussed the growth of 'blogging' and the changes it has wrought within the world of traditional media publishing. Other commentators are increasingly referring to a social practice referred to variously as 'grassroots journalism,' 'open source' journalism, or 'participatory journalism.' The very newness of these developments, combined with the excitement brought about by the promise of greater democracy through technology, has led a number of usually sober and serious-minded people to wax rhapsodic about the impact of the new practice.

Alluding to the growing decentralization and fragmentation of the mainstream press, Orville Schell, dean of the University of California at Berkeley School of Journalism, has argued that "the Roman Empire that was mass media is breaking up, and we are entering an almost-feudal period where there will be many more centers of power and influence" (Bianco, 2005). In an essay in the *Online Journalism Review*, Mark Glasser has pushed the claims of bloggers still further, writing that "newspapers represent all that is old and moldy about journalism: printed on dead trees, distributed by underpaid teens, and read by an aging audience. Weblogs represent all that is edgy and hip about journalism: written in a personal voice, encompassing divergent modes of thought, and distributed on a global platform" (Glasser, 2003). Of course, along with the celebration has come the inevitable backlash; Steve Lovelady of the *Columbia Journalism Review* has publicly referred to bloggers as "salivating morons who make up the lynch mob" (Lovelady, cited by Rosen, 2005).

Despite the far-reaching claims made by many of the proponents and detractors of grassroots journalism, serious academic study of this social phenomenon remains in its infancy. Few scholars of journalism—perhaps due in part to the tenuous place of so-called 'journalism studies' within the academy (Zelizer, 2004)—have begun to advance serious theoretical claims about the social impact of grassroots journalism. Even less common are studies that analyze the specific varieties of content produced by various participatory journalism projects. This chapter aims to address these concerns. I begin by unpacking the relationship between 'participatory journalism' and common theoretical understandings of 'alternative media.' After working through and situating these various definitions of alternative media, I undertake a provisional examination of what we might call, following Bourdieu, the boundaries of the participatory journalistic field (Bourdieu, 1992). I compare the mission statements of three organizational participants in the field—U.K. Indymedia,Wikinews, and The Northwest Voice and analyze their journalistic output along three dimensions: level of participation, adherence to 'journalistic' norms, and ties to radical social movements, as well as the architecture of their websites. I conclude by noting some apparent discrepancies between theoretical speculation and my empirical overview, and outline avenues for future research.

GRASSROOTS JOURNALISM
AND 'MEDIA POWER'

Any study of 'grassroots' or 'participatory' journalism immediately faces a series of definitional hurdles. How do we identify the object of our study? What exactly is participatory journalism? Where do its analytical boundaries begin and end? This conceptual confusion is only exacerbated by the ambiguity surrounding the field of 'alternative media studies,' an academic field that can both include and exclude different participatory journalistic websites, depending on how we define 'alternative media.' In short, confusion reigns with regard to the analysis of participatory journalism, alternative media, and indeed, journalism itself. This confusion makes it difficult to determine what exactly it is we should be studying when we look at some of the independent journalism being produced online.

Perhaps the most useful definition of participatory journalism comes from Shayne Bowman and Chris Willis, who define it as the practice "of citizens play-

ing an active role in the process of collecting, reporting, analyzing and disseminating news and information" (Bowman & Willis, 2003). Participatory journalists,
in this model, push journalism beyond a traditional top-down model of news distribution in which journalists collect information and transmit it to the public via
their editors and bureaucratic news organizations. Instead:

> What is emerging is a new media ecosystem where online communities dis-
> cuss and extend the stories created by the mainstream media. These commu-
> nities also produce participatory journalism, grassroots reporting, annotative
> reporting, commentary, and fact-checking, which the mainstream media feed
> upon, developing them as a pool of tips, sources, and story ideas. (Bowman &
> Willis, 2003)

Such a definition is useful because it focuses almost entirely on the *process* of
grassroots journalistic production rather than the *content* of journalism produced.
Grassroots journalism, imply Bowman and Willis, is only 'radical' insofar as it
mounts a challenge to concentrations of media power; radicalism is not inherently based on oppositional content but rather on a decentralization of traditional
journalistic processes. Under the definition provided by Bowman and Willis,
grassroots journalism can be progressive or fascistic, politically grounded within
left-wing anarchist collectives or Republican blogging groups. The key test is
whether the process employed challenges the concentration of *previously 'authorized' forms of media power.*
  On the face of it, such a seemingly apolitical definition poses a special challenge for scholars of what has been called 'alternative media,' calling into question the oppositional bias of many previous alternative media studies. Many of
the most celebrated analyses within the alternative media tradition might find it
difficult to absorb the full range of grassroots journalism projects (left-wing,
right-wing, and, increasingly, overtly apolitical) into their field of analysis. This
is unfortunate, because much of the work of alternative media theorists has maintained a critical perspective that seems missing from the more utopian specula-
tions on the power of blogging and other forms of online media. John Downing
(2001), perhaps the leading scholar of the alternative media since the 1970s,
argues that this media must *inherently contest* established blocs of political power
with a view towards wider social emancipation. Likewise, Chris Atton (2002)
provides one of the most detailed recent overviews of the different scholarly definitions of alternative media; echoing Duncombes' work on 'zines, Atton argues
that the key to conceptualizing alternative media is to understand it both in
terms of the attitude toward the dominant system of capitalist control and the
position within that system.
  Both Downing's focus on radical media and Atton's emphasis on alternative
media's "attitude toward the dominant system of capitalist control" (Atton, 2002:
24) nevertheless render any attempt to understand the wide swath of grassroots

journalism online more problematic. Although there are a number of participatory journalism websites whose content focuses on traditionally 'progressive' concerns, a number of the most cited and influential weblogs on the internet are of the right-wing variety (Glasser, 2003), and at the same time a growing movement emphasizing locally based 'citizens journalism' is seemingly apolitical in character. Does the field of alternative media scholarship offer us any other definitional tools through which to analyze the broad sweep of citizen engagement with the journalistic process? Can we combine the critical focus of many alternative media studies with the broader political range emphasized by Bowman, Willis, and other grassroots journalism scholars?

Some recent work by Nick Couldry and James Curran shifts the focus of alternative media study away from political orientation and toward questions of *media power*. Drawing on the work of media scholar John Thompson (Thompson, 1995), Couldry and Curran argue persuasively that much of the work on alternative media inherently excludes "any media on the right of the political spectrum, even those whose challenge to the concentration of media resources in central institutions is explicit and direct" (Couldry & Curran, 2003: 7). Instead of focusing on the media as either a conduit for or influence upon traditional systems of power—political, economic, ideological—Couldry and Curran see media power as a *form of symbolic power in and of itself*. Alternative media can then be seen as "media production that challenges, at least implicitly, actual concentrations of media power, whatever form those concentrations take in different locations" (Couldry & Curran, 2003: 7).

In this spirit, Couldry and Curran's conclusion to their analysis of media power and alternative media might serve as an equally valid preface to my own study of grassroots journalism online:

> What we bring together ... may or may not be a practice that is politically radical or socially empowering; but in every case, whether directly or indirectly, media power is part of what is at stake. (Couldry & Curran, 2003: 7)

By welding Bowman and Willis' definition of participatory journalism to Couldry and Curran's focus on challenges to traditional concentrations of media power, we can offer a preliminary definition of the object of our study. This chapter focuses on online projects in which formally uncertified citizens engage in traditional journalistic practices with the stated or unstated aim of challenging formal concentrations of socially authorized media power. This definition limits our field of analysis to the online world, places our emphasis on journalistic rather than nonjournalistic practices (excluding online personal diaries from the analysis, for example), and retains a working conception of power that implicitly maintains a critical edge while avoiding ideological prejudments about acceptable content.

PROBLEMS AND METHODOLOGY

We can now begin to formulate additional questions about the participatory journalistic field, that is, the field in which citizens play "an active role in the process of collecting, reporting, analyzing and disseminating news and information" (Bowman & Willis, 2003). These questions interrogate and further elaborate upon the central theoretical claim made above—that participatory journalism challenges traditional concentrations of symbolic media power. Among other questions, we can ask:

- Do 'participatory journalistic' organizations produce original material? Or do they mostly reprint the material of other, professional journalistic organizations? A debate has raged within the blogosphere about the degree to which participatory journalism is itself dependent on the work of professional journalists (see, for example, Neiman Reports, 2003).
- Do social actors who define themselves as participatory journalists 'commit journalism'? In other words, do they 'pound the pavement,' take pictures and video, conduct interviews, and rifle through government documents? Or do they merely pontificate, comment upon already existing news, and confine themselves largely to opinion? (Neiman Reports, 2003).
- How common is *objective* participatory journalism? Is it entirely biased? Although I do not attempt to 'measure' objectivity, I do seek to analyze the degree to which grassroots journalism groups align themselves with insurgent social movements. To date, this question has not been debated much within the field; I contend, however, that it will become a question of primary importance as grassroots journalism goes increasingly 'mainstream' (see, for example, Anderson, 2005b).

As noted above, these questions are designed to probe the degree to which participatory journalistic organizations challenge traditional concentrations of symbolic media power. If participatory journalists, using traditional news-gathering methods, produce their *own original* content, one could argue that this activity represents a serious challenge to the traditional symbolic authority granted to the mainstream media insofar as the news-gathering functions traditionally carried out by large, professional organizations are now being undertaken by formerly disempowered individuals and groups. If, on the other hand, participatory journalism simply regurgitates content already gathered by more formal media organizations, its challenge to concentrations of symbolic power could be seen as correspondingly muted. Finally, we can ask whether some or all of the new participatory groups go so far as to embrace an older notion of journalistic 'objectivity.'

The pages below move from theoretical speculation to empirical analysis and detail the results of a multilevel examination of three leading participatory journalism websites: Indymedia U.K., the Northwest Voice, and Wikinews. Indymedia is an on and offline news service which was born out the 1999 antiglobalization protests in Seattle and now has over 150 chapters around the world. The Northwest Voice is the internet-based extension of a small community newspaper in Bakersfield, California. Wikinews grew out of the widely praised 'wikipedia project,' an open-source encyclopedia on the Internet. Each of these organizations can be seen as standing in for three broadly conceived 'ideal types' within the participatory journalistic field: participatory media produced by a social movement group (Indymedia); participatory media as an extension of traditional, mainstream journalism (the Northwest Voice); and participatory media as citizens-based, 'open-source' journalism (Wikinews).

In the course of my analysis I first compare the mission statements of the three journalistic organizations. Then, I analyze their content along three dimensions: level of participation, adherence to 'journalistic' norms, and ties to radical social movements. Finally, I briefly analyze the 'digital architecture' of their websites. Both the architecture analysis and mission statement overviews are primarily descriptive in nature, and content analysis fleshes out the theoretical structure already discussed.

MISSION AND SELF-UNDERSTANDING

How do grassroots journalists define who they are and what they do? Any adequate understanding of participatory journalism as a field would need to grasp both how its actors view themselves and how they view the other actors in their field. Any analysis of grassroots journalism online should be *intersubjective*, that is, it should seek to determine relationships between various social agents. In my analysis of Indymedia U.K., Wikinews, and the Northwest Voice, I have analyzed the mission statements of the three participatory journalistic organizations that were the object of my study, along with a brief overview of the key secondary literature on each media outlet.

Indymedia U.K.

The worldwide Independent Media Center (IMC) movement was born during 1999 protests against the World Trade Organization (WTO) in Seattle (Downing, 2003). Convinced that the corporate press would neither cover the antiglobalization protests accurately nor give adequate voice to those opposing corporate globalization, activists created their own web-based media network through which anyone could, via a process of 'open publishing,' publish photos, text, and video about the protests to the website. Following in the wake of antiglobalization protests that were, in the early years of the 21st century, spreading from trade summit to trade summit, Independent Media Centers proliferated. By early 2000, permanent IMCs were being established to provide coverage of local activist struggles, apart from and in addition to the coverage of mushrooming antiglobalization protests. By April 2005 there were over 160 Independent Media Centers on six continents, one of which was located in the United Kingdom (http://www.indymedia.co.uk).

In late 1999, with a number of technical barriers still in place that discouraged individual publishing on the Internet, the concept of 'open publishing' was a major theoretical and technical plank within Indymedia's larger mission. According to Matthew Arnison:

> Open publishing means that the process of creating news is transparent to the readers. They can contribute a story and see it instantly appear in the pool of stories publicly available. Those stories are filtered as little as possible to help the readers find the stories they want. (Arnison, 2001)

Other Indymedia partisans simply echoed the words of punk singer Jello Biafra: "Don't hate the media, become the media."

True to the circumstances behind its founding, the United Kingdom IMC mission statement grounds its exhortation to 'be the media' in a commitment to activism. The editors of U.K. IMC emphasize the participatory journalistic aspects of the site—"the content of the Indymedia U.K. website is created through a system of open publishing: anyone can upload a written, audio and video report or a picture directly to the site through an openly accessible web interface" (Indymedia U.K., 2004)—but precede the invitation to publish with this statement about Indymedia's goals:

> The Indymedia U.K. website provides an interactive platform for reports from the struggles for a world based on freedom, cooperation, justice and solidarity, and against environmental degradation, neoliberal exploitation, racism and patriarchy. The reports cover a wide range of issues and social movements—from neighbourhood campaigns to grassroots mobilisations, from critical analysis to direct action. (Indymedia U.K., 2004)

One can expect that the journalistic content of the U.K. IMC will not be 'balanced' in any traditional sense. At the same time, however, there exists some anecdotal evidence that the political passions of those who agree with U.K. IMC's mission statement encourages them to 'commit more journalism.' As IMC participant Cayce Calloway writes on an Indymedia email list-serve:

> That's why I post to the IMC. I think what most people are trying to do
> when they say they're being 'objective' is attempting to tell both sides of a
> story. As a result, at the most simplified level, that means the truth and the
> lies get equal weight. I can only speak for myself, but I'm only interested in
> telling the truth and that seems to be true for a lot of people I know who post
> to the IMC. *Because I have strong beliefs, the need to tell it is passionate for me*
> (http://regenerationtv.com/pipermail/imc-la/2001-July/002403.html,
> emphasis added)

In addition, the fact that Indymedia was born in the act of providing actual on-the-ground coverage also distinguishes it organizationally from many 'weblogs,' which see their mission as providing commentary and analysis to supplement the reporting of more traditional journalists.

Wikinews

At first glance, Wikinews has the same mission as Indymedia:

> We seek to create a free source of news, where, provided that we can over-
> come the digital divide, every human being is invited to contribute reports
> about events large and small, either from direct experience, or summarized
> from elsewhere. Wikinews is founded on the idea that we want to create
> something new, rather than destroy something old. . . . We seek to promote
> the idea of the *citizen journalist*, because we believe that everyone can make a
> useful contribution to painting the big picture of what is happening in the
> world around us. The time has come to create a free news source, by the
> people and for the people. (Wikinews, 2004)

At the same time, however, the Wikinews project differs from Indymedia in at least one significant way—it embraces a 'neutral point of view policy' (NPOV). Whereas Indymedia revels in its biases—"Indymedia U.K. does not attempt to take an objective and impartial standpoint," the IMC mission statement notes (Indymedia U.K., 2004)—Wikinews holds fast to notions of journalistic objectivity. "The neutral point of view policy states that one should write articles without bias, representing all views fairly," writes Wikinews. "The policy says that an article should fairly represent all, and not make an article state, imply, or insinuate that any one side is correct" (Wikipedia, 2005).

In some interviews, Wikinews organizers specifically contrast their mission to that of Indymedia. "At Wikipedia, we have very, very strong neutral policy," says Wikipedia cofounder Jimmy Wales.

> We call it a neutral point of view, and it's really one of the central organizing
> principles of everything we do, including the news project. Unlike some

other grassroots journalism type of projects like Indymedia, which is a very far left type of thing written by activists, we strive to be a neutral, high-quality source of basic information. (Wales, cited by LaMonica, 2005)

In the same interview, Wales highlights some of the possibilities and limitations of grassroots journalism:

> I don't really see how we could take over the mainstream media. One of the things they can do well that we can't do is send a trusted reporter out to the Ukraine, for example, and get a report back that can be trusted. We're not going to be able to send people places. *We can rely on people who are local, but if we don't know who they are, then we can't trust them as sources.* Because typically, people who would be attracted to writing original reports would tend to be activists, not necessarily journalists. (Wales, cited by LaMonica, 2005)

Unlike Indymedia, Wikinews emphasizes the problems raised by allowing strangers to contribute grassroots journalism: Can readers believe the journalism these contributors produce, especially if they are obviously biased in favor of certain political positions?

At the same time, while restricting the range of its journalistic input, Wikinews makes its editorial process highly transparent. The changes made to each and every Wikinews article are visible online, and readers can scroll through the different versions of a story to see how it was changed and the degree to which the different changes adhere to the NPOV policy. In all respects, Wikinews' primary mission seems to be that of building trust by limiting first-hand reports, Wikinews can remove potential confusion regarding the veracity of an article while at the same time allowing its editorial process to be completely open.

The Northwest Voice

In many ways, The Northwest Voice resembles a traditional, local newspaper. Indeed, that's how it began. As *Wired* described it:

> A small California newspaper has undertaken a first-of-its-kind experiment in participatory journalism in which nearly all the content published in a regularly updated online edition and a weekly print edition is submitted by community members. It's all free. Following in the footsteps of past community journalism projects that sought to give individuals a voice in local news, as well as the growing trend in news-like blogs, The Northwest Voice is giving residents of Bakersfield's northwest neighborhoods near-total control of content. (Terdiman, 2004)

The Northwest Voice is somewhat unique insofar as it is an example of what Jeff Jarvis and others call 'hyperlocal' grassroots media (Miller, 2005), a website specifically geared towards the input and needs of a geographically localized community, usually a small suburb. "The Northwest Voice welcomes all contributions from the community," notes the site's online submission form, "including articles, pictures, information about community events, letters to the editor and most anything else you'd like to share." Site editor Mary Lou Fulton explains:

> In our community, people immediately liked the idea of a neighborhood publication, but they didn't get the content model at first. We'd explained about how we wanted people in the community to write all the articles, and inevitably we'd hear, "OK, but can you come out to cover my event?" And we'd politely say, "No, but if you'd like to write something up, we'd be glad to publish it." I think it simply had never occurred to many people that such participation was possible. It's interesting and exciting to see passive consumers turn into active participants, which is exactly what we want. (Terdiman, 2004)

Beyond simply hoping that area residents would stumble onto the site and start contributing, Fulton and others recruited an 'advance team' of important community members to provide journalistic content—school superintendents and principals, leaders of parent-teacher organizations, and pastors. As of July 2004, 50% of the site's content was coming from this core group, with another 25% being submitted by paid staff and 10% by nonrecruited area residents. The advance team concept also helped mitigate the fears expressed by Wales and other Wikinews editors regarding the problem of trust. "Most of our community contributions come from 'trusted' individuals like school teachers, youth sports coaches and ministers," Fulton told Cyberjournalism.net, "so we don't feel the need to double-check on everything they write. If we receive contributions regarding a public controversy, we do make sure the facts are correct but the presentation of the information is entirely up to the individual."

When asked to elaborate upon her vision of participatory journalism, Fulton couched her response in the rhetoric of democracy:

> The open source model offers us a new way to connect with readers, to better understand their worries and joys, and to enable them to share some of themselves with the world. It gives readers a personal and emotional stake in our products, and I believe that is critical to the future of our industry. (Dube, 2004)

CONTENT ANALYSIS

Next I undertake a comprehensive content analysis of the journalism produced by each of the three sites. During a seven-day period, March 20-26, 2005, I examined a total of 318 articles. It is through this content analysis that I attempt to flesh out the primary theoretical claim made above: that participatory journalism represents a challenge to traditional concentrations of 'media power.' The content analysis is undertaken at the story level and attempts to define certain surface-level features. Each article is coded along three axes—level of adherence to 'journalistic' norms, ties to social movements, and grassroots participation. Although this level of qualitative generality might be troublesome, I argue that, to date, the actual amount of content analysis performed on online participatory media has been so limited that we must begin with broad brushstrokes in an attempt to construct even a simplistic model of the participatory journalistic field (Anderson, 2004, 2005a).

My content analysis begins by identifying the *type* of article posted and determining its adherence to traditional journalistic norms (i.e., is it a reprint of an already existing article in the mainstream media, a formal announcement made by an organization or activist group, a press release, original commentary, or original 'reporting' in the classic sense). I next identify whether each article has a political focus, and, if it does, whether that focus is limited to political parties or includes social movement groups 'outside' the traditional political arena. Finally, I analyze whether each article was produced by a 'grassroots journalist,' or whether it was authored by an already empowered member of the mainstream media or government (see Figure 2.1).

	Indymedia 2.273	Wikipedia .320	NW Voice 2.625
Journalistic Norms			
Reprint	10.9%	92.0%	0
Announcement	32.8%	0%	43.8%
PR (Post-Event)	4.7%	0%	0
Commentary / Analysis	18.7%	0%	6.3%
Reporting	32.8%	8.0%	50.0%
References to Politics			
No Link	2.3%	82.7%	93.8%
Political Activity	13.3%	6.7%	0%
Radical Activity	84.4%	10.7%	6.3%
Participatory Nature			
Other (paid reporter, etc)	14.1%	92.0%	25.0%
Grassroots Journalist	85.9%	8.0%	75.0%

FIGURE 2.1. Coding results for online grassroots media content analysis.

Indymedia U.K.

Most of the journalism found on the Indymedia U.K. website for the time period selected centered around protests on the second anniversary of the invasion of Iraq. A number of grassroots journalists posted pictures and video of marches and speakers. A typical report about an antiwar protest march goes something like this:

> An eyewitness account of today's antiwar demonstration in London, followed by a brief restaurant review, then a synopsis and diagnosis. Here's what happened: Started off in Hyde Park, with a temperature in the early 20s Celsius, bright sun and a mild breeze. Ranks of vans were situated about the place, especially up near the Marble Arch. The march stretched back to some distant end of Hyde Park that I didn't care to amble down to. (Lenin, 2005)

These numerous reports were eventually collected and turned into a 'center column feature' by U.K. IMC editors. I will describe editorial features of Indymedia U.K. shortly. For now, suffice it to say that more than 32% of the material posted to IMC U.K. from March 20 to March 24 2005 was some type of firsthand reporting (i.e., category 5 on our scale of 'adherence to traditional journalistic practices').

An equal amount of material (32.8%), however, was in the form of pre-event announcements or press releases (category 3). For instance, a March 21 article began: "Birmingham Indymedia Cinema presents a screening of *Trading Freedom: The Secret Life of the FTAA* and *Workers Without Bosses* on Tuesday 22 March 2005 at the Midlands Arts Centre, Birmingham." Another posting read: "Social change philosopher and activist Joanna Macy will be visiting Oxford to give a talk and lead a two day workshop in May 2005. She is an author, scholar and spiritual teacher who has been active worldwide in movements for peace, justice and deep ecology." One can assume that these announcements were designed to increase awareness about particular activist events. We can see that Indymedia's identity as both journalistic endeavor and movement facilitator is reflected in the equal number of postings devoted to news and to movement building. The remaining third of the articles were roughly evenly split between reprints (category 1), post-event press releases (category 2), and original commentary and analysis (category 4).

Wikinews

Of all the grassroots journalism websites examined, Wikinews contained the least amount of entirely original content. Indeed, it is probably accurate to say that, so far, Wikinews is not really even in the participatory journalism business; rather, it is doing something more along the lines of 'grassroots editing.' Ninety-two percent of the articles on Wikinews during the period examined combined reprints of articles from various other major news outlets such as the BBC, the AP, and *The New York Times*. Only 8% of the articles examined were first-hand reports; one reported on a recent earthquake in Japan, a second discussed the conversion of a landmark Cambridge gas station into a Hess station, and a third reported how a woman in Wendy's found a human finger in her chili. Indeed, as of May 2005, there had only been 25 grassroots journalism stories published on Wikinews out of the more than 700 published.

Much of this can probably be attributed to the extraordinary difficulty in practicing grassroots journalism under the current Wikinews model. For example, an article about the possible eruption of Mt. St. Helens in early March, submitted by an actual witness to the volcano's tremors, was headlined "Ash and Steam Reported Over Mt. St. Helens." A second Wikinews contributor immediately asked, "Who saw this? I can't tell from looking at the article? Who is this mysterious Wikinews correspondent?" A third Wikiuser asked, "How can Wikinews claim that someone reporting for Wikinews is a firsthand witness without attributing that report to someone with a name?"

Of course, one could conceivably encounter the same questions on any of the grassroots sites examined, especially Indymedia; nevertheless, a certain type of 'web culture' has grown around these sites, a culture in which firsthand posts are generally either accepted as accurate or are disputed through a comments section. Based on my own research, as well as some anecdotal evidence obtained from Indymedia participants, much of this difference in trust can be attributed to Indymedia's grounding within a large social movement. Why, after all, would an activist lie to his or her allies? Wikinews, on the other hand, seeks to create a grassroots journalism practice that transcends the boundaries of activism and politics. In this realm of radical uncertainty, much of the reporting that is not somehow authoritatively certified is automatically suspect.

These difficulties with firsthand reporting on Wikinews have not gone unnoticed. One anonymous blogger attributes the problem to differences between running an encyclopedia and running a news site:

> A collaborative news service is a different creature than a collaborative encyclopedia. . . . If people are motivated to engage in DIY [do-it-yourself] media, they mostly want to talk about themselves and their lives. In the 1980s, these people did personal zines. Now they run blogs. Finding people to volunteer time to write collaborative journalism is just very hard. This is one of the huge factors working against the Wiki News project. (*Problems with Wikinews*)

A second anonymous blogger takes aim at Wiki's much touted Neutral Point of View Policy:

> One potential pitfall of Wikipedia's NPOV philosophy is that the goal of
> neutrality makes it very difficult to write articles that make politically con-
> tentious fact-based conclusions. . . . If a NPOV philosophy is unwilling to
> 'adjudicate factual disputes,' then it only seems to be raising the amount of
> 'informational uncertainty.' (*What's Wrong with Wiki*).

One way to avoid the pitfalls of having to 'adjudicate factual disputes' is to
concentrate largely on summarizing the products of already existing news media.
Wikipedian John Kearney may be right when he writes: "These articles on controversial topics that devolve into a polemical essay by one side, followed by a
refuting polemical essay by the other side, are tiresome" (*What's Wrong with Wiki*).
But so far, the alternative produced by Wikinews offers little that a savvy news
consumer cannot obtain from other, already existing, nongrassroots news sources.

The Northwest Voice

The most intriguing of the three grassroots journalism sites may have been the
Northwest Voice. It contained the largest percentage of articles coded as 'traditionally journalistic,' but was also the least politically militant in terms of content.
Its contributors wrote about new high school gyms, cheerleading contests, and
music recitals. In many ways, the Northwest Voice resembled the media form
that it had replaced: the small town newspaper.

Although a fairly high percentage of the articles on the Northwest Voice
were announcements (43.8%), another 50% were straight reporting. Much of this
reporting was, at least on the surface, highly depoliticized. In an article entitled
Norris Welcomes New Gym, for example, the local school superintendent Wallace
McCormick proudly described the reaction of students as they entered their 'real
gym:' "As the students entered the gym there were many exclamations of 'Wow!'
and This is cool.' Each advisory class selected a male and female student to try
half-court shots with a basketball. Three shots were actually made." A second
article on March 21 regaled readers with lunch stories from Fruitvale Junior
High. "Meet the lunch ladies and learn what the right ingredients are for packing
a healthy lunch from home," the story promised.

Compared to antiwar protests, these subjects appear, at least at first blush,
mundane. Why did reporting about such seemingly trivial occurrences attract
such a high degree of participation? And why did the Northwest Voice invalidate
some of my initial speculation, which posited that a website's levels of grassroots
participation would directly correlate with its degree of political engagement?
There are at least two intriguing possibilities that I can only allude to here, but
would be well served by further research into various forms of hyperlocal or
community-based online journalism. The first would involve a deeper exploration of the degree to which participatory journalism on a local level represents
the emergence or extension of an online form of what A.J. Secor has called the

"quotidian politics of making do" (Secor, 2003). One cannot simply understand 'politics' exclusively in terms of activism in social movements; there are more everyday aspects of political commitment as well, and some of these aspects may have been on display in our analysis of contributions to the Northwest Voice. A second line of research would further elaborate upon the theoretical ground laid down by Escobar in his research on the idea of "place as a concept, and a politics of place as a social process" (Escobar, 2000: 167). Do projects like the Northwest Voice contribute to a highly localized 'defense of place?' And what are the larger social and political implications of this move towards the quotidian and local? Again, further research in this area is needed. For now, we can document the empirical fact that an *overtly depoliticized* form of grassroots journalism is thriving on the world wide web.

WEBSITE ARCHITECTURE

By itself, a content analysis is insufficient to establish a website's adherence to categories such as 'journalistic norms,' 'ties to social movements,' and 'grassroots participation.' To supplement my content analysis I examined the 'site architecture' of Wikinews, U.K. Indymedia, and the Northwest Voice. By looking at the layout of the different websites we can gain additional insight into the ways that each participatory journalistic enterprise conceives its mission and its users. As Beczkowski writes:

> Processes of media choice and interface design can be, at least partly, understood by looking at the *inscription of a vision of the user.* . . . In Akrich's terms, in the very fabric of what they create, [web] designers 'inscribe' by whom and how an artifact will be used. (Beczkowski, 2004: 77)

How do the various architecture choices employed by the website designers of Indymedia U.K., Wikinews, and the Northwest Voice 'inscribe their vision of the user?' How does this vision of the user supplement or contradict the results of our content analysis?

Indymedia U.K. is divided into three columns and is dominated by a center column (see Figure 2.2). This center column functions as a 'feature' page and allows volunteer site editors to collect thematically related or important stories that grassroots journalists post to the website. The left-hand column contains the IMC 'cities list,' a list of more than 200 formally recognized IMC sites around the world. The right-hand column is topped by a list of upcoming protest events and is followed further down the page by the IMC 'open newswire,' which is where grassroots journalists submit their stories, in reverse chronological order. Above the right-hand column is a large grey box that reads: "Publish your news."

Indymedia UK is a network of individuals, independent and alternative media activists and organisations, offering grassroots, non-corporate, non-commercial coverage of important social and political issues.

(((i))) INDYMEDI@ UK

Skip Nav | Home | Editorial Guidelines | Mission Statement | About Us | Contact | Help | Support Us

Kollektives

Cambridge
Leeds Bradford
Liverpool
London
Manchester
Oxford
Scotland
Sheffield
South Coast
West Country
World

Other UK IMCs
Bristol
Scotland

Seize the media

Indymedia needs your support for it to survive

Not the servers

Radio projects >>
Video projects >>

07-04-2005 12:44 | Indymedia | Cambridge | Leeds Bradford | Liverpool | London | Manchester | Oxford | Scotland | Sheffield | South Coast | West Country

Technical Problems

There are currently problems with our publishing server and as a result, some posts and comments are not appearing on the site as quickly as they should and some seem not to be appearing at all.

The problem might be caused by an update to the search engine, the search for the site has been switched to google to see if this makes things work better.

Read more | 8 comment(s) >>

14-04-2005 12:18 | G8 2005 | Genoa | Free Spaces | Indymedia | Repression | Technology

Police, Lies, and Video Tape

While dozens of police are on trial for abuses in Genoa in 2001 (including the **violent raid** on the Indymedia Centre which left British independent journalist Mark Covell critically injured [...] taking place in New

Calendar – Announce an Event:

EVENTS COVERAGE:

UK

May 14-15 London G8 Independent / Alternative Media Convergence
June 15-17 Sheffield G8 Justice and Home Affairs Meeting
July 2-8: Gleneagles, Scotland: G8 Summit
Protests | Dissent! | G8 Alternatives | Make Poverty History | Links and Resources

EUROPE AND AMERICAS

April 15-17 DC: IMF/World Bank
June 16-18 Luxembourg Days of Action Against the European Union Summit!

ONGOING

Iraq Occupation:
Al-Muajaha | Electronic Iraq

Search

FIGURE 2.2. Indymedia UK homepage.

There are no ads on the site, but at the same time, Indymedia's function as an activist portal is trumpeted by its list of protest events at the top of the right-hand column. U.K. Indymedia also devotes a large amount of screen space to the other cities that also have Indymedia websites—in a sense, the very notion of Indymedia as a *network* is integrated into the webpage itself. We should also note the prominent placement of the 'publish your news' button on the IMC site, immediately making clear that the site allows anyone and everyone to contribute.

Finally, this relative openness to participation is somewhat compromised by the dominance of the center (or 'editor's') column. Despite the fact that grass-roots journalists contributed 85% of Indymedia's articles, many of these journalists are dependent on site editors for highlighting their stories. In other words, on the IMC U.K. website, all stories are equal, but some stories are more equal than others (the stories that the volunteer editors think are important). A number of formal and informal internal Indymedia policies strive to limit this power differential; nevertheless, it would be naïve to deny its existence. At the same time, however, it is possible to argue that the relative 'flatness' of most of the IMC site—the prominent placement of the publish button, the listing of stories in reverse chronological order—combined with the wide diversity in its content, necessitates some degree of editorial control.

Wikinews' is probably the most elegant of the four websites I examined, especially in comparison to the particularly text-heavy Indymedia. The site echoes the Indymedia design, embracing a three-column layout with a single, 'featured' story and additional stories below the fold (see Figure 2.3). The right hand column allows readers to browse stories by subject and highlights a list of breaking material, as well as stories that are currently in violation of the NPOV policy. The right-hand column also features useful news like the weather and global stock market reports. The left-hand column provides additional information about the purpose and mission of Wikinews.

In its relative simplicity, Wikinews is both clean and easy on the eye. Wikinews also clearly announces its mission and the fact that it aims to be a site for participatory, grassroots journalism; the top banner tells visitors that the site is a "free content news source that you can edit." The site's registration system, however, is a bit more complicated, and the manner by which one actually becomes a Wikinews contributor or editor is not spelled out clearly anywhere on the front page. Like Indymedia U.K. but unlike the Northwest Voice, there are no advertisements on the Wikinews website.

Like Indymedia U.K. the Northwest Voice clearly invites its readers to participate, with a visible 'share your Voice' button dominating the top of the page (see Figure 2.4). The Northwest Voice also utilizes a three-column layout, although the content of these columns differs little compared with the content of a more traditional newspaper. The right column is composed entirely of classified ads, and the left column is made up of category headings that echo those found in a normal paper: 'letters,' 'classifieds,' 'church news,' and so on.

article | discussion | view source | history

Please participate in the Wikinews design contest for our multilingual portal and skin!

Water cooler – Mailing list – Site news (April 18) – Real-Time Chat

WIKINEWS

navigation
- Main Page
- Article workspace
- Upload media
- Recent changes
- Random page
- Help

search

[ ] Go | Search

toolbox
- What links here
- Related changes
- Special pages

other languages
- Suomeksi
- Deutsch
- Español
- Français
- Italiano
- Nederlands
- Polski

Main Page

From Wikinews, the free news source

Welcome to Wikinews, the free-content news source that you can write!

April 18, 2005 12:56 UTC

LATEST NEWS | GET INVOLVED | SUBMIT STORY | NEWSROOM | CROSSWORD | RSS 🔗

British National Fingerprint Database begins without parliamentary consultation

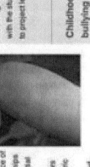

Starting in 2006, HM passport service of Britain will begin use of biometric chips in the issuance of passports. Essential to this scheme is the creation of a central database for passport holders that contains fingerprint and biometric data. This database, along with fingerprinting facilities, will be shared by the controversial Identity Card scheme.

Critics say this is an attempt by the British government to introduce by the back door many elements of the Identity Card scheme. Full story for info

Internet censorship study group reports on China

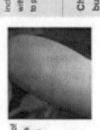

An international study group report released Thursday calls China's internet censorship "the most sophisticated effort of its kind in the world," and details measures used within China to limit citizen access to internet resources, including the BBC. Volunteers in China who assisted with the study did so at "substantial risk," according to project leader John Palfrey. Full story

Childhood exposure to TV linked to bullying

An Archive of Pediatrics & Adolescent Medicine report found there is a statistically significant

FIGURE 2.3. Wikinews homepage.

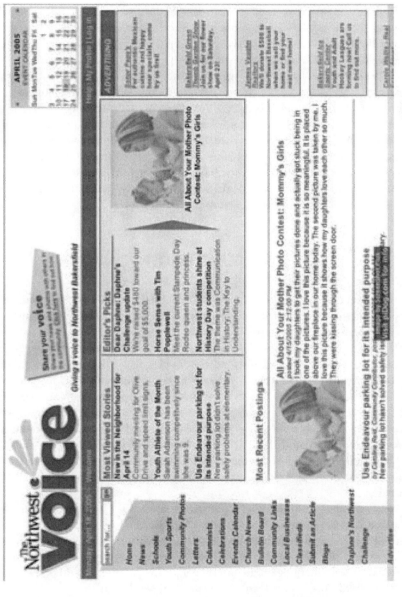

FIGURE 2.4. The Northwest Voice homepage.

Although the top of the center column is largely constructed by the site's editor (with its 'editors picks' and 'most viewed stories') the hierarchy between editor and contributor is much less noticeable than it is on the Indymedia U.K. website. Indeed, the right-hand column on U.K. IMC (also called the 'open newswire') is transported to the center column of the Northwest Voice, with every story, in effect, featured, even those that consist of a single line or picture. I suspect that this can be attributed to the relative infrequency of reader contributions (the Northwest Voice receives between 2 to 5 submissions a day, whereas Indymedia U.K. receives between 10 and 50).

From this analysis of different website designs we can see ways in which the layout of a website both reinforces and contradicts the data we obtained during our content analysis. Indymedia's call for everyone to 'be the media,' for example, is rendered somewhat more complex by its reliance on a highly visible 'editor's column,' and the difficulties in actually becoming a Wikinews contributor are reiterated by the additional problems in getting access to editorial control from the news site's front page. In many ways, the design of a website crystallizes the assumptions, both about mission and about readership, that I discussed earlier in my overview of organizational mission statements.

CONCLUSION

Pulling together my analysis of mission statements, content analysis, and website architecture overview, what general conclusions can we draw with regard to the state of the participatory journalistic field?

To begin with, the posts on most sites appeared to correlate strongly to the mission of that site. For example, Indymedia U.K. had a large number of posts by political activists, whereas the Northwest Voice was entirely local in character. It is interesting to speculate, however, what might happen to the Northwest Voice should Bakersfield enter a highly politically charged period. For example, what if corruption in the mayors' office was uncovered or if there was a terrorist strike on Sacramento? Would there be a rash of political postings? And would those who maintain the site tolerate them? Only additional research, particularly interviews with the founders and maintainers of these websites, can answer these questions.

In addition, grassroots media outlets are committed, at least theoretically, to the deprofessionalization of journalism. Despite the wide variation in political and ideological perspectives, the mission statements of all three websites—Indymedia U.K., Wikinews, and the Northwest Voice—argue that a new type of journalism was emerging on the internet, a journalism that should be encouraged and nurtured. At the very least, these sites believe that there is now room in the journalistic dialog for ordinary citizens. At the most extreme, journalists were denounced as 'agents of modernity'—privileged and out-of-touch representatives of a pseudo-scientific caste whose time was running out.

The commonly accepted notion that there is little original reporting on the Internet, defined in the traditional sense, was incorrect. With the exception of Wikinews, contributors to all three sites did more than simply link to already written news stories and comment on them—they 'committed journalism,' filing on the spot reports, conducting interviews, and taking photographs. The question of whether this journalism is actually useful for the 'public'—whether it presents new information, encourages the growth of a robust public sphere, or reinforces political commitment via engagement with quotidian politics—is another area that demands further investigation.

Although we did see the provision of original online content, no participatory journalistic website I studied was either entirely participatory or entirely journalistic. The amount of original reporting on each site ranged from 50% (Northwest Voice) to 8% (Wikinews). On average, this means that about two-thirds of the content was something else—commentary, announcements, or reprints. All three sites also had editors, either to create feature stories, to make sure content was newsworthy and factual, or to make sure it was locally relevant. Pure participatory democracy did not exist on any of the sites I examined.

Finally, the healthiest websites seemed to be those that maintained connections with 'actually existing' communities. Organizations like Wikinews that function largely in virtual space sometimes seemed to struggle with a democracy deficit or a lack of grassroots participation. The Northwest Voice, on the other hand, was grounded in an actually existing local community, the town of Bakersfield, California. Indymedia U.K. was also geographically limited (to the United Kingdom) and based within an active political community. Sites that allowed their readers to contribute journalism that had an impact on their lives seemed more likely to encourage participation than sites which aimed for neutral content.

To conclude on a cautious note: It remains unclear whether or not the explosion in online participatory journalism will result in any concrete radical change, either within the profession of journalism itself or in the larger political and economic structures as a whole. The idea of 'participatory journalism' is extremely flexible and is compatible, as we have seen, with websites that advocate 'old fashioned objectivity' as well as 'hyperlocal' (and rather nonmilitant) citizens reporting. The type of radical participatory content produced by Indymedia seems, in this instance, to be the exception rather than the rule. At the same time, it remains to be seen whether the growth in citizens' journalism will result in any larger changes in the structure of journalism as a whole, or whether the democratization of the press will be absorbed back into larger journalistic structures against which they only recently rebelled.

REFERENCES

Anderson, C. (2004). Information circulation in the blogosphere: Analysis of media patterns in coverage of electronic voting in the United States. Paper presented at the Halifax Media Symposium, June 24, 2004.

Anderson, C. (2005a). *Blogging the DNC.* Unpublished paper.

Anderson, C. (2005b). *San Fran smackdown— Indymedia / Blogosphere divide rages on KRON Blog,* Retrieved February 11, 2007, from http://indypendent.typepad.com/academese/2005/07/httpwwwthebayar.html

Arnison, M. (2001). *Why open publishing is the same as free software.* Retrieved April 21, 2005, from http://www.cat.org.au/maffew/cat/openpub.html

Atton, C. (2002). *Alternative media.* London : Sage.

Beczkowski, P.J. (2004). *Digitizing the news innovation in online newspapers.* Cambridge, MA: MIT Press.

Bianco, A. (2005). *The future of the New York Times.* Retrieved May 5, 2005, from http://www.businessweek.com/magazine/content/05_03/b3916001_mz001.htm

Bourdieu, P. (1992). *An invitation to a reflexive sociology.* Chicago: Chicago University Press.

Bowman, W., & Willis, C. (2003). *We media: How audiences are shaping the future of news and information.* Retrieved May 5, 2005, from http://www.hypergene.net/wemedia/weblog.php

Couldry, N., & Curran, J. (Eds.). (2003). *Contesting media power: Alternative media in a networked world.* Lanham, MD: Rowman & Littlefield.

Downing, J. D. H., with Ford, T. V., Gil, G., & Stein, L. (2001). *Radical media: Rebellious communication and social movements.* London: Sage.

Downing, J. (2003). The Independent Media Center movement and the anarchist socialist tradition. In N. Couldry & J. Curran, (Eds.), *Contesting media power: Alternative media in a networked world* (pp. 243-57). Lanham, MD: Rowman & Littlefield.

Dube, J. (2004). *Interview with Mary Fulton.* Retrieved July 31, 2005, from http://www.cyberjournalist.net/news/001487.php.

Escobar, A. (2000) Place, power and networks in globalization and postdevelopment. In K. Wilkins, *Re-developing communications for social change* (pp. 163-174). Lanham, MD: Rowman & Littlefield.

Gillmor D. (2004). *We the media: Grassroots journalism by the people, for the people.* Sebastopol, CA: O'Reilly.

Glasser, M. (2003). *Weblogs are pushing the newsroom envelope.* Retrieved November 22, 2005, from http://www.ojr.org/ojr/glaser/1064357109.php

Indymedia U.K. (2004). *IMC U.K. mission statement.* Retrieved November 22, 2005, from http://www.indymedia.org.uk/en/static/mission.html

LaMonica, M. (2005). *Interview with Jimbo Wales.* Retrieved July 31, 2005, from http://news.com.com/Open-sourcing+the+news/2008-1025_3-5515166.html

Lenin. (2005). *Iraq protest report.* Retrieved January 4, 2007, from http://www.indymedia.org.uk/en/2005/03/307106.html

Miller, D. (2005). *Hyperlocal journalism.* Retrieved November 19, 2005, from http://www.radioopensource.org/hyperlocal-journalism

Neiman Reports (2003). Weblogs and journalism. *Neiman Reports,* 57(3), 61-64.

Northwest Voice (2004). *About the Northwest Voice.* Retrieved November 1, 2005, from http://www.northwestvoice.com/home/staticfull.php?page_id=305

Problems With Wikinews. Retrieved June 1, 2005, from http://chuck.mahost.org/weblog/index.php?p=752

Rosen J. (2005). *Eason Jordan resigns.* Retrieved May 5, 2005, from http://journalism.nyu.edu/pubzone/weblogs/pressthink/2005/02/11/esn_res.html

Secor, A. J. (2003) Belaboring gender: The spatial practice of work and the politics of 'making do' in Istanbul. *Environment and Planning, 35*(12), 2209-2227.

Terdiman, D. (2004). *Open arms for open source news.* Retrieved January 4, 2007, from http://www.wired.com/news/culture/0,64285-0.html

Thompson, J. B. (1995). *The media and modernity: A social theory of the media.* Stanford, CA: Stanford University Press.

What's wrong with wiki? Retrieved August 1, 2005, from http://www.echochamber project.com/blog/archives/000081.html

Wikinews. (2004). *Mission statement.* Retrieved November 22, 2005, from http://en.wikinews.org/wiki/Wikinews:Mission_statement

Wikipedia. (2005). *Neutral point of view.* Retrieved November 21, 2005, from http://en.wikipedia.org/wiki/Wikipedia:Neutral_point_of_view

Zelizer, B. (2004). *Taking journalism seriously: News and the academy.* London: Sage.

THEORIZING CITIZENS' MEDIA
A Rhizomatic Approach

Tanja E. Bosch

Community radio station Bush Radio is nestled at the foot of Table Mountain in Cape Town, South Africa. When a child goes missing, broadcasts are immediately interrupted with urgent calls to the public until the child is found. On Mondays *Positive Living* takes radio into the high schools with its outside broadcast unit, facilitating frank discussions about sex and HIV. The continent's only gay talk show airs on Thursdays, and on Saturdays, children as young as six years old broadcast from the on-air studio. During the war in Iraq, Bush Radio printed several hundred T-shirts sporting the eye-catching slogan 'Bush Against War' and organized antiwar protest marches in the city center. As station director Zane Ibrahim said,

> When the war started, Bush Radio had to immediately inform the people of the townships how this war is going to affect them, their lives—gasoline, petrol will go up, every foodstuff, imports would go up, so they had to be informed, so they could make informed decisions about how they feel about the war. When President Bush gave the world a 48-hour ultimatum we decided to give him an ultimatum for peace, and we suspended all our programming for 48 hours, and played John Lennon's "Give Peace a Chance" 576 times, again and again. We had T-Shirts printed "Bush Against War," so this is the kind of thing we do. (Z. Ibrahim, personal communication, 29 July 2003)

Grounded on a case study of Bush Radio, the purpose of this chapter is to propose a new theoretical approach to community radio. Drawing on Deleuze and
Guattari's (1987) notion of rhizomes as 'grasslike,' heterogeneous entities with
multiple entry points and routes rather than roots, this chapter theorizes Bush
Radio as a connector and bridging mechanism that impacts the social fabric.

THEORIZING ALTERNATIVE MEDIA:
A HISTORICAL APPROACH

Scholarship on citizens' media emerged out of traditional development communication theories and continue to frame the study of these media in "rigid categories of power and binary conceptions of domination and subordination that
elude the fluidity and complexity of alternative media as a social, political and
cultural phenomenon" (Rodríguez, 2001: 3-4).

Recent shifts in the theoretical terrain abandon these totalizing theories to
embrace more critical approaches. Rodríguez (2001) has drawn on the theory of
radical democracy proposed by Ernesto Laclau and Chantal Mouffe (1985), who
suggest that attempts by nonmainstream groups to contest legitimate discourses
and to redefine their identity should be interpreted as political action. Rodríguez
(2001) coined the term 'citizens' media' in an attempt to overcome binary categories traditionally used to theorize alternative media, arguing that terms like
'alternative' suggest their own lesser relationship to dominant media.

Couldry (2000) has also deconstructed the binary relationship between alternative and mainstream media, describing how people become active within the
mainstream media frame and attempt to introduce alternative forms of mediation
and media activism that challenge the authority of existing media institutions.
Similarly, Atton (2002) draws on Foucault's writings on the 'insurrection of subjugated knowledges' and prioritizes the term 'alternative media,' based on the
assumption that the Other is able to represent itself.

Drawing on Habermas' notion of the public sphere, and from Emma
Goldman's feminist anarchism and Sheila Rowbotham's Marxist feminism,
Downing (2001) proposes several conceptual moves that include first, the need to
acknowledge oppression as a heterogeneous and fragmented reality; second, the
need to build lateral links between fragmented movements against oppression(s);
third, the need to visualize the struggle against oppression in terms of movements
and not as institutions; and fourth, the need to think of liberation as an everyday
process that disrupts immediate realities (18-24). Downing (2001) further argues
that alternative media provide a forum that is relatively free from economic and
editorial constraints, permitting the "discursive reinterpretation and refutation of
media forms and symbols" (318).

These theories only explain certain aspects of alternative media, such as
democratic participation or the subversion of traditional power dynamics.

Similarly, overarching theories on national development are useful to frame the phenomenon, but—although community radio falls within the paradigm of communication for development as a form of participatory communication—do not always provide a complete frame of analysis for understanding how alternative media play a role in community dynamics.

METHODOLOGY

My relationship with Bush Radio started unexpectedly in 1995, on one of Cape Town's notorious speeding, overcrowded 15-seat minibus taxis, traveling home from undergraduate classes at the University of Cape Town. My copy of the campus newspaper sparked a conversation about community media with another passenger, the late Ghanaian freelance journalist and Bush Radio volunteer, James Brew, who recruited me to join his production team. Brew was the producer of a current affairs magazine program called *African Rhythm*, which aired Saturday afternoons at 5pm. When I left Bush Radio for graduate studies on a Fulbright scholarship at Ohio University in 1999, I was eager to explore the theoretical aspects of the environment I had experienced first hand.

This chapter is based on a larger ethnographic study of Bush Radio (Bosch, 2003), with the researcher as instrument and reflective heuristic device. Given my extensive involvement in the organization that I was proposing to study, reflexive or narrative ethnography seemed a logical methodological choice. In reflexive ethnographies the researcher's personal experiences are critical to illuminate the culture under study. Reflexive ethnographies range on a continuum—from starting research from one's own perspective, to confessional ethnographies as described by Van Maanen (1990), where the researcher's stories of doing the research become the main focus (Denzin & Lincoln, 2000).

Fieldwork was carried out between June 10 and August 31, 2002 while working at the station as a producer of *Abantu Abakhulu* (meaning 'The Elderly' in the Xhosa language), an eight-part, 30-minute series, dealing with health and social issues relevant to the elderly and aging; also during work at the station in a voluntary capacity during November and December 2000, and from July to September 2001. I also spent three months at the station during June and August 2003. During these times I presented programs, facilitated training workshops, assisted with scheduling, wrote and edited jingles, and studio engineered for some programs. The primary data-gathering methods during these periods were participant observation and in-depth interviews.

OVERVIEW OF COMMUNITY RADIO

The terms "alternative" or "community media" refer to a diverse range of media including newspapers, magazines, radio, television, and electronic network initiatives. Community radio in the developing world emerged within the context of participatory communication projects in Latin America in the 1960s, following the criticisms of the failures of the dominant, capitalist paradigm of the West and the Marxist/socialist paradigm of the East (Nwosu, Onwumechili & M'Bayo, 1995). Led by Third World scholars and activists, Paulo Freire (1970, 1985) in particular, these critics pointed out that the mass media privilege agendas irrelevant to Third World citizens. Scholars and activists searched for alternatives, leading to the consequent global rise of participatory communication initiatives, which include community radio (Rodríguez, 2000).

> Today, small-scale, locally owned media are developing to counter the spread of global media corporations. Groups in developing countries have been empowered to express their opinions and needs by using modern technologies to gain participation in the public sphere. (Mowlana, 1998)

In general, radio remains the most pervasive medium with the greatest potential for participatory communication strategies due to its low cost and accessibility to illiterate populations, particularly in rural areas. Community radio has provided groups with access to media and an opportunity to articulate their views through direct and indirect participation. The rise of radio as a vehicle for popular, participatory communication began with the Bolivian miners' radios in the 1940s (O'Connor, 1990), but extended beyond its Latin American origins to the Caribbean, Asia, Australia, Europe, and Africa. In South Africa, over 80 community radio stations were granted broadcast licenses in 1994. By December 2006 there were 150 stations broadcasting with community radio licenses.

The key concepts underlying community media are access, participation, and self-management (Lewis, 1993). The defining characteristic of community radio is thus its operation by specific groups of people who participate in all aspects of running the station, from fundraising and management to programming, production, and on-air activities. Volunteers, drawn from the audience, usually staff community radio stations. In this sense, the traditional boundaries between sender and receiver are blurred through the creation of an active audience. As managing director, Zane Ibrahim, tells staff members at the Monday morning staff meeting:

> You don't work for Bush Radio, you work for the community! We're not chasing listeners; we're chasing empowerment and development [of the community]. I'm not your boss; the community is your boss. Those people that live in shacks [informal housing] in Langa, those people that were robbed last night in Khayelitsha, those are your bosses. (Z. Ibrahim, personal communication, 21 July 2003)

RHIZOMATICS AND COMMUNITY RADIO

A rhizome has no beginning or end; it is always in the middle, between things, interbeing, intermezzo. (Deleuze & Guattari, 1987: 21)

As explicated by Deleuze and Guattari (1987) in *A Thousand Plateaus*, the rhizome generates connections through its characteristics of heterogeneity, disjunction, multiplicity, multiple entry points, and routes rather than roots. In a botanical sense, a rhizome is an underground tuber that ramifies and diversifies, producing new buds, as opposed to what Deleuze and Guattari call 'arboric systems of knowledge' based on the model of a tree, which symbolizes linear thinking and hierarchical structures. The rhizome moves between the lines established by the arboric systems, and as such is 'fuzzy' rather than aggregated, with both 'this' and 'not this' co-existing simultaneously (Deleuze & Guattari, 1987).

Community radio develops in rhizomatic fashion, growing globally more like the grass than the trees. Hundreds of low-powered FM stations have sprung up in the United States as a result of assistance from nonprofits like the Prometheus Radio Project, and the World Association of Community Radio Broadcasters (AMARC) has almost 3,000 members and associates in 106 countries (www.amarc.org). It may be argued that community radio is not necessarily becoming more powerful than media conglomerates, but is growing horizontally, creating ripples under the surface. Like a rhizome, community radio stations form networks of connections across which people and ideas flow and disperse.

In the South African case of Bush Radio, both the airwaves and the physical space of the radio station serve as a meeting point for the various communities of Cape Town and their interest groups and organizations. People involved in different types of struggles are often brought together by Bush Radio, which also assists them in various ways. The gay and lesbian service organization *Triangle Project* is currently being strengthened through the training of some of their members to participate in production activities on *In The Pink*, the gay and lesbian program. The Red Cross Society of South Africa gains assistance via its partnerships with Bush Radio, which brings outside broadcast equipment into different areas under the joint banner of the two organizations. As Sarah Stevens of the Red Cross said at one outside broadcast:

> With the help of Bush Radio, we're getting a lot of members who want to become a part of the Red Cross Society, and that plays a big role for us because we want to recruit more volunteers, and actually Bush Radio is making us famous because people know, okay, they have a volunteer community outreach, and Bush Radio's going to be there, and people are running to Bush Radio to see the faces behind the voices that are actually here, so we really appreciate that. (S. Stevens, personal communication, 29 July 2003)

Connection and Heterogeneity

There are several key points to Deleuze and Guatarri's theory of the rhizome that will each be addressed in turn below, with specific reference to Bush Radio. Firstly, the principle of connection and heterogeneity, which states that any point of a rhizome can be connected to any other point. In other words, the rhizome is not hierarchical in structure as no point comes before another. At Bush Radio this heterogeneity is expressed through the fact that job titles have no real meaning and responsibilities are shared. A producer may also be expected to present programs or read the news. Everyone has to learn how to operate the on-air studio and to learn basic editing, as unlike most radio stations, Bush Radio has no assigned studio operators or editors. For example, the AIDS producer is constantly encouraged to produce features on other topics and to invite other presenters on to her program, *Positive Living.* When she once asked someone else to present her program, the other presenter admitted that she thought programs about AIDS were 'boring' and did not usually listen to this type of program. However, after interviewing an HIV positive musician who humanized the issue and made it more real for the audience, she changed her attitude toward HIV and AIDS. Although staff members do have specific responsibilities, they are encouraged to be flexible in the interpretation of their job descriptions.

This lack of hierarchies is further significant in that it often affects content as well as who becomes a participant. Instead of leaving program development in the hands of programmers alone, anyone can come up with ideas for new programs. This different articulation of leadership and authority thus allows for more participatory democratic practices. More than once people who came in as a guest on a show eventually became part of the production team. For example, local musician Lu Chase, once interviewed, was then later recruited to be a presenter for the Arts and Culture show. Individuals learn about all aspects of radio instead of being confined to specific areas only.

The rhizomatic heterogeneity of Bush Radio can also be seen in the manner in which staff interact. Unlike in most other work environments, at Bush Radio people interact as equals regardless of gender, race, class, or educational level. Those in different roles and decision-making power levels communicate as equals and even socialize with each other outside of work.

Linear thinking and hierarchical structures have thus been subverted rhizomatically to allow for tasks to be completed, while not allowing titles to control individuals. Although Adrian Louw holds the title of Program Integrator, at a commercial station his role would be described as operations manager or even station manager. Producer Erna Curry said:

> For the first time I've got to do the kind of work that falls in with basically what I believe my principles are about. So it's very comforting in that respect. Bush Radio is a very progressive organization. So working at Bush I

think really changed my life. Bush Radio's got its own politics and its own
organizational difficulties as well, but I've just always felt that, I don't know,
I just found that there was a place I could really utilize all my skills—and
that's not something you can do in a lot of other organizations. (E. Curry,
personal communication, 21 August 2002)

Bush Radio offers access and participation for nonprofessionals with a range
of individuals from students, the unemployed, activists, teachers, and lawyers
presenting programs in their free time. The presenter of the Sunday night blues
program is a surgeon employed at Groote Schuur, the biggest hospital in the city,
prestigious as the site of the world's first heart transplant. The presenter of the
jazz program is an internationally acclaimed jazz musician and returnee from the
United States. A former Truth and Reconciliation Commission[1] investigator
hosts a Friday afternoon current affairs program. The principal of an elementary
school on the Cape Flats is a volunteer news reader. Fixed identities such as
'sender' and 'audience' are systematically broken down, as the so-called audience
at times also become senders through the participatory practices of the radio station. At Bush Radio volunteers listen to each other's shows, offering feedback to
their colleagues at the monthly producers' meetings, and they are simultaneously
being positioned as sender and receiver.

Bush Radio offers the audience numerous opportunities for feedback, from
letters to phone-calls to an Open Forum meeting, which is open to all members
of the community. On many occasions suggestions for programming are incorporated, and in some cases individuals who offered feedback came aboard as volunteers. Communication does not follow the traditional one-directional sender-
receiver model.

Although Bush Radio has always targeted a specific geographic area, after
the end of apartheid and abolition of the Group Areas Act, black people are no
longer concentrated in those areas. The station's broadcast range extends to areas
outside of the Cape Flats, and many listeners call the station from these areas.
The audience is no longer a black audience. Some white presenters work at the
station, and there are many calls from white South Africans who live within the
station's geographical footprint. The station has attempted to redefine its understanding of community as a group of people who are interested in alternative
information—in other words, critical information about global political issues
such as that provided by the Michael Parenti and Alternative Radio cassette
tapes, which come from the United States. As Adrian Louw said:

One of Bush's aims, which I think it's done very successfully, is also to build
bridges between those communities. If there's a more advantaged community listening that's okay, but we're not catering for them. So if our listenership
is increasing they're either listening because they want to find out what's
happening or we are actually spreading the message of understanding. (A.
Louw, personal communication, August 20, 2002)

Similarly, Bush Radio's policies on issues such as HIV/AIDS or gender further demonstrate this rhizomatic subversion of hierarchy. Rather than ghettoizing these issues by relegating them to a specific slot, HIV and gender awareness is raised throughout the programming day. Even music programs have scheduled public service announcements (PSAs) on topics from gay rights to domestic violence. These PSAs are dispersed across the entire program schedule, are locally produced, and often contain interesting angles that take into account local values or myths in common currency. Bush Radio's programming is thus rhizomatic, comprising pockets of information located at various times. For example, one PSA deals with the myth that having sex with a virgin can cure AIDS. Another uses drama and comedy to encourage men to play active roles in child-rearing.

The content of broadcasts does not follow the linearity often preferred by commercial radio, as Bush Radio often supplements or contradicts dominant discourses or representations. This is seen in the daily approach to programming, which constantly seeks new angles to stories covered by the mainstream, focusing on the human experience and the impact of national issues on local lives. Interviews with local taxi drivers have been used to explain the relevance of a national fuel increase. News policy further states guidelines that include gender neutral language, sensitivity to race, and ethical considerations in story selection.

Unlike commercial radio, which has a distinctive format, Bush Radio's programming is unique for its heterogeneity. In one day audiences are exposed to every genre of music from blues and jazz to hip-hip, kwaito or drum 'n bass on Bush Radio. Commercial R'nB, rap, and traditional music are also played on the station. Talk programs range from call-in programs on African politics to informational programs on AIDS. On Friday evenings audiences can listen to talks by U.S. political commentator and academic Michael Parenti, and on Sundays they can hear *Conversations with Writers,* which engages local authors. On Saturday afternoons teenagers talk about fashion, sex, and drugs, and on Sunday afternoons *Abantu Abakhulu* broadcasts programs to the elderly. This diversity of formats and genres creates room for experimentation with content and form, and in this way community media can be seen as a breeding ground for innovation, later often re-appropriated by mainstream media (Carpentier, Lie, & Servaes, 2003). One example of this is how the formats of certain shows on Bush Radio have been copied by mainstream radio stations that have the resources to improve upon the original concept. In several instances this has included the use of the name itself. Shows such as *Backchat* and *The Morning Cruise* and the slogan *It's All Good* showed up on commercial stations long after their existence on Bush Radio.

The listeners' ability to choose a program is much like the rhizome, where many points are linked together, not necessarily in sequence, allowing them to move from one point to another. Unlike listeners to many other radio stations, although dedicated, Bush Radio listeners often do not listen to the station for an entire broadcast day. Rather, they tend to listen passionately to certain programs only, showing unfamiliarity with others, even those that may occur directly before or after the ones they listen to on a regular basis. A recent in-house audience research survey (Ogada, 2005) showed that in fact, the most popular programs are the ones that cater to specialized tastes, such as music. In particular, the Tuesday night Drum 'n Bass show, Thursday night reggae show, and Friday night's hip hop show were found to be the most listened-to shows. While the survey shows that generally audiences do not connect to the rest of the program schedule, their rhizomatic relationship with Bush Radio means that they use the station to connect with each other on the basis of these specialized music genres. In Cape Town, for example, Drum 'n Bass is generally perceived to be popular only among white youth. The survey surprised Bush Radio staff by showing that the audience of this show is much more diverse than originally thought, and that black and white youth interact with each other via the show. These kinds of specialized music shows thus generate grasslike links that grow among audiences, as different identity communities use the radio as a space to cross artificially created boundaries that separate their ethnic identities.

Speaking before a panel at the Independent Communications Authority of South Africa (ICASA) licensing hearing in June 2001, Ibrahim said:

> One of our mandates is to demystify radio to the community; for so long we've been spoken at not spoken with; for so long we've had radio thrown at us and it was the worst kind of radio, telling us that we were useless, no good. So now, from the age of four we are teaching children, it's your radio; the airwaves belong to the people.

The community Ibrahim speaks about refers not only to the station's audience, but also to a group of people whose interests Bush Radio attempts to represent. But it is not always clear to Bush Radio who its 'community' is. To staff's surprise, an auto mechanic called in one Monday morning from a previously black township for a copy of the Michael Parenti commentary that aired the previous Friday night. Although the target audience is predominantly working class, staff always assumed that Parenti listeners would be mostly lower middle class, perhaps students, or members of nongovernmental organizations. On the other hand, a DJ from the hip-hop show described how he was surprised to encounter a professor at the University of Cape Town who was an avid listener of the station and of his program. This was a surprise because the station assumed that the hip-hop show's audience comprised mostly black youth.

> Who is it that we're serving and who is actually listening? It's not an easy question to answer because we don't have the resources to do proper audience research. The station is geared towards a younger audience currently. We try and service as many people in the broader community as possibly, community of Cape Town very broadly speaking. We always say if you want to find out about HIV and AIDS, if you want to find out about children, gender issues, then you can listen to Bush. We don't try and entice

people with sexy presenters that pose half naked. We're not that kind of
radio station. We're not a sexy radio station. (A. Louw, personal communication, 20 August 2003)

Multiplicity

The next principle of the rhizome is that of multiplicity, which Deleuze and
Guattari explain, saying that the will of the puppeteer does not control the
actions of the puppets, and that it is the lines between the points that are most
important. In South Africa the formal policies and systems that control the
broadcast industry do not always extend to community radio. With the liberalization of the airwaves after the first democratic elections in South Africa in 1994,
the Independent Broadcasting Authority (IBA) made special provision for the
licensing and monitoring of community radio stations. However, community
radio stations have resisted and continue to challenge many of these policies.
Bush Radio for example, is currently in the process of challenging ICASA license
conditions that preclude the broadcast of foreign programming.

Whereas ICASA's concerns are grounded in the potentially hegemonic
nature of foreign programming and the need to keep multinational programming
at bay, Bush Radio argues that internationally produced programs such as
Alternative Radio or *Making Contact* are of local relevance. These weekly 90-
minute public affairs programs, originating from the United States, provide
analyses and views that tend to be ignored or distorted in most mainstream
media. Bush Radio thus builds bridges internationally as well through its connections with progressive media communities abroad. In an environment where
alternative news sources are scarce, linking up with critical voices abroad and
making their programming available to Bush Radio's local audience strengthens
the lines between the points.

Another example of multiplicity is the increasing involvement of the government's Department of Communications in the community sector, through
their funding and setting up of stations around the country. This has been perceived as the insidious advent of possible government control of stations that
should be community run and owned. Although the license is given to the community, some media activists have raised fears that these stations will be less likely to hold government accountable on and off the air, due to this funding. Against
this trend, many stations have chosen to operate independently of government
funding. In this case, the will of the puppeteer (government) definitely does not
control the actions of the puppets (community radio stations).

The Principle of Asignifying Rupture

Deleuze and Guatarri (1987) propose the principle of asignifying rupture, which
states that "a rhizome may be shattered at any given point, but will start up again

on one of its old lines or on new lines" (9). This principle is most clearly demonstrated by briefly looking back at Bush Radio's early history. In August 1993, Bush Radio students and volunteers pressured the government to free the airwaves and grant Bush Radio a broadcast license. However, during this period of negotiations the apartheid government was still in power, and two right-wing community radio stations were given licenses, while two applications by Bush Radio were rejected. The station then held its first illegal broadcast on April 25 1993, and the authorities arrived within a few hours to confiscate the equipment. According to one of the founders, the late Edric Gorfinkel:

> There were 20, 30, 40 of them with guns and dogs and patrolling outside, I mean it was a serious military operation, it was hilarious! The people who were there also found it amusing. They were obviously very threatened by it. And in a funny kind of a way it's just confirmation that one's on the right wicket. And to a large extent that's how we treated it. You want to take our equipment away, no problem; we'll see you in court. And they picked a couple of people to charge and that was me and Mervyn Swartz, Mervyn was the trade union representative. The tide of history was going in the other direction; nobody was going to be going to jail. (E. Gorfinkel, personal communication, 28 August 2003)

Another founder, Lumko Mtimde, agreed that this did not derail the process:

> People were not disappointed. Even after that confiscation we had demonstrations, which were successful, which were supported by a number of people and actually strengthened our campaign to free the airwaves, that very action that the enemy did. So people were not demoralized, instead they began to say we have to fight until we win this battle. And one can say safely we won that battle. (L. Mtimde, personal communication, 28 August 2003)

In true rhizomatic fashion, the Bush Radio story did not end here. According to the principle of asignifying rupture, in a rhizomatic network movements and flows can be rerouted around disruptions, with the severed section regenerating itself and continuing to grow, forming new lines and pathways. The emergence of Bush Radio out of a cassette production facility (CASET) and the perseverance of its founders against the political situation of the time is proof of this regeneration of the rhizome. CASET emerged at the height of this increased internal resistance and the defiance campaign against the apartheid regime. Founder Edrik Gorfinkel explained how the political context informed CASET's mission:

> The initial work that we did was recording what happened in the defiance campaign. Going to mass rallies, recording toy-toys[2] as well as recording

some of the ANC-IDASA[3] safaris where people from inside South Africa were going to meet ANC people outside. And CASET recorded those conferences to be transcribed, and quite a few audio productions were made out of that as well and distributed through the democratic movement. (E. Gorfinkel, personal communication, 28 August 2002)

I traced the late Gorfinkel to the end of a dusty gravel road, on a farm in the middle of the desert in the Karoo, 700 kilometers outside of Cape Town.

Basically the idea for me after I'd been working in radio in Zimbabwe for a number of years was that at some point South Africa's broadcast environment was going to need to be transformed. I had the idea basically of using audio cassette as a way to play radio, began to train people and I had a hunch that audio cassette could actually be quite a useful mechanism for organizing and education and that kind of stuff within the mass democratic movement. So I registered for an adult education course at UCT [the University of Cape Town], and I did the Talking Newspaper as my student project. It was repression days and as an academic project it wouldn't necessarily attract the same kind of attention from the top people and so on. And because it was an adult education course I targeted people with handicaps to independent reading, that's how I put it, so blind people and also aimed at illiterate people. The blind thing was also just to make it look like a social project. (E. Gorfinkel, personal communication, 28 August 2002)

CASET produced audiotapes with recordings of conferences and political meetings, local music, poetry, and story telling. Recordings were mostly in English, the unofficial lingua franca. Poet and writer Sandile Dikeni was the first employee of CASET. I met the effervescent Dikeni for the first time at Bush Radio where he was recording a documentary on the enrobement of Saartje Baartman[4] as part of his current work at the Government Communication and Information System (GCIS).

We used to work together as a team. We'd discuss projects and I'd go and implement that. We'd receive requests from organizations and political organizations to produce tapes on them and their history. I would go out with my Marantz [field recorder], then come back and remix and so on. Much of the stuff that was produced organizations requested from us. We worked on recording history. You must remember that at this time the country was under a state of emergency. So we packaged material and we also received material from outside. Material was sent by mail order. We'd create profiles of tapes, which were put together in a newsletter called *Mamela*.[5] People were starved for information. What really was amazing was people's reception of the tapes. We got letters from the Northern provinces, people would come down to Cape Town to buy the tapes. Radio's got this beautiful thing about it. You can hear your own voice on tape, it just gives you goose-bumps, it does something to you. And so many people that never thought they'd ever be heard, suddenly heard themselves through the speakers of a ghetto-blaster. And I recorded them, and I could look in their eyes and see this excitement in their eyes of recognizing their own voices on the air. And those small things were for me the most beautiful stuff. (S. Dikeni, personal communication, 22 August 2002)

After elections in 1994, a coalition government of national unity took power, with the ANC having secured a parliamentary majority. Community broadcasting was recognized for the first time and defined as "initiated and controlled by members of a community of interest, or a geographic community, to express their concerns, needs or aspirations without interference, subject to the regulation of the Independent Broadcast Authority–IBA" (Duncan & Seleoane, 1998: 216). According to administrator Brenda Leonard (personal communication, 30 August 2003), the IBA first allocated licenses in provinces where there was little contestation over frequencies. Bush Radio thus only received a license to operate as a community radio station on August 9, 2005.

Deleuze and Guattari (1987) state that the rhizome continues to grow and expand through constant re-emergence in new forms. There is an origin, but the rhizome expands so far from the original that it becomes nearly impossible to relate much of the growth to the beginning. According to Deleuze and Guattari, the rhizome does not really have a beginning or an end, but grows from the middle. In the same way, Bush Radio originated as a cassette production facility and eventually transitioned into a community radio station; more recently, plans are being discussed to reorganize Bush Radio as a training institution.

The people who work at Bush Radio often end up following paths quite far removed from broadcasting, though they may carry with them many of the Bush Radio principles. One popular music DJ quit his position as presenter of the afternoon drive-time show to pursue a career as a quantity surveyor. Two blind presenter/producers who originally considered broadcasting as a career choice because of their disabilities became known for their work at Bush Radio and were consequently recruited for public relations work by the national electricity utility company. One of the producers who worked with the children's project went on to study law. Through such people, Bush Radio expands rhizomatically in ways that are not even related to radio. As managing director Zane Ibrahim says:

I'm happy when people leave Bush Radio. Those with potential and talent must move on, or they'll stagnate and end up hating Bush for holding them back. They must use Bush Radio to develop themselves to the point when they can go out there and make a difference to society because they've learned to serve their community at Bush Radio. If you look at CREW [the Children's Radio Education Workshop], how many of those kids will go on to become broadcasters? That's not the intention. The idea is that through

their involvement with Bush Radio they'll become more critical media consumers. (Z. Ibrahim, personal communication, 12 December 2005)

Even a loss of the broadcast license will not necessarily mean the end of
Bush Radio—like the rhizome, it does not ever really end but just evolves. In
many ways, Bush Radio thus becomes a connector and bridging mechanism that
impacts the social fabric of a community. Like the rhizome, it is just constantly
growing, evolving, needing constant nourishment and care to survive. In the
words of Managing Director, Zane Ibrahim:

> I look at life in terms of the plant life. And I looked at Bush Radio like that, I
> looked at the roots and I said okay. It was rooted in the struggle, so some of
> the roots needed to be cut, trimmed and these roots were mostly ANC roots
> and I cut the political roots off. Then I looked at the stem and it was fine, it
> comes from a good community, it's rooted in the community, Salt River's
> fine, to get back on the campus you have to deal with campus politics and I
> haven't got time; and then the leaves were fine. So what about nutrients and
> soil and that's where the funders came in—money, training, information. I
> contacted all the underground structures that I knew in the world and asked
> them for materials. Michael Parenti and all of that, and they came on board,
> and I was done, I had my nutrients, I had my fertilizer and my soil and that
> was Bush Radio and I've run that ever since. (Z. Ibrahim, personal communi-
> cation, 25 February 2002)

To extend the metaphor, the rhizomatic is nonlinear, anarchic, and nomadic,
and as rhizomes, community radio and citizens' media become a crossroads for
organizations and movements linked to civil society, cutting across borders and
building linkages between pre-existing gaps (Carpentier, Lie & Servaes, 2003).
As Deleuze and Guattari (1987) write, "a rhizome ceaselessly establishes connections between semiotic chains, organizations of power and circumstances relative
to the arts, sciences and social struggles" (7). In its early days, Bush Radio staff
perceived the station's role as mouthpiece for community based and nongovernmental organizations that had no access to other media outlets. Today, the relationship with these organizations continues, often bringing them together at the
radio station.

One example is the station's deliberate strategy of consulting NGOs around
specific programs. When the gender program was created, representatives from
all the gender-related and women's organizations were called to a meeting to
brainstorm topics, provide resources, and in some cases also to make staff available for radio training of these organizations' personnel. In this way, like many
others, Bush Radio often becomes a space where people from different types of
social justice struggles and movements can meet and collaborate, functioning as a
catalyst and allowing groups, activists, and social justice organizations to find

each other, launch new alliances and collaborative projects, learn about each other's struggles, and, in sum, strengthen the grasslike growth of organized civil society and social movements.

CONCLUSION

This ethnographic examination of Bush Radio demonstrates that Deleuze and Guattari's theory of the rhizome could help us theorize citizens' media. But despite its utility, this theoretical use of the rhizome can also be questioned. One concern is that the rhizomatic growth of community radio may not necessarily be positive, in that some control of distant offshoots may eventually be necessary to ensure that community radio remains loyal to its basic principles of accessibility, participation, and democracy. Another negative aspect of community radio as rhizome is that its very fluidity and uncertainty obscures possibilities for networking and unifying the sector. This lack of a common ground has complicated the functioning of organizations such as The World Association of Community Radio Broadcasters (AMARC) and has prevented the emergence of a well-defined community media movement (Carpentier, Lie, & Servaes, 2003). In South Africa, this is seen through the inability of organizations such as the National Community Radio Forum (NCRF) to create powerful networks for lobbying around policy issues, making regulatory reform initiatives very difficult, as activists and organizations cannot even come up with a clear definition of community radio.

However, in the absence of an alternative, the use of the rhizome makes for some interesting and perhaps useful theoretical conjectures. Like the rhizome, community radio cuts across borders and builds linkages. Bush Radio is clearly rhizomatic in terms of Deleuze and Guattari's (1987) principles of connection and heterogeneity, multiplicity, and asignifying rupture. Through the application of rhizomatic theory to community radio, we further see that Bush Radio is not so much an organization as it is a rhizomatic organism, held together by a complex set of interlinked networks of relationships and interactions, with the concept of community pulsating as its central life-force.

In conclusion, this chapter highlights the importance of media as direct catalysts on political, economic, and social processes. Media are not only conduits for governments, political parties, and citizens, but have become autonomous power centers in constant competition with other power centers. Bush Radio is one of many spaces of resistance in South Africa. Drawing on an ethnographic methodology, this chapter has further argued that Bush Radio provides a mirror image for struggles of community and identity in post-apartheid Cape Town. In short, this chapter is about identity construction in South Africa through the eyes of one community radio station in Cape Town. It argues for rethinking old theoretical conceptualizations of community radio and for more theoretically creative, rhizomatic approaches.

NOTES

1. The South African Truth and Reconciliation Commission (TRC) was set up by the new Government of National Unity to help deal with human rights abuses under apartheid.
2. Toy-toying is a Zulu protest dance almost always used by protesters at marches and demonstrations.
3. IDASA is the Institute for Democracy in Southern Africa.
4. Baartman was a local Khoi woman taken to London in 1810, where she was displayed naked in freak shows. She died 5 years later in France. After years of negotiations between South African historians and French authorities, Baartman's skeleton, brain, and genitalia were finally returned from a French museum. A traditional Khoi enrobing ceremony was held, a sacred rite performed by Khoisan elders to prepare a body for burial.
5. 'Mamela' is Xhosa for 'listen.'

REFERENCES

Atton, C. (2002). *Alternative media.* London, Thousand Oaks: Sage.

Bosch, T. (2003). *Radio, community and identity in South Africa: A rhizomatic study of Bush Radio in Cape Town.* Unpublished doctoral dissertation, School of Communications, Ohio University.

Carpentier, N., Lie, R., & Servaes, J. (2003). Community media: Muting the democratic media discourse? *Continuum: Journal of Media and Cultural Studies, 17*(1), 51-68.

Couldry, N. (2000). *The place of media power: Pilgrims and witnesses of the media age.* London: Routledge.

Deleuze, G., & Guattari, F. (1987). *A thousand plateaus: Capitalism and schizophrenia.* London: Athlone Press.

Denzin, N., & Lincoln, Y. (2000). *Handbook of qualitative research.* Thousand Oaks, CA: Sage.

Downing, J. D. H., with Ford, T. V., Gil, G., & Stein, L. (2001). *Radical media: Rebellious communication and social movements.* London: Sage.

Duncan, J., & Seleoane, M. (Eds). (1998). *Media and democracy in South Africa.* Pretoria: HSRC and FXI.

Freire, P. (1970). *Pedagogy of the oppressed.* New York: Continuum.

Freire, P. (1985). *The politics of education: Power, culture and liberation.* South Hadley, MA: Bergin and Garvey.

Laclau, E., & Mouffe, C. (1985). *Hegemony and socialist strategy.* New York: Verso.

Lewis, P. (Ed). (1993). *Alternative media: Linking global and local.* Paris: UNESCO.

Mowlana, H. (1998). *Communication technology and development.* Paris: UNESCO.

Nwosu, P., Onwumechili, C., & M'Bayo, R. (Eds). (1995). *Communication and the transformation of society.* Lanham, MD: University Press of America.

O'Connor, A. (1990). The miners' radio stations in Bolivia: A culture of resistance. *Journal of Communication, 40*(1), 102-110.

Ogada, J. (2005). *A participatory audience research study of Bush Radio.* Unpublished research report conducted for NiZA-Nederlands Instituut voor Zuidelijk Afrika

Rodríguez, C. (2001). *Fissures in the mediascape: An international study of citizens' media.* Cresskill, NJ: Hampton Press.

Rodríguez, C. (2000). Civil society and citizens' media: Peace architects for the new millennium. In K. Wilkins (Ed.), *Redeveloping communication for social change: Theory, practice and power* (pp.147-160). Boulder, CO: Rowman & Littlefield.

Van Maanen, M. (1990). *Researching lived experience: Human science for an action sensitive pedagogy.* Albany: State University of New York Press.

SECTION II
Communications
for Social Change Projects

INTRODUCTION TO SECTION II

Dorothy Kidd

All three chapters in this section examine the contribution of community-based media projects to social change in rural communities of the global south, in Zimbabwe, India, and Colombia, respectively. They share a common framework, in which change is linked to *participation,* in all stages of communication, of and by groups that have been historically and persistently marginalized by the mainstream media, national governments, and international development. Participation has become such a commonplace and so plastic, stretched to describe the dynamics of every kind of communication, from those of the alternative and citizens' media to the social networks of the commercial Internet, that it is particularly worth re-examining some of the theoretical and practical distinctions between frameworks and what these chapters can illuminate about the value of popular participation in communication and in social change.

The framework of *participatory communication* and *social change* traces back to the international debates about the democratization of communication of the 1970s and 1980s [see Introduction to this volume]. Although the larger political project of the New World Information and Communication Order (NWICO) was defeated at UNESCO, several of its arguments began to echo in the very different quarters of national governments, multilateral institutions, commercial media industries, nongovernmental organizations (NGOs), and social justice movements. Although each spoke of a common intent to actively involve "people who were the subjects of development in shaping the process," this was where the similarity ended, marking a turn towards "a diversity of differences" and "numerous unresolved disagreements"(Yoon, 2006: 799).

In her 1994 review of women and grassroots communication, Pilar Riaño argued that participatory communication had been mainstreamed. The more powerful state and multilateral institutions took the concept on board because it could provide better ways to engage constituencies to support their programs and to fortify consent. All the major approaches of that period that attracted international funding—diffusion of innovations, social marketing, and entertainment-education—placed a greater emphasis on community input and the use of indigenous communications networks. However, local people were primarily consulted only in the early stages of development project designs and were not involved in defining the problem and the overall goals or in producing the programming (Riaño, 1994:5).

The small-scale media projects championed by nongovernmental organizations (NGOs) and social movements went further in their attempts to deepen the engagement of local people in all stages of communication, from the initial "needs assessment through media production to final evaluation and effectiveness"(Riaño, 1994: 5). Nevertheless, many of these projects failed to account for the multitude of differences of power and control of resources within populations and for the larger structural conditions of "dependency and domination of Third World societies" (Riaño, 1994: 5). Riaño called for moving the debate beyond institutional agendas concerned with state-related policies and towards a practice of democratization rooted in the "active and dynamic interaction of the people, the social movements, the institutions and the cultural industries" (Riaño, 1994: 3). She argued that the way forward was already being demonstrated by the emerging praxis of women's communication groups, in which the production practice and the programming content derived from the cultural repertoires, knowledges, lived experiences, and felt needs raised from the grassroots.

This is where these accounts come in. All three of the chapters in this section derive from this contest over the meaning and practice of *participatory communication* projects. Chido Matewa describes a series of videos produced by the Women Filmmakers Trust (AWFT) of Zimbabwe from the mid 1990s to the early 2000s. Critical of the exclusion of rural women from pre-and post-Independence development programs, the AWFT set out to remedy this through participatory video. However, they had little prior knowledge or experience. In her self-reflexive account, she notes how this NGO moved away from a top-down model to instead work more closely with local women and men and inventively create production and exhibition practices that emerged directly from local cultural, economic, and political needs and knowledges. Drawing on strong narrative traditions of song and drama, the AWFT collaboratively scripted video dramas that allowed participants to play with different dimensions of a problem and to collectively act out solutions. Based on the needs of particular communities, the AWFT developed a number of different video series that dealt with the entrenched challenges of economic survival and structural adjustment policies, the social and economic discrimination of girls and women, HIV-AIDs, local systems of governance, and pre-and postindependence legacies of violence.

Through a longitudinal study of AWFT's work, the chapter provides a coherent representation of two distinct approaches to participatory media. AFWT shifted from an initial orientation based on the 'epidemiology' approach, which focuses on 'messaging' and in which effectiveness is measured via changes in audience behavior and attitudes (Rodríguez, 2004). Instead, they began to adopt what Rodríguez calls the 'social fabric' approach, facilitating the opening of local communication spaces, which allowed for more complex and multidirectional social interactions (2004). Matewa describes a wide variety of changes in social solidarities and power relations, from the smallest unit of the family to the national political sphere.

Clemencia Rodríguez's chapter takes this process of participatory communication one step further; the communicators themselves participate in the evaluation. Based on the model of community radio researcher Jo Tacchi,[1] processes of social and cultural change at the local level were evaluated within three concentric circles: the people directly working or participating in media production; all the grassroots organizations, collectives, and social movements that use the medium to engage with the public sphere; and finally, the listeners. This chapter is a multiperspectival report from the most innermost circle, the participatory evaluation carried out by the radio producers from the network of community stations in the Magdalena Medio region of Colombia, working with Rodríguez and other Colombian communication scholars.

Using Pilar Riaño's memory workshop methodology, the evaluation team mapped the impact of the radio station's work on the local social and political ecology of this resource-rich but conflicted region where civilians are often cornered by guerrilla organizations, paramilitary groups, and drug traffickers. Many of the producers played key roles in mediating conflict between factions within their communities, among local political figures, and with armed groups. Moreover, Rodríguez concludes that the real contribution of the stations was not the broadcasting of messages per se, but rather the facilitation of communications spaces in which local people could express their identities, reflect on their differences, and practice nonviolent ways of relating to one another and dealing with conflict.

Pavarala and Malik also compare the three concentric circles of participation in community radio projects directed by nongovernmental organizations in four rural villages in India that are not well served by either the commercial or state-operated broadcasting systems. Their study shows that social change was greatest among the inner circle of women radio producers. Largely illiterate and from the poorest of castes, their professional skills and their community standing among other women and men grew immensely. Radiating outwards, the women members of local self-help organizations, the principal program contributors and audiences in three of the four projects, witnessed a greater recognition of their social and political concerns, as well as increased confidence and ability to negotiate, among male relatives, village leaders, and government officials. However, the women listeners of the third circle were often unable to listen to the programming because of intense work-loads and family constraints, and this circle realized far fewer social benefits. Pavarala and Malik conclude that significant social changes will only result from the integration of poor women throughout the entire circuit from production to listening. Moreover, they argue that the parameters of participation must also include women's leadership in directing and managing community radios, independent of state or corporate entities.

These projects provide a much different profile of participatory communications than the more celebrated web-based social networks. First, the face of many of the participants is poor, female, and rural, in contrast to the largely professional, male, and urban web 2.0 users. Secondly, although many of the initiators, as in the Indian example, are middle class, poor women from the most excluded castes are beginning to take leadership roles. Finally, in both the Indian and Zimbabwean cases, the strong participation of women has introduced new concerns into the public sphere, from the more intimate dimensions of personal health, to the gendered inequalities of inheritance, water distribution and political representation.

The inclusion of people whose knowledges and perspectives tend to be marginalized also required a different approach to the choice and design of information and communication technologies (ICTs). Media such as radio and video, which reinforce collective processes of media production and reception and respond to the economic resources, cultural backgrounds, languages, aesthetics, and narratives of grassroots groups, are chosen over those that privilege a minority of well-off early adopters, or the individualized production and reception of consumer content. In these case studies, participatory production is a core goal of each project, and not just a way to produce cheaper content, or a more efficient means of attracting and delivering audiences to advertisers and marketers. In addition, the authors underscore the necessity for social and political solutions, and the consideration of means by which persistently marginalized groups can be actively involved in governance, decision making, and operations at all stages of communication.

These three chapters can also provide lessons about the relationship between participatory communication and social change. They document a complexity of individual and collective changes in the communities most directly involved, with repercussions outward to the national stage. They also provide examples of more robust democracies fed by complex and multivocal public spheres that continue to expand the social imaginary, even in communities beset by tense social and political conflict. Facilitating the engagement of these local sets of social actors may not lead directly to the national and international level policy reforms covered by mainstream media; nevertheless, the growing circuits of distribution of these kinds of locally originated media is beginning to weave a much more dynamic and stronger social fabric.

NOTES

1. Writing about the participatory dynamics in public art, Suzanne Lacy developed a similar evaluative model of six circles, which grow in size as they reach a greater number of people. Starting from the inside, the circle includes: "origination and responsibility, collaboration and co-development, volunteers and performers, immediate audience, media audience, and audience of myth and memory" (Lacy, 1995; 178). Thanks to Megan Petersen for drawing my attention to this.

REFERENCES

Lacy, S. (1995) Debated territory: Toward a critical language for public Art. In *Mapping the Terrain: New Genre Public Art.* Washington, DC: Bay Press.

Riaño, P. (Ed.). (1994). *Women in grassroots communication.* Thousand Oaks, CA: Sage.

Rodríguez, C. (2004, December 6). *Communication for peace: Contrasting approaches. The Drum Beat, 278.* Retrieved December 10, 2006, from http://www.comminit.com/drum_beat.html.

Yoon, C. S. (2006). Excerpt from participatory communication for development. In A. Gumucio-Dagrón & T. Tufte. (Eds.), *Communication for social change anthology: Historical and contemporary readings* (pp. 799-800). South Orange, NJ: Communication for Social Change Consortium.

COMMUNITY RADIO AND WOMEN
Forging Subaltern Counterpublics

Vinod Pavarala
& Kanchan Kumar Malik

As part of a national campaign for community radio in India,[1] four nongovernmental organizations (NGOs) have been experimenting with community-based participatory communications among the rural poor, and particularly among women. All four operate in marginalized communities with limited access to electricity, broadcast channels, and digital information and communications technologies (ICTs) (see Figure 4.1).

Two of the projects, *Namma Dhwani* (Our Voice) in Budikote, in the southern state of Karnataka, and the Deccan Development Society (DDS) project, in the Medak district of the adjoining state of Andhra Pradesh, began without access to FM radio broadcasting and have experimented with other kinds of narrowcasting. Two projects in northern India, Kutch Mahila Vikas Sanghatan (KMVS) in the northwestern state of Gujarat, and Alternative for India Development (AID) in the Palamau District of Jharkhand, rent services on local All India Radio (AIR) stations. Three of these four community radio projects are developing community-based programming in cooperation with local women and their voluntary associations, using local dialects and indigenous cultural forms, to provide relevant local information and discussion about issues of governance, agriculture, natural resources, and gender inequities. The community radio programs of AID are produced by both men and women and mainly include youth groups and other community representatives identified by the NGO itself.

This chapter is based on these four case studies.[2] The research combines analysis of focus group discussions with local audience members, interviews with

FIGURE 4.1. Map of community radio projects in India.

women producers, self-help group members and NGO staff, and reviews of programming and policy documents. After a brief profile of each of the projects, we
describe women's participation in five dimensions, as listeners, program content
contributors, producers, planners and managers, and review the extent to which
the women participants have been able to create avenues for social change. We
then examine the value of these projects as models for community radio independent of state and commercial interests. Finally, drawing on Nancy Fraser (1992),
we discuss how the work of the women in these four projects contributes toward
the creation of counter public spheres that articulate and give visibility to
women's realities and bring their concerns, identities, and issues to the dominant
public agenda.

GENDER, MEDIA, AND PARTICIPATORY DEVELOPMENT

This chapter is set against the background of insights from participatory communications and feminist theorizing, both of which have sought to redefine existing
approaches to development in order to make them more responsive to gender
and to the involvement of those who have suffered systematic and systemic

inequalities and deprivations as 'partners' in development. The gender main-streaming practices stirred by the dominant Women in Development (WID) framework are giving way to Gender and Development (GAD) approaches that question the prevailing structures that generate and underpin a disadvantageous status for women relative to men, as well as to the sociocultural, economic and political status quo (Abbot, 1997; Bhasin, 2000; Connelly, Li, Mc Donald, & Parpart, 2000; Humble, 1998; Kabeer, 1994; Knobloch, 2002; Ramamurthy, 2000; SinghaRoy, 2001; Verma, 2004).

The paradigmatic shift towards participatory development, with aims of handing over control of natural and shared resources to marginalized people, appears to offer the prospect of giving all the stakeholders a voice and a choice (Chambers, 1997; Gujit & Shah, 1998). In reality, the legacy of a highly unequal and hierarchical society, with embedded notions of male superiority, caste, and class dominance, affects women's options to intervene in discussions or partici-pate in decision-making processes (Cornwall, 2000). Unless a feminist, class, and caste perspective is unambiguously integrated into the design, implementation, monitoring and evaluation of all existing and prospective development initiatives, their outcome will rarely enhance gender equality or lead to empowerment of women.

There is an increasing consensus among communication and feminist schol-ars and organizations that media and new technologies of communication, informed by a gender perspective, can be harnessed as indispensable tools for reversal of women's marginalization. Women's organizations in the first-ever international conference on empowering women and communication in Bangkok in 1994 argued that women's empowerment through communication was not enough; it was necessary to promote:

> forms of communication that not only challenge the patriarchal nature of media but strive to decentralize and democratise them; to create media that encourage dialogue and debate, media that advance women's and people's creativity, media that reaffirm women's wisdom and knowledge, and that make people into subjects rather than objects or targets of communication, media which are responsive to people's needs. (Frankson, 2000: 20)

Since then scholars have developed these ideas, arguing for the necessity of communications spaces for expression of women's issues; dissemination and exchange of authentic information and images about women; enhancement of women's equal participation in civil and public life; women's representation in development; and the inclusion of women's active participation in solidarity campaigns and collaborative actions for their own futures (Chambers, 1997; Connelly et al., 2000; Cornwall, 2000; Gujit & Shah, 1998; Pavarala & Kumar, 2002; Riaño, 1994). A growing school of scholars and practitioners have also argued for more attention to the ways that women's social movements are building new communication alternatives for change at the grassroots level and contributing to the democratization of communication (Gujit & Shah, 1998; Kidd, 1992; Nair & White, 1987; Riaño, 1994).

The intersection of these two movements, of women and participatory communication, plays a critical role among the rural projects profiled below. Although national and state legislatures in India have consistently enacted legislation to overcome gender discrimination, this has made little difference to the lives of the majority of women. They still rank the lowest in most social indicators including literacy, health, skill development, sustainable livelihoods, and so forth. The regions where these community radio projects are located are among the most neglected and the least developed parts of the country. The majority are poor and landless, by and large at the mercy of nature. They are often forced to leave their native places on a seasonal basis to look for wage labor. Most women have extremely low levels of literacy and lack access to basic information and resources. In addition, they must survive with the dual burden of household tasks and income generation, and suffer from poor nutrition, early marriage, and frequent child bearing. All of these forms of subjugation are compounded by the spiteful forms that patriarchal norms and behavior take in the face of economic pressures, leading to a rise in the incidents of mental and physical violence against women (Ramachandran & Saihjee, 2000).

Radio is particularly well-suited to the largely nonliterate oral storytelling cultures of India, and has a proven track record of being a catalyst for social change all over the Third World. It is an affordable medium in terms of production, management, and reception, and can reach communities at the very end of the development road—people who live in areas with no phones and no electricity. Even in very poor communities, radio has a far-reaching penetration; its widespread usage makes it potentially a people's medium.

THE FOUR COMMUNITY RADIO PROJECTS

Namma Dhwani: The Community Radio Project of Voices/Myrada

In September 2001, *Namma Dhwani* (Our Voice) community radio production center was inaugurated at Budhikote village in the Kolar region of the southern state of Karnataka. Only 100 kilometers from Bangalore, the cyber capital of India and one of the fastest growing cities in the world, Budhikote could not be more different. The millet and tomato-growing sector has suffered through several years of drought, rising poverty, below-average education levels, and rampant corruption. After a decade working as part of the UNESCO-funded *Assessing Impact of ICTs for Poverty Reduction*, Voices, a Bangalore-based media NGO and the Mysore Resettlement and Redevelopment Agency (Myrada), conducted a base-line survey of information needs. They found that local people did not have access to relevant information about crops, market prices, health, and particularly women's health. Mirroring the national communications gap between urban and rural centers, rich and poor, neither the state nor the private media provided this crucial information. With the prevailing high rates of illiteracy, the survey respondents wanted this information in an accessible audio format, in their own dialect, which is a mix of Kannada and Telugu.

Voices and Myrada decided to pilot a project that would demonstrate the feasibility of community radio in India and "act as an instrument of persuasive advocacy supporting community radio legislation in India" (ICT in the Hands of the Poor). Partnering with over 35 women's self-help groups, Voices and Myrada inaugurated *Namma Dhwani* in September 2001 as the audio studio component of the Community Multi Media Centre. The primary aim of *Namma Dhwani,* according to Seema Nair, the project coordinator, is "to bring poor women who are at the periphery of information and communications networking into the centre of it, thus giving them the power to make more informed decisions, better organise themselves and take actions." *Namma Dhwani* has a well-equipped recording station and three trained local persons to run the audio production center. Ten local women and two men, representing their local self-help groups and the two NGOs, comprise the management committee. They, in turn, recruit volunteers from Budhikote and the adjoining villages to help in the production of radio programs. The two hours of daily programs focus on local development and governance issues, including the *panchayat* (local government) meetings, water quality, crop and market information. They also have regular slots devoted to gender issues, including family planning, reproductive health, HIV/AIDs; as well as cultural programs of stories, plays and poems, a quiz show, and a game show for teenagers.

Unable to get a broadcast license to operate community radio, they have developed some innovative ways of distributing their programs. They decided in March 2003 to cablecast their programs to the village households and now reach 250 television-owning families, the village school and those who have bought radio sets with cable jacks made available at subsidized prices by Voices. Community narrowcasting sessions are also held regularly to reach a cluster of 35 villages (Nair & Menon, 2004). They also play the program on loudspeakers in three other villages and sell and rent tapes to other villages and resource centers.

Women Speak to Women: The Community Radio Project of DDS

The Deccan Development Society (DDS) has been working in about 75 villages of the Medak district of the adjoining state of Andhra Pradesh with rural, poor, and primarily Dalit women for over two decades on "a string of sovereignty issues: food sovereignty, seed sovereignty, autonomy over natural resources, market sovereignty" (Mukhopadhyay, 2004: 30-31). The district is not served by any of the Local Radio Station projects of All India Radio, nor do stations in the state's capitol, Hyderabad, broadcast in the local dialect (Satheesh, 2004: 30-31). In 1998, DDS set up an FM radio station in the Machnoor village of Zaheerabad *mandal* (block), with a recording studio, control room, two transmitters, and a transmitting tower.

This station is managed and run by a team of Dalit women, including 'General' and Algole Narsamma. According to them, the programming content seeks to serve the information, educational, and cultural needs of the women in the region and to communicate their problems, raise their issues and find solutions through the medium of radio. The women record programs on topics related to women's empowerment, regional development problems, and indigenous knowledge and cultures. The programs are produced in a magazine format, mixing interviews and discussions with folk and/or traditional songs and drama.

At the time of writing, in early 2007, DDS was applying for a broadcast licence. Up until then they had circulated the programs via the network of women's *sangams*. The tapes were distributed to 75 of the nearby villages, where they were played back on tape recorders at each *sangam*. Feedback from the women was then recorded by field workers and brought back to the station. In late 2006, when the Union Government finally cleared the national community radio policy, the DDS women initiated the process to acquire a license which would give them 'permission' to broadcast their programs from their community radio station in Machnoor.

Ujjas Radio: The Community Radio Project of KMVS

Kutch is an isolated and desolate region in the westernmost corner of India, next to Pakistan. The women's NGO, Kutch Mahila Vikas Sangathan, (KMVS) has been active in the villages since 1989, helping to develop local women's leadership on a wide array of issues (Soni, 2004). KMVS has grown rapidly to a federation of 10,000 members, organized through the *mahila mandals* (women's groups) in 165 villages. In the late 1990s, women involved in *Ujjas* (rural women's newsletter), women *sarpanchas* (local level leaders), and other KMVS members demanded a radio program to cater to their information needs. Most of the programming of the regional AIR station, Radio Bhuj, is in the state language of Gujarati and not the local Kutchi dialect. KMVS therefore decided to produce a radio program by purchasing a commercial slot on Radio Bhuj in December 1999.

Their first program, the 30-minute *Kunjal Paanje Kutch Ji* (KPKJ)—or Saras Crane of our Kutch—featured a dramatic serial about an imaginary village named Ujjas (or Light), plus investigative reports, folk songs, and a travelog, all in the Kutchi dialect. They focused on "gender issues on the one hand, and *swaraj* or democratic self-governance on the other" (Soni, 2004). This emphasis was partly in response to state legislation, which had set aside a third of the *panchayat*, or local government seats, for women. Gradually the serial interwove story lines and themes about other gender inequities and how to build sustainable socioeconomic transformation. Produced by KMVS, with funding from UNDP, it was directed by the Ahmedabad-based Drishti Media Collective, written by Paresh Naik, with assessment support from the Center for Alternatives in Education and the Indian Institute of Management, in Ahmedabad. The Saras Crane was very successful. Almost two-thirds of the one-and-a-half million Kutchi population tuned in every Sunday (Kennedy, 2003), and the series was conferred the prestigious Chameli Devi Jain Award 2000 by the Media Foundation in New Delhi.

After completion of 53 episodes in December 2000, KMVS began a 15-minute biweekly program called *Tu Jiyaro Ain* (To be Alive), broadcast twice a week from March 2001. This program aimed at addressing the needs of the earthquake-devastated people of Kutch in an interview format. In July 2002, they launched *Kutch Lok Ji Bani* (KLJB, Voice of the People of Kutch) which is handled entirely by the media unit of rural reporters from the different villages, half of whom are women, and guided by a network of women village leaders (Kennedy, 2003). Their programming has moved away from the complex format of the first serial, which required specialized writing and professional skills, to one that is increasingly managed, technically and editorially, by the local team (Virmani, 2002).

Chala Ho Gaon Mein: The Community Radio Project of NFI/AID

Chala Ho Gaon Mein (Come, Let's Go to the Village) also serves a poor and relatively isolated rural region, in Palamau, in the state of Jharkand in northern India. It has been broadcast on the local AIR-FM Daltongunj station in the Palamau district since August 5, 2001. The program was initiated by Alternative for India Development (AID), an NGO umbrella organization that provides institutional, financial, social, and technical support for several smaller community-based groups and is not tied with any established political parties (Pavarala, 2003). Founded in 1982 as part of the mass movements against corruption, AID believes in grassroots democracy and participatory development, enabling the more disadvantaged to analyze and deal with their problems themselves, to bring about total transformation, and to create a just society (All India Development).

The 30-minute *Chala Ho Gaon Mein* is the only radio program in the local dialect linked with gender equity and justice and produced with participation of the local communities. It is supported by the strategic and financial backing of the National Foundation for India (NFI) and in technical collaboration with *Manthan Yuva Sansthan* (a media activist group). Broadcast every Sunday at 7:20 pm to 45 villages, the program was put together with the help of village reporters and digital postproduction work carried out in the state capital Ranchi (165 kms from Daltongunj).

Today, *Chala Ho Gaon Mein* is broadcast twice a week, every Sunday and Wednesday from 7:15 pm to 7:45 pm, and covers more than 160 villages of Palamau, Latehar, and Garwah districts of Jharkhand. A team of community reporters motivate people to participate in program production and develop story ideas and scripts. The magazine format includes radio dramas, music, folk songs, discussion, news, and letters. All postproduction, such as dubbing, recording, and editing takes place in the new studio set up in the Loknayak Jayaprakash Narayan Community Technical College of AID in Garwah. This studio is 50 kms away from Daltongunj, where the programs are fully produced by the local volunteers without any external assistance.

WOMEN'S PARTICIPATION IN PROGRAM PRODUCTION

In a review of the contribution of community media, Cicilia Peruzzo argues that participatory projects represent a significant advance in the democratization of communications (Peruzzo, 2006: 802). Participants may learn new knowledge, embrace their own cultural identities, and come to a better understanding of existing social relations, power structures, and political issues as well as developing new skills and competencies (802). She outlines five dimensions of participation: message reception, message participation (as for example, interview subjects, or in song or theater components); program production and dissemination (preparing, editing, and transmitting content); planning (setting policy, developing formats, and management objectives and principles); and management (administration and control of the community medium) (Peruzzo, 2006: 801).[3]

Voices/Myrada's decision to strengthen the women's self-help groups, or *sanghas*, has provided a communications network that encourages all five dimensions of participation in the *Namma Dhwani* project in Bandikote, Karnataka. *Sangha* members are the most active listeners. "If *Namma Dhwani* programme is coming we leave all our work and listen to it," a middle-aged *anganwadi* teacher, Uma affirms. "There is no TV at my place. My neighbour calls me when the programme is on and I leave my work and go to her house and listen." The *sangha* members also participate in message making through their contribution to the segment *Mane Maddu* (Home Remedies) or through their discussion of the issues within the various *sanghas*. Bhavani, a volunteer, spoke about how self-conscious she was about talking in public, but now, "I love participating in live radio programmes." To prepare for the task, she reads newspapers, participates in self-help group meetings, and uses the computer to access information. The women in her group are now asking for news about Panchayat and its activities.

The *sanghas* also provided the structure for program production and management. The program producers received their training in radio production through the *sangha*s. Mangala Gowri, a young and once shy member of a poor daily-wage earner family, now proficiently manages the audio studio in her village along with a few other women and volunteers. Together they carry out planning, recording, scripting, editing, narration, mixing, mastering, and voiceovers in the local dialect (Kumar, 2004). The management committee consists of at least one representative from each of the women *sanghas*. They exchange feedback and program ideas in their *sangha* meetings and also motivate their members to participate. Seethamma, a Management Committee member who is illiterate, has learned to keep the program logs and calculate the accounts through the Myrada trainings. She says, "I think *Namma Dhwani* is a way that all people in the village can use to develop themselves. Why watch all those serials and listen to those cinema songs when we can listen to our own songs and programmes that will help poor people like us?" (Nair, 2004).

The value of participation is greatest for women in the *sanghas*. Those outside this network, 'the poorest of the poor,' suggests the project coordinator, Seema Nair, "are preoccupied with day to day needs, scraping a living from daily work, and then returning to cook and clean in their households; they have very little time to participate in the *sanghas*, or listen to the radio. At the other end of the income scale, television, and especially the regional soaps, are starting to lure those with access" (Nair, 2004).

The *sangams* are also the basic network of participatory communication for the DDS Project in Pastapur in Andhra Pradesh. It was the *sangam* women who had asked for the radio station as a way to communicate among themselves, to dispense timely information that is helpful to the community, and to discuss the things that women are doing at DDS. The women in the *sangam* are very active listeners. They have found especially useful those programs with information specific to their agricultural needs and about indigenous knowledge systems, health and hygiene, food security, gender justice, and the narrative traditions of song and drama. Fifty-year old dalit, a nonliterate woman, Sunderamma, of Kalimela village, identified with the programs about crop and biofertilizers; the 'other radio' gives them only film songs. She also appreciated the possibility of listening to the cassettes more than once.

The design, production process, and management are all based on working with the *sangams*. The *sangam* members participate in generating program material. They get together to sing songs composed by DDS women themselves and to talk about various issues at the radio station where the recordings are produced. The 'local' experts as well as the production staff are women of their own community. The DDS Community Media Trust, which owns the community radio and handles its production, has eight radio and video women who represent the *sangams* as trustees.

In the Kutch, the most active participants are those already involved in the extensive networks of KMVS. Hawa Bai is the 35-year old *sarpanch* of Mohaldi village of Abdasa *taluka*. She told us:

> We all wait for this programme, gather together and listen to it. Some
> women in my village started listening to radio only after this programme was

started. I make my daughters write letters and send feed back to the programme. I am illiterate but I have come to know about panchayat and about
our own history. I get jankari (information) from radio only. (Focus Group
Discussion—FGD)

Ramba of Kalatalav village is 70 years old, a venerable age for people of this
region, and plays the role of the 'Parma *dadi,'* or grandmother, in the *Kunjal* radio
program. She is an enthusiastic *sangathan* member and actively involved in the
Savings and Credit program when she was chosen for the role. Now she is a dedicated listener and promoter of the radio program in her village. She says that the
women in her village are enthusiastic about the program and listen to radio even
if they have work to do.

Many other women are unable to listen because of lack of time and cultural
constraints. Thirty-year-old Amina Bai of the Jhumara village of Kutch reported:
"I normally don't sit to listen to radio. I don't get time, I have to look after children, go to get fodder for the cattle, it is not easy to find, and animals are dying.
When I listen, I cannot understand anything, so why should I listen" (FGD).

The radio programs in the Kutch are planned and managed by a mix of
small town urban/rural field workers and staff and the participants of the various
village-based collectives (Virmani, 2002). Perhaps the one aspect that KMVS
can boast most about is its team of community radio reporters. Significant capacity building efforts have enhanced the abilities of the rural women, who had neg-
ligible exposure to media production prior to their involvement in these projects, to be eloquent radio reporters. Vijayaben, a middle-aged woman with four
years of formal education, reports from the Mohaldi and Abdasa *talukas.* She
attended workshops on conscientization, confidence-building, technical training,
and the art of seeking *mahiti* (information) and community participation. She and
her fellow reporters are aware that theirs is a *bhagidari wala* radio (participatory
radio), which means they have to go out to the people, unlike All India Radio
that asks people to come into their studio for recordings. Most of the women
reporters in KMVS confessed that earlier they were shy and even scared to
move out of their homes or to talk to men. But with suitable training and field
exposure they have now gained confidence and are not afraid of handling any
aspect of radio production.

Women are much less actively involved in all five dimensions of participation in *Chala Ho Gaon Mein* in Jharkand. Given the prevailing social order, it is
almost impossible for women to sit in the midst of men and listen to a program.
Often their male family members take the radio set outside the house to listen
with friends. Chatni Devi, a 50-year-old agricultural labourer of Kundari village
in Lesliganj block, said: "We have FM radio at home. I try to listen to *Chala Ho*
every Sunday. But I can only listen while doing housework. When my husband
or his brother takes the radio outside the house, I can't listen" (FGD).

As a result, many women said that they listen to the community radio broadcast while cooking—"*roti banate hue sunte hain*"—and are therefore not able to lis-

ten to the programs attentively (*dhyan se nahi sun paate*), and even if they do listen, they forget what was said—"*yaad nahin rahata*"—some attributing it to the fact that they are uneducated. Although some want to be regular radio listeners, they would only listen to radio "when men are not around." Many women felt that listening sessions during meetings of women's groups or collectives in the village could provide a more conducive environment for reception of radio.

Although many of the older women seemed alienated from the radio program, some of the younger women we interviewed insisted that the program has many benefits. Kamala Devi, who married into a literate family, was enthusiastic about two different radio dramas, one of which was about the dowry problem and the other on overpopulation. Sonamati, an articulate middle-aged woman at Rajhara village, involved in *van samitis* (forest protection committees) and *mahila sanghatans* (women's collectives), was enthusiastic and articulate about the role of the radio program in various development efforts in the region. Her interview reminded us that participation of women in radio production is amplified when there is some amount of prior mobilization and conscientization.

Listenership among women in the Jharkand project is also tied in to their participation in program production. At Nawadih, several adolescent girls had participated in discussions, drama, *lok geet* (folk songs), and so forth. They recalled in great detail a short play they had recorded on the issue of postnatal health of the mother and the child. The active participation of these young girls in program production was also owed, in large measure, to the tireless efforts of the community reporter who works with them and operates as facilitator as well as director and producer. Shilwanti Biranchi, the dynamic reporter at Bhalmanda village confirmed this; she told us that she had made her own family members participate in plays and other programs for *Chala Ho Gaon Mein* to convince others that it was not only harmless, but could also be fun. Many women felt that participation could be further enhanced through changes in the content and process of program production. They wanted more woman-centered programming on issues such as dowry, child marriage, literacy, reproductive health, and so forth. They also suggested that women other than reporters be given opportunities to participate in discussions.

All of these projects are based on the active participation of women in communications as part of a wider strategy of social change. Although the socially ascribed roles for women inhibit their frequency of listening to radio and their full participation in the community radio programs, their capabilities to develop messages cannot be underestimated. All of these projects have demonstrated that women will participate if the programs are in their local dialects, use familiar cultural forms, their choice of local issues, and actively involve them in program production. Women, and especially those who are part of the social networks of *sangams* or other voluntary associations, with skills and confidence enhanced through media production, will act as agents to mobilize other women to participate.

ADDRESSING WOMEN'S ISSUES
AND CONTRIBUTION TO SOCIAL CHANGE

These four projects have a lot in common with the growing numbers of grass-roots groups around the world that are constructing democratic 'we' spaces for women to develop their own narratives, "voice their concerns, name who they are, share and build projects of change" (Riaño, 1994: xi). The programmes of community radio have enabled women to change accepted 'media languages' by providing them with a space and a process for expressing ideas and issues linked to their unique experiences. For women media producers, the first tough task is to adequately address the concerns of their own village/community and have a *pahchan*—identity that imparts other women with faith in them and the potential of the medium to bring about *sudhar*—improvement and prompts them to participate in media activities. In this section, we discuss some of these and other changes that have occurred.

Seema Nair, the project coordinator of *Namma Dhwani*, cautions against burdening the already overloaded rural communities with unrealistic expectations (2004). Citing Prof. John van Zyl, she suggests it is best to avoid "the belief that individuals have the capacity to change their circumstances once it has been pointed out to them what is in their own best interests. In other words, that there is a clear, linear relationship between knowledge and action." Instead, she argues that the value of *Namma Dhwani* has been in participants creating their own content, which has given them increased confidence in themselves and restored dignity to their local knowledge (of which they had been deprived).

Still limited by their dire situation of poverty and constraints on their social roles, the women we interviewed have already noticed some changes. Twenty-one-year-old Byatappa, from the management committee remarked:

> Whether it is the question of eating well for the sake of our health or the facts that help women progress economically, such programmes are useful. There are programmes about legal help that women need in case of dowry harassment. Earlier women used to fear going to the police station for any help because there were wrong notions that they lock you up in the room or exploit you. Now women are more aware of their rights. (FGD)

Some women mentioned the change in the attitudes of men close to them. Some of their family members had not always been supportive of their participation in the *sanghas*. "But now, they say, it is time for the *sangha*."

"I will do the remaining cooking, you go." Sujata of Navjyoti *sangha* clarified that:

> All this happened slowly, step by step. The change did not happen all of a sudden. The other day my husband asked me to go with Amaresh on his

scooter because it was late—they have come for you. How long do you make them wait, he said.

The changes in the DDS program are similar, resonating outwards from the women most involved to the wider community. Tuljamma, who is a health supervisor and also a member of the radio committee, believes that participating in DDS activities, including making radio programs, have made women more confident. "Before that, we were scared about meeting and talking to people. Now we discuss matters in our *sangams*, make radio programs and even talk to higher officials including *Patwari*." Zaheerabad Anuradha adds:

> Women are now participating in Panchayat meetings. We sit along with men and we participate in decision-making. Earlier, there were no women in Gram Panchayat. Nowadays women are *Sarpanchs* and Ward members. These women are no longer just dummies, they are questioning also. (FGD)

The women in the focus groups of DDS told us that earlier there had been little communication on developmental issues among women within a village or from different villages. The *sangams* had increased the interaction, and new relationships are being forged. They are now discussing their problems with each other. Kalimela Tukkamma affirms that the attitude has changed.

"If we talk about an issue, it will be solved. Because of the *sangam* activity and discussions on radio, we can talk now. Otherwise we used to sit silent. Government officials will come and we let them talk. Now we question them."

Almost all the women in the focus groups were convinced that their involvement in collective developmental activities and their relative improvement in financial status have led to an observable, and in a few cases, major changes in the attitudes of their husbands towards them. Kishnapur Chilkamma is a board member of DDS; she recalls the time when men would not allow their wives to go out for *sangam* meetings in the night and would beat them up if women wanted to go for a radio station meeting. Now the men are gradually recognizing the potential of women and giving respect. "Today men even come forward to facilitate our work." The women in Raipally reported on the impact of a radio program that highlighted the importance of saving:

> Previously our husbands were irresponsible, now they work more for the well being of the family. At work, the wage for women is Rs.10 and for men it is Rs.20. Out of that Rs.20 they used to give only Rs.10 to us and rest they would keep for tea, bidi (hand-rolled cigarette) and toddy. Now they give it to us for saving in our bank account that we have learnt to operate. (FGD)

The social changes have not been so swift for everyone. Many women pointed out the problems they faced with men who were habitual drunkards. The experience of Nagamma of Pastapur, in her late 20s and already a mother of five, is typical of some.

> After all other efforts had failed, I brought a DDS cassette home, which had songs about the ill effects of drinking, but my husband switched off the tape recorder saying this is "nonsense'. *Sunane wale sunte hain, nahin sunane wale nahin sunte; galian dene wale dete hain, rahne wale rehte hain.* Some men listen and change, but others don't even listen. I continue to stay with him even though he drinks and uses abusive language. (FGD)

DDS has built a shelter for destitute women who are beaten by their husbands or tortured by in-laws, and the radio producers have tried to discuss these issues. One program presented information about the shelter and the legal aid committee. They also discussed the attitude of parents who tell their daughters that their life is with their husbands; often the women feel they have no choice but to stay back and suffer, or to commit suicide. Although radio programming cannot possible change behaviors overnight, Humnapur Laxmamma, a senior media activist with DDS's participatory video team, thinks that it can help bring issues that were before endured in silence to public consciousness:

> Previously we used to bother only about our own problems. We were not keen on the problems of others. Now we are doing collective work. We share each other's sorrows and happiness. We want to help women in other villages and expect the same for them. Before radio, we used to do lot of good things which were not noticed by society. But now everyone knows all our activities. We cannot write all these things in a book, we are recording it in the cassette. It is easy for the people to understand. Moreover, after me, my next generation can also hear this cassette and know about the works which we have done. (FGD)

The programs in Kutch have also prompted discussion about many new issues that are seldom brought to the public sphere. These have included discussions of local governance. The third weekly radio series, *Kutch Lok Ji Bani* (Voice of the People of Kutch), includes regular investigative reports that cast light on government malfeasance and local corruption. As a direct consequence, some instances of malpractice were redressed even before the reports were broadcast for fear of the exposé (Virmani, 2002: 2). They have also included programs that affect women intimately, such as the harassment of brides for dowry, violence against women, unnatural deaths and suicides of women, pressure on women to produce boys, and maternal mortality. In many cases, the programs and ensuing discussions have come up with small solutions, recommending better distribution of resources and responsibilities to make them more equitable.

The community radio projects have also contributed to creating awareness about social problems that perpetuate women's subordination to men in the Jharkhand region. The tradition of *tilak/dahej* (dowry) is quite deeply rooted in the culture there, and it is unrealistic to expect that the AID radio program would make a dent so soon. However, it is apparent that the program has managed to put the issue firmly on the agenda. Thirty-year-old Kamoda Devi, the only literate woman in the focus group in Bhalmanda village (AID), said:

> If I take dowry for my son now, I will realize the problem later when my son has a daughter and he has to give dowry. So it is important to stop this practice. If this can be done through the programme, it will be good for society. (FGD)

Adolescent girls at the Nawadih village (AID) also condemned the practice as a blot on society and hoped that the radio program can address the issue. Surendra Thakur, one of the community reporters, offered another example of a specific outcome of *Chala Ho Gaon Mein* in the area of gender equity:

> Before this radio programme started, people used to send only their sons to school and make their daughters work at home. However, after this program started talking about treating sons and daughters equally, many parents came forward and, with our help, enrolled their daughters in school. (FGD)

The extent to which changes have taken place may be difficult to assess. However, all of the programs have achieved some success in helping women to become aware and to consolidate their views and perspectives on gender subordination and social transformation. This participatory process further helps women in raising their collective consciousness and understanding their own social reality and problems. Changes in traditional attitudes, behaviors and roles that perpetuate gender stereotypes and inequalities are more perceptible. As women create, control, and listen to the information presented by the community radio, they are seeking, despite the odds, to correct these imbalances.

A RADIO OF THEIR OWN

All four of the projects have recognized the value of putting ownership, control, and management of community radio into the hands of local women and men, independent of state and commercial forces. All four have participated in lobbying for legislation and resources to do so. P.V. Satheesh, Director, DDS, says,

"For us, a community radio is total control of the communities over the radio. And that includes everything, it includes the language, it includes the format, it includes the expression and entire sequence of what will come there." He recalls the answer that the women gave when they rejected the offer of a slot on the state-controlled All India Radio network to air their programs.

> Look, that is a kind of a continuous chain of broadcast and within that they will give us a particular position. And we don't know what comes before that and what comes after that. Like for example, we are all talking about organic agriculture and may be there is a pesticide advertisement before that and then our organic agriculture comes, after that somebody from an agricultural university may give a talk about hybrid seeds. So, we don't want our programmes to be positioned in a radio channel where that positioning may be very awkward for us.

Chilukapalli Anasuyamma from Pastapur, a 30-year old nonliterate *dalit* single woman, told him:

> The mainstream radio is still steeped in the traditional gender roles. If we depend on it, we have to go back in time. All that we have done in our *sangams* will come to a nought. If we have our own radio it can help us continue this progress we have made on gender issues.

Although the women radio reporters of Bhuj and the community radio representatives of Palamau had negotiated with the previous state policy for airing their programs, their voices harmonized with those in Budhikote and Pastapur for demanding a radio of their own. All of them believe that in order to deploy radio as a tool of empowerment, participation of people is not enough. The ownership, control, and management of the radio station must be in the hands of the community for it to function as an autonomous media space open to the need for self-expression by the socially and culturally marginalized sections of society, especially women.

FORGING SUBALTERN COUNTER PUBLICS

Community media provide women an arena, outside the state apparatus, that may be used as a potent instrument for democratic deliberations and negotiations. Such an institutionalized space for discursive interaction and for political participation through the medium of talk could be looked at as an alternative postbourgeois model of public sphere that Habermas stops short of developing in *The Structural Transformation of the Public Sphere*. Following Nancy Fraser, we would argue that community radio better promotes the ideal of participatory parity than does a single, comprehensive overarching public sphere, offering the possibility to accommodate contestations among a plurality of competing publics. These spaces, among the most marginalized, help to counteract the communications advantage of dominant groups that have rendered subordinate social groups less able to articulate and defend their interests.

As *subaltern counterpublics*, spheres parallel to the dominant social category, "members of subordinate social groups invent and circulate counter discourses to formulate oppositional interpretations of their identities, interests and needs" (Fraser, 1992: 123). They function both as spaces of withdrawal and regroupment; and on the other hand they also function as bases and training grounds for agitational activities directed towards wider publics. This dialectic enables these *subaltern counterpublics* partially to offset, although not wholly to eradicate, the unjust participatory privileges enjoyed by members of dominant social groups. Our research on community radio initiatives suggests that if we could forge *subaltern counterpublics* through a process of shifting control of media technologies to those excluded and marginalized from the dominant public sphere, they would help expand the discursive space, which could eventually facilitate collective action and offer a realistic emancipatory potential.

NOTES

1. Nonprofit development organizations and media-activist groups in India campaigned for more than 10 years for the right to set up low-cost local radio broadcasting facilities to support their community development work. In November 2006, the Union Cabinet finally cleared the community radio policy marking a much-delayed, but well-deserved victory to communities and civil society groups that have been waiting patiently for the right to broadcast to be extended to them.
2. This chapter is a more focused, reorganized, and updated version of the paper "Community Media And Women—Forging Subaltern Counterpublics" presented at the South Asia Pre-WSIS Seminar on Gender Perspectives in the Information Society held in Bangalore in April 2005. The authors thank Dorothy Kidd and the reviewers for their valuable suggestions and comments that contributed substantially to the revision of this chapter.
3. Peruzzo adapted these principles of participation in communications from Merino Utreras' work with the Latin American International Center for Advanced Communications Studies (CIESPAL) and UNESCO.

REFERENCES

Abbot, D. (1997). Who else will support us? How poor women organise the unorganisable in India. *Community Development Journal, 32*(3), 199-209.

All India Development. About us. Retrieved December 26, 2006, from http://www.aidindia.net/aboutus.htm.

Bhasin, K. (2000). *Understanding gender.* New Delhi: Kali for Women.

Chambers, R. (1997). *Whose reality counts? Putting the first last.* London: Commonwealth Secretariat.

Connelly, M. P., Li, T. M., Mc Donald, M., & Parpart, J. L. (2000). Feminism and development: Theoretical perspectives. In J. L. Parpart, M. P. Connelly, & V. Barriteau, (Eds.), *Theoretical perspectives on gender and development.* Ottawa, Canada: International Development Research Centre (IDRC). Retrieved June 6, 2007, from http://www.idrc.ca/es/ev-9419-201-1-DO_TOPIC.html.

Cornwall, A. (2000). *Making a difference? Gender and participatory development.* University of Sussex: Institute of Development Studies, Discussion Paper 378.

Frankson, J.R. (2000). *Gender mainstreaming in information and communications: A reference manual for governments and other stakeholders.* London: Commonwealth Secretariat.

Fraser, N. (1992). Rethinking the public sphere: A contribution to the critique of actually existing democracy. In C. Calhoun (Ed.), *Habermas and the public sphere* (pp. 109-142). Cambridge: MIT Press.

Gujit, I., & Shah, M. K. (1998). Waking up to power, conflict and process. In M. K. Shah (Ed.), *The myth of community: Gender issues in participatory development* (pp. 1-23). London: Intermediate Technology Publications.

Humble, M. (1998). Assessing PRA for implementing gender and development. In I. Gujit & M. K. Shah (Eds.), *The myth of community: Gender issues in participatory development* (pp. 25-35). London: Intermediate Technology Publications.

Kabeer, N. (1994). *Reversed realities: Gender hierarchies in development thought.* London: Verso.

Kennedy, M. (2003). Radio Ujjas. *The Nation.* Retrieved December 26, 2006, from http://www.thenation.com/docprint.mhtml?i=20030224&s=kennedy.

Kidd, D. (1992). *Alternate media, critical consciousness and action: The beginnings of a conversation about women and grassroots media.* Unpublished paper. Simon Fraser University, Burnaby, Canada.

Knobloch, U. (2002). *The contribution of Martha Nussbaum's capabilities approach to feminist economics: Questioning the gender-based division of labour.* Paper presented at Promoting Women's Capabilities: Examining Nussbaum's Capabilities Approach, 9-10 September at Von Hügel Institute, St Edmund's College, University of Cambridge, Cambridge.

Kumar, K. (2004). Community radio waiting to go on air. *Grassroots, 5*(2), 15.

Mukhopadhyay, B. (Ed.). (2004). *Community radio in India: Step by step.* Bangalore: VOICES and UNDP India.

Nair, S. (2004). Namma Dhwani: Taking the local route. ICT in the hands of the poor. Retrieved December 25, 2006, from http://ictpr.nic.in/nammadhwani/2jul.htm.

Nair, S., & Menon, D. (2004). Namma Dhwani. In B. Mukhopadhyay (Ed.), *Community radio in India: Step by step* (pp. 37-40). Bangalore: VOICES and UNDP India.

Nair, K., & White, S. (1987). Participation is the key to development communication. *Media and Development, 34,* 3640.

Pavarala, V. (2003). Building solidarities: A case of community radio in Jharkhand. *Economic and Political Weekly,* 2188-2197.

Pavarala, V., & Kumar, K. (2002). Civil society responses to media globalization: A study of community radio initiatives in India. *Social Action, 52*(1), 74-88.

Peruzzo, C. (2006). Excerpt from right to community communication, popular participation and citizenship: Popular participation in communication as a strategy for enhancing the exercise of citizenship. In A. Gumucio-Dagrón & T. Tufte, (Eds.), *Communication for social change anthology* (pp. 801-805). South Orange, NJ: Communication for Social Change Consortium.

Ramachandran, V., & Saihjee, A. (2000). *Flying with the crane: Recapturing KMVS's ten-year journey.* Bhuj: KMVS.

Ramamurthy, P. (2000). Indexing alternatives: Feminist development studies and global political economy. *Feminist Theory, 1*(2), 239-256.

Riaño, P. (ed.) (1994). *Women in grassroots communication.* New Delhi: Sage.

Satheesh, P.V. (2004). The DDS audio initiative at Pastapur. In B. Mukhopadhyay (Ed.), *Community radio in india: Step by step* (pp. 30-33). Bangalore: VOICES and UNDP India.

SinghaRoy, D.K. (Ed.). (2001). *Social development and the empowerment of marginalised groups: Perspectives and strategies.* New Delhi: Sage.

Soni, P. (2004). Kunjal Panchchi KutchJi. In B. Mukhopadhyay (Ed.), *Community radio in India: Step by step* (pp. 34-36). Bangalore: VOICES and UNDP India.

Verma, V. (2004, December 4). Engendering development. Limits of feminist theories and justice. *Economic and Political Weekly,* pp. 5243-5252.

Virmani, S. (2002). Radio Reyaan: Reflections on radio experiments in Kutch. Development by Design. Think cycle. Retrieved December 27, 2006, from http://www.thinkcycle.org/tcfilesystem/download/development_by_design_2002/publication:_radio_reyaan:_reflections_on_radio_in_kutch/radio_reyaan_shabnam_virmani.pdf

PARTICIPATORY VIDEO AS AN EMPOWERMENT TOOL FOR SOCIAL CHANGE

5

Chido Erica Felicity Matewa

The Africa Women Filmmakers Trust (AWFT) has pioneered the use of participatory video in development in Zimbabwe. After some experimentation, they adopted a community-based production and viewing process, which facilitated community discussion about local development among rural women and men, furthering processes of participatory democracy. The AWFT project moved beyond earlier communication for development initiatives (Hornik, 1988), which had failed to recognize the important role of women in development programs (Amadiume, 1987; Balit, 2000; Boserup, 1970) and especially as participants in development communications processes. This chapter examines the AWFT's emerging model of participatory video production by reviewing several community videos produced in rural Zimbabwe from 1994 to 2001 in the communities of Gwanda, Mutoko and Umzingwane District, and Mubaira and Mhondoro in Chegutu District.

Frequently academics and activists mention how participatory media processes 'give voice to the voiceless' and 'empower marginalized communities.' However, with few exceptions (Caldwell, 2003; Dowmunt, 2001), systematic ethnographic fieldwork and thick descriptions (Geertz, 1973) of these processes of change are rare. The following pages provide examples of the complex ways in which participatory video practices trigger processes of individual and collective change (Rodríguez, 2001). Based on ethnographic observations, interviews with participants, field diaries, and content analysis of the AWFT video productions, I flesh out how participation in video production processes had an impact on individuals and communities at different levels. My research articulates how participatory video production processes create public spaces for dialogue and collective self-reflection, allowing participants to shift their attention toward local resources, skills, and competencies to solve their own problems. I further analyze how communities in Matebeleland used these processes to document important events and recover historical memories, providing an opportunity for postconflict expression and dialogue for peoples victimized by armed violence. Finally, I examine how circulating the videos opened horizontal communication channels between rural communities separated by natural and other barriers.

My fieldwork with AWFT took place between December 2000 and March 2002. Participants of the six video screenings also participated in the focus group discussions, which had an average of 35 participants. In-depth interviews were also conducted with three founding members of AWFT, two members of the Board of Trust, five project staff, and eleven individuals who had previously worked with AWFT. The research also benefited from personal reflections of the author, one of the founder members.

Africa Women Filmmakers Trust (AWFT) was launched in 1992 by a group of young Zimbabwean women moved by a desire to use media to help improve the situation of rural women in Zimbabwe. Although their aim was to find ways to use the media for the empowerment of the marginalized and for giving a voice to the voiceless, they had no experience or knowledge of participatory video, either in Zimbabwe or in Southern Africa. Their only point of reference was the propaganda mobile films circulated by the Ministry of Information during the colonial era, which had allowed them to witness the effectiveness of film, but whose purpose was to maintain the imperial status quo (Cruz, 1999).

One of their first inspirations was the work of Reverend Stephen Matewa, who had used the participatory approach in mission and development projects in Makoni and Nyanga District during the 1970s and 1980s. He had encouraged communities to come together, to identify areas of common interest, and to mobilize themselves to achieve specific goals using locally available resources and skills. Through this process, communities were able to build schools, clinics, and community halls; they also initiated income-generating projects such as soap-making and established gum tree plantations to combat deforestation. The process had an empowering effect on the communities. Reverend Matewa himself observed that the participants, most of whom were women, felt isolated, yearned for an opportunity to speak, to be heard, and to share their experiences with other communities (C. Matewa, personal communication, January 22, 1991).

Reverend Matewa challenged the founders of AWFT to come up with a project that would give an opportunity to marginalized communities to set their own agendas for social change. During an informal meeting in 1991, Reverend Matewa encouraged the founder members to develop projects that empowered the whole person and particularly women, as they were the most marginalized (AWFT, n.d.: 3). The participants at this initial meeting agreed that they would focus on gender empowerment, using media for self-definition and for sharing experiences. They were also interested in highlighting the role that women play in the making and shaping of history. Providing an example of women's legacy, Reverend Matewa told the story of Aunt Madziire, whose husband, Nyakurukwa, later became Chief of the Makoni people. Aunt Madziire was famous for her wisdom and courage and had saved her husband when he was attacked by a lion. The meeting concluded that young women needed to hear such stories to encourage and motivate them to achieve greater things in life (C. Matewa, personal communication, January 22, 1991).

THE SITUATION OF RURAL WOMEN IN ZIMBABWE

AWFT's emphasis on women's empowerment was a response to the extreme subordination of rural women in Zimbabwe. Although legislative reform has removed some of the legal barriers to gender discrimination in waged work and family relations, Zimbabwean women remain at a severe disadvantage. In the media, women remain under-represented as producers, and little attention is given to women's issues. Rural women are virtually absent from both print and electronic media (Matewa, 1997).

Women's secondary status traces back to the economic policies, legal practices, and patriarchal ideologies of the colonial period. Black women were both members of an oppressed people and subject to discrimination as women. During English colonial rule, women in Zimbabwe lacked access to land and other resources, mobility due to family commitments and social cultural restrictions, and control over their own labor (Gaidzanwa, 1992). The colonial-era legal system only recognized men as the heads of households and property owners (Weinrich, 1979). Women could only control the income they earned as craftswomen and those gifts given to mothers when their daughters got married (Schmidt, 1992; Weinrich, 1979).

Reinforced by Western notions of patriarchy, which relegated women to the domestic sphere, this marginalization of women and women's concerns continued in western-funded development program. During the 1950s, women were unable to secure any agricultural extension services and were only provided with home-economics training (Kabeer, 1994: 20). Although the Women in Development (WID) approach of the 1970s attempted to better integrate women into development initiatives, the projects did not look at the sources and nature of the subordination and oppression of women (Boserup, 1970). The subsequent Women and Development approach (WAD) of the late 1970s highlighted the importance of women and development processes (Tinker, 1997). However, both approaches focused on the role of women in the cash economy, and not on their crucial roles in social reproduction in domestic and community economies (Østergaard, 1992).

After independence in 1980, legal reforms attempted to improve the legal status of Zimbabwean women in the waged workplace and in marriage.[1] Despite these legislative reforms, women in Zimbabwe remained disadvantaged, and women in rural areas continued to be the majority among the poorest of the poor. Most rural women lived in areas characterized by poor soils and low rainfall, with limited access to credit and few financial resources to develop the farms and had to eke out a living from a precarious combination of agricultural and nonfarm activities. The constantly changing structure of the community and family, on the other hand, continued to burden them as wives, mothers, caregivers, and home managers, leaving women with limited time to participate in both social and developmental activities. The aim of the AWFT was to highlight these concerns.

PARTICIPATORY VIDEO PRODUCTION

The first project that AWFT embarked on was a series of videos under the title *Women of Will.* The first production was perhaps most notable because of what they learned about the participatory production process. Initially, they set out to portray prominent African Zimbabwean women as a way to provide role models for young rural women. They consulted widely to identify the women who would be featured. After a period of research, the series producer selected the issues to be highlighted and developed a script. However, as they had no experience with participatory communications, they ended up implementing a project that was hierarchical and noninclusive. The limitations of this top-down approach became evident in their first production with Jane Ngwenya in 1995.

Jane Ngwenya grew up in the 1930s when Zimbabwean women were doubly discriminated against, first as part of the oppressed African majority and secondly as subservient appendages of men. Against such odds Ngwenya had played an important role in Zimbabwe's armed struggle, and later in postindependence politics. Considered a moving spirit among the women in Matebeleland in the late 1950s, she was trained in Zambia in the early 1960s to be the first leader of the initial contingent of women to reach the battlefront. After independence, she became a Member of Parliament, and was appointed Deputy Minister of Labour Manpower Planning and Social Welfare in 1982.

A conflict immediately arose during shooting of the video over what Jane considered to be important and what had been scripted. Jane yearned for an opportunity to tell her story from her own perspective. She criticized the project coordinators for imposing views and agendas and in the process treating others as mere objects. She wanted to include examples from her childhood that would show how her upbringing and the attitudes of the church and the larger society towards women had been serious obstacles to her advancement. For example, her schooling almost ended when she had asked "Is Heaven meant only for Africans?" as it was only Africans she had seen suffering. She was suspended from school pending expulsion. Later, during the 1950s, she found it difficult to balance her interest in politics with the traditional role of a wife. Politics was seen as a man's domain, and her involvement as an activist disgraced her family. Courageously, she wrote to the Vatican asking them to grant her a divorce. "What do you consider as a worse sin, killing or letting me divorce my husband, the man who has brought untold suffering into my life?" (C. Matewa, fieldnotes, 11 March 1996, Bulawayo). Jane saw herself as a heroine when her divorce was granted, but later as a victim when her husband sold the family home and deserted with their children without consulting with her.

Jane Ngwenya also wanted to include her experiences during the struggle to liberate Zimbabwe. She had been in the same room with other Zimbabwe African Peoples' Union (ZAPU) leaders preparing for an important Organization of African Union (OAU) meeting, when one of the most prominent leaders Jason Moyo, was killed by a parcel bomb.[2] Several others were injured and left in shock and confusion. Auntie Jane thought that these events should be given more prominence than her contribution as a Deputy Minister.

Ngwenya's challenge to the script and to AWFT's top-down approach prompted AWFT to review their objectives. If their goal was for women to use media to define their futures, they would have to move beyond the traditional production techniques, in which the producers developed the script separate from the participants. Although Ngwenya had not known about AWFT's goal of enabling participants to set their own agenda, she helped to steer the project back on course. She was given an opportunity to select the issues that were important to her and to help decide how she would be seen by the outside world.

By enabling Ngwenya to set her own agenda, AWFT reversed the usual mass media decision-making process. Rather than the media professionals setting the agenda for the discussion (Eilers, 1994: 67), Ngwenya assumed that role. After evaluating this experience, AWFT realized that they needed to develop production techniques that were robust enough to allow participants to set their own agenda. As a result, they set up the Participation in Production Program to further develop the participatory approach.

THE PARTICIPATION IN PRODUCTION PROJECT

The Participation in Production Project was launched in 1995 and funded mainly by the World Association for Christian Communication until 2001. The target group was rural women and marginalized communities. The aim of the project was to make the means of video production accessible to rural women and to counteract the gross inequalities inherent in centralized control of media production. The project demonstrated several benefits that could not have been achieved using traditional methods of video production. The second series of videos produced between 1995 and 2001 were determined by AWFT working with the communities.

Survival and Community Transformation

Survival was the first documentary video produced with the refined participatory production approach. This documentary focused on how women were coping with structural adjustment programs (SAPs) and was produced in 1995 with communities in Mubaira in Chegutu District, Mutoko and Gwanda District.[3] The AWFT chose the topic as one for which they could easily secure funding, because the negative effects of the SAPs, particularly among women, were becoming increasingly evident. Although the general theme was decided by AWFT, each community had the opportunity to determine the specific program content. Cases profiled included a widow, a woman deserted by her husband, a young woman involved in the illegal and dangerous trade of gold panning, and several market women. Participants perceived themselves as survivors, not as victims of economic policies, and they selected women who were doing something to change their fate; hence the title *Survival*.

The first profile was Mrs. Mpofu, a widow. When her husband—the family's main breadwinner—died, his relatives took away the family wealth. The video shows Mrs. Mpofu growing and selling tomatoes to make ends meet, but then running into difficulties when others in the village also took up tomato growing and flooded the market. Mrs. Mpofu is then shown going to the nearby town of Victoria Falls, to buy second hand clothes for resale in the village. This venture, too, fails; although the villagers wanted second-hand clothes, they had no money to buy them, and Mpofu had to turn to barter trading. The video summarizes her story in a song, with lyrics urging other women to work hard to change their condition and discouraging economic dependence on husbands, as husbands could die and leave the wives to bring up the family alone.

The video provided an environment that promoted an exchange of ideas and learning through the portrayal of the real day-to-day experiences of village members. The participants talked about the intricacies of portraying the challenges facing women. For example, several women initially felt that the selection of Mrs. Mpofu's story was not appropriate, nor highlighted the connection between national economic policies and local communities. Others drew a link; if the relatives had been better off economically, they would not have taken the inheritance from the widow and her children. Still others argued that the husband's family had opportunistically interpreted the traditional practices for their own selfish gain. Although these arguments were not resolved, the process enabled participants to look critically at several issues while they collectively identified factors that were causing the problems and how these could be resolved or prevented.

The second profile featured Mrs. Ndlovu, a woman who had been deserted by her husband. Her husband had left their rural home to look for a job in town; six years later, he had not returned nor had he contacted his family. He left Mrs. Ndlovu pregnant and with the responsibility of caring for four young children. During the community's discussion, several people concluded that the man's failure to return might have been caused by his inability to secure a job, a result of the Structural Adjustment Policies, in which companies had drastically cut their work forces to reduce expenditures.

In addition to the important points of view and analysis presented, the video of Mrs. Ndlovu was notable because of the active involvement of the community in trying to improve her situation. During the filming process, and without the knowledge of the AWFT video coordinators, the local women producers had collected cash and bought household provisions, which they intended to hand to Mrs. Ndlovu during one of the scenes. Much to the surprise of the AWFT personnel, the local women producers added a scene in which they introduced Mrs. Ndlovu to a cattle-fattening project and then incorporated her as a full project member. Finally, the Councilor of the area arrived to announce that he was going to help Mrs. Ndlovu get birth certificates for her children so that they could get assistance from the Social Services Department. These two events made AWFT realize the degree to which participatory video can bring about real off-screen social change.

In her discussion of participatory video among Colombian women (2001) Rodríguez distinguishes between video as product and video as process. Rather than emphasizing the finished video, or product, 'process video' emphasizes the richness of the production process, which directly involves people in discerning and prioritizing their own problems and finding the information and resources to solve these problems. According to Richardson, "in participatory video work, the communication process is more important than the production of a video" (1997: 22). The success of the initiative often depends on the extent to which people feel involved (Burke, 1999: 28). The process of production with Mrs. Ndlovu and her community helped build a sense of community responsibility and assisted the community in looking for solutions within their own reach. With the collaboration of communities, AWFT discovered a technique and process that would enable women to articulate their own voice(s), empowering them to take steps to improve their situations, and as well, integrate the cultural forms and media already used by participants, such as drama and music.

Community Video and Historical Memory

AWFT also discovered the value of participatory video in documenting historical memory in a project in Matebeleland Province. The majority of the populace in Matebeleland had belonged to the Zimbabwe African People's Union (ZAPU), the second largest nationalist organization after Robert Mugabe's Zimbabwe

African National Union (ZANU). During the struggle for independence, ZAPU and ZANU had allied in the Patriotic Front (PF). However during the post-Independence elections of 1980, Robert Mugabe decided that ZANU would contest the elections on their own, and won a smashing victory to form the new government; and ZAPU became the main opposition party. Civil war between the former allies erupted after Independence, lasting until the late 1980s.

In 1999, the production of *The Untold Story* allowed the local communities to play a crucial role in identifying the shooting locations, determine the content, and narrate their experiences of the war. The video was also remarkable because it presented the plight of civilians, who were often trapped between two armed groups. In some instances, participants in the video were not sure whether it was government agents, local dissidents, and/or South African–trained dissidents who had perpetrated atrocities against them. As one of the survivors noted to the prominent Zimbabwean historian, Professor Ranger, "We were like beasts between two cannibals. The dissidents mauled at one side of us and the fifth brigade mauled at one side of us and there was nothing left but our bones" (Ranger, *The Untold Story* [video], 1999). After the shooting of the video, Mrs. P. Ndlovu remarked,[4]

> I feel relieved now that I have had an opportunity to tell my story of what happened during this period. It has been weighing on us heavily. At least our grandchildren will be able to know what really happened. (Ndlovu, *The Untold Story* [video], 1999)

Mrs. Moyo said:

> Accepting to come and visit the sites, where some of our loved ones are buried or were murdered, has enabled us to revisit our past. It has enabled me to put that past behind me so that I move on with my life knowing that a permanent record has been made which will outlive us, a record depicting what happened and how we suffered. (Moyo, *The Untold Story* [video], 1999)

This project also demonstrated the aural and visual capacities of video to assist both the literate and illiterate to create historical records for a variety of purposes. For example, for many women, *The Untold Story* provided an opportunity to tell their story, making sure that it would be passed on to the next generation just as they had said it. For some, the video provided a record of the places where atrocities had been committed; others wanted to record the ruins of their deserted villages to highlight the magnitude of the problem. Still others wanted to highlight the steps they had taken to establish the fate of their loved ones. Finally another group scripted the footage having in mind the many villagers who had fled their homes during the massacres and never returned.

Using Participatory Video for the Discussion of Democracy

AWFT also discovered the value of participatory video in promoting community discussions about democratization. Generally, Zimbabwean communities understand democracy to comprise a range of dimensions, including consultation, participation, and the selection, via voting, of representatives who would be committed to the welfare of the people who vote for them. In reality, the electorate are seldom consulted and are frequently denied a voice and a place in the process of deliberation or governance.

In 1996, *Democracy-Community Participation* was produced in collaboration with women and youth in the communities in Mhondoro, in Chegutu District. In the video, the community in Mutoko stressed that democracy was not new in Zimbabwe, or in Africa. Historically, women had played important roles in the governing process as spirit mediums, with some rising to become chiefs. In Mutoko, one of the tribes still believes that chieftainship should rotate between men and women. If women are not appointed during their turn, the land is cursed. The cleansing of the land only starts with the installation of a woman as chief. Apart from being the intermediary between the community and God, the spirit medium has the tasks of advising the King, helping to settle the disputes of the royal family, and dividing the deceased King's property. She also plays an important role in the election and installation of the King, as the stabilizing factor (Schmidt, 1992).

In their video production process, the community in Mhondoro identified four issues of paramount importance for which they wanted urgent redress: access to water, the rights of handicapped persons, better education, and the eradication of poverty. As well, they wanted to discuss the idea that leaders should be chosen on the basis of who could best address these problems. Using drama, they decided to contrast the behavior of bad leaders with that of more ideal leaders.

The Councillor of the area, Mr. Zvoma, was cast to play the role of a bad leader. He was always drunk and never addressed any of the problems affecting the community he represented. During shooting, the AWFT production team realized that Mr. Zvoma was not just role-playing, but was actually portraying himself. During the production process, the open dialogue and discussion among participants gave Mr. Zvoma the opportunity to see himself as others saw him. At the end of filming, Mr. Zvoma emerged as a transformed person who vowed to work hard for the community he represented. He decided to restrict his drinking to the weekends with the hope of quitting altogether. He began paying attention to the issues and concerns of the community and promised to do something about them.

The video production process enabled the community to state what they expected from their leader. Collectively, participants were able to reflect and identify issues that needed attention. The participatory video production approach also assisted the councilor's transformation. When AWFT visited the community a year latter, Mr. Zvoma had been re-elected as councilor. He had facilitated a number of development activities in the community, including the digging of boreholes to assure safe drinking water and the involvement of some members of the community in dairy production.

YOU HAVE BROUGHT LIGHT TO THE COMMUNITY: MOBILE VIDEO SCREENINGS

In addition to the immediate benefits for communities directly involved in production, the Africa Women's Filmmakers Trust recognized that circulating the videos could also help teach new skills and stimulate debate on topical issues in other communities. In 1999, they decided to launch the Access to Media Program, the first of its kind in Zimbabwe. In order to reach remote communities, which often had no access to electricity, they used generator-powered mobile vehicles to screen the videos. After a screening in Chipinge, one of the most underdeveloped districts in Zimbabwe, one man said, "Maunza chiedza kwedu" which literally means "You have brought light to our community" (Matewa, 1999, personal communication, Chipinge). It was the first time this community had seen a video or a moving picture. The mobile screenings helped to connect communities that had no direct link or were separated by physical and other barriers.

Discussions after the screenings created spaces for community members to open up and identify areas needing redress, exchange new information on difficult subjects, and discuss sensitive issues. This process was similar to the Egyptian Video and Community Dreams Project, described by Gumucio-Dagrón, where video played a role in crystallizing the debate around extremely delicate cultural issues (Gumucio-Dagrón, 2001: 316). For example, the video *Side by Side* which deals with AIDS issues, prompted one woman to ask about the safety of condoms, as she had heard rumors that the substance inside condoms was actually spreading the HIV virus.[5] In the ensuing discussion, facilitated by members of the community and the AWFT team, the community ultimately decided that statements about the substance inside condoms infecting people were false and that condoms were safe when used correctly in the prevention of HIV. They concluded by encouraging others to remain faithful to their partners and recommending abstinence among youths and widows.

In another location, the community raised the issue of the rights of the girl child among people of the apostolic faith—who generally give away their children at a tender age for marriage to older men. Although the women participants acknowledged the plight of the girl child, the women collectively concluded that the men needed to be equally convinced to make any lasting change. As the women were hesitant to discuss the subject with their husbands, more video screenings were required and men were invited. The discussions that followed the video screenings created a conducive environment to discuss the subject. Thus, screenings not only provided an opportunity for participants to discuss sensitive issues but also to learn from each other and to deal with some of the myths surrounding health issues.

The video screenings also stimulated communities to think and reflect about their community's economic condition and how they could change it. After watching the videos *Survival* and *An Entrepreneur,* one of the participants in Zimunya, in Manicaland Province, said;

> When we came we thought at the end we will be given some money to start a project or some blankets like other organizations are doing with orphaned children in this area, but no, you came to inform us, to empower us, to challenge us to stand up like those women in the film *Survival* and be survivors like them. Here we have no gold, so we cannot do gold panning. But, we have plenty of trees. We should sit down and think what we can do with the resources, which are locally available, and in abundance. But, as we have been shown in the film *An Entrepreneur,* we have to look at our skills and markets before we embark on anything, otherwise we will fail as many have failed before us. (AWFT Annual Report, 1999: 2)

The screenings and discussions provided an opportunity for communities to deliberate on the importance and relevance of new topics for production. In Mubaira, the community decided to produce a film highlighting their lack of safe drinking water. During the production and screening, participants discussed the options available and realized that they could collectively harness their limited resources to solve their problems. The screening was therefore a platform that enabled them to set a collective agenda. The process also enabled participants to look within themselves for ways they could use local and personal resources to tackle development challenges in their area and to become less dependent on donor funding.

Gumucio-Dagrón observed a similar process with *Television Serrana,* the Community Video and Television Project that operated in the heart of the famous Sierra Maestra in Cuba:

> New topics for production usually emerge from debates. During one of the after-show discussions the crew discovered an 82-year-old man that had been writing poems on Sierra Maestra for 20 years; he became the subject of video production. Likewise, the contamination of River Yao by a coffee processing plant was first mentioned after a video show; a critical video documentary followed and pushed for the implementation of corrective measures. (Gumucio-Dagrón, 2001: 209)

CONCLUSION

AWFT has discovered that video is a reflexive medium, which enables actors in a participatory project to be both the subject and the object of reflection. Participants realised that they could do things, and say what they thought, knowing that it would be heard beyond their local boundaries, and so video helped to build their confidence. When a video produced using the participatory approach was shown to other communities, it enabled members of these communities to see themselves through the lives and experiences of others and reflect. So, video, when used in a participatory way, is extremely powerful in giving recognition to marginalised individuals and communities, which then generates the sense of empowerment that enables them to take action for social change. (Matewa, 2003: 11)

The African Women's Filmmakers Trust was established to explore how video could be used to give women a voice and bring about social change. They soon realized that the more top-down professional model of script development would not allow communities to present issues of interest and concern to them in their own way. In response, the AWFT adopted the participatory communications approach, working with 'real' people with whose experience the audience can relate, thereby making the video more believable and effective for attitude change (Gumucio-Dagrón, 2001: 184).

Thanks to their ability to truly hear what project participants demanded, AWFT coordinators shifted from what Rodríguez calls an 'epidemiology approach' to the more complex 'social fabric approach' to social change. In the 'epidemiology' approach, experts dissect social reality for people and transmit predesigned messages to change their behavior. In the 'social fabric approach,' communication facilitators open social spaces to invite people to interact among themselves in more complex, multidirectional, and long-term collective processes (Rodríguez, 2004). The AWFT video productions demonstrated how communities appropriated these technologies and created new public spheres at the local level. These novel communication spaces were soon put to use among community members. Processes of self-examination are then facilitated by the production process; in the case of *Democracy-Community Participation*, for example, the use of the actual councillor in the drama allowed him to recognize his weaknesses and to commit to work with the community for the development of the region.

Perhaps one of the most significant issues is to what extent a new local public sphere contributes to enhancing democratic dialogue, self-reliance, and community solidarity. The mere act of speaking in public, for example, was impacted by participating in these video production processes. Participants built confidence that enabled them to participate more actively in other fora. During the evaluation of the Access to Media Program by AWFT in 2003, participants narrated stories of how they had courageously challenged aspiring members of parliament during the 2002 campaign for having neglected them and not lived up to their promises. Politicians could no longer take the rural electorate, particularly the women, for granted.

Viewing the videos collectively allowed participants a communication space where they could exchange information and dispel rumors (as in the HIV and condoms case); consider alternative interpretations of local issues (as in the case of the video about the plight of girl child); discuss local solutions to local problems (as in the case of lack of safe drinking water); and collectively develop local inventories of competences, skills, and resources (as in the case of availability of trees for potential income-generating projects). These are the threads that weave a dynamic public sphere; fleshing out this type of communication processes is how we can see the link between alternative media and stronger participatory democracies.

Participatory video production and screening enabled the building of a greater sense of community. During the shooting of *Survival*, for example, all the participants in Gwanda, including the AWFT staff, decided to attend a funeral, suspending the shooting until afterwards. The local production collective felt that the project belonged to them, so they requested that the project vehicle collect provisions for the funeral at a nearby town. For the Gwanda collective, the participatory approach was paving the way for community-based ownership.

In *Survival* the community not only demonstrated their capacity for sharing resources and skills with Mrs. Ndlovu, they also took control of the video production process to highlight the importance of this approach. In both *Democracy-Community Participation* and *Survival*, the attitudes of the individuals and communities involved changed just by having participated in the process.

Another significant finding of my research on the impact of the AWFT video projects on the social fabric of local communities is how these processes contributed to postconflict reconstruction. In Zimbabwean communities ravaged by armed conflict, the AWFT video project allowed them to articulate their past experiences in a way that could be shared with others and stored as part of the local historical memory. As Pilar Riaño-Alcalá has written,

> [T]he sustained relationship with violence by individuals and societies transforms the fabric of everyday life as the place of taken-for-granted relations. . . . Under the impact of sustained violence, the basic referents of trust in everyday life seem to disappear and people find themselves constantly struggling to recover some of the qualities of an ordinary daily life. (Riaño-Alcalá, 2006: 14)

The representation of images, sounds, and memories allowed the people in Matabeleland to re-organize their experience of surviving armed conflict; to have 'a communication object' around which to have a collective dialogue about how they had coped and survived violence; and to leave a document about an easily 'erasable' community history. Also, the case of the *Untold Story* should leave us with a more complex and nuanced rendition of communities impacted by war and armed conflict. Instead of seeing them merely as victims trying to survive, we need to be able to appreciate the creativity that goes on. As Caldwell says: "I found expression and creativity under the worst conditions" (Caldwell, 2003: 662).

This shift in power relations, in which rural communities empower themselves and begin to challenge the status quo, has also made it more difficult to find sustainable funding for video projects like these. Generally, donors do not want to fund projects that are controversial, which challenge existing power structures or criticize government policies and practices. Most donors prefer to fund top-down projects, in which the marginalized communities are mere recipients of aid and where the identification of needs, and the allocation of resources, is out of the control of the recipients. These projects deny the women and youth the opportunities to determine issues of concern to them, to represent themselves, actively participating in the creation of knowledge and in finding remedies for problems in their communities. More importantly, they miss the opportunity to strengthen local public spheres, where local solutions to local problems could emerge. When government-controlled and commercial media deny rural communities the opportunity to articulate their voice and engage in debate on issues of social interest and national importance, a vital opening for basic human rights and democracy is denied.

NOTES

1. The Minimum Wages Act (1981) set a minimum wage for all jobs and the Equal Pay Act (1981) legislated equal pay for equal work. The 1985 Labour Relations Act prohibited discrimination, on any grounds, in relation to recruitment, wages, training, promotion, and retrenchment. The Amendment to the Customary Law and Primary Courts Act (1981) improved the maintenance provision for women. The Matrimonial Causes Act (1985) improved divorce law; and the Deceased Person's Family Maintenance Act (1987) gave women some rights to matrimonial property.
2. The OAU was formed to foster solidarity among the African countries.
3. SAPs were policy changes set up by the International Monetary Fund (IMFO) and the World Bank (WB) as conditions for loans for developing countries. They included programs of privatizing state institutions and social services, reducing the public service staff, deregulating private industries, and encouraging trade liberalization or the reduction of import and export restrictions. They have been widely criticized for increasing the debt of poorer nations and increasing poverty, particularly in rural areas (SAPRIN, 2002).
4. Ndlovu is one of the most common names among the Ndebele speaking people. Mrs. Ndlovu mentioned in the profile featured in the video film *Survival* is different from Mrs. Ndlovu featured in the video film *The Untold Story*.
5. *Side by Side* is one of the video films AWFT sourced from other independent producers for use in the mobile video screenings project

REFERENCES

AWFT. (n.d.). *Project document.* Photocopy.

AWFT. (1999). *Annual report.* Photocopy.

Amadiume, I. (1987). *Male daughters female husbands: Gender and sex in an African Society.* London: Zed.

Balit, S. (2000). *Voices of change: Rural women and communication.* Retrieved December 15, 2001, from http://www.fao/docrep/x2550E/x2550e04.htm

Boserup, E. (1970). *Woman's role in economic development.* London: Earthscan.

Burke, A. (1999). *Communication and development: A practical guide.* London: Department for International Development, Social Development Division.

Caldwell, J. (2003). Alternative media in suburban plantation culture. *Media, Culture and Society, 25,* 647-667.

Cruz, M. (1999). Africa women film-makers trust: Using media to empower communities. *Churchwoman-May Friendship Day 'God's Sweet Surprises: Angels, Mentos, and Friends, 1,* 11-12.

Dowmunt, T. (2001). *Dear camera. Video diaries, subjectivity and media power.* Paper presented at the OURMedia I conference, Washington DC, May 24. Retrieved December 12, 2006, from http://www.ourmedianet.org/om2001/ica2001.html

Eilers, F. (1994). *Communicating in community: An introduction to social communication.* Manila: Logos.

Gaidzanwa, R. (1992). The ideology of domesticity and the struggles of women workers— the case of Zimbabwe. *Working Paper Sub-Series On Women's History and Development,* No 16. The Hague: Institute of Social Studies.

Geertz, C. (1973). *The interpretation of cultures.* New York: Basic Books.

Gumucio-Dagrón, A. (2001). *Making waves: Stories of participatory communication for social change.* New York: The Rockefeller Foundation.

Hornik, R. C. (1988). *Development communication: Information, agriculture and nutrition in the third world.* Lanham, MD: University Press of America.

Kabeer, N. (1994). *Reversed realities: Gender hierarchies in development thought.* London: Verso.

Matewa, C. (1997). *The role of the media in the subordination of women in Africa.* Unpublished master's thesis, The University of Manchester, England.

Matewa, C. (2003). Media and the empowerment of communities for social change. Unpublished doctoral dissertation, The University of Manchester, England.

Østergaard, L. (1992). *Gender and development: A practical guide.* London: Routledge.

Riaño-Alcalá, P. (2006). *Dwellers of memory: Youth and violence in Medellín, Colombia.* New Brunswick, NJ: Transaction.

Richardson, D. (1997). *The internet and rural agricultural development: An integrated approach.* Rome: FAO.

Rodríguez, C. (2001). *Fissures in the mediascape: An international study of citizens' media.* Cresskill, NJ: Hampton Press.

Rodríguez, C. (2004 December 6). *Communication for peace: Contrasting approaches.* The Drum Beat, issue 278. Retrieved December 10, 2006, from HYPERLINK "http://www.comminit.com/drum_beat.html" http://www.comminit.com/drum_beat.html

Schmidt, E. (1992). *Peasants, traders and wives: Shona women in the history of Zimbabwe, 1870-1939.* Harare: Baobab.

Structural Adjustment Participatory Review International Network (SAPRIN). (2002) *The policy roots of economic crisis and poverty.* Retrieved July 7, 2007, from http://www.saprin.org/global_rpt.htm

Tinker, I. (1997). The making of a field: Advocates, practitioners and scholars. In N. Visvanathan, L. Duggan, & L. Nisonoff (Eds.), *The women, gender and development reader* (pp. 33-42). London: Zed.

Weinrich, A. K. (1979). *Women and racial discrimination in Rhodesia.* Rome: UNESCO.

KNOWLEDGES
IN DIALOGUE
A Participatory Evaluation of Citizens' Radio Stations in Magdalena Medio, Colombia[1]

Clemencia Rodríguez

The Colombian internal armed conflict is considered one of the worst in the world. Some estimates speak of 35,000 violent deaths, over 1,000 kidnappings, and 800 citizens missing every year; all these with a staggering impunity rate of over 90% (Garcia & Uprimmy, 1999: 40).[2] In 1990 the homicide rate per 100,000 in Colombia was 80, four times as much as in the rest of Latin America (Romero, 2003: 27). In the last 40 years armed conflict has claimed the lives of 200,000 Colombians and has forced 2 million others to flee their homes in terror (Berrigan, Hartung, & Heffel, 2005).

Although Colombia endures a 'multiplicity of violences' (Sánchez, 2001) that includes leftist guerrillas, right-wing paramilitaries, drug trafficking networks, and common delinquency, all these forms emerge from power struggles engendered by unequal access to material resources; social violence in Colombia is not related to cultural, ethnic, or religious differences. However, more than half a century of continuous social and political violence has had a tremendous impact on Colombians' collective imaginaries and everyday cultural practices. The mixture of patron-client relationships; an absent, corrupt, or negligent state; and the presence of armed groups and their militaristic options have normalized a cultural fabric that de-legitimizes the rule of law, privileges individual agency, perceives difference as something to be overpowered and annihilated, and favors violent forms of conflict resolution.

Proposals to move Colombia from violence and armed conflict to peaceful coexistence range from the militaristic solutions implemented through Plan

Colombia to more comprehensive initiatives that intend to impact the social fabric in the hope that strong communities will themselves reject armed solutions to
life problems. In this chapter I document one of the latter proposals, in which a
network of eighteen citizens' radio stations operating in a Colombian region
known as *Magdalena Medio* [Middle Magdalena or MM] intend to change the
social and cultural fabric in each of their municipalities.

In 2004 I went back to my native Colombia to conduct fieldwork to continue
research on citizens' media. In *Fissures in the Mediascape* (Rodríguez, 2001), I articulated my version of how citizens' media (also called community media, alternative media, autonomous media, or radical media) facilitate social change.
Although my previous studies shed light on how these media truly impact the
social fabric in which they operate, another set of questions led me back to the
field: How can we demonstrate these changes? How can we document this
impact? How can we truly evaluate citizens' media impact on the social fabric?

A FELT NEED:
CITIZENS' MEDIA EVALUATION

The year 2001 also marked the emergence of OURMedia (www.ourmedianet.
org), a global network of citizens' media academics and activists.[3] Ultimately, the
goal of OURMedia is to design and develop initiatives to strengthen citizens'
media, community media, and alternative media in national and international
policy arenas. At the annual conference of OURMedia in Barranquilla,
Colombia, in 2003 my preoccupation with citizens' media evaluation resonated
with many other OURMedia presentations—coming from both academics and
practitioners.

At the conference, Alfonso Gumucio-Dagrón, from the Communication for
Social Change Consortium, emphasized the urgency to design evaluation
methodologies and indicators to document processes of social change to donors,
communities, legislators, and project participants themselves. Victor Van Oeyen
(from ERBOL-Bolivia), Lucho Dávila and Andree Geerts (from ALER-Ecuador)
presented what is perhaps the most comprehensive evaluation study of community radio in Latin America. Published as *La Práctica Inspira* [Practice that
Inspires], the study documents how the best practices of Latin American community radio have triggered processes of social change at the local level (Van Oeyen
& Geerts, 2004). Jo Tacchi and Peter Lewis discussed their work in Sri Lanka.
Developed around the idea of 'communication ecology' and using ethnography
to gain insight into subtle processes of social and cultural change, Tacchi's and
Lewis' team designed and implemented innovative evaluation methodologies
(Tacchi, Slater, & Lewis, 2003). Gustavo Gómez of AMARC Latin America,
surely the most knowledgeable expert on community media regulation in Latin
America, confirmed the importance of this work when he insisted that if we are

to demand more frequencies and better policies for community media, we need to 'demonstrate' to legislators why these media matter.

I arrived in Colombia on January of 2004 with all these evaluation debates in mind. To my surprise, before I was finished explaining my intentions, I found great enthusiasm from academic colleagues wanting to participate in the design of an evaluation methodology especially tailored for citizens' media, and also from community media leaders wanting their media initiatives to be evaluated. With communication professors Jair Vega (Universidad del Norte in Barranquilla, Colombia) and Amparo Cadavid (Universidad Javeriana, Bogotá, Colombia) I formed an academic team that operates with some fundamental assumptions: first, we believe that academic research should be *at the service* of praxis; in other words, that the knowledge we produce within academia is most valuable if and only if it becomes useful for those in the field trying to make our societies better places to live—in this case citizens' media practitioners. All our research questions, outcomes, publications, reports, and so forth, are determined more by the needs of citizens' media practitioners than by academic priorities. I believe it is important to clarify this, because more than once I have been in discussion circles in which academics complain about the difficulties of working side-by-side with activists. I am always puzzled, as our own experience as a team has been very different, being always more than welcomed by activists to conduct research 'about them.' However, from the beginning it has been very clear, for our academic team as well as for the activists with whom we work, that it is *their* needs and not ours that drive everything we do. Academic output is secondary to the production of knowledge usable by the projects themselves.

Second, our team is strongly committed to a process of collective construction of knowledge. Every step of the design and implementation of the evaluation methodology is decided collectively between the academic team and our practitioner colleagues; we maintain a high level of ownership of the methodology on the part of the media practitioners whose project we are evaluating. Because we assume that the evaluation should respond to the questions they need answers to, their input is needed every step of the way. Although I have been familiar with Freirean dialogue-of-knowledge proposals for more than twenty years, this is the first time I have been able to witness and to participate in a process that fully assumes the Freirean commitment to dialogue of equals.[4] As we work together and discuss issues, theories, data gathering techniques, and samples, I can see how we, as academics, learn so much about actual citizens' media practice while at the same time our media colleagues appropriate academic languages, theories, and ways of reflecting about practice.[5]

Third, our team assumes the relationship between academics and citizens' media as a long term commitment. We are aware that the projects cannot undertake the evaluation on their own because it is very expensive and time consuming.[6] We believe that as academics, our research skills should be put to use for purposes like these; thus our goal is that the evaluation does not drain off resources (in terms of time, money, labor) scarce within community media projects. In general, citizens' media leaders are already stretched very thin, strapped for funds, and constantly having a million fires to put out. Thus most of the actual labor of gathering, transcribing, classifying and analyzing data is done by our academic team. At every step of the way we meet with our media colleagues to discuss next steps, to reflect on results, and to reach agreements about what to do with the results (A video? A report for donors? An academic publication? A conference presentation? Materials to return the results to the community?).

At present our academic team is completing evaluation studies of three Colombian citizens' media projects: the *Colectivo de Comunicación de Montes de María*, a participatory radio and television production initiative in the Colombian Caribbean; *Radio Andaquí*, a municipal citizens' radio station located in Caquetá, in the Colombian Amazon; and finally, of AREDMAG, a network of eighteen citizens' radio stations in *Magdalena Medio*. These three citizens' media projects operate in regions of intense armed conflict; however, social unrest and political violence take a specific form in each case. This chapter will focus exclusively on the *Magdalena Medio* case.

OUR PROPOSAL TO EVALUATE CITIZENS' MEDIA

We have adopted the 'concentric circles' approach to citizens' media ecologies from Jo Tacchi and her team (Tacchi, Slater, & Lewis, 2003). Thus, we understand each citizens' medium as existing at the center of at least three concentric circles: the most immediate circle is the people directly working or participating in media production; the second circle consists of all grassroots organizations, collectives, and social movements that use the radio station as a way to engage with the public sphere; the third circle is the listeners. We assume that citizens' media impact each of these three circles differently, and thus each circle merits the design of a specific evaluation methodology that can allow us to document and analyze processes of change.

Working collectively with our citizens' media colleagues, our academic team developed a methodology especially designed for each circle. The methodology for the first circle is based on qualitative verbal and visual narratives based on memory recuperation—an adaptation of Riaño-Alcalá's memory workshops developed as part of her participatory research on memory and violence (see Riaño-Alcalá, 1998, 1999, 2000a, 2000b, 2003, 2006). For the second circle we use a combination of in-depth interviews and visual and verbal testimonies. Data collection for the third circle combines quantitative listeners' surveys and qualitative in-depth interviews with specific listeners whose lives have been strongly impacted by the station (for example, in one case a community leader and long-time listener of the station was rescued from the hands of a guerrilla group thanks to the station). The remaining pages focus exclusively on the evaluation of the first circle.

WEALTH AND WAR:
MAGDALENA MEDIO AND ITS PARADOXES

Local scholars have labeled Colombia *un país de regiones* [a country of regions], meaning that the historical processes of colonization, economic development, and formation of cultural identities are better understood when examined region by region and not through a national lens (see Aldana et al., 1998; García, 1996; González, 1994, Guzmán & Luna, 1994; Jimeno, 1994; Uribe, 1992).

As a region, the *Magdalena Medio* (MM—Middle Magdalena) lies in the center of the country, covering the middle course of the Magdalena River, which flows from south to north and forms a long valley between the eastern and central Andean mountain ranges. The MM covers 30,000 square kilometers, which approximately 800,000 Colombians call home. Crucial national communication and trade infrastructures go through the core of this region, including the Magdalena River; the main interstate highway and railroad; fiber optic lines; oil production facilities; and gas and oil pipelines. Well connected to national and international markets, 27 of the region's municipalities make the highest tax contributions to the budgets of their respective departments of Antioquia, Bolívar, Santander, and Cesar.[7, 8] Six of these municipalities are oil producers; five stand over the country's richest gold deposits; and several others are important agricultural and livestock centers.

However, some of these same municipalities are the poorest and most marginalized in the region, a paradox that Colombian economists describe with the term 'perverse economy.' Although the products exploited for international markets have shifted from quina, the source of quinine, rubber, and wood to oil, coca, palm oil, sorghum, and cotton, the economic model has not changed since the nineteenth century. The rich natural resources have been extracted with very little ending up in the pockets of the local communities.

The *Magdalena Medio* has some of the highest violence rates in the country; from 1997 to 2002 the people of MM experienced 930 massacres, 5,200 murders, 465 disappearances, 211 attacks on villages, 16,000 kidnappings, 96,000 displaced refugees, and 130,000 landmines (Cadavid, 2003). In 2002 the rate for homicides per 100,000 inhabitants was 250 (Katz García, n.d). Widespread forms of violence in both rural and urban areas in the region include guerrilla and paramilitary activity, drug trafficking, oil mafias, and common delinquency.

In this context, the *Programa de Desarrollo y Paz del Magdalena Medio* [PDPMM or Peace and Development Program for Middle-Magdalena] was born in 1995 in an attempt to decrease levels of violence and increase the quality of life of local communities in MM. The PDPMM was developed by several institutions including ECOPETROL, the Catholic Diocese of Barrancabermeja, and CINEP *Centro de Investigación y Educación Popular*—a well known Colombian NGO—that, concerned with the growth of armed conflict, decided to join forces in a comprehensive development project for the entire region. Based on the economic theories of Amartya Sen (1999) and his proposal to include economic indicators that measure happiness and not just economic growth, the PDPMM is an experiment in regional development that attempts to tackle all needs and hopes of local communities simultaneously; the program includes 300 initiatives to activate local economies; strengthen civic participation and consensus-building in local and regional decision-making processes; rebuild transportation, energy, health, and educational infrastructures; encourage local cultures; and nurture pluralism, diversity, and tolerance. The PDPMM partnership has had the financial support of ECOPETROL, the United Nations Development Program, Caritas, the governments of Japan and Sweden, and the World Bank. In 2002, in an attempt to counter the militaristic angle of Plan Colombia, the European Union decided to invest in the PDPMM as a Peace Laboratory.[9]

Toward the early 1990s media activists had begun developing citizens' radio initiatives throughout the country. As part of its communication and culture component, the PDPMM decided to support five citizens' radio stations that were already operating in *Magdalena Medio*, run by citizens' groups and collectives. These stations had emerged as attempts of local collectives to strengthen their capacity to participate in local governance, monitor public institutions, and express local concerns. Common participants in these citizens' media ventures were teachers' associations, cultural collectives, religious organizations and churches, community leaders, and local authorities.

Between 1995 and 2000 five more radio stations secured broadcasting licenses and the necessary technical infrastructure. Today, thirteen citizens' radio stations and five communication collectives in eighteen municipalities throughout the region are organized as the Network of Community Radio Stations of *Magdalena Medio*—AREDMAG (*Asociación Red de Emisoras Comunitarias del Magdalena Medio*).[10]

THE EVALUATION STUDY OF AREDMAG

Working collectively with AREDMAG's board of directors we designed a sample and set of data collection strategies that would provide us with evidence to evaluate the first circle, or how people directly involved with AREDMAG's radio station experience social change. AREDMAG's board of directors consists of six members popularly elected by the people involved with AREDMAG's eighteen community radio initiatives. The board decided that two of its members would assume the evaluation study as one of their main responsibilities, but at different times of the process other board members participated.

The academic team and the board designed a sample of 60 community radio participants/producers who would participate in the data collection for the first circle. The sample was designed according to criteria to ensure balance by: (a) type of radio initiative (i.e., stations already operating and members of ARED-

MAG; stations operating and not members of AREDMAG; communication collectives applying for a radio license and members of AREDMAG); (b) roles within the radio initiative (i.e., station director, producer, member of the programming board, etc.); (c) gender and age.[11] The 60 participants of the sample were invited to travel to a central location for three days for a series of data collection workshops.

The data collection strategies used in the first circle evaluation study are based on the memory workshops developed by Pilar Riaño-Alcalá in her ethnographic studies of youth and violence. Riaño-Alcalá's memory workshop emerges at the intersection between critical ethnography, participatory action research, oral history, and popular education (see Riaño-Alcalá, 2006). In a memory workshop, participants join around a series of methods that elicit individual and group narratives about past experiences. They share memories, listen to verbal testimonies, create visual displays through means such as mapping, paper quilts, or visual biographies, discuss group process, negotiate and construct understandings of experiences, and reflect on the stories shared. Using questions specifically designed to trigger individual and collective memories about specific past experiences, a series of visual and verbal narratives are collected as data in the research process.

Although a detailed description is beyond the scope of this chapter, in a nutshell the memory workshop consists of a series of first-person accounts of situations actually experienced and/or witnessed by workshop participants, elicited by a memory-trigger question. The workshop begins by asking participants to remember a specific type of memory, such as, for example, "please remember a moment in which you felt that the radio station was in some way contributing to nonviolent conflict resolution in the community." Workshop participants are also asked to try to re-create their individual memories "as if you were in front of a movie" and to express the memory visually on a map, a collage, a drawing, or some other visual narrative. The next step is a round of individual verbal narratives in which each participant tells his/her story while the rest listen. The visual testimonies are then assembled into a collective 'memory quilt' and "each participant narrates his or her memory, and then the group reflects on what they have heard" (Riaño-Alcalá, 2008: 272).

The memory workshop was valuable for several reasons: it shared our commitment to collective construction of knowledge; it allowed for data collection on both individual and collective memory and experience; it triggered participants to express both their first hand experience and their analysis of what that experience means; and it elicited different types of data that range from visual to verbal narratives. Riaño-Alcalá says: "From a popular education standpoint, the workshop constitutes a practical-theoretical moment with a collective and participatory dynamic. It embraces praxis as a method—learning by doing—and as an epistemological point of departure—knowledge starts from the experience (stories) of participants—that encourages critical thinking towards social change" (Riaño-Alcalá, 2006: 273).

But more important, memory workshops connect well with our assumption that when it comes to social change, community members know how they have changed both individually and collectively. Our role as evaluators became then to design and implement methodologies to facilitate communication processes in which people can tell us how they and their communities have experienced social change. The analysis presented in the following pages attempts to give voice to local knowledges about social change and not only to academic interpretations; thus the long quotations and the inclusion of visual narratives. As we embarked on this research study, our team shared a strong commitment to a critique of anthropological research that negates community voices and interpretations as it emboldens academic knowledge as the only legitimate voice (Behar & Gordon, 1995; Clifford, 1983; Clifford & Marcus, 1986; Rosaldo, 1989). Our approach to fieldwork and to presenting anthropological data is in line with recent calls for "a practice of ethnography as made up of the subject's own texts . . . in a way that takes subjects as knowledge-producers in their own right" (Restrepo & Escobar, 2005: 117-118) in order to open the field to "novel forms of writing more sensitive to . . . the polivocality of any representation of culture" (Restrepo & Escobar, 2005: 108). The following pages attempt to offer a 'place of encounter' where readers can dialogue directly with the people of *Magdalena Medio* and not only with my academic voice. The research is positioned as what some anthropologists have called a 'multivocal ethnography' (Conquergood, 1991; Quantz & O'Connor, 1988, as cited by Murphy & Kraidy, 2003: 13), which attempts to incorporate local voices—and not just the researcher's—into the process of knowledge production. The verbal and visual narratives obtained from the memory workshops articulate how and why these Colombian citizens' radio stations play important roles in the lives of individuals and in the social and cultural fabric of the local communities.

Working with our sample of 60 participants from AREDMAG's eighteen citizens' radio stations and collectives, we collected a total of 160 individual narratives and eighteen group discussions about the role(s) of citizens' radio in processes of social change. The evaluation study of AREDMAG sheds light on how these radio stations are having an impact on the social and cultural fabric of their communities. Our entire evaluation study tackles the following questions:

- Are AREDMAG's stations generating stronger public spheres?
- Are these stations increasing participation in community decision-making processes?
- Are they improving transparency of local governments?
- Are they enhancing conditions of governance?
- Are they strengthening local cultures and values?
- Are they contributing to the formation of a collective cultural imaginary?

- Are they nurturing processes of peacebuilding, mediation and/or non-violent conflict resolution?
- What follows are just a few fragments of the overall analysis of the first circle.

CITIZENS' RADIO
AND COLLECTIVE IMAGINARIES

The *Magdalena Medio* can easily be labeled an 'imagined community' (Anderson, 1991). As mentioned earlier, the region includes parts of four different departments; traditionally, Colombia has always been fragmented culturally in regions that more or less match departmental boundaries. The term *Magdalena Medio* was originally coined by the Colombian army to designate a region particularly difficult to control due to social unrest and the presence of illegal armed groups. One of the fundamental PDPMM design goals was to consolidate the MM as its own territory, aware of its own history, cultures, languages, economic potential, political identities, and dreams for the future. The PDPMM understood that only a strong territorial collective imaginary could help the MM delineate its own utopia—understood as a vision for the future.

The consolidation of a collective imaginary that speaks to the MM is an arduous and challenging goal because the region is such a mix, from the riverine culture of the Magdalena River to the Andean cultures of the higher altitudes and the coastal cultures of the Caribbean, made even more complex as these territorial cultures hybridize with the cultures of four different departments. During my fieldwork I have learned to see the MM as a region of borders, meaning that everywhere is a point of intersection and encounter of very different cultures.

AREDMAG's radio stations are supposed to play a role in contributing to the consolidation of a MM collective imaginary. But are they? Some of the visual and verbal narratives elicited by the memory workshops provide some answers:

> Well, one element that I see coming back again and again in all these drawings is the physical space of the territory, the place where we move, where we exist, where we are all together ... if we were to remember, especially those of us older than thirty, when did we start talking about *Magdalena Medio*? I remember my years as a student when you only heard the term *Magdalena Medio* as a military reference, to talk about a region of war, of armed conflict ... but this *Magdalena Medio*, this new term used to refer to this region has lost its war meanings little by little and is now used to refer to the geographical place, to this territory that little by little we are making our own, ... we are not from Antioquia, we are not from Santander, we are not from Bolívar, we are not from Cesar, we are from *Magdalena Medio*, even at

the national level, when we go to national meetings they don't say "there's the people from Santander;" instead they say "there's the people from Magdalena Medio" . . . and in one way or another the stations have contributed to this with their daily work . . . .[12]

This radio producer is aware that *Magdalena Medio* is a code-in-construction. The feeling of belonging to the *Magdalena Medio* is a product of daily interactions; in some way AREDMAG's community radio stations have contributed to cultivating the type of interactions and symbolic practices that will ultimately consolidate the collective imaginary of Magdalena-Medio-as-territory.

[Man – Barranca] I was working for a series called *Region of Life, Region of Sounds* together with Carlos Vásquez and Melba Quijano. And so they assigned me three topics: 'places of encounter,' 'tangible and architectural patrimony,' and 'architecture,' this last one having to do with parks, plazas, markets, all that. The first place I went to visit was Simití. I got there and I had no idea what to do about the 'places of encounter.' So I asked Sofía, and she told me that the *enramadas*[13] are important meeting places here in Simití … she was making me breakfast, and so I was listening to her while I was eating this awesome cheese *bollo* with scrambled eggs, coffee … so after that great breakfast I went to the wetlands and sure enough, at the *enramadas* (or *ramá*, like they pronounce it there) what I found was a heated discussion among about twenty fishermen, and their debate was all about if a doctor was more important than a teacher or visa versa. So immediately I turned on my mini-disk and began recording the discussion. Then I began to ask them questions, and at that very moment I realized that real journalistic work is not the great stories about major political figures, but it is here, among the people that produce our daily life, that produce everyday life in our region: a fisherman, a common person, talking and expressing himself, expressing his world, expressing his vision of the universe using his own languages, his own ways of naming things, his own ways of talking, of laughing, of gossiping. I took all that and produced a series of radio programs about Simití's *enramadas*.

[Man – Gamarra] I drew a fisherman as a kind of representation of our municipality; that and kids' and youth participation. The station's signal and its listeners. With this what I want to express is something that I always have in mind, something I want to bring back from memory, and it is one day when we wanted to dramatize for a radio program a story about these fishermen that found a statue of the Immaculate Virgen … they found it in the river … they threw their net and caught her. The question for us was, how are we going to reproduce the effect of the fishing net falling in the water? And so we went to the river with all our equipment, to capture the sounds ….

In these two narratives we can see how the very need to produce radio programs makes these radio producers shift their gaze and focus it on their own local contexts; this need to capture the local context using the technology induces them to search, capture, and reflect local identities. It is through these processes that community radio stations trigger processes that ultimately lead to the consolidation of a *Magdalena Medio* collective imaginary—understood as a shared notion of place, a notion of territory with its own identity grounded in historical context, geography, and cultural features.

Once all the 60 visual narratives had been posted on the walls the participants themselves seemed surprised at how much of the region had been expressed and captured in the drawings (see Figures 6.1 and 6.2):

> [all these drawings] exude the scent of our region ... just look ... everything we are is captured here ... our landscapes. Our mountains, our rivers, they are everywhere, they traverse every one of our stories, our region has a strong presence in every one of the scenarios where we produce community radio

Traversed by local landscapes—both natural and cultural—and also by the particular forms that armed conflict takes in the region, the feeling of belonging to the *Magdalena Medio* instead of one of the four departments, is shared and cultivated by AREDMAG's radio stations.

Specific features emerge to describe the *Magdalena Medio* as territory in the visual and verbal narratives. For these citizens' media participants, *Magdalena Medio* is acknowledged as a hybrid, as a site of cultural difference, cultural borders, intersections, and *mestizajes*. Higher altitude Andean cultures intersect with low-land riverine and coastal ones. In terms of ethnicity this means white *campesino* communities share the *Magdalena Medio* with Afro-Colombian peoples; cattle ranching communities with agricultural and fishing communities; however, ultimately the *Magdalena Medio* exists somewhere at the intersection between different ethnic groups, economies, and landscapes. Ultimately, as seen by its community radio people, the *Magdalena Medio* lives 'in the middle'—a place of *mestizajes*.

FIGURE 6.1. Visual narratives focus on local landscapes.

FIGURE 6.2. Visual narratives focus on local landscapes.

AREDMAG'S RADIO STATIONS AS CONFLICT MEDIATORS AND PEACEBUILDERS

The role of AREDMAG's radio stations in local processes of peace-making are complex, multifaceted, and context driven. In each different situation, the community radio station has found its own way to cultivate nonviolent conflict resolutions and to buffer or protect civilians from the negative impact of armed violence.

Citizens' Radio as Mediator in Inter communal Conflict

The radio stations of AREDMAG serve as peacebuilders in the region as they mediate among groups when everyday conflicts emerge that can easily escalate into aggression and violence. In all communities conflict is a necessary element of everyday life. However, in communities such as those of *Magdalena Medio*, where the violent resolution of quotidian conflicts has been legitimized and normalized for generations, simple conflicts can easily end in bloodshed. Tensions over the use of public space, or land tenure, or a community celebration can easily turn into violent episodes. In the narrative cited below we can see how the local radio station was used as a tool to mediate and help solve a conflict among local parties:

> [Man – Gamarra] I have drawn a lot that a government agency had assigned to some people.... But the owners completely neglected it, no one did anything with it for five or six years, until the radio station started a campaign against neglected vacant premises in the community, because they become a nuisance, invaded with tall weeds, a refuge for burglars, a place where people congregate to do drugs ... and all of a sudden, a bunch of houses appeared on the lot that had been vacant for so long. So a conflict started between the owners of the lot and the owners of the houses; lot owners wanting to vacate home owners and home owners refusing to leave the premise. This issue was brought to the radio station, and each party presented their arguments in front of the microphone, to the entire community. Meanwhile, the conflict escalated to such a level that at one point the two parties went at each other with machetes and sticks. So the radio station became involved as a mediator. What did the station do? We invited both parties again, to explain the entire case and their arguments in front of the microphones, and the station pleaded with both parties and the call-in listeners to find a non-violent way to resolve the conflict. Finally the home owners agreed to pay the lot owners for the land, but later the problem started again because the home owners were not paying the appropriate price; so the mayor had to be brought in. He decided to assign a new lot to the lot owners and to allow the homeowners to keep the land where they had built their homes.

This narrative shows how the communication space opened by the radio station impacts this local community's social fabric. The radio station creates a communication space that operates as a public sphere accessible to the parties in conflict. The station cultivates a space for nonviolent conflict resolution and encourages the parties in conflict and the listeners to find a nonviolent way to resolve the conflict. Clearly in this case the station had enough legitimacy within the community to be accepted as a mediator; both lot and home owners agreed to allow the station to intervene; both parties accepted the station's invitation to explain their position in front of the microphones and in front of their opponent; members of the community called in to offer their opinions and to propose conflict resolution strategies. The technology itself played a significant role because it forced the parties in conflict to face not only their opponent, but the entire community. Issues of public face and public legitimacy become salient when personal arguments have to be defended in a public arena as opposed to a private realm. When what I say can be heard by the entire community, my identity and social image is at stake. Anything I say will be used by my community to construct their image of me; in this sense, I have to be much more careful about what I say. This technology-mediated communication space allows subjects to engage in a process of self-reflection about the social image they want to cultivate, thus keeping impulsive hot tempers in better check.

Nevertheless, the station was not able to come up with a definitive solution to the conflict; local authorities had to be brought in. In this sense, the station is putting pressure on public authorities to assume their responsibility to protect and defend citizens' rights, and to help resolve community conflicts. However, if local authorities do not follow through with the commitments assumed on the radio, the station could ultimately lose its legitimacy in the community.

Citizens' Radio as Mediator in Conflicts Among Local Political Figures

A common theme that emerged in our study revolves around instances in which the radio stations play a role defusing conflict among opposing local political parties or political figures. During the first half of the twentieth century Colombia was marked by intense and violent conflict among the two traditional political parties (the Liberals and the Conservatives). As a result, the idea of solving political dissent by violently eliminating one's opponent has been 'normalized' in the Colombian imaginary. In *Magdalena Medio*, citizens' radio stations are playing a significant role by redirecting the resolution of political violence from the realm of violence and aggression to the realm of discourse.

[Man – Gamarra] (see Figure 6.3.) What I have drawn here is three political personalities—three candidates in the forthcoming election for mayor in our municipality—and, every time they talked to each other, or met in a public space, they began insulting each other; I drew little red bombs under them, because the situation was becoming a time bomb in our community. Seeing this, the youth collective at the radio station decided to organize what became known as the First Forum for Democracy in Gamarra; we wanted to seek ways to enhance peaceful coexistence in the municipality; that is one of our objectives. The three candidates agreed to come to the station and the Forum began at nine in the morning; it was supposed to end at ten, but the conversation was so exciting that the Forum kept going until twelve thirty; and the three candidates, who had insulted each other just ten minutes before the Forum started, left the station arm in arm—here [in my drawing] you can see them draped by the yellow, green and white of Gamarra's flag. How did we accomplish this? well, as the dialogue began, we realized that the three had gone to high school together; so they each began remembering all their escapades, when they skipped school together to go to the river, or to play pool . . . this changed the mood of the conversation, they felt at ease with each other, they began looking at each other as human beings, and not just as rivals in a political race ... we managed to lower the volume of the violent tone among the three candidates and to cultivate a more fraternal relationship. A woman —and school teacher—is the director of this program; she works with the radio production youth collective and the way she conducted the interview was key to our success.

FIGURE 6.3. Deflating aggression among political candidates.

The key, in this case, is the mediating role played by the program director. Originally, the producers of the Forum had planned thirty minutes during which the youth collective would ask questions about the candidates' own youth and school years; then more mature interviewers would take over to focus on more 'serious' subjects such as the candidates' political agendas. However, during the first part of the interview, the director realized that the young interviewers were enabling the candidates to find common ground around their teenage past. On the spot, she made the decision to change the production plan and to allow the young interviewers to conduct the entire three-and-a-half hour Forum.

This type of ad hoc knowledge—or communication competence—seems to have played a key role in this situation. First, the director was able to detect the emerging bonds of identification and solidarity among the political opponents; second, she valued these as the building blocks of conflict resolution and peace-building. She envisions peace as the product of quotidian gestures and interactions among the members of a collectivity; she understands the nature of these gestures and interactions, including nonverbal expressions, and, as she began detecting them among the three political candidates, she took the necessary decisions to nurture them. The radio station is simply allowing this community leader to use her competence and wisdom to intervene in the public sphere; her wisdom and competence are now part of the social and cultural capital with which the community of Gamarra will shape its future.

Citizens' Radios as Mediators in Conflict with Armed Groups

Without doubt the most dramatic and significant aspect emerging from our evaluation study is the role that citizens' radio stations play in processes of mediation and conflict resolution between the community and illegal armed groups. For decades the *Magdalena Medio* has seen a strong presence of armed groups and guerilla organizations. The Ejército de Liberación Nacional [National Liberation Army] (ELN) itself was born in 1965 in San Vicente de Chucurí, one of the *Magdalena Medio* municipalities. During the late 1990s right-wing paramilitary groups broke into the region with the intention of 'cleansing' it from left-wing guerrillas, which led to some of the highest levels of bloodshed in the history of Colombia. In the following narratives we begin to understand the complex role(s) that citizens' media can take in contexts of armed conflict. The first narrative says:

> [Man – Santa Rosa del Sur] Five years ago I had a horrible experience, when our station director, José Botello, was kidnapped by the ELN; they took him to the Serranía de San Lucas, fifteen hours away from downtown Santa Rosa. No one knew what had happened until a farmer who witnessed the kidnapping came to the station and told us. At the station we discussed what to do, because to say something on the air could make the station a military target of the guerrillas. But we decided to broadcast a press release where we

demanded that the captors respect his life and wellbeing as a civilian. As soon as we aired this, messages, letters, and official press releases from hundreds of local grassroots organizations and citizens began pouring into the station, all with similar demands and words of support for José. In all we got more than 1000 letters and more than 2000 signatures in a document that was sent to the President and also to the ELN. As messages continued to pour in, we shifted to a kind of sad musical selection as an expression of protest. The ELN responded with a challenge to the community: if we wanted José back, if it was true that the community loved him so much, the community had to go get him. Immediately the station began communicating this new demand and in six hours we had 480 people willing to travel the 20 hours to the place known as Micoahumado, high up in the mountains ... we gathered in more than forty cars and trucks; there were women, children, men, all carrying white flags . . . it looked like a snake of cars and trucks going up the mountain! We arrived at the camp and asked to speak with the *comandante.* They told us he wasn't there and we had to wait, so in no time we set up tents and began lighting fires ... we had brought pots and pans, potatoes, yucca, we bought a steer and we proceeded to feed everybody 'cause we were not going to leave until we reached a resolution. The next morning the so-called *comandante* showed up and we told him we needed José back, and not just his family but the entire community, as they could see; he didn't know what to do, so he called his superior and they told him to just make us wait, that we would surely give up and leave; when they real-

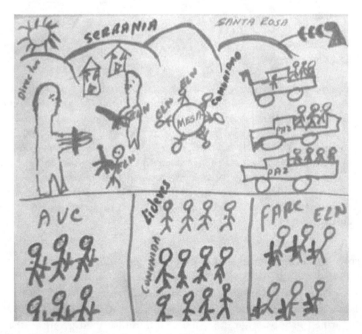

FIGURE 6.4. Rescuing José Botello from the ELN.

ized we were not leaving and that we had formed a negotiating commission, they freed José Botello . . . from beginning to end it was seven days of horror and seven days of hope . . . when we came back to Santa Rosa with José we had two days of festivities, everybody in the central plaza celebrating, which the station also transmitted live from the streets, thanks to our mobile unit.

The second narrative in this section comes from San Vicente de Chucurí, where right-wing paramilitary groups attempt to intimidate young men and women by imposing strict codes of fashion, hair styles, piercing, and everyday life practices and behaviors; for example, paramilitaries commonly forbid long hair for young men, low-cut jeans for young women, and piercing in general. Blacklists with the names of young people who defy these codes are then posted on visible public places, and if the questionable behavior continues, these marked youth can end up dead or "disappeared":

> [Man - San Vicente de Chucurí] Our communities are cornered by the terror imposed by armed groups. There was a moment in San Vicente where the black lists began multiplying, especially targeting those youth that wanted to be themselves. So one day I'm listening to the station and I hear this short message that addressed the black lists issue; all you heard was someone taking attendance and a second voice responding:
> —"so and so"
> —"present!"
> —"so and so"
> —"present!"
> —"so and so"
> And then, complete silence . . .
> "he is not here. He is on a different list!"
> The message was so strong! What I am expressing in my drawing is how the community is cornered and in the middle of all this the station is trying to open a communication space to play, to sing, to love, and also to scream, because we are all terrified but at the same time we are listening to these different proposals coming from the station. The station is playing an important role, especially for young people, who are the ones more affected by the war, and at the same time, they are the ones with different life options, alternative proposals, including their musics . . . they are using the station to put forward their voice and their proposals in the middle of the generalized terror and death.

As explained earlier, our evaluation methodology elicited qualitative data of two kinds: verbal and visual. Respondents were asked to add to their narrative with a drawing or collage that would express what they were trying to convey. The central theme of Figures 6.4 and 6.5 is the permanent state of siege imposed on civilians by armed groups. Figure 6.4 shows different armed groups—the ELN and

FIGURE 6.5. A radio station trying to offset the terror of war.

FARC guerrillas on one side and the paramilitary (AUC) on the other. The community is depicted literally in between these three armed groups. The drawing about San Vicente de Chucurí (Figure 6.5) shows the community surrounded by gigantic weapons that represent the strong presence and impact of armed groups in this municipality; these visual testimonies aptly express the intense levels of fear and feeling 'cornered' experienced by civilians confronted with the annihilating power of armed force. Ironically, even though the role of the station as an important voice in the community is stressed in both cases, it is depicted as a miniature entity. The visual narratives seem to be saying that although the station tries to maintain a communication space autonomous of the armed groups, it, too, feels intimidated and terrorized by these groups. The stations emerge as communication spaces for peace, but also a vulnerable space that exists in permanent tension with the presence of armed groups.

These two narratives express two very different ways in which the stations are contributing to peaceful conflict resolution with illegal armed groups in *Magdalena Medio*. In the first narrative the station mediated between the ELN and the community when a community leader was kidnapped; the station decided to make the kidnapping a public event, and not just a private tragedy that only affected the family and friends of the victim. The station addressed the entire community as victims of the ELN, and the community responded as a unified and very strong front. Assured by the resolute response from the community, the station decided to go one step further and engaged the guerrilla group in a process of negotiation. Clearly the station benefits from a high level of legitimacy among the local community; it is *because* the community feels one with the station and feels that the station is truly at its service that the station can trigger such a strong response (see issues of sustainability of community media as explained by Gumucio-Dagrón, 2003).

In this case, thanks to the station, the community was able to galvanize forces and to act collectively and peacefully to confront the guerrilla group. Here again the station has opened a communication space that can be used by the community on an *ad hoc* basis; peaceful conflict resolution emerges from communication and interaction, more as communication competencies that the community has learned to use in moments of crisis than as predesigned messages or communication strategies about peaceful co-existence (which is the case in most communication/media for peace projects).

The role of the station in the second narrative is of an entirely different nature. In a case of bravery (that could easily be suicidal), these young radio producers in San Vicente de Chucurí produced a high impact and well-designed message protesting the blacklists of paramilitary groups in their municipality; they protested the demonization of difference and the pressure to conform imposed on local youth. Here the station allows these young radio producers to open a communication space where difference is not only accepted but also celebrated, where being young means to be different, to explore, to play with and tease out social and cultural codes that are not yet legitimized.

CONCLUSION

Without doubt our evaluation methodology deviates from the traditional forms of evaluation implemented by most development projects in general and communication for social change initiatives in particular. It came as a surprise—to our academic team as well as to AREDMAG's board of directors—that the evaluation experts responsible for overseeing the European Union's Peace Research Lab projects not only accepted but also welcomed our evaluation methodology and its results. My feeling is that the lack of appropriate indicators and evidence is felt not just on the part of the project leaders but also on the part of international donors; in other words, it seems that all stakeholders in the field of social and cultural change are somewhat frustrated with traditional forms of evaluation and in search of new ones. In this sense we hope to make a contribution that others could adopt and adapt to different contexts, projects, and needs.

The narratives of citizens' radio producers of *Magdalena Medio* are clear evidence of how citizens' media open communication arenas in which conflict management has shifted from the realm of aggression and violence to the realm of discourse. I cannot stress enough that these are not communication discourses *about* mediation and conflict resolution; rather, they are communication spaces to be used to mediate and interact (Rodríguez, 2004). The stations are not sending messages to the community *about* how to solve conflict in nonviolent ways. Instead, the stations themselves are mediating conflicts; their communication competence is not being used to design messages about peaceful co-existence, but instead the stations are constructing peaceful co-existence through communication. Here, citizens' media open communication spaces in which communities can consider, experiment with, and witness other, alternative, nonviolent ways of dealing with conflict; other, alternative, collective imaginaries; other, alternative ways of interacting with others; and other, alternative, ways of understanding difference. In this sense, I am almost tempted to say we should call these 'alternative radio stations.' In sum, more than transmitting messages about peace and reconciliation, AREDMAG's citizens' radio stations are opening communication spaces in which peace can be performed, felt, learned, and appreciated. In *Magdalena Medio*, citizens' media's hope for the future rests on the assumption that individuals and communities who learn to perform and value everyday life and peace will protect it.

NOTES

1. A few sections of this chapter were published in Rodríguez, C. & Cadavid, A. (2007). From violence to discourse: Conflict and citizens' radio stations in Colombia. In R. Isar & H. K. Anheier (Eds.), *The cultures and globalization series. Volume I. Conflict and tensions* (pp. 313-327). Thousand Oaks, CA: Sage.
2. Many thanks to Orley Durán, Melba Quijano, Julio Oyos, Manfry Gómez Ditta, Omaira Arrieta, and all the other people from the citizens' radio stations in Magdalena Medio who believed in us and trusted us with their stories and their lives. It is thanks to their faith in the power of communication, their courage, and especially their love for Colombia that this text is possible.
3. OURMedia/NuestrosMedios emerged from annual conferences collectively organized by Nick Couldry (then at the London School of Economics and now at Goldsmith's, University of London), John Downing (then at the University of Texas at Austin and now at Southern Illinois University), and myself.
4. Brazilian philosopher Paulo Freire proposed a process of knowledge construction based on the inclusion of diverse voices and interpretations of social reality (Freire, 1980, 2005).
5. The level of ownership and appropriation of academic discourse has been so intense for some media activists that they are making their own—very successful—presentations about our evaluation study in Colombian academic circles. Also, as a result of participating in the evaluation study, a radio producer participant decided to enroll in a masters program.
6. All our time as researchers, the statistical work needed, and most of the fieldwork costs are funded by our universities and by a research grant from the Communication for Social Change Consortium; the media projects have used evaluation funds from inter-

national donors to cover research assistants in the field, photocopying, and some of their own time.

7. The municipalities of the Magdalena Medio are: Cimitarra, Landázuri, El Peñón, Puerto Parra, Puerto Berrío, Bolívar, Puerto Nare, Barrancabermeja, San Vicente, Bajo Ríonegro, Sabana de Torres, Betulia, El Carmen, Puerto Wilches, Yondó, Bajo Simacota, San Alberto, Aguachica, San Martín, Gamarra, La Gloria, San Pablo, Morales, Cantagallo, Santa Rosa del Sur, Simití, Río Viejo, Regidor.

8. Departments are the geographic units in which the national territory is divided; the Colombian equivalent to states in the United States.

9. For more information on the PDPMM see the web portal of the *Programa de Desarrollo y Paz del Magdalena Medio*, available at http://www.pdpmm.org.co (retrieved February 11, 2007).

10. These five communication collectives are in the process of securing a broadcasting license.

11. The academic team attempted to bring in the issue of ethnicity but—with good reason—the board shot it down because in a region strongly marked by mestizaje, it becomes impossible to delineate different ethnic groups. This actually became a source of many jokes in which board members questioned the value of certain academic discourses to interpret their social realities.

12. All testimonies are originally in Spanish.

13. Natural platform formed by trees on the wetland's shore.

REFERENCES

Aldana, W., Atehortúa Cruz, A., Correa, H.D., Escobedo, R., García, N., García, C., Pardo, A., & Romero, M. (1998). *Conflictos Regionales. Atlántico Y Pacífico* [Regional conflicts. Atlántico and Pacífico]. Bogotá: FESCOL and IEPRI.

Anderson, B. (1991) *Imagined communities: Reflections on the origins and spread of nationalism.* London & New York: Verso.

Behar, R., & Gordon, D. (1995) *Women writing culture.* Berkeley: University of California Press.

Berrigan, F., Hartung W. D., & Heffel, L. (2005) Promoting freedom or fueling conflict? U.S. military aid and arms transfers since September 11. A World Policy Institute Special Report. Retrieved November 14, 2006, from http://www.worldpolicy.org/projects/arms/reports/wawjune2005.html#6.

Cadavid, A. (2003). *Communication: Building nation from the regions.* Paper presented at the Global Fusion conference, Austin, Texas, October, 24-26 .

Clifford, J. (1983). On ethnographic authority. *Representations, 2,* 118-146.

Clifford, J., & Marcus, G. E. (1986). *Writing culture. The poetics and politics of ethnography.* Berkeley: University of California Press.

Conquergood, D. (1991). Rethinking ethnography: Towards a critical cultural politics. *Communication Monographs, 58,* 141-156.

Freire, P. (1980). *Educación Como Práctica De La Libertad* [Education and the practice of freedom] Mexico: Siglo XXI.

Freire, P. (2005). *Pedagogía del oprimido.* [Pedagogy of the oppressed]. México: Siglo XXI.

García, C. I. (1996). *Urabá: Región, Actores Y Conflicto, 1960-1990* [Urabá: Regions, actors and conflict]. Bogotá: CEREC.

García, M., & Uprimny, R. (1999). El nudo gordiano de la justicia y la guerra en Colombia [The Gordian knot of justice and war in Colombia]. In A. Camacho & F. Leal (Eds.), *Armar La Paz Es Desarmar La Guerra*. [To arm peace is to disarm war] (pp. 33-72). Bogotá: CEREC, IEPRI, and FESCOL.

González, F. (1994). Poblamiento y conflicto social en la historia colombiana [Population and social conflict in Colombia's history]. In R. Silva (Ed.), *Territorios, Regiones, Sociedades* [Territories, regions, societies] (pp. 13-33). Bogotá: Universidad del Valle and CEREC.

González, J. J. et al. (1998). *Conflictos Regionales. Amazonía Y Orinoquia* [Regional conflicts. Amazonia and Orinoquia]. Bogotá: IEPRI and FESCOL.

Gumucio-Dagrón, A. (2003). *Arte de equilibristas: La sostenibilidad de los medios de comunicación comunitarios* [The art of aerialists: Community media sustainability]. Paper presented at the OURMedia III Conference, Barranquilla, Colombia.

Guzmán, A., & Luna, M. (1994). Violencia, conflicto y región. Perspectivas de análisis sobre el Valle del Cauca y el Cauca [Violence, conflict and regions. Analytical perspectives about Valle del Cauca and Cauca]. In R. Silva (Ed.), *Territorios, Regiones, Sociedades* [Territories, regions, societies] (pp. 180-207). Bogotá: Universidad del Valle and CEREC.

Jimeno, M. (1994). Región, nación y diversidad cultural en Colombia [Region, nation and cultural diversity in Colombia]. In R. Silva (Ed.), *Territorios, Regiones, Sociedades* [Territories, regions, societies] (pp. 65-78). Bogotá: Universidad del Valle and CEREC.

Katz García, M. (n.d.). *A regional peace experience. The Magdalena Medio Peace And Development Programme*. Retrieved November 14, 2006, from http://www.c-r.org/accord/col/accord14/regionalpeaceinit.shtml.

Murphy, P., & Kraidy, M. (2003). Toward an ethnographic approach to global media studies. In P. Murphy & M. Kraidy (Eds.), *Global media studies. Ethnographic perspectives* (pp. 3-19). New York and London: Routledge.

Restrepo, E., & Escobar, A. (2005). 'Other anthropologies and anthropology otherwise': Steps to a world anthropologies framework. *Critique of Anthropology, 25*(2), 99-129.

Riaño-Alcalá, P. (1998). Recuperar las memorias y elaborar los duelos [Recovering memory and processing pain]. In I. Cepeda & C. Girón (Eds.), *Duelo, Memoria, Reparación* [Mourning, memory, reparation] (pp. 103-118). Bogotá: Fundación Manuel Cepeda.

Riaño-Alcalá, P. (1999). La piel de la memoria [The skin of memory]. *Nova y Vetera, 36*, 79-85.

Riaño-Alcalá, P. (2000a). Recuerdos metodológicos: El taller y la investigación etnográfica [Methodological memories: Workshops and ethnographic research]. *Revista de Estudios Sociales, 7*, 48-60.

Riaño-Alcalá, P. (2000b). La memoria viva de las muertes. Lugares e identidades juveniles en Medellín [Living memory of death. Place and youth identities in Medellín]. *Análisis Político*, 41: 23-39.

Riaño-Alcalá, P. (2003). Encuentros artísticos con el dolor, las memorias y las violencias: Antropología, arte público y commemoración [Artistic encounters with pain, memories and violences. Anthropology, public art, and commemoration]. In P. Riaño-Alcalá (Ed.), *Arte, Memoria Y Violencia. Reflexiones Sobre La Ciudad* [Art, memory, and violence. Reflections about the city] (pp. 19-60). Medellin: Corporación Región.

Riaño-Alcalá, P. (2006). *Dwellers Of memory. Youth and violence in Medellín, Colombia.* New Brunswick, NJ: Transaction Publishers.

Riaño-Alcalá, P. (2008). Seeing the past, visions of the future: Memory workshops with internally displaced persons in Colombia. In P. Hamilton & L. Shopes (Eds.), *Oral histories and public memories.* Philadelphia: Temple University Press.

Rodríguez, C. (2001). *Fissures in the mediascape. An international study of citizens' media.* Cresskill, NJ: Hampton Press.

Rodríguez, C. (2004, December 6). *Communication for peace: Contrasting approaches.* The Drum Beat, issue 278. Retrieved November 14, 2006, from http://www.comminit.com/ drum_beat.html

Romero, M. (2003). *Paramilitares Y Autodefensas* [Paramilitaries and self-defense militias]. Bogotá: IEPRI And Editorial Planeta.

Rosaldo, R. (1989). *Culture and truth. The remaking of social analysis.* Boston: Beacon Press.

Sánchez, G. (2001). Introduction. Problems of violence, prospects for peace. In C. Berquist, R. Peñaranda, & G. Sánchez (Eds.), *Violence in Colombia, 1990-2000. Waging war and negotiating peace* (pp. 1-38). Wilmington: Scholarly Resources.

Sen, A. (1999). *Development as freedom.* New York: Alfred Knopf.

Tacchi, J.; Slater, D., & Lewis, P. (2003). *Evaluating community based media initiatives: An ethnographic action research approach.* Paper presented at the OURMedia III conference, Barranquilla, Colombia. Retrieved November 14, 2006, from www.ourmedianet.org

Uribe, M. V. (1992). *Limpiar La Tierra: Guerra Y Poder Entre Los Esmeralderos* [Cleaning the land: War and power among emerald extractors]. Bogotá: CINEP.

Van Oeyen, V., & Geerts, A. (2004). *La Práctica Inspira.La Radio Popular Y Comunitaria Frente Al Nuevo Siglo* [Practice that inspires. Popular and community radio in the new century]. Quito, Ecuador: ALER.

SECTION III
Examining Internal Structures, Dynamics, and Forms

INTRODUCTION TO SECTION III

Ellie Rennie

An irritating question hangs around community-based media, afflicting the domains of critique and practice: "Why can't it work better?"

The chapters in this section take on the internal structures of community media organizations. They address concerns of efficiency and process and raise deeper issues to do with the exclusivity of communities and the egalitarian ideal of participatory media. Examining the structure of community media organizations may seem perfunctory—a matter for committees and regulators rather than practitioners and theorists—but it can also lead us to the heart of 'our media' and the assumptions we make about it.

The structure of community media has an importance beyond the day-to-day running of a media outlet: it includes the mechanisms by which participation and access are achieved, ultimately facilitating the circulation of ideas that might not otherwise become part of the public sphere. When community media made it onto the international communications agenda in the 1970s, 'access' to the media began to be discussed not only in terms of nonprofessional content, but also as community participation in the management of stations (International Commission for the Study of Communication Problems, 1980). Bolivian miners' radio was raised as one potential model. From its haphazard beginnings in the 1950s, miners' radio remained local, independent, self-funded, and established to meet the needs of a particular community. This organizational structure ensured that the miners received politically important information (such as news of impending military attacks) and culturally relevant entertainment (O'Connor, 2004). Self-governance thus became an important goal, the primary means to what was expected to be the production of significantly different media content. Since that time, community media has expanded and diversified, experimenting with and instituting various organizational models along the way. It has also attracted its share of critics who have questioned whether community governance is the most efficient means to the circulation of new ideas. Why does participation by ordinary folk necessarily lead to alternative, democratic communication? What obstacles do community media groups face?

Two examples are presented in this section. The first chapter discusses community radio in Australia, which has grown in both size and diversity over the course of its 30-year history. The principle of participation guides the structural character of community radio; community broadcasting licenses specify that stations must be owned and operated by the community to which the license was granted and that they are run as not-for-profit enterprises. This regulatory structure has accommodated a diverse range of communities across the political spectrum and allowed for some degree of flexibility in station management. As this chapter demonstrates, issues such as non-commercialism, community representation, quality, and training continue to be played out—tensions that define the sector as much as its achievements.

The remaining chapters discuss Indymedia, a global, Web-based network committed to open publishing, a system whereby anyone can upload written articles, audio, or video content to the site with minimal gatekeeping. As well as providing a simple, no-cost means for activists to publish first-hand accounts and publicize events, Indymedia seeks to be transparent and egalitarian in its processes. The authors in this section discuss the importance of Indymedia as an activist network, and how new technologies have helped extend practices in that field. They also examine the issues arising out of these practices, revealing that although Indymedia may have eliminated some hierarchies, it has also inadvertently created new structures that encourage exclusivity and elitism within the group. Communities are not inherently democratic structures—even with the right principles, self-critique and internal challenges will cause dissension and hopefully correction.

COMMUNITY ORGANIZATION

The unique internal structures of community media organizations are an attempt at what can be termed "community governance" (Rose, 1999). Community media fits within a wider sphere—often called the third sector or civil society—which has a different system, or technology, of governance to commercial enterprise and government provision. The concept of 'community' includes social ties or networks, group affiliations, and loyalties. It can be a disparate, confusing domain that, at first glance, appears to function in spite of rules or political constructs. However, its advocates see community as a sphere that, with some nurturing and regulation, can provide a level of social coherency not otherwise achievable. We do not live as isolated individuals, concerned only for our own welfare (as a society based purely on commercial interaction would suggest), nor do we need to rely entirely on government when it comes to building institutions that work in the public's interest. Community advocates see a role for groups and networks in the provision of independent support and services and for the maintenance of a healthy and vibrant public sphere (or spheres). If our political systems take this into account and provide communities with the resources they require to function (in the case of community radio this might mean broadcast licenses and spectrum), then a fairer, more equitable society will result. If we, as citizens, dismiss community—or consider it only a by-product of individual liberty—we risk instituting policies that may result in social fragmentation, isolation, and economic division. Community media therefore endorses community governance in that it aims to maintain and progress community concerns, valuing community expression as a necessary alternative to public service and commercial media (Rennie, 2006).

Therefore, a starting point for identifying community organizations is that they will aspire to put group concerns and maintenance before individual gain. Legal mechanisms, such as not-for-profit status and democratically elected boards may be adopted in order to ensure that the community is adequately represented. Even in the absence of legally binding structures, a community organization will develop rules or practices designed to work in the interests of the group. To expect community media to perform in the same way as the professional media is to deny this inherent difference.

So what outcomes flow from the democratic structures of community media? The chapters in this section discuss changes in the relations between media producers and consumers as well as the production and circulation of community-centered content. Community media organizations do not generally differentiate between the audience and those qualified to speak to them. Through participation, consumers (audiences) of the media become producers, or readers become writers. Participation provides a means to self-expression and learning, potentially transforming the individual's status or power. However, community media cannot be defined by participation alone. Individuals can become reader-writers outside of community media formations as can be seen by the user-generated content that is appearing across various media forms, public and private. What distinguishes community media is that community involvement takes place at the governance level, with consequences for content and social change (for instance, community development and new social movements). Community media encourages individual expression but seeks to extend this to others via accessible systems and structures.

The implications for content are somewhat difficult to gauge. In early discussions of community media, democratically structured media was justified as a means for the production and circulation of alternative viewpoints. Giving ordinary citizens a voice, it was hoped, would stimulate diversity and challenge the increasing homogeneity of mainstream outlets. The first chapter in this section successfully demonstrates that community involvement does have consequences for content and audiences. Through focus groups with community radio audiences, Michael Meadows and his colleagues have found that listeners consider community stations as familiar, a 'part of the family,' and can perceive interaction between the audience and producers. This research also uncovered substantial support for community radio's less formal methods of content production as well as local and alternative viewpoints. However, researchers generally have abandoned hope that community media might somehow reverse tendencies in the commercial media towards networking and ownership concentration. As the Australian example demonstrates, the growth of community media has coincided with a loss of localism and ownership diversity in the commercial radio sector, a trend that looks set to continue across the globe.

In addition, the chapter charts the various subsectors of community radio, portraying the diversity of stations and the circumstances under which they operate. Many of these stations are far from 'radical,' although station managers still identify provision of access and participation to community groups as the primary contributions of community radio. This suggests that a dedication to community organization in the media realm is not limited to alternative, anarchist, or socialist ideals, but may stem from the broader desire to sustain a sphere of activity beyond government and the economy. The chapter states that not all community stations see themselves as *necessarily* resisting the mainstream. In fact, some aspire to mainstream status in terms of both programming and philosophy—but they work within the discursive arena of the local community or from a perceived minority status.

ALTERNATIVE MEDIA ORGANIZATION

The internal structures of alternative media organizations will often reflect their political objectives. Consensus decision making, collaboration in production, and attempts to flatten management hierarchies deliberately invert commercial mechanisms at every stage of the production process. Where community media organizations emphasize participation and openness, alternative media take this a step further, identifying themselves as 'disorganizations,' collectives, or networks in a direct challenge to the perceived establishment (Atton, 2002). This does not necessarily make alternative media more representative than commercial or public service media. Even with democratic structures in place, this media is essentially representative of the group involved, rather than society as a whole. Downing usefully describes democratic, consensus-led media as 'zones' that stand deliberately outside of the capitalist order. This is a form of prefigurative politics, "an attempt to practice socialist principles in the present, not merely to imagine them for the future" (Downing, 2001). In other words, alternative media seek the experience of a different social order, designing their groups and processes accordingly.

The Internet has provided an opportunity to develop new practices and technologies that progress these goals. The end-to-end structure of the Internet (which means that information can pass without needing to go through a central point) allows for access and participation on a global scale. Although many web applications have been built with gatekeeping mechanisms that result in selective access or payment for use and so forth, movements such as the free software movement and open publishing create spaces for common use (Stallman, 2002). Indymedia has been one such space, in that it enables people to publish with minimal editorial interference and even to collaborate in the development of the technology itself. By keeping the source code visible and available for reuse and adaptation by other groups, Indymedia propagates an ethic of open architecture and extends its network.

As a result, Indymedia has been discussed as a 'communications commons,' a space that exists for the benefit of the community that anyone can use. The commons concept is a fairly recent addition to communications theory (Kidd, 1998; Lessig, 2001). Traditionally, a 'commons' might be a stretch of land designated for communal use, where participants might grow crops or graze cattle without infringing on the rights of others to do the same (Neeson, 1993). It signifies a different order to individual ownership—the prevailing property model of contemporary democracies—in that it privileges collective activity and shared resources over private property and individual authorship. Although a commons is accessible, it is not a 'free for all' and will have its own set of agreements and rules of conduct (which may be informal) set out by the community that uses the space. The communication commons can also exist outside of electronic media. Zines, for instance, will often encourage readers to photocopy and distribute at will, defying copyright norms (Atton, 2002).

The second chapter in this section (Skinner, Uzelman, Langlois, & Dubois) examines the limitations that Indymedia Centres (IMCs) face in their attempt to perform as sites of resistance. The authors compared three IMCs in Canada, groups that vary in their processes and size. Issues such as fund-raising, editorial control, and volunteer recruitment are shown to be potentially divisive, raising issues of noncommercialism, censorship, and whether such groups can continue in perpetuity. The chapter shows how a diversity of models and standards characterize the community media sector even at the most alternative end of the spectrum.

The article by Brooten and Hadl demonstrates the way in which seemingly horizontal structures that are intended to promote access can inadvertently create their own hierarchies. Even with policies of consensus decision making and antidiscrimination, Indymedia groups can inadvertently sustain dominant personalities, which devalue and silence others. The authors discuss how a culture of critique and dissent favors a masculine perspective, which can result in victimization and exclusion of some members. The language of 'independence' hides power structures and "allows those who hold power (however informal) to ignore the responsibilities of that power". Jones and Martin similarly analyzed the power structures within Indymedia U.K., showing that technology in and of itself does not lead to media democracy. IMCs rely upon technical expertise—knowledge that is likely to be contained to a small group within the collective. This can be used to dominate and determine the group's direction and exclude existing or new participants. Seemingly small issues, such as who has access to the passwords required to alter how the site works, reveal the potential for dominance.

These dynamics can destroy a community organization. An IMC in Brisbane, Australia, was shut down by the regional Oceania group (on the advice from IMC Brisbane founders) for infringements of the IMC Code of Conduct. In the documentation of this drastic move, hostility, mistrust, and bullying appear to have become entrenched in the group, causing irreparable damage. It goes to show that communities are not immune from power plays and narrow-mindedness. Like state-based democracy, community groups require constant vigilance, self-reflection, and transparent structures. This does not mean that alternative media is unachievable or that it fails in what it sets out to achieve. As the authors in this section point out, the democratic ambition of alternative and community media inspires self-critique and renewal. This is inconceivable for hate-based or propaganda media (Downing, 2001). Although community media groups can still fall victim to inconsistencies, factional differences, misinterpretation, and human failings, these instances are not what distinguish them from other organizations; it is their attempt at democracy and participation that produces some extraordinarily important and unique results.

The final chapter also discusses some of the problems that community researchers face. During the course of their research, Jones and Martin were categorized as 'outsiders' and were blocked to collect data by one of the group's founders. Attempts to expose and understand the internal dynamics of alternative media organizations can be met with suspicion and hostility from practitioners. Not only are universities sometimes perceived to be elitist and politically influenced (which is possibly true), alternative organizations will often reject researchers who claim 'expertise' and use it to define and direct the field or bolster their own status. But it is also the case that understanding the unique structures of community media can help us to better understand its aspirations and achievements. Without such research, community media will continue to be judged against the commercial and public service media, according to inappropriate criteria. For that reason we need to stop asking "why can't it work better?" and concentrate our efforts on why it works the way it does.

REFERENCES

Atton, C. (2002). *Alternative media.* Thousand Oaks, CA: Sage.

Downing, J. D. H. with Ford, T. V., Gil, G., & Stein, L. (2001). *Radical media: Rebellious communication and social movements.* London: Sage.

Kidd, D. (1998). *Talking the walk: The communications commons amidst the media enclosures.* Unpublished doctoral dissertation, Simon Fraser University, Burnaby Canada.

Lessig, L. (2001). *The future of ideas: The fate of the commons in a connected world.* New York: Random House.

International Commission for the Study of Communication Problems. (1980). *Many voices one world: The MacBride Report.* Paris: UNESCO.

Neeson, J. M. (1993). *Commoners: Common right, enclosure and social change in England, 1700-1820.* Cambridge: Cambridge University Press.

O'Connor, A. (Ed.). (2004). *Community radio in Bolivia: The miners' radio stations.* Lewiston: The Edwin Mellen Press.

Rennie, E. (2006). *Community media: A global introduction.* Lanham, MD: Rowman & Littlefield.

Rose, N. (1999). *Powers of freedom: Reframing political thought.* Cambridge: Cambridge University Press.

Stallman, R., Lessig, L., & Gay, J. (2002). *Free software free society: Selected essays of Richard M. Stallman.* Cambridge, MA: Free Software Foundation.

MAKING SPACES
Community Media and Formation of the Democratic Public Sphere in Australia

7

*Michael Meadows, Susan Forde,
& Jacqui Ewart, and Kerrie Foxwell*

I see the role of community radio to be or I believe it should be based on exactly what it is saying: community radio and community involvement opportunities for the community, serving the community, educating if you want to . . . informing, entertaining but with the community always in mind. It obviously goes beyond that as well but that is the basis. I think that is a good way to start myself. Even providing opportunities for the community, because every one of us belongs to a community. (Melbourne Community Radio Focus Group, 2001)

Community media around the world are attracting increasing attention from audiences who see them as genuine alternative sources of information to dominant forms of media. The term 'community' is itself problematic, taking on many different meanings from place to place, culture to culture, including 'local,' 'access,' 'radical,' 'alternative,' 'rural,' or 'nonprofit.' Although such media have tended to emerge where communities are denied access to existing forms of expression, this in no way seems to limit the desire by communities to seek their own voice. Community media include all manner of communication technologies—from the 'old' forms like radio, television, video, popular theater, and print to 'new' technologies such as videoconferencing, photocopying, fax, SMS (text messaging), and, of course, the Internet (Magno, 2002). Our concept of 'community' will be interrogated a little later in this chapter, but suffice it to say here that it is a definition that embraces the multifarious ways in which a wide range of extraordinarily diverse 'communities of interest' *define themselves.* In this chapter, we are concerned with the nature of local radio in Australia produced by such 'communities of interest' whether limited by geographic, linguistic, social, political, or cultural boundaries.

The rise of community media outlets and the subsequent increasing research attention given to them and their products is undoubtedly linked to the content crisis currently being experienced by global mainstream media. At the same time as profit margins increase for major media conglomerates, their audiences have been in steady decline—particularly in the daily newspaper market. In the United States, the majority of journalists seem unhappy with the state of their profession, primarily because of the increasing impact of commercial pressures on their work. Two-thirds feel that increased economic pressure is 'seriously hurting' the quality of news coverage and eroding the quality of journalism and news (Kovach, Rosenstiel, & Mitchell, 2003; Pew Research Centre for the People and the Press, 2003). The emergence of community media has been touted as the "most vibrant and hopeful response to the trend towards globalization and commercialism" because local communities identify more strongly with local cultural issues (Herman & McChesney, 1997: 200). This is strongly supported by early findings from the first qualitative audience study of the Australian community broadcasting sector (Forde, Meadows, & Foxwell, 2002). The evidence suggests, too, that community media may be the only sector that is actually growing in the Western mediascape, and their connection to the local may be a critical reason for this growth.

The number of community radio stations in Australia now surpasses the number of commercial broadcasters. In 2006, Australia had 483 licensed, independent, community-owned and operated radio stations with a further 37 temporary and aspirant broadcasters. Around 120 of these produce programs in 97 different ethnic community languages. There are 96 stations producing Indigenous programming and an additional 80 Remote Indigenous Broadcasting Services (RIBS) serving communities in the vast, sparsely-populated areas of regional and remote Australia covering most of the continent although most are engaged in retransmitting available satellite programming, both mainstream- and community-produced (AICA, 2006; CB Online, 2006; Community Broadcasting Foundation, 2006). The community broadcasting sector includes four, long-term community television license holders in Brisbane, Sydney, Melbourne, and Perth with two community television stations operating on open narrowcasting licences[1] in Adelaide and Lismore.[1] In addition, there is the Aboriginal-owned and run Indigenous Community Television (ICTV), which reaches an increasing number of regional and remote communities with the facility to downlink the satellite signal (PY Media, 2006). A federal government commitment of an additional AUD$48 million over four years to develop a National Indigenous Television service was under discussion at the time of writing (Department of Communication, Information Technology and the Arts, 2006). By comparison, there are currently 261 operational commercial radio licenses operating around the country (Gardiner-Garden & Chowns, 2006).

Quantitative audience surveys in 2004 and 2006 have revealed that around four million Australians listen to the Australian community radio sector for an average of 7.5 hours each week with twice that number tuning in each month (McNair, 2004, 2006). This is a startling result, supporting the largely anecdotal evidence that has flowed in from sector activists for a decade or more. It offers concrete evidence of the significant reach and influence of what has been termed the third tier of Australian broadcasting. Commercial radio, which uses markedly different criteria to define its 'consumers,' claims to reach around 80% of Australians who tune in for around 2.5 hours each day (Commercial Radio Australia, 2006). Clearly, community radio in Australia is a significant and growing cultural force.

In this chapter, we will outline the nature of community broadcasting in Australia using both qualitative and quantitative methods. Although quantitative research alone can be useful in determining demographics—numbers of stations, listeners, programming hours, for example—our approach here is more holistic, seeking to answer the 'how' and 'why' questions: Why do people engage with community radio? What are their expectations? How are these expectations being met? What role do stations play in creating or expressing community culture? Complementary qualitative and quantitative approaches, we argue, enable us to critically assess the full impact of this burgeoning sector. The first major study of the Australian community radio sector (Forde, Meadows, & Foxwell, 2002) revealed the important cultural role local stations were playing in disparate communities around the country. But what was lacking from that first investigation was information about audiences. Our current work seeks to address that void.[2]

THE AUSTRALIAN MEDIA ENVIRONMENT

The cultural importance of alternative, independent, or 'citizens' media' is particularly pertinent in relation to the present Australian mediascape—arguably the most concentrated in the Western world. There has been a shift in the past ten years away from strict, centralized and government-controlled broadcasting regulation to an 'arm's length' regime in which broadcasters take more responsibility for determining and monitoring broadcasting standards. This approach by the Australian Broadcasting Authority (now called the Australian Communications and Media Authority) has accelerated the transformation of citizens to consumers, narrowing the range of public sphere debate. A movement towards concentration of media ownership in Australia began early in the 20th century and has resulted in the establishment of 'irrevocably commercial'—and conservative—press and broadcasting sectors in Australia. Media control is primarily in the hands of Rupert Murdoch's News Corporation (newspapers, pay television, magazines, book publishing, film production, online news, recording industry production, National Rugby League, and Australian Associated Press); John Fairfax Holdings (newspapers and magazines); and Australia's richest man, Kerry Packer's Publishing and Broadcasting Limited ([PBL; television, pay television, magazines, cinema exhibition, online news, and gambling interests). Late in 2006, further relaxation of ownership rules by the federal government heralded another phase in Australia's media concentration stakes—one in which questions of program diversity seem to be taking a back seat (Australian Government, 2006). This is exactly where community radio can claim to have filled a growing void. In addition, the global trend towards falling daily newspaper circulation is reflected in Australia where it has dropped by more than 50% since 1950—evidence of fragmenting audiences along with the creation of monopoly newspaper markets in all but two of Australia's capital cities (Schultz, 1994).

Australia's broadcasting system emerged in the early 1920s and became a hybrid of the United States virtually unregulated and Britain's highly regulated approach. Within a few years, separate commercial and government-funded radio sectors had been established. The first television station in Australia in 1956 (in time for the Melbourne Olympics) was commercial, just preceding the government-funded Australian Broadcasting Commission channel to air. The commission became the Australian Broadcasting Corporation (ABC) in 1983, 51 years after its inception. The ownership pattern in the Australian broadcasting industry followed that of the newspaper industry, and since the late 1980s, Australian commercial television has been controlled by three corporations—Seven Network Ltd (television, pay television, publishing, and online interests), Publishing and Broadcasting Limited (PBL), and Ten Network Holdings (television and advertising interests). Ownership is more diverse in the commercial radio sector, although several large organizations control the profitable city-based FM licences (*Communications Update*, 2005). Radio reaches about 95% of Australians, with an average of five radio sets per household. Satellite delivery of program content remains a central organizing element of national networking for all Australian television stations along with ABC radio. Australia first launched its own domestic communications satellite—AUSSAT—in 1985 following pressure from commercial television stations. The community radio sector established its own satellite distribution network—ComRadSat—in 1993. It offers a range of core programs to community stations that subscribe, along with a 24 hour, seven-days-a-week national feed for participating stations. Around 180 community radio stations access ComRadSat in varying degrees. Stations pay a quarterly flat fee, based on their income, to access available programming (Community Broadcasting Association of Australia, 2005).

Community radio—first known as public radio—emerged in the mid-1970s through lobbying by a collection of fine music, education, and left-wing political groups. In 1992, Australia's 50-year-old broadcasting legislation was remodeled into the Broadcasting Services Act, creating seven discrete categories to cater for a diversifying broadcasting environment. 'Community' was one of the categories identified in Section 15 of the legislation, defining it as free-to-air, nonprofit, and community-orientated (Broadcasting Services Act, 1992). Australia's growing multicultural community gained access to two specialist community radio stations in 1975, leading eventually to the establishment of the Special Broadcasting Service (SBS) in 1980 and its national free-to-air multicultural television channel in 1984. Albeit with a limited audience, SBS TV broadcasts English language–subtitled programs translated from 60 languages and is still the only Australian 'mainstream' broadcaster to openly adopt a policy of antiracism. Within a few years of Pay TV's introduction in 1995, company names linked to these 'new' stations bore a striking resemblance to those in the so-called 'free-to-air' sector. Pay TV (or 'cable') reaches less than one-quarter of Australian homes (Gardiner-Garden & Chowns, 2006). Both the ABC and the SBS have been under sustained funding pressures from indifferent federal governments who seem persuaded by the economic rationalist approach that treats media like any other business, regardless of its role. So like many other countries around the world, publicly funded broadcasting in Australia is under threat. Recent moves to lift restrictions on foreign and cross-media ownership in Australia have created even more opportunities for mainstream media dominance.

This is the modern Australian communications environment in which minority voices have increasingly turned to community media to find communication spaces.

A COMMUNITY PUBLIC SPHERE

The community media sector is a cultural resource that facilitates cultural citizenship in ways that differentiate it from other media. Embodied in this process is the nature and definition of the term, 'community.' Rodríguez (2001: 164) warns that the polymorphic nature of community or citizens' media rejects tight definition and offers a useful framework, describing citizens' media as the result of "a complex interaction between people's attempts to democratize the mediascape and their contextual circumstances." Downing supports this notion in his theorization of 'radical' media. He acknowledges (2001: 3) that popular cultures "are not automatically oppositional or constructive" and defines radical alternative media as constituting "the most active form of the active audience" expressing "oppositional strands, overt and covert, within popular cultures." The community radio sector in Australia is unique in that it incorporates a broad range of popular cultures. It represents views ranging from the extreme left to the far right with the majority of stations identifying with middle of the road politics. So in this way, it does not easily fit into definitions drawn from particular social, political, and cultural arenas because all are represented. Perhaps the common bond is that each subsector sees itself as operating in a particular public sphere in which it is viewed as a minority.

Following on from this, rather than adopting the idea of a single, all-encompassing public sphere, we might think of media operating in terms of a series of parallel and overlapping 'public arenas'—spaces where participants with similar cultural backgrounds or 'communities of interest' engage in activities concerning issues and interests of importance to them (Fraser, 1992: 126). This, then, helps to define our notion of 'community' in terms of how we use it in this chapter. Communities of interest articulate their own discursive styles and formulate their own positions on issues that are then brought to a wider public sphere where they are able to interact "across lines of cultural diversity" (Fraser, 1992: 126). What we might term a 'community public sphere' or 'community public arena' could be seen as a discrete formation or space that develops in a unique context and is the product of contestation with the mainstream public sphere. And, as Fraser (1992: 127) reminds us, "the unbounded character and publicist orientation of publics allows people to participate in more than one public, and it allows memberships of different publics to overlap." It is clear from our research in Australia that not all community stations see themselves as *necessarily* resisting the mainstream. In fact, some aspire to mainstream status in terms of both programming and philosophy—but they work within the discursive arena of the local community or from a perceived minority status. Rodríguez' concept of 'citizens' media' provides some support for our idea. She urges us to move beyond definitions of community media that rely on *what it is not* and to consider the "transformative processes they [media] bring about within participants and their communities" (Rodríguez, 2002: 79). Thus, community media should not be seen as the starting point for organizing people, but rather as an extension of an *existing desire to communicate* to establish a sense of personal and community power (Hochheimer, 1999: 451).

This transformative process is clearly evident in some Indigenous and ethnic media enterprises where production practice and organization have strong links to traditional community frameworks (Morris & Meadows, 2001; Roth, 2005). A national inquiry into broadcasting acknowledged in 2000 that Indigenous media in Australia was providing 'a first level of service'—in other words, the primary media service—to its communities as well as acting as a 'cultural bridge' between Indigenous and non-Indigenous people (Productivity Commission, 2000: 3). Our recent audience research has underlined this critical role. So how have the transformative processes evident in the community media sector elsewhere been given substance in Australia?

THE AUSTRALIAN COMMUNITY RADIO SECTOR

Community radio emerged in Australia in the mid-1970s on the newly available FM band. In line with similar developments with the independent press, the sector has seen the rise of Indigenous and multicultural radio—claimed as the world's most linguistically diverse (SBS, 2006)—and local community radio serving a wide range of communities of interest. Community broadcasting has become one of the largest growth sectors in the Australian media industry (Forde, Meadows, & Foxwell, 2002: 9-19).

Station Demographics

The vast majority of community radio stations in Australia produce general programming, with the remainder divided into specialist groupings: Christian, Indigenous, radio for the print handicapped, fine/classical music, ethnic, and educational. By the turn of the new millennium, almost 65% of community radio stations in Australia were broadcasting in more conservative regional areas. These are sparsely populated zones outside major urban areas that tend to hug the eastern and southern coastline of the continent. Around 20% of community stations are in capital cities with a further 15% in near-city areas. The emphasis on broadcasting to regional Australia is partly a response to the increasing withdrawal of local commercial radio from nonurban areas, leaving community radio as the only source of local news and information for many small towns around the country. This shift to servicing regional Australia—generally more conservative politically than urban areas—could explain trends in political preferences that emerged from our study. Overall, the sector considers itself more left of centre than right of center, although it is most likely to place itself in the middle of the road politically. However, at the time of our survey (2000), the voting intentions of station managers would have resulted in a conservative federal government being re-elected—which is precisely what happened in 2004 (Forde, Meadows, & Foxwell, 2002: 1-7). These responses can be clearly contrasted with findings from a study of the independent press in Australia, which found journalists and editors were overwhelmingly from the 'left' side of the political spectrum—almost 65% identified with the left, with only 11% nominating 'middle of the road' as an apt political description (Forde, 1998).

Personnel Demographics

The average community radio worker in Australia is male, over 40 years of age, and probably lacks a university education. He is most likely to have been born in Australia of British or Irish descent and is most likely to place himself politically in the 'middle of the road.' He is slightly more likely to vote for the left-leaning Labor Party, although if he is a station manager, he is slightly more likely to be a supporter of conservative politics. Almost two-thirds of people working in the community radio sector are male, and this is consistent with other areas of media work. Almost 69% of community radio workers are over 40, and nearly 41% are over 50. There is some concern throughout the sector over the small proportion of younger people working as volunteers, although several stations that specialize in youth issues (radical news, current affairs, and music, etc.) do have higher proportions of young people on staff. Compared to the general Australian population, community radio workers are reasonably well-educated. Almost one-third have completed tertiary (university) study, and about 40% have at least some level of tertiary study. This compares with about 15% in the general population with a university degree. Almost half of community radio workers have at least some form of post-school qualification, comparable with the figures for the general population.

Three-quarters of community radio workers were born in Australia, which reflects almost exactly the proportion in the broader Australian community. A further one in 10 community radio workers were born in Britain, which is slightly above the general population figure of 6%. About 2% of community radio workers were born in either Africa or Asia, with continental Europe comprising the most popular non-Anglo/Celtic place of birth. More than 50% of station managers are volunteers and of these, about one-quarter are pensioners or retired from full-time work (Forde, Meadows, & Foxwell, 2002: 21-34).

Almost two-thirds of respondents in our survey reported producing 100 or more hours of local programming each week. On average, Australian community radio stations have 65-70 regular volunteers. A conservative national estimate of regular volunteering would be 20,000 regular unpaid participants. This is equivalent to around AUD$145 million a year in work for the Australian community. Community radio workers spend two and a half times longer at their work than general volunteers working across the country. This is indicative of a focused, committed workforce and suggests a significant contribution by community radio in providing many in Australian society with a sense of belonging and identity. Unlike most other nations, Australia has developed discrete community broadcasting legislation with the overall aim of encouraging community access and participation in broadcast media.

More than 90% of radio station managers identified (without prompting) "provision of access and participation to community groups" as the important contribution their station makes to the local community. Other identified roles included a commitment to community cultural events and 'other contributions' to the community, including the representation of 'specialist groupings' such as ethnic communities, young people, and so forth. 'Other contributions' frequently referred to the station's existence as a local alternative to mainstream radio stations and as a forum for broadcasting local music (Forde, Meadows, & Foxwell, 2002: 21-34).

The community sector undertakes an extensive training role, with around 4,000-5,000 people involved annually in mostly unaccredited programs. Around 70% of the sector is engaged in training programs involving external organizations, usually universities. There is a significant flow of trained personnel from the community radio sector into mainstream media organizations. However, the important training role being undertaken by community broadcasters remains largely unacknowledged by either the government or the mainstream media sector (Forde, Meadows, & Foxwell, 2002: 63-81).

Funding

The major focus of conflict across the community media sector in Australia is in trying to balance station independence with an increasing need to generate funds from local sponsors. Although there are some paid positions within community radio stations, 30% of stations operate entirely on a volunteer basis and 35% of stations employ three people or fewer. The majority of paid positions are in sales and administration. Thus, volunteers, rather than paid staff, are responsible for program/content production. Unlike commercial broadcasting, service to smaller and heterogeneous audiences characterizes community radio. Community radio volunteers often see themselves as a "community within the station as well as a community outside the station" (Melbourne Focus Group, 2001). Ironically, it is the diversity of aims and audiences that unites the sector. Annual funding for permanently licensed stations from the Federal Government Department of Communication, Information Technology and the Arts (DCITA) has remained virtually on the same levels in real terms since 2000—at around AUD\$22,000 per station. Overall, the funding for the sector has fallen in real terms since 1996, with the 2005-2006 federal government contribution just under AUD\$8 million—a fraction of the sector's total income (2003-2004) of around AUD\$51 million (CB Online, 2006: 12; *Community Broadcasting Foundation*, 2006: 2). This has placed increasing pressures on community stations to generate their own funds through sponsorship announcements, subscriptions, donations, and/or other events. As a result, stations are finding it increasingly difficult to remain afloat without significantly adjusting content to attract a larger audience. Some stations feel this is forcing them to adopt more commercial formats, which is against the principles of community radio as outlined in the Broadcasting Services Act. Many focus group participants voiced concerns that this commercialization will further compromise program production, with more controversial material being abandoned in favor of programs that please local sponsors. On the other hand, there is a strong feeling across the sector that it has to become independent of government, and many participants see an increase in local sponsorship as the answer. Under the terms of the Broadcasting Services Act, community stations cannot carry advertising. They can run sponsorship announcements only (mentioning only the name and address of the sponsor), and these are limited to five minutes per hour (Forde, Meadows, & Foxwell, 2002: 95-108).

Diversity

Given the shared philosophy of access and participation across the sector, there are some significant differences in the services offered by regional and metropolitan areas. In the cities and large towns, there are often several community stations that serve specific communities. For example, in Brisbane 98.9 FM is an Indigenous station that has focused on country and Indigenous music, attracting an audience of around 100,000. Radio 4MBS caters for fine music tastes (from jazz to opera), 4EB caters for ethnic groups, and 4ZZZ caters for 'alternative'/marginalized groups and opinions and local music and arts talent, particularly for young female listeners (Meadows & van Vuuren, 1998). Metropolitan stations perform a different cultural role in their communities. As one metropolitan volunteer commented, "city stations see their role as 'alternative' because there is no point in replicating that which already exists [in mainstream radio]" (Adelaide Focus Group, 2001). Regardless of location, the strategies employed to service local communities are often taken for granted in the day-to-day operation of Australia's community broadcasters:

> We have a local news as well as a national news service. We have community announcements, we have interviews, and just comments that presenters make on air about things, etc. We have our council that's actually involved with the station and is supportive of the station. They have airtime talking about issues. We have our local member talking about things, so it's through a whole range of things. A little bit of talk back, from time to time. (Brisbane Focus Group, 2001)

Not enjoying a similar 'critical mass,' regional stations often adopt a generalist format catering to a local geographic community and/or to communities of interest within the region. Further, regional stations are often the only local broadcasters and thus serve a broader or more diverse community than their metropolitan peers. There are around 30 regional areas in Australia in which community radio now provides the only radio service. As such, stations like these play a critical role in disseminating local news and current affairs and information about cultural events (Forde, Meadows, & Foxwell, 2002: 35-46).

Australian and Local Content

Around 80% of community stations broadcast a news service, although this is usually syndicated. The sector's own satellite-distributed National Radio News (NRN) service is the most used, followed closely by commercial networked news from either the Macquarie or Southern Cross news networks. National Radio News is run by three full-time journalists working with journalism students at Charles Stuart University, Bathurst, in New South Wales. Around 90 community radio stations take the news feed each day, compiled from a variety of local and international sources (including the BBC World Service). Overall, around one-fifth of the community radio sector is producing original news and current affairs, in most cases, on a daily basis. Those stations that produce their own content are providing high levels of training for their workers in news and current affairs production, and a large number of the workers or volunteers have formal training in journalism. The news and current affairs services are strongly anchored in their communities of interest, with news workers relying heavily on local meetings, conversations, regular contacts, and local newspapers for story ideas. Three-quarters of the news and current affairs produced by the sector is specifically relevant to the local community, and news workers feel they have complete autonomy to select and report on stories of importance. Additionally, the majority of workers producing local news identify provision of this service as their station's most important role, along with its ability to provide 'alternative' information from mainstream media. These ideas resonate strongly with those of their counterparts in the independent press sector.

The production of Australian content, such as radio drama, poetry readings, live recordings of Australian music, new Australian classical music, and regular support of local theater and literature, is clear evidence of the contribution community radio makes to Australia's cultural landscape. The network of 'fine music' stations has long-standing strong connections to the arts community through their support of Australian composers and live recordings of new jazz and classical music. With Christian radio stations making up around 15% of community stations across Australia, this network has made concerted efforts to link with relevant local arts communities, particularly with musicians and theater groups. There are several national projects funded by the federal government and designed to facilitate the development of contemporary Australian music for broadcast on community radio via the sector's satellite channels (Forde, Meadows, & Foxwell, 2002: 43-44; Owens, 2000: 3-4).

INDIGENOUS BROADCASTING

The community sector has proved to be a major communications outlet for Indigenous voices in Australia, with around 80 licensed stations in remote regions broadcasting more than 1,000 hours of Indigenous content weekly and a further 50 stations in regional and urban areas. There are three Indigenous narrowcast radio services (one is an open narrowcast licence) and an Indigenous commercial radio station. Aboriginal and Torres Strait Islander people have won access to the airwaves following persistent campaigns. Most major urban and regional areas have an Indigenous broadcaster complementing existing media. In addition to the community stations, there are two Indigenous radio networks. The National Indigenous Radio Service (NIRS) was launched in 1996 and enables Indigenous community radio stations across Australia to either link into national programming or choose to broadcast locally. In 2001, the National Indigenous News Service (NINS) began operating out of studios in Brisbane, providing a general, independent, national news service that features Indigenous stories and Indigenous perspectives on general news (Molnar & Meadows, 2001).

Community broadcasting is the largest component of Indigenous media in Australia. The value of hearing local voices and stories is difficult, if not impossible, to quantify and is the distinguishing feature of all community broadcasting. This is particularly evident in the report of the national review of Indigenous media, *Digital Dreaming* (ATSIC, 1999). Where local radio production was being undertaken regularly, stations were perceived to be playing an important role in maintaining local cultures and languages. Where local and culturally appropriate frameworks are used to structure community media, then these media become part of the local community, that is, part of local culture. For example, 5UMA (Port Augusta, in South Australia) estimates there are 10 Indigenous languages still spoken in the area, and two have been chosen for broadcast because of their intelligibility across many tribal groupings. The station prides itself on covering Indigenous issues in these languages and in 'plain English,' thus accommodating those in the Port Augusta community for whom English is a second, third, or even fourth language (Forde, Meadows, & Foxwell, 2002; Port Augusta Focus Group, 2001).

ETHNIC BROADCASTING

The National Ethnic and Multicultural Broadcasters' Council (NEMBC) identifies 104 stations (58 regional and 42 metropolitan) across Australia producing in excess of 1,700 hours of local programming weekly in 100 different languages (NEMBC, 2006). Ethnic media have become core elements of Australia's multicultural society—both the government-funded arm (SBS) and the community arm. Notably, the community arm produces about three times as much broadcast content as the government-funded SBS (Francis, 2001). Our most recent research has revealed innumerable practical examples that demonstrate the pivotal role played by ethnic and multicultural broadcasters and the crucial community services they perform—confirmed by focus group discussions with audiences from 10 different language communities.

In late 2000, when a group of Albanian refugees were brought to Australia to escape the Kosovo conflict, Radio 3ZZZ in Melbourne arranged an Albanian language program to be delivered each day to inform the refugees of happenings in their home country as well as their status in Australia. In the Tasmanian capital, Hobart, radio station 7THE responded to the needs of Albanian refugees and found journalists within the refugee community. Volunteers from the station drove 40 minutes each way to pick up the Albanian journalists to enable them to deliver their programs (Hobart Focus Group, 2001).

More recently, our research has revealed the critical role played by ethnic community radio in providing access to specialist information about Australian society for specific audiences, as well as promoting cross-cultural understanding for the broader Australian community. This has been identified by audiences as central to the role of multilingual ethnic community radio, identifying it as an essential service. Ethnic community radio audiences see it as especially important at a time when Australian government policy towards refugees has been seriously questioned by human rights organizations locally and internationally (Filipino Focus Group, 2006; Forde, Meadows, & Foxwell, 2002: 55-60; Macedonian Focus Group, 2006; Turkish Focus Group, 2006).

AUDIENCE RESEARCH

In November 2004, the first national quantitative audience study of the Australian community radio sector startled critics (mainly commercial broadcasters) by reporting that around one quarter of Australians (4 million listeners) tuned into community radio each week—and the figure increases to almost 50% over a month. The survey of 5,000 people around Australia revealed that almost 700,000 people were *exclusive* community radio listeners. The study found audiences fairly evenly split on gender lines (male 53%; female 47%) with just over half aged 40 and above (McNair, 2004). Two years later, the national survey was repeated—confirming the data gathered in the earlier study (McNair, 2006). Although numbers alone are limited in what they can tell us about 'how' and 'why' people listen and/or watch, for example, there is little doubt that the community radio sector in Australia has attracted a significant audience.

Preliminary findings from the first qualitative audience study of the sector in late 2006 suggest strong support for the important cultural role being played by community radio in Australia. Responses from around 50 focus groups and scores of 'key people' interviews (individuals and organizations who use community radio and television) have enabled us to delve more deeply into the processes that create and sustain communities. Local radio has clearly become a central organizing element of Australian society.

Audiences have welcomed diversity in programming—from talk to music— and have articulated significant support for alternative ways of receiving factual information through individual programs rather than using traditional formats such as news bulletins. And they are emphasizing the importance of community radio providing an alternative by focusing on local rather than global news events, arguing that existing publicly funded organizations like the Australian Broadcasting Corporation (ABC) and the Special Broadcasting Service (SBS) already provide independent sources of news and information and have the resources to cover national and international news—so why should community radio compete (Bay FM Focus Group, 2005)? One focus group participant summed it up like this:

> ... news isn't just, you know, 'bombs went off in London' or 'the football.' I mean, we don't have to listen to endless shows about football or cricket. I

mean, it is your definition of news. There's a lot of news on it [the station] but it's not necessarily the way it can be defined on other stations. (3RRR Melbourne Focus Group, 2005)

Our research has revealed an extraordinary level of passion for community radio, with almost all audience focus group participants describing their relationship with a local station as like being 'part of a family.' Others speak about the strong appeal of 'ordinariness' in being able to identify with a presenter or a person being interviewed on air. Many confess they would be 'devastated' if their local community radio station went off air (Bay FM Focus Group, 2005; 3RRR Focus Group, 2005). These are powerful indications of the varied ways in which audiences are engaging with community radio. It suggests that a high level of interaction—either perceived or actual—between audiences and producers would seem to be fundamental to the very definition of community radio. It suggests a significant dismantling of the idea of an audience-producer barrier.

One stark example comes from Indigenous audiences in north Queensland. In November 2004, Aboriginal people on Palm Island, near Townsville, stormed and burned down a police station on the island following the death in custody of a young local man. Whereas mainstream media have branded the incident 'the riot,' Indigenous voices on the Indigenous airwaves speak about 'the resistance' with a locally produced and nationally broadcast talkback program, *Talkblack*, providing listeners with views other than those from sources such as state politicians and the police—in short: 'black voices and black issues' (Palm Island interviewee, 2006). The program won an award for the best coverage of Indigenous Affairs at the 2006 Queensland Media Awards. Indigenous audience representatives have identified their community radio as the only real alternative available to them in such times of community crisis. One avid listener captures the feelings of many when he observes:

> I think the only tool the community has to use is using places like 4K1G [a local Aboriginal radio station] to make sure that what was being brought out of the Palm [Island] community as a whole was projected in the right manner, not in a negative manner. That's only one part of the importance of Murri [Aboriginal] media or Indigenous media. It provides places like Palm, Woorabinda, the Cape [York] and other Indigenous communities, particularly the Indigenous population in the mainstream, with a voice, a balance, projecting our stories, our culture, our language the way we want to hear it but giving it to the wider audience too, people who live in the mainstream, people who don't often come in contact with Indigenous people. (4K1G listener, 2005)

There is strong evidence from other audience focus groups to suggest that the multiple roles of community radio are not confined to the Indigenous sector alone. Preliminary analysis of audience responses are not only reinforcing earlier perceptions of the sector and its role, but also extending our understanding of community radio *processes* by providing an insight into the often intimate, diverse, and intensely personal relationships listeners have developed with their local community radio stations in Australia. Audiences are telling us of the significant role played by community radio—and *only* community radio—in crisis situations like floods, bushfires, and major weather alerts; of dealing with multiple deaths in a community by offering on-air counselling for listeners; of offering the alternative views of 'citizen journalists' who challenge mainstream versions of events; by providing listeners with a sense of community likened to being part of a family; and of rejecting globalizing information processes in favor of what affects the local and the everyday lives of listeners.

Audiences in the ethnic community radio sector reveal similar responses: the importance of radio in maintaining languages and cultures, sustaining community networks, and providing a crucial medium for music. Focus group participants identified the prime importance of community radio in providing new immigrants with local news in their own languages *as well as* information from their countries of origin. It suggests an important unifying element inherent in this extraordinarily diverse sector.

Conflict is not entirely absent from the sector: there is tension between individuals, subsectors (generalist, indigenous, ethnic), dissatisfaction with some aspects of the representative body—the Community Broadcasting Association of Australia—and awareness of pressure to perform with minimal levels of government funding. But as the annual conference each year confirms, an extraordinary level of cooperation is a hallmark of the community media environment in Australia. Our audience study confirms this, revealing overwhelming support for the current direction stations are taking. Although our audience research participants were to a large degree self-selected (listeners to particular stations were invited to nominate for focus groups), the wide range of stations involved in the study, a 'theoretical sample' (Glaser & Strauss, 1967; Macnaghten & Myers, 2004: 68) and random selection minimized possible bias. The single most obvious critique offered by audiences, sector-wide, was simple—they want more of the same: diversity, 'ordinariness,' accessibility, local music, news, and information. All of these core elements are notably absent from, or devalued by, mainstream media.

CONCLUSION

When broadcasting first began in the early 1920s, it came with a promise of real communication between audiences and producers. But, instead, it has delivered mostly a one-way information flow. The emergence of Australia's unique independent broadcasting sector challenges this. The very idea of focusing on local audiences has meant that community media must be a part of local communities of interest. They cannot exist otherwise. And if they are part of local communities, then they play an important cultural and political role because they are part of community culture. Any suggestion of taking media away from communities where it is well established brings a lively response. One *Anangu* elder spoke proudly of community television started in her communities in the remote central desert in the early 1980s. She speaks of media and culture as one (APY interviews, 2006):

> Travelling in any way in the country, they can listen to music; they can put a TV there—make everybody happy; make everybody awake and think about the land: this is my grandmother's land; this is my *tjamu's* land; this is my *kami's* land, my grandfather's and grandmother's and uncle's and mother's. That's the media we started for *Anangu* children and we can't give it to anybody.

How local media achieve this and the form they take varies widely across Australia, with each working to reflect the community of interest being served. For this to work, communities must establish a process—through dialogue—that enables the diverse elements of their community to work together to produce a 'citizens' media,' and thus, 'public arena' activity. Rather than blindly copying outside models, independent media 'invent' their own ways of making sense of the world.

As national and commercial media policy shifts continue to abandon or neglect remote and regional Australia in favor of more cost-effective urban-centered infrastructure, community media have taken on an increasingly important cultural role—providing communities with a first level of service. Producing community broadcasting might be thought of as a *process* of cultural empowerment, and it may be that the *ways* in which community media facilitates community organization are more important than content production per se. Community broadcasting in Australia 'imagine' notions of culture and citizenship through shared meanings, values, and ideals. Put simply, it is a process of 'making sense' of the world and our place in it. In this way, community media workers *both produce and maintain* the culture of a community and in doing so play a central role in creating a community public sphere. Community media are thus resources for building multiple and complex media and cultural literacies through participation on a localized and personalized scale. As Hochheimer (1999) reminds us, community broadcasting should not be seen as the starting point for organizing people, but rather as an extension of an *existing desire to communicate* to establish a sense of personal and community power. Through the processes and practices we have outlined in this chapter and are slowly beginning to understand, community broadcasting plays an important cultural role by encouraging dialogue between diverse 'public arenas'—a unique way of 'making spaces' integral to formation of the broader public sphere and enhancing the democratic process.

NOTES

1. Open narrowcasting licences are offered by the Australian Communications and Media Authority to broadcasting services with a limited and specified audience reach. The limits could be special interest, location, time frame, or audience appeal. For more detail, see http://auction.acma.gov.au/current_projects/lpon/index.asp, retrieved November 23, 2006.
2. Focus Group Discussions and listener interviews: Brisbane, 27 April 2001; Melbourne, 28 June 2001; Warrnambool, 29 June 2001; Hobart, 1 July 2001; Adelaide, 4 July 2001; Port Augusta, 6 July 2001; Albany, 10 September 2001; Bay FM Byron Bay, 26 August 2005; 3RRR Melbourne, 12 July 2005; Katherine FM Katherine, 4 August 2005; 4K1G Townsville and Palm Island, 19-21 August 2005; APY interviews Umuwa, 27-28 October 2006; Turkish Focus Group, Melbourne, 4 April 2006; Macedonian Focus Group, Melbourne, 3 April 2006; Filipino Focus Group, Darwin, 13 June 2006.

REFERENCES

AICA (2006). Australian Indigenous Communication Association: About. Retrieved November 23, 2006, from http://www.aica.asn.au/.

ATSIC. (1999). *Digital dreaming: A national review of indigenous media and communications. Executive summary.* Canberra: Aboriginal and Torres Strait Islander Commission.

Australian Government. (2006). Meeting the digital challenge: Reforming Australia's media in the digital age. Discussion paper on media reform options. Retrieved November 23, 2006, from http://www.dcita.gov.au/__data/assets/pdf_file/37572/Media_consultation_paper_Final_.pdf.

Broadcasting Services Act (1992) Retrieved November 23, 2006, from http://www.austlii.edu.au/au/legis/cth/consol_act/bsa1992214/.

CB Online (2006). Community broadcasting database: Public release report. Retrieved November 23, 2006, from http://www.cbonline.org.au/index.cfm?pageId=37,0,1,0.

Community Broadcasting Foundation (2006) Annual report. Canberra: Department of Communications, Information Technology and the Arts.

Commercial Radio Australia. (2006). Commercial radio. A snapshot. Retrieved November 23, 2006, from http://www.commercialradio.com.au/ssl/documents/ACF41FF.pdf.

Communications Update (2005, April). Media ownership update.

Community Broadcasting Association of Australia (2005). Community radio network: Australian community radio satellite network. Retrieved November 23, 2006, from http://www.cbaa.org.au/content.php/199.html.

Department of Communication, Information Technology and the Arts. (2006). Backing indigenous ability. Retrieved November 27, 2006, from http://www.dcita.gov.au/communications_for_business/funding_programs__and__support/connect_australia/backing_indigenous_ability.

Downing, J. D. H., with Ford, T. V., Gil, G., & Stein, L. (2001). *Radical media: Rebellious communication and social movements.* London: Sage.

Forde, S. (1998). *Reviving the public sphere: The Australian independent and alternative press industry.* Unpublished doctoral dissertation, University of Queensland, Brisbane, Australia.

Forde, S., Meadows, M., & Foxwell, K. (2002). *Culture, commitment, community: The Australian community radio sector.* Brisbane: Griffith University.

Francis, B. (2001). Personal interview with the authors, July 5, 2001.

Fraser, N. (1992). Rethinking the public sphere: A contribution to the critique of actually existing democracy. In C. Calhoun (Ed.), *Habermas and the public sphere* (pp. 109-141). Cambridge: MIT Press.

Gardiner-Garden, J., & Chowns, J. (2006). Media ownership regulation in Australia. Retrieved November 23, 2006, from http://www.aph.gov.au/library/intguide/SP/Media_Regulation.htm .

Glaser, B. G.., & Strauss, A.L. (1967). *The discovery of grounded theory: Strategies for qualitative research.* Chicago: Aldine.

Herman, E., & McChesney, R. (1997). *The global media: The new missionaries of corporate capitalism.* London: Cassell.

Hochheimer, J. L. (1999). Organising community radio: Issues in planning. *Communications: The Journal of European Communication Research, 24*(4), 443-455.

Kovach, B., Rosenstiel, R., & Mitchell, A. (2003). A crisis of confidence: A commentary on the findings. In *Pew Research Center for the People & the Press national survey of journalists* (pp. 27-32). Washington DC: Pew Research Center.

Magno, A. (2002). Seeing is believing: Using new technologies to change the world. Videotape/website produced by Necessary Illusions, CBS Newsworld, and SRC/RDI. Retrieved November 23, 2006, from http://www.seeingisbelieving.ca/ .

McNair, I. (2004). Community broadcasting audience survey. Retrieved November 23, 2006, from http://www.cbonline.org.au/index.cfm?pageId=44,149,3,941 .

McNair, I. (2006). Community broadcasting audience survey. Retrieved November 23, 2006, from http://www.cbonline.org.au/media/mcnair_survey_06/National_Fact_Sheet.pdf.

Macnaghten, P., & Myers, P. (2004) Focus groups. In C. Seale, G. Gobo, J. F. Gubrium, & D. Silverman (Eds.), *Qualitative research practice* (pp. 65-79). London: Sage.

Meadows, M., & van Vuuren, K. (1998). Seeking an audience: Indigenous people, the media and cultural resource management. *Southern Review, 31*(1), 96-107.

Molnar, H., & Meadows, M. (2001). *Songlines to satellites: Indigenous communication in Australia, the South Pacific and Canada.* Leichhardt: Pluto Press.

Morris, C., & Meadows, M. (2001). *Into the new millennium: Indigenous media in Australia.* Final Report. Brisbane: Griffith University.

NEMBC. (2006). National Ethnic and Multicultural Broadcasters Council. Retrieved November 23, 2006, from http://www.nembc.org.au/ .

Owens, J. (2000, January 14). Report to the contemporary music project committee of the community broadcasting foundation, pp. 3-4.

Pew Research Center for the People & the Press (2003). Press going too easy on Bush: Bottom-line pressures now hurting coverage, say journalists. *National Survey of Journalists.* Washington DC: Pew Research Center.

Productivity Commission. (2000). *Broadcasting: Final report.* Canberra: Ausinfo.

PY Media. (2006). Pitjantjatjara Yankunytjatjara Media Association. Retrieved November 23, 2006, from www.waru.org .

Rodríguez, C. (2001). *Fissures in the mediascape: An international study of citizens' media.* Cresskill, NJ: Hampton Press.

Rodríguez, C. (2002). Citizens' media and the voice of the angel/poet. *Media International Australia, 103,* 78-87.

Roth, L. (2005). *Something new in the air: The story of first peoples' television broadcasting in Canada.* Montreal: McGill-Queens University Press.

SBS (2006). Special Broadcasting Service Online. Retrieved November 23, 2006, from www.sbs.com.au .

Schultz, J. (1994). The paradox of professionalism. In J. Schultz (Ed.), *Not just another business* (pp. 35-51). Leichhardt: Pluto Press.

INDYMEDIA IN CANADA
Experiments in Developing Glocal Media Commons

David Skinner, Scott Uzelman,
Andrea Langlois & Frédéric Dubois

The Independent Media Centre (IMC) network, or Indymedia, has been touted as a major innovation in alternative media form. Since its establishment in the lead-up to the 1999 World Trade Organization (WTO) protests in Seattle, Indymedia has broken new ground in developing open and dialogic processes of news production and generating novel forms of organizational networking (Atton, 2003b; Downing, 2002, 2003; Kidd, 2003a, 2003b, 2004).

Focused primarily at the organizational level, this chapter considers these innovations in the context of the growth and operation of three IMCs in Canada.[1] Situating their development in the global Indymedia movement, it compares and contrasts their founding, structure, and operation, and the challenges they have faced in their growth from largely event-based sites established to document local protests to long-term 'glocal' open publishing media outlets that serve a range of interests operating at both (and between) global and local levels.

In the face of waning numbers and diminished activity at IMCs in Canada, as well as recent criticism regarding the content of IMC websites and the diversity of their collectives, this research considers the limits and pressures on their abilities to function as sites of resistance to dominant forms of social and media power, as well as whether or not the Canadian sites might be seen as part of a larger IMC social movement (Couldry, 2003; Rodgers, 2004; Whitney, 2005).

BACKGROUND

The first IMC was established in Seattle in November 1999 to cover the WTO meetings and protests and to provide a counterpoint to reports from corporate media, police, and other official sources. The media room acted as a dispatch center, workspace, and distribution point for over 400 media activists and independent journalists (Rinaldo, n.d.). Hundreds of hours of audio and video footage, as well as photos, written news stories, and background reports were produced using the Center's facilities. The IMC website drew over a million visits, and by the time the WTO meetings finished, the anticorporate globalization movement had established a new media voice (Galatas, 2001).

The Center's organizers coupled a long heritage of alternative media activism with nonproprietary open source software used by Australian activists to create a website that allowed anyone with Internet access to instantly upload text, photos, and digital audio and video files (Halleck, 2003; Kidd, 2004). This do-it-yourself 'open publishing' system challenged the hierarchical or vertical relationship between producers and consumers that characterizes traditional media by facilitating participation and dialogue.

The success of the Seattle IMC in providing a counterpoint to corporate media quickly led to a network of Centers being established around the world, most in connection with major demonstrations against institutions of global neoliberal governance.[2] Some of these projects were event-specific; others have continued to function as long-term community resources. At the time of writing, Indymedia.org lists more than 150 IMCs operating in 31 countries, with the bulk of them in North America and Europe.

Although there is often sharing of experience, expertise, software, and personnel—particularly in the start up stage—after joining the network IMCs generally operate autonomously. Although each collective crafts its own mission statement, IMCs are founded upon a shared set of ideals, or 'Principles of Unity,' by which all centers strive to operate. Among these principles are commitments to: operate on a not-for-profit basis; be 'non-hierarchical and anti-authoritarian' in terms of structure and process; build 'diversity' within their localities; use 'free (open) source' and nonproprietary software; be committed "to the principle of consensus decision making; the development of a direct, participatory democratic process"; be "committed to the principle of human equality," and avoid "discrimination based upon race, gender, age, class or sexual orientation" (Indymedia, 2001). IMCs also often share similar editorial principles, although each collective develops its own set of policies and procedures in this regard as well.[3] Some collectives have also developed specific governance policies and procedures, including anti-oppression statements, and membership and decision-making policies.[4]

But although the network is, in part, given form by common commitments to democratic practice and social justice, IMCs are very flexible organizations, and the kinds of activities they undertake can vary considerably from location to location (Herndon, 2003; Levy, 2004: 114; Mamadouh, 2004; Whitney, 2005). However, to better understand the structure and operation of these sites we must first review some of the distinctive characteristics of Indymedia and the qualities that set it apart from other alternative media projects.

PERSPECTIVES ON INDYMEDIA

Indymedia is often described as an example of a new movement in the context of an emerging networked civil society in which political ideals are combined with new information and communications technologies (ICTs) to help create a global network for the production and dissemination of news and information that is independent from corporate and state interests (Surman & Reilly, 2003; *cf* Castells, 2001).

Working along these lines, Kidd (2003a: 59-60) equates IMC activists with the commoners who struggled against the enclosure of common lands in precapitalist Europe and sees IMCs as part of an emerging 'global communications commons.' She argues that the "roots of the IMC derive from ... struggles over control of the cyber and terrestrial commons" and suggests that during its formative moments in Seattle, the IMC was the product of cooperation between four sets of contemporary 'commoners': antiglobalization social movements, local Seattle community activists, open source technicians, and activist media producers. The Seattle IMC drew upon a broad legacy of technical and organizational skills and "consciously built upon the experience of earlier networks, inviting many of the activists from the independent video, community radio, micro-radio, and open source movements to participate very early on in the planning, fundraising, and gathering of production equipment" (61). Together, these people worked to constitute a new media space "relatively autonomous from the direction of the corporate and state media, in which unpaid workers share cyber and real territories, labor time, and communications technologies, techniques, and techne" (Kidd, 2003a: 51).

This notion of 'relative autonomy' has also been taken up by activist-scholars who have used the term 'autonomous media' to highlight a particular political logic employed by IMC activists and others seeking to create new modes of democratic communication (Dyer-Witheford, 1999; Langlois, 2004; Langlois & Dubois, 2005). For instance, Uzelman (2002, 2005) distinguishes between 'alternative media' strategies and 'autonomous media' strategies. The former are employed by activists who focus primarily on media content by endeavoring to create new avenues for counterinformation or to open up existing media institutions to a broader range of messages. Autonomous media strategies like IMCs, on the other hand, in addition to creating new means of disseminating counterinformation, also focus heavily on the form and processes by which democratic communication occurs. They privilege radically democratic internal organization as well as participatory and dialogic forms of communication. In so doing, IMCs challenge not only the gate-keeping function of mainstream media but also the heavily professionalized, hierarchical, point-to-mass nature of corporate, public, and even many alternative media outlets. Uzelman (2002: 81) argues that, at the organizational level, these aspects of the IMC network impart relative autonomy not only from established forms of constituted power such as states and corporations but also from the logics of command and accumulation that drive them.

Further highlighting the organizational characteristics of the IMC movement, Downing (2002: 219) argues that Indymedia provides a refreshing counterpoint to the generally centralized and hierarchical Leninist model that dominated radical politics through much of the twentieth century. Instead, he argues IMCs are the somewhat unconscious inheritors of anarchist socialist thinking and share three key principles with that tradition: "the priority given to *movements* over institutions, the attention given to *pre-figurative* politics, and the place allocated to *direct* action" (original italics) (2003: 248). Although Indymedia is sometimes characterized as a movement itself, IMCs are most often associated with the anticorporate globalization or anticapitalist movements (Atton, 2003b; IndyMedia Documentation Project, n.d.). But IMCs are also points at which a range of social justice movements intersect—antiracist, feminist/women's, queer, environmental, peace, and postcolonialist—to name only a few. Because these radical politics inform both the structure and practices of these organizations, such that a commitment is made to provide 'safe' and egalitarian working environments, they are also sites of "pre-figurative politics" (Langlois, 2005).

Taking yet another perspective, although some authors, and indeed many IMC activists, characterize the network as a movement unto itself, IndyMedia can also be understood as a *tactic* drawn upon by a multiplicity of activists engaged in numerous, overlapping movements. To be sure, given its function in critiquing and bypassing the mainstream, corporate media, it can also been seen as one (particularly widespread and dynamic) element of a larger media democracy movement (*cf.* Hackett, 2000). However, thinking of IMCs as a tactic draws attention to the implicit strategy or logic of struggle guiding these interventions. For instance, Day (2005: 34-45) understands IMCs as a "non-branded tactic" similar in nature to Reclaim the Streets, Food Not Bombs, factory occupations, neighborhood assemblies and social centers in that no one has, or can, take ownership over these modes of political action and thus, proving effective in practice, they have been taken up by groups all over the world. IMCs thus represent the expression of a radical, nonhegemonic strategy or logic of struggle that aims not to extract concessions or reform by placing demands on the powerful but rather to take direct action in order to make the powerful, and the institutions that serve them, redundant (Day, 2005: 45).

EXPERIMENTS IN ORGANIZATIONAL FORM

Despite its seeming novelty, much of what has been undertaken by the Indymedia network is not new in either theory or practice. The participatory politics of the collectives' operations are rooted in a number of traditions, including socialist anarchism and Ghandian nonviolence (Downing, 2002: 219-222). As well, ideas regarding the horizontal possibilities of electronic media can be traced to at least the early twentieth century (*cf.* Benjamin, 1968; Vatikiotis, 2004). However, the ways in which the logics of participatory communication were carried into the context of the Internet has been innovative. In particular, Indymedia's commitment to open publishing and the critique of centralized forms of organizational control and the general gate keeping functions of the mass media that this practice carries, set it apart from both traditional and other Web-based media (Surman & Reilly, 2003: 33-35).

Open publishing software permits the widespread decentralization of work among many activists and independent journalists. As Atton (2003b: 54) points out, coupled with Indymedia's "non hierarchical methods of organization and its democratization of production techniques that encourage thousands of contributors," this global network "appears to successfully overcome the economies of scale that have for so long bedeviled print-based alternative media projects." Over the last several years the open publishing function of IMCs has been used not only to share reports from amateur journalists and 'native' reporters but also news and commentary, announcements, event listings, and Web-links gleaned from a wide range of sources. In this guise "Indymedia is a content aggregator ... a reducer and its activists (work) as editors and diffusers of radical news and opinion" (Atton, 2003a: 13).

Additionally Langlois (2005: 48-9) illustrates that the flexibility of the various generations of open source software underpinning Indymedia's open publishing project has also enabled collectives to adapt it to their own circumstances and values. From this perspective, she argues that "open publishing can be seen as a theory, or philosophy, which is put into practice, rather than a technology that determines how the Indymedia network develops" (2005: 49).

The practice of open publishing has not been without problems, however. In the wake of being bombarded with spam and racist, sexist, homophobic, and right-wing posts, many Indymedia collectives have wrestled with imposing editorial controls on the wide open character of open publishing (ChuckO, 2002; Jay, n.d.). Focusing on the nature of 'free speech,' these debates have often been long, drawn-out affairs and the source of dissension within many collectives. Where collectives have imposed controls, concerns over the exclusionary nature of these practices have been raised. Where controls have been eschewed, there are concerns that vitriolic content works to alienate and marginalize the people and groups targeted by these posts (*cf.* ChuckO, 2002; D'Annibale & Chehade, 2004: 371; Rodgers, 2004; Whitney, 2005). At the same time, concerns have been raised that increased moderation of the news wires will lead to a creeping professional-ization of news writing and editing (Kidd, 2004: 337).

THREE CANADIAN IMCS

At the time of writing there are links to eleven Canadian IMCs on the main Indymedia site. Of these, seven appear operational (Hamilton, Maritimes, Ottawa, Québec, Thunder Bay, Victoria, and Winnipeg). One has been shut down (Montreal), one is dormant and offline (Ontario), one (Vancouver) has been folded into a recently launched provincial site (BC Indymedia), and the status of the fourth (Windsor) is not clear.[5]

Based on both interviews with members of their respective collectives and the first-hand experience of the authors, this section examines the development and operation of IMCs in Hamilton, Québec, and Vancouver. These sites were chosen because they have been among the most active in Canada and provide both a regional and linguistic cross-section of Canadian IMCs. The interviews were conducted by the authors during the fall of 2004 and spring of 2005. Fourteen people were interviewed: three from Hamilton, five from Vancouver, and six from CMAQ in Montreal. These numbers include interviews with the most active members of these organizations during these times as well as 'self-interviews' conducted by authors Andrea Langlois (CMAQ), Frédéric Dubois (CMAQ), and Scott Uzelman (Vancouver), who were long-time working members of these collectives. The interviews were based upon two open-ended questionnaires that were comprised of over 100 questions and explored topics ranging from the history and operations of these organizations, the affiliations of the centers and their personnel, the technologies they deployed, and their roles in the production and circulation of public knowledge.

Founding, Structure, and Operation

All three IMCs examined here were founded in 2000 and were inspired directly by the events in Seattle. Each was also created in relation to a local protest, although the protests were different in scope and the centers came together under quite different circumstances.

Hamilton was founded by a group of men who had organized protests against a militaristic air show. After uploading a considerable amount of material to the Ontario IMC, they were approached by one of its founders and asked if they might like an IMC of their own.

The initial goal of the Vancouver IMC was to provide coverage of anticipat-ed protests against the Pacific Rim Biotechnology Conference and an accompa-nying counter conference/teach-in taking place in the city in the fall of 2000. A group of eight to ten people, three of whom had experience building IMCs in other cities, met weekly to establish process and policies. They struck a partnership with TAO Communications[6] to open a work space that was later also shared with a local alternative newspaper. For the first three months the IMC's share of the rent was donated by a member of the collective; after that the collective struggled to raise the rent.

The *Centre des média alternatifs* du Québec (CMAQ), also known as Indymedia Québec, was initiated by a man who worked for Alternatives, a Québec nongovernmental organization (NGO). He wanted to establish a center to cover the Summit of the Americas in Québec City in April 2001. He obtained a grant from the Québec provincial government to set up an IMC, and a website was running by October 2000. Because the organizers wanted a trilingual site and, at the time the Indymedia code was unable to accommodate this concern, a private company was hired to build it. The site was constructed using the company's own proprietary language, which, because it was not open source, became a problem in acquiring an Indymedia domain name and affiliation with the larger network. After several rounds of negotiations a domain name was obtained, and about six months later the site was converted to open source. During the Summit, CMAQ operated a media room in Québec City, following which this space was closed and a work space opened in Montreal. Alternatives continued to subsidize the operation of the Center for almost two years, supplying bandwidth and some personnel.

Although they have moved a few times, CMAQ has always had an office space. At the time of writing, their space and Internet access are provided by Québec Public Interest Research Group (QPIRG), at McGill University, as part of an exchange of services. Server-related costs are split with the computer collective Koumbit, which supplies services to a number of organizations, including CMAQ.[7] Vancouver maintained their office until the fall of 2002 when a lack of money and members led them to close the space. After that, the collective held sporadic face-to-face meetings in numerous locations. Alternatively, Hamilton has never had an office or physical space but holds monthly meetings to facilitate its work. CMAQ was a provincially registered nonprofit for three years and recently dismantled the legal entity; the other two organizations have no legal status.

The volume of content on each site varies according to the level of public and collective member participation, as well as local and global events. Although users contribute several stories and announcements to the newswires every day, interviewees from all three IMCs expressed concern that little content had been generated by the collectives in the year prior to our interviews. However, interviewees reported that, at times, the collectives have made marked contributions in distributing news that is ignored or underreported by the dominant media. For instance, although cameras are not allowed in Canadian courtrooms, in early 2001 the Vancouver IMC won the right to videotape and stream through their website the proceedings of an appeal by the Mexican government against a decision in which Metalclad, an American corporation, was awarded damages for lost profits under the North American Free Trade Agreement. In Hamilton, the collective regularly produced coverage of protests against the construction of the Red Hill Expressway—a highway slated for an environmentally sensitive area—as well as stories on the detention and 'secret trials' of several men detained in Canada under suspicion of links with terrorists. And in Montreal, CMAQ's coverage of student strikes in February/March 2005 over changes in the provincial government's education policy drew extensive comments and discussion from the community at large.

Even though content can be slow to change, the sites all appear to support reasonable traffic. According to interviewees, the Vancouver site receives 2-3,000 unique visits per day, and Hamilton and Montreal averaged 500-1,000 per day.[8] However, traffic can vary substantially depending on what is featured and what links stories have to other sites. It can also spike when protests are planned or expected.

Because of the online and volunteer nature of their organizations, interviewees found the size of their collectives hard to gauge. None of the collectives enact a formal membership policy, and not all the people who work on the Web sites attend meetings.[9] That said, as one might expect, participation appears to rise around large actions and at times of pronounced local activism. For instance, during the Summit of the Americas in Québec City, volunteers at CMAQ numbered in the hundreds. After the Summit, participation fell to about twenty people, and, in the year prior to the interviews, there appeared to be about 8-10 people involved. In Vancouver, membership has also fluctuated and interviewees' estimates of the number of active members there ranged from four to fifteen. In Hamilton, interviewees reported that the number of people in the collective has remained relatively steady over the last few years, with an average of six people attending monthly meetings and another six regularly contributing to the work and discussion on line.

Interviewees indicated that increasing the size of their collectives was key to increasing the content they produce and the range of activities they undertake. Although all three organizations had engaged a variety of methods to attract new members—including tabling at events, visiting schools and universities, and hosting public events—only Vancouver reported any ongoing or systematic efforts in this regard, and this without much success. Membership retention was also a problem. As a Vancouver interviewee noted, these problems may have arisen in part because "(t)here was no organizational capacity for welcoming and incorporating new members … (and new) people often don't have capacities to self-organize." Similarly, interviewees from the other collectives reported that new recruits did not generally have the skills or confidence to immediately become fully participating members and often drifted away after coming to one or two meetings.

As with most alternative media organizations, money is generally in short supply at IMCs (cf. Atton, 2002: 33-34). Moreover, the possible clash of values between potential donor organizations and IMCs makes fundraising a controversial activity.[10] Interviewees from both CMAQ and Hamilton expressed concern over the 'strings' that might be attached to possible sources of revenue such as grants, donations, or advertising. With a large unpaid bill for bandwidth, generating money to maintain their operations was particularly important to interviewees from Vancouver. But with expenses covered in both Hamilton and Montreal, fundraising was not a pressing concern. To meet expenses, all three IMCs have undertaken a number of small fundraising activities such as showing films, hosting music fundraisers, selling T-shirts, videos, stickers, and buttons. Using another NGO's society status, CMAQ received a few small grants that were used to pay bills and hire short-term employees. Members then acquired society status for CMAQ in order to be able to apply for funds independently of the parent organization.

The collectives' democratic nature was evidenced in the process underlying the development of their mission statements and editorial processes. Interviewees reported particularly extensive debates over editorial policies and what might comprise 'free' or admissible speech. But in the end, consensus prevailed, and all three collectives adopted positions that allow them to 'hide' or relocate offensive posts to less accessible parts of the website or delete them altogether, although there are variations in the editing process at each location.

Because editorial controls are generally based upon subject matter rather than quality, interviewees were generally not concerned about the possible 'professionalization' of content on their sites. However, some did report that differences in technical knowledge and access to the Internet limited the participation of some of their members in creating articles, performing editorial duties, and posting content to the sites.

Given Indymedia's commitment to social equality, an often voiced criticism is that young, white men are generally overrepresented in IMC collectives (Kidd, 2004; Rodgers, 2004). This was the case with the three considered in this study. In terms of both gender and, particularly, race, all three reported little diversity, although this too has fluctuated over time and according to events.[11] And although all the interviewees saw increasing diversity within their collectives as a priority, none had any specific plans or strategies in place to accomplish this goal.

Interviewees from Vancouver and Montreal also reported trouble with sexism in their collectives. In Vancouver, controversy focused on the participation of a man with a history of aggressive behavior toward women. At CMAQ, the posting of sexist material by a group of antifeminist men— self-styled 'masculinists'—precipitated heated debates over editorial policy. These incidents contributed to problems in maintaining a solid base of volunteers in both collectives.

Networking

The interviews revealed networked relationships at a number of different levels. For example, all three IMCs reported a range of relations with other Indymedia collectives. As noted, Hamilton was in part founded by someone from another collective. In addition, Hamilton's site has been hosted by a server located and maintained by IMCs in New York State. Recently, Hamilton set up their own server and began to host IMC Cyprus. CMAQ sent people to help start new alternative media rooms at the 2003 and 2005 World Social Forms in the Brazil and had help from other collectives in setting up their media rooms for the 2001 Summit of the Americas and the 2003 anti-WTO protests in Montreal. Three of Vancouver's members helped initiate the Calgary IMC (subsequently renamed Alberta IMC) for the World Petroleum Congress in 2000. One of these people also received sponsorship from Alternatives to help set up an IMC in Argentina. Interviewees from Vancouver also reported regular connections and sharing of resources with IMCs in Victoria and Seattle. Vancouver also hosted the Victoria, Thunder Bay, and Alberta websites on its server.

Several interviewees noted that they or other members of their collectives had helped establish other alternative media outlets. For instance, three of Vancouver's members created Squeegee Media—a worker's co-operative that builds and hosts Web sites for nonprofit and activist organizations. Similarly, several CMAQ activists were key in setting up the Québec Alternative Media Network (RMA), which works to build relationships between 25 alternative magazines, newspapers, websites, and radio and TV stations (Dubois, 2005: 139-140). As well, members of CMAQ's technical team have gone on to create Koumbit, a nonprofit workers' collective that provides information technology services.

All three IMCs also have (or had) key relationships with other grassroots organizations. CMAQ's agreement with Québec PIRG, for example, has that organization supplying office space in exchange for e-mail accounts, server space, Web-hosting, technical expertise, and journalistic/media workshops. Vancouver has an agreement with Squeegee Media that provides storage space and voice mail. And, until recently, Hamilton had an arrangement with a local Internet service provider (ISP) that gave them bandwidth. Similarly, most of the interviewees reported that they had been, or continued to be, active in other local activist organizations, thereby demonstrating connections to local activist communities.

At another level, interviewees from all three IMCs also stated that they viewed their sites as community resources that both individuals and organizations might use to develop and share a range of different types of information. In this regard, all three IMCs carry news and information from a wide range of public interest, environmental, and social justice organizations. Other alternative media outlets—such as community radio and television outlets, other Web-based organizations, and print publications—also regularly use the sites to publish and publicize their work. From this perspective, these IMCs are part of a larger web of media activism; they are nodes in a network that includes not only Indymedia but a range of media outlets.

DRAWING FROM THE CANADIAN EXPERIENCE

Despite the diversity evident amongst the three IMCs, they all, to a degree, provide the basis for a developing 'media commons.' Additionally, they have at times offered direct challenges to the general gate-keeping function of the corporate media. At other times, their contribution rests on aggregating and distributing content culled from other radical or alternative media outlets or, on occasion, stories from commercial media outlets. They also act as vehicles for political organization, providing venues for debate and distributing information about lectures, meetings, and other events related to political activism. Still, as both the dwindling numbers of Canadian IMCs and the often slow turnover of content on their sites illustrates, the sustainability of their operations appears to be a growing issue.

But before detailing some possible directions for bolstering IMC operations, it is important to consider whether the seemingly tenuous nature of these organizations is in fact a problem. As Rodríguez (2001: 22) points out, too often we view what she calls "citizens' media" projects as "chaotic and politically frail." Instead, she posits, "we should approach democratic communication as a live creature that expands and contracts with its own very vital rhythms." From this perspective, media are historically bound, their effectiveness situated in specific historical circumstances. Working from this position one needs to consider whether apparently 'frail' citizens' media outlets are in fact in need of 'saving' or whether, perhaps, their condition is indicative of a particular stage (or end?) in their life cycle. As with many IMCs, a number of Canadian Centres were established to report on protests. Some have made a transition to serving a larger set of purposes and/or communities. Others such as IMC Ontario and IMC Alberta have not. Following Rodríguez, we can see that this is not necessarily indicative of problems within the logic of Indymedia itself or some kind of failure on the part of the collectives that created those organizations. Rather, their purposes served, they have fallen dormant, perhaps to be revived as circumstances change. However, given that CMAQ and the Hamilton and Vancouver IMCs have more or less adapted to changing circumstances, this study raises some considerations regarding how IMCs might cope with the challenges they face in the context of such change.

Recruitment and Diversity

Although volunteer labor is central to IMCs' autonomy from corporate and professional imperatives, the most cited challenge was finding and, particularly, keeping new recruits. Consequently, developing and regularly undertaking recruitment strategies would seem to be an important step toward increasing the size of collectives and the range of activities they undertake. Equally important are strategies for retaining new members. Although all three IMCs reported having programs for developing the skills of their members, problems with retention suggest that a more systematic approach is needed to help reduce 'barriers to entry' into the collective, such as developing media literacy programs to help people better understand the role and purposes of the Center, as well as more comprehensive skills-building programs. At the same time, however, as pointed out by one interviewee, if one considers IMCs to be a community resource, then those who post to the site might be seen as 'members', and the issue of recruitment is not so pressing. From this perspective, what might be required to boost the material posted to IMCs is not more collective members, but a better awareness of the aims and purposes of IMCs among local activist communities. As an interviewee from Hamilton noted, not only was he surprised by the fact that local activists were often not aware of the IMC but they also did not seem to understand the way open publishing works and the IMC often received requests from local progressive groups to send out someone to 'cover' their events. All this accents the need for community outreach.

Inside IMCs, a more structured approach to recruiting might also help address inequities in gender and racial diversity. The fact that organizations tend to reflect the inequities of social power present in the societies in which they operate is not a novel observation and is the reason that many have adopted equity policies to guide hiring and other aspects of their operation. In the case of IMCs, 'barriers to entry' include knowledge of both the operation of the equipment and the underlying social issues that drive Indymedia, as well as access to sources of income or support that enable voluntarism. Consequently, IMCs are more accessible to those who possess these resources. One way to expedite change in this area would be to have collectives adopt a diversity statement (and strategy) that provides form and direction to how they deal with issues of gender and racial diversity, particularly in terms of recruiting. (The adoption of anti-oppression statements might help stave off conflicts around sexism, as well).[12] To be effective, however, recruiting strategies must be designed to increase diversity. Consequently, orienting training programs and resources to support the participation of specific groups of people is important. Working in this direction IMCs might engage in projects that are founded upon overt antiracist organizational commitments or ally themselves with organizations representing minority interests (Conway, 2004: 135).

Education for new members on the ideals and ambitions of the collectives may also be in order. For instance, as one member of the Montreal collective pointed out, during the 'masculinist' crisis a number of men in the group did not seem to understand the ways in which the views expressed by the group were not simply 'free speech' but, more importantly, elements of larger ideological discourses that contributed to the ongoing subordination of women. Similarly, as an interviewee from the Vancouver IMC noted, often the organization seemed to operate on a 'naïve faith' that people understood the democratic concepts that underpinned its operation. However, when it was revealed that all members did not understand basic principles of social equity (such as when the issue of sexism arose) some felt alienated and betrayed. Interviewees from both Vancouver and Montreal attributed drops in participation to the crises over sexism their collectives experienced. Because IMCs generally draw from a set of young and diverse activists, it is understandable that all volunteers may not be familiar with the critiques and concerns of all the different interests that animate the group. However, ensuring that all members understand the practical dimensions of the policies that inform the collective might well improve member retention.

Funding

As we have seen, increasing the income of IMCs is somewhat controversial. In the short term, increased revenues might be used for organizing media literacy, news writing, and Web site management training, as well as more fundraising and recruitment activities. In the longer term, money might be employed to hire someone to help develop and co-ordinate the collectives' activities, as well as raise funds to maintain them. However, this path towards institutionalization is not without its price and pursuing funding raises three important questions. First, does the funding source act to shape or constrain the organization's development? Second, does the very process of fundraising and resource acquisition have negative political effects? And third, does formal institutionalization of a grassroots project place constraints on praxis?

The first question concerns the familiar problem of political independence, either actual or perceived. The second question, however, is more subtle. The more IMCs extend themselves to become more concrete, community-based projects, the more they either have to generate volunteer labor power or have to insert themselves into well-established mechanisms of revenue generation, whether through grant writing, alliance formation, or entrepreneurialism.[13] Thus, even if grassroots organizations can maintain independence from direct political influence, the act of soliciting revenue has political impacts. Volunteers with Vancouver IMC were very aware of this and often worried about instrumentalizing their events and diverting too much energy into revenue generation.

Finally, although formal institutionalization facilitates revenue generation by making grants and donations more accessible, it may act to constrain the political activities of a grassroots organization in many ways. For example, incorporating as a nonprofit society requires enacting a formal hierarchical structure. There is also the question of how a collective's energy might become channeled into sustaining the institution itself (e.g. reporting to funders) and away from community engagement.

Networking

As some writers have suggested, developing stronger relationships with other social movements and progressive organizations that share similar values might also help strengthen IMCs (Kidd, 2004; Setchell, 2001). As Hamilton (2000: 371) notes, such relationships build capacity "without capital outlay" and also help integrate organizations into "other realms of life." All three IMCs examined here benefited from such relationships. Given the opportunities for working together in terms of sharing office space, equipment, and bandwidth, creating and distributing content, and organizing local communities, developing more of these kinds of relations would seem to be in order. Again, however, Canadian experience illustrates some possible pitfalls here. For instance, at CMAQ interviewees reported that the link they had with Alternatives led to mistrust of the organization from grassroots communities and raised questions internally about the power the NGO held over the collective by virtue of paying for its bandwidth and being the parent organization signing for the receipt of grant funds. Relationships based upon exchange of services tend to have fewer problems than ones based on money, but as members of CMAQ noted, it is always important to have a clear written contract in this regard.

EDITORIAL AND INTERNAL PROCESSES

On another note, some Canadian IMCs appear to have overcome some of the problems commonly haunting other Indymedia outlets. For instance, both Hamilton and Montreal successfully met with the challenge of spammers, trolls, and posts that clash with the sites' progressive social mandates. On the CMAQ site, postings must be validated by editors before they appear on the newswire. In Hamilton, editorial vigilance seemed to be the key.

Finally, CMAQ has moved to reduce the friction caused by the internal division between the technical crew and other members of the collective that often haunts IMCs. Because technical issues concerning computers and software are complex and specialized, there are often complaints that technical discussions exclude other members and dominate meetings, as well as charges that the 'techies" mastery of the software allows them to exert undue control over the functioning of the collective (Rodgers, 2004: 7). In the face of such problems, the technical crew at CMAQ left the IMC and formed their own collective. They continue to provide the necessary maintenance and troubleshooting services to the IMC, but don't participate in decision-making processes.

CONCLUSION

To some extent, the IMCs examined here all negotiated transitions from their beginnings as protest-based sites to local sites for political organization that enjoin issues at local, regional, and transnational levels. But in these configurations, the three Canadian IMCs are very different from the first IMC established in Seattle. As Atton (2003a: 13-14) notes, these developments underscore the "evolutionary capacity of radical Internet projects to reconfigure themselves as circumstance and necessity suggest." But although these three sites more or less adapted to changing circumstances, their operations were hampered by a lack of resources. It would appear that once the initial enthusiasm of most volunteers wears off and reserves of individual energy are depleted, it becomes very difficult to maintain a high level of participation. Given ongoing trouble with spammers and trolls, participation—in terms of editorial vigilance—became a particular problem for both Vancouver and Hamilton. This problem also raises issues concerning the efficacy of a pure, open access regime.

Are the IMCs examined here part of a larger social movement? To the extent that they were inspired by the Seattle IMC, established as part of the larger IMC network of centers, and continue to aid and inspire other IMCs, they might be viewed as such or, at least, as part of a larger media democracy movement. At another level, however, they are given form and focus by local conditions and people that have been radicalized by a range of critical social movements. At this level, IMCs are both part of a larger set of movements and a 'tactic' drawn upon by activists that are, to various degrees, associated with those movements. To some extent, however, it would appear that individual IMCs cannot be understood without reference to local conditions and the identities and relationships of those who use them (Bennett, 2003). Similarly, to the extent that the IMCs examined here are indicative of a larger movement, their survival may hinge on their abilities to respond to shifting political environments at the local level. Given the opportunities for creating a range of synergies—with certain caveats—developing relationships with other progressive social movements and organizations also seems central to this project.

But just as IMCs built upon the work of activists before them, their work now forms the basis for new media activism and, although it may be too early to speak of legacies or to write the epitaph of Indymedia, perhaps the greatest contribution of IMCs will be as incubators for a new generation of activist ideas and practices.

NOTES

1. The authors would like to thank the Canadian Media Research Consortium for a grant that made this research possible, as well as the members of the Vancouver (Kelli Gallagher, David Maidman, Tammy Lea Meyer, and an anonymous member), Hamilton (Andrew, John, and Randy), and CMAQ (Pat, Frederic, Andrea, Pat,

Isabelle, Oana, Omar, and an anonymous member) IMC collectives who so generously gave their time to the interviews underlying this work.

2. For example, among others, IMCs were present at the following demonstrations: the 2000 IMF/World Bank meetings in Washington DC in April and in September in Prague; the 2001 Free Trade Area of the Americas in Quebec City; and the 2001 meeting of the Group of 8 nations in Genoa, Italy.

3. Developing a decision-making structure at the global level has been much more difficult, and, as Milberry (2003: 77) illustrates, "efforts to develop network-wide processes for decision-making and planning have failed."

4. Such policy statements can be found on many IMCs Web sites under 'about us' or 'info' links. See, for example, Urbana-Champaign IMC which is incorporated as a nonprofit organization and has a complex structure and substantial list of bylaws: www.ucimc.org/mod/info/display/bylaws/index.php, retrieved February 11, 2007.

5. 'Alberta' continues to be listed on many IMC sites, but it was shut down in 2004 due to a lack of a editorial activity.

6. TAO was an activist organization that provided computer services for the Vancouver activist community. It has since transformed into Resist.ca which continues to provide Internet services but also hosts a moderated newswire.

7. See http:www.koumbit.org, retrieved February 11, 2007.

8. To protect the identities of contributors, Indymedia sites generally do not record the Internet Protocol addresses of visitors. Consequently, it is difficult to know with any certainty who is visiting these sites.

9. Vancouver Indymedia attempted to establish a membership policy after a crisis of sexism within the collective in order to formally exclude disruptive individuals. However, the policy was not put into practice.

10. The receipt of a $50,000 grant from the Ford Foundation in 2002 by Urbana-Champaign IMC elicited extensive debate and led to the declining of the funds (Shumway, 2003; Whitney, 2005).

11. There is greater diversity in terms of occupation. For instance, Hamilton's collective includes a graduate student, a daycare worker, a store owner, one person who is unemployed, and another on a disability pension. No single group of people—such as 'students'—dominates any of the collectives.

12. In the wake of the problem they experienced Vancouver did adopt an anti-oppression statement from the San Francisco collective. However, one respondent noted that it was too late and the damage to the collective had already been done. The Montreal group did add their names to a list supporting an antidiscrimination policy circulated on the Global list by the 'Indymedia women' listserv, but then didn't see the need to have antidiscrimination policies integrated into their collective processes.

13. This raises the interesting question of how autonomous organizations can generate revenues without inserting themselves into these funding streams by developing new forms of revenue (e.g. community currencies, barter, theft and piracy, and so on).

REFERENCES

Atton, C. (2002). *Alternative media.* Thousand Oaks, CA: Sage.

Atton, C. (2003a). Reshaping social movement media for a new millennium. *Social Movement Studies, 2*(1), 3-15.

Atton, C. (2003b). Organisation and production in alternative media. In S. Cottle (Ed.), *Media organization and production* (pp. 41-54). Thousand Oaks, CA: Sage.

Bennett, W. L. (2003). New media power: The Internet and global activism. In N. Couldry & J. Curran, (Eds.), *Contesting media power: Alternative media in a networked world* (pp. 17-37). Lanham, MD: Rowman & Littlefield.

Benjamin, W. (1968). *Illuminations.* New York: Shocken.

Castells, M. (2001). *The internet galaxy: Reflections on the internet business and society.* Oxford: Oxford University Press.

ChuckO. (2002). The sad decline of Indymedia. Retrieved August 6, 2005, from http://www.infoshop.org/inews/article.php?story=02/12/08/2553147.

Conway, J. M. (2004). *Identity, place, knowledge: Social movements contesting globalization.* Halifax, NS: Fernwood.

Couldry, N. (2003). Beyond the hall of mirrors: Some theoretical reflections on the global contestation of media power. In N. Couldry & J. Curran (Eds.), *Contesting media power: Alternative media in a networked world* (pp. 39-54). Lanham, MD: Rowman & Littlefield.

D'Annibale, V. S., & Chehade. G. (2004). The revolution will not be televised, but it might be uploaded: The IndyMedia phenomenon. In M. Moll & L. Shade (Eds.) *Seeking convergence in policy and practice: Communications in the public interest* (Vol. 2, pp. 363-379). Ottawa: Canadian Centre for Policy Alternatives.

Day, R.J.F. (2005). *Gramsci is dead: Anarchist currents in the newest social movements.* Toronto: Between the Lines.

Downing, J. (2002). A multi-local, multi-media challenge to global neoliberalism. In M. Raboy (Ed.), *Global media policy in the new millennium* (pp. 215-232). Luton: University of Luton Press.

Downing, J. (2003). The independent media center movement and the anarchist socialist tradition. In J. Curran & N. Couldry (Eds.), *Contesting media power: Alternative media in a networked world* (pp. 243-257). Lanham, MD: Rowman & Littlefield.

Dubois, F. (2005). Networks unite! Strengthening media solidarity. In A. Langlois & F. Dubois (Eds.), *Autonomous media: Activating resistance and dissent* (pp. 135-149). Montréal: Cumulus Press.

Dyer-Witheford, N. (1999). *Cyber-Marx: Cycles and circuits of struggle in high-technology capitalism.* Chicago: University of Illinois Press.

Galatas, E. (2001). Building Indymedia. In P. Philips (Ed.), *Censored: The news that didn't make the news—and why.* New York: Seven Stories Press. Retrieved Jan 14, 2007, from http://www.thirdworldtraveler.com/Independent_Media/Building_IndyMedia.html

Hackett, R. (2000, Autumn). Taking back the media: Notes on the potential for a communicative democracy movement. *Studies in Political Economy, 63,* 61-86.

Halleck, D. (2003, April). Indymedia: Building an international activist Internet network. *Media Development.* Retrieved September 20, 2004, from http://www.wacc.org.uk/ modules.php?name=News&file=article&sid=240

Hamilton, J. (2000). Alternative media: Conceptual difficulties, critical possibilities. *Journal of Communication Inquiry, 24*(4), 357-378.

Herndon, S. (2003). Indymedia USA. Paper presented at the OURMedia III Conference, Barranquilla, Colombia. Retrieved August 24, 2005, from www.ourmedianet.org/papers/om2003/Herndon_OM3.pdf

Indymedia. (2001). Principles of unity. Retrieved July 25, 2005, from http://docs.indymedia.org/view/Global/PrinciplesOfUnity.

Indymedia Documentation Project. (n.d.). Indymedia's frequently asked questions (FAQ). Retrieved July 9 2005, from http://docs.indymedia.org/view/Global/ FrequentlyAsked QuestionEn#goals

Jay, D, O. (n.d.). Three proposals for open publishing: Towards a transparent, collaborative editorial framework. Retrieved September 20, 2004, from http://dru.ca/1mc/ open_pub.html

Kidd, D. (2003a). Indymedia.org: A new communications commons. In M. McCaughey & M. D. Ayers (Eds.), *Cyberactivism: On-line activism in theory and practice* (pp. 47-69). New York: Routledge.

Kidd, D. (2003b). Become the media: The global IMC network. In A. Opel & D. Pompper (Eds.), *Representing resistance: Media, civil disobedience and the global justice movement* (pp. 224-240). Westport, CT: Praeger.

Kidd, D. (2004). From carnival to commons: The global IMC network. In E. Yuen, G. Katsiaficas, & D. Burton-Rose (Eds.), *Confronting capitalism: Dispatches from a global movement* (pp. 330-340). New York: Soft Skull Press.

Langlois, A. (2004). How open is open? The praxis of open publishing. *Open Journal*. Retrieved September 20, 2004, from http://openj.touchbasic.com:8088/journal/ archives/00000004.htm>

Langlois, A., (2005). How open is open? The politics of open publishing. In A. Langlois & F. Dubois (Eds.), *Autonomous media: Activating resistance and dissent* (pp. 47-59). Montréal: Cumulus Press.

Langlois, A., & Dubois, F. (Eds.). (2005). *Autonomous media: Activating resistance and dissent.* Montréal: Cumulus Press.

Levy, M. L. (2004). *We are millions: Neo-liberalism and new forms of political action in Argentina.* London: Latin America Bureau.

Mamadouh, V. (2004). Internet, scale and the global grassroots: Geographies of the Indymedia network of Independent Media Centres. *Tijdschrift voor Economische en Sociale Geographie, 95*(5), 482-497

Milberry, K. (2003). *Indymedia as a social movement? Theorizing the new global justice movements.* Unpublished MA thesis, University of Windsor, Canada.

Rinaldo, R. (n.d.). Indymedia mobilizes for the sequel to Seattle. Retrieved August 4, 2005, from http://www.alternet.org/story/131/

Rodgers, J. (2004). *Online media: Franchising the alternative?* Unpublished paper. Presented at IAMCR conference, Porto Allegre Brazil, July.

Rodríguez, C. (2001). *Fissures in the mediascape: an international study of citizens' media.* Cresskill, NJ: Hampton Press.

Setchell, L. (2001). Making a difference: In Boston, Indy Media takes simple steps and tests relationships. *Toward Freedom, 49*(7), 7.

Shumway, C. (2003). *Democratizing communication through community-based participatory media networks: A case study of the independent media center movement.* Unpublished MA thesis, New School University, New York, USA.

Surman, M., & Reilly, K. (2003). Appropriating the Internet for social change: Towards the strategic use of networked technologies by transnational civil society organizations. *Social Science Research Council.* Retrieved September 20, 2004, from http://www.ssrc.org/ programs/itic/civ_soc_report/

Uzelman, S. (2002). *Catalyzing participatory communication: Independent media centre and the politics of direct action.* Unpublished MA thesis, Simon Fraser University, Burnaby, Canada.

Uzelman, S. (2005). Hard at work in the bamboo garden: Media activists and social movements. In A. Langlois & F. Dubois (Eds.), *Autonomous media: Activating resistance and dissent* (pp. 16-29). Montréal: Cumulus Press.

Vatikiotis, P. (2004). Communication theory and alternative media. *Westminster Papers in Communication and Culture, 1*(2), 4-29.

Whitney, J. (2005). What's the matter with Indymedia? Retrieved July 28, 2005, from http://www.alternet.org/mediaculture/23741/

GENDER AND HIERARCHY
A Case Study of the Independent Media Center Network

Lisa Brooten & Gabriele Hadl

> The true focus of revolutionary change is never merely the oppressive situations that we seek to escape but that piece of the oppressor that is planted deep within each of us and that knows only the oppressor's tactics, the oppressor's relationships.
>
> Audre Lorde (1984: 123)

This chapter illustrates that a gender perspective is essential if social movements are to develop practical alternatives to the status quo, taking as a case study the network of Independent Media Centers (IMCs), or 'Indymedia.'[1] IMCs are committed through their Principles of Unity[2] to work toward "the development of non-hierarchical and anti-authoritarian relationships, from interpersonal relationships to group dynamics" (Indymedia Documentation Project, 2002: No. 6). Nonetheless, a number of Indymedia activists have argued that at least in terms of gender relations, these principles are less than widely realized. Which issues have they highlighted? Which patterns can be identified in these debates? Drawing on internal IMC discussion forums, posted articles on gender and the discussions they trigger, and interviews with IMC activists, we analyze how issues of gender have been discussed within the network. How do participants in these debates view the network's relationship to patriarchy? Who is accorded the right and ability to speak (and for whom) and how is 'normatively feminine' labor valued? How do they reflect on Indymedia's self-imposed challenge to confront and replace hierarchical relations? Our analysis of these debates suggests that measures designed to improve access and level the playing field, in some cases ironically reinforce hierarchical structures. These findings hold lessons not only for Indymedia, but for all movements for more just communication societies.

THE NETWORK OF INDEPENDENT
MEDIA CENTERS (NIMC OR INDYMEDIA)

The Indymedia network of alternative and radical media collectives emerged as a result of strong global resistance to corporate-led globalization (Kidd, 2004). A specific concern is to challenge and support alternatives to the imperialism, elitism, and authoritarianism embodied in the economic neoliberalist paradigm and the commercial media that support it. At the time of data collection (September 2005), 152 IMCs, publishing in 25 languages, formed this network of autonomously run, nonprofit media collectives. The network's face to the world is its global site (www.indymedia.org), with stories culled from the local sites. The ideological common ground between the network's diverse local collectives is spelled out in the Draft Principles of Unity (Indymedia Documentation Project, 2000) and the NIMC Draft of NIMC Membership Criteria (Indymedia Documentation Project, 2002). IMCs primarily present 'news,' with a special focus on social justice movement events, challenging traditional journalism and the concept of 'objectivity' by privileging firsthand accounts from activists (Brooten, 2004). The network calls on its participants to 'be the media' by becoming their own producers of news content.

IMCs are committed to open publishing and the consensus process, key elements of the network's Membership Criteria (Indymedia Documentation Project, 2002). In open publishing, anyone with Internet access can publish instantly and with minimal 'gate keeping.' IMC websites typically provide newswire posting forms (for adding items to the news column) and a similar comment posting function for adding comments about a newswire post. The consensus process calls for "open, transparent and egalitarian processes" so that "diverse people and groups are welcome to attend and that no attempt is made to exclude people based on their sex, race, gender, class, age, ability or religion" (Indymedia Documentation Project, 2002: g). Process tools include wikis—websites that can be accessed and edited by any IMC volunteer (docs.indymedia.org)—and electronic mailing lists ('listservs') (lists.indymedia.org).

There is an informal distinction between 'users' (content and discussion contributors, and audiences) and 'volunteers' or 'collective members' (regular contributors, editors/facilitators, techies, translators, network liaisons, etc.), though these roles are often blurred. Some IMCs are only websites maintained by a few people, whereas others involve a large number of volunteers participating in a variety of projects and different media, including audio, video, and print media, not least to facilitate participation among those without Internet access.

One of Indymedia's most effective tools for development and progress has been consistent self-critique. Well-debated challenges facing the network include uneven participation, North-South tensions, overemphasis on tech work, and English language dominance. In most IMCs, the core volunteers come from relatively privileged groups. Within the international network, young, white, English speaking, well-educated men from the global North are arguably most visible. IMCs generally have minimal funding and rely almost exclusively on volunteers and donated time and equipment. In addition, IMCs have suffered attacks by governments, police surveillance, and right-wingers, and have been subject to the seizure of servers and a 'continuing plague' of spam and hate speech (Kidd, 2003: 9). Further, IMCs are influenced by their local mainstream cultures, social movements and subcultures, each with their own ideological limitations.

RESEARCHING INDYMEDIA

Research on Indymedia has been controversial. In response to a slew of inappropriately conducted research projects, the IMC U.K. has developed a set of guidelines for researchers, favoring qualitative and participatory methods and requiring communication from researchers explaining their projects to concerned IMC electronic mailing lists (Indymedia Documentation Project, 2004). Our approach meets and exceeds these guidelines. The research is thus also consistent with feminist research methodologies, which challenge the traditional quest for 'objective truth' and the hierarchical relationship between the 'researcher' and 'researched' in favor of a coproduction of knowledge and the recognition of multiple subject positions.

Drawing on our own experiences and personal contacts as participants in local and global IMC spaces, we posted calls for collaboration to gender-related lists and a number of local IMCs in the Americas, Europe and Asia. We developed an IMC wiki to solicit input and publish the progress of the project (cf. Indygender Researchers, 2005). We identified and contacted fifteen key volunteers known for their involvement in gender debates. Of these, three contributed e-mail interviews and analyses, and others pointed us to what they had identified as key texts in the ongoing debates on gender in the network. We systematically reviewed these texts, as well as relevant debates on gender-related English-language electronic mailing lists and IMC newswires. We analyzed these key texts using an inductive process of textual analysis, in which themes arose from the texts themselves, rather than being imposed upon the data. Our goal was not to provide a 'representative sample' of such debates, or to show that the central concerns in these debates are consistent for all chapters of the network. Our goal was rather to identify recurring patterns and assumptions seen as problematic by key activists within the network and to assess how these patterns could be used as a basis for furthering the discussion and identifying the impact of gendered discourse and stereotyping within Indymedia. Our hope is that the patterns and assumptions discovered here will be helpful for other social movements attempting to address gender issues as well.

GENDER AND HIERARCHY

Feminist scholarship has developed nuanced conceptualizations of how the maintenance of hierarchies is strongly linked to patriarchy and how patriarchy is integral to the 'relations of ruling' in contemporary societies at multiple levels: in the behavior of individuals, groups, and even internationally in the 'maneuvers' between nations (Enloe, 2000; Smith, 1990; Taylor & Bernstein Miller, 1994). Though there is no universal set of gender codes, some argue that "no nation in the world grants women and men the same access to the rights and resources of the nation-state" (McClintock, 1997: 89). Feminist scholarship shares with social movements an emphasis on the need to struggle against hierarchies of class, race, gender and imperialism (Alexander & Mohanty, 1997; Mohanty, 1991). Acknowledging that gender is not a stable category, that women can and do use 'normatively masculine' strategies, and that individuals may embody both privilege and oppression is not to deny gender-based oppression or its connection with hierarchy. Any project committed to challenging hierarchies and building alternatives to the global system of domination must thus seriously undertake to challenge gendered power dynamics and normative gender roles.

As a move towards counteracting hierarchy, feminist activists and scholars have promoted an alternative conception of power that moves away from *power over* others, to a conception of *power-to* or *power-with*, or the ability to empower oneself and others (Taylor & Bernstein Miller, 1994). Rather than seeing power as a limited commodity in a zero-sum game in which players have to compete, this conception sees power as unlimited and generative, increasing with every application. Rather than requiring dominance and hierarchy to maintain itself, this type of power is thwarted and destroyed by hierarchy and dominance, which are dependent on and made manifest in highly gendered systems and structures (Rakow, 1988; Taylor & Bernstein Miller, 1994).

FEMINIST PERSPECTIVES
ON GENDER, COMMUNICATION, AND MEDIA

Such reconceptualizations of power have emerged from a vibrant history of thought on gender and communication and from earlier women's movements that have worked to democratize alternative media. Numerous women's media movements have challenged existing hierarchies of power not only by fore-grounding voices unheard in mainstream (or 'malestream') media, but also in providing women with access to resources and in the development of collective, consensus-based, and nonhierarchical organizational structures. They have emphasized production processes rather than end products, challenged concepts of objectivity, and promoted the blurring of the producer/consumer dichotomy and the use of personal testimonials (Cottingham, 1989; Crafton Smith, 1989; Riaño-Alcalá, 1994; Sreberny-Mohammadi, 1996; Werden, 1996).

Women's movements have also shifted over time. Second-wave feminism focused on legal equality and integration of women into the (patriarchal) public sphere, but critiques revealed the notion of 'global sisterhood' as essentialist and problematic, especially its assumption that all women share the concerns of white, professional-class western feminists. The shift from this essentialist approach to a commitment to embrace multiple identities, tactics, and causes has emerged from feminism's 'third wave,' which recognizes differences of race, class, sexual orientation, and geographical location. The resultant emphasis on building solidarity across differences "is analogous to the structural differences between traditional social movements and new social movements," which are more loose-ly structured and fragmented than earlier, more centralized structures (Lotz, 2003).

Despite these developments, the most influential among feminist approaches to communication technologies has been the *women in technology* perspective, a remnant of second-wave feminism focusing on the small proportion of women in computing and information technology. This perspective suggests concrete mea-sures to increase women's involvement, in which 'more women is better' becomes axiomatic (Association for Progressive Communication WNSP, 1997). Where this perspective fails to take into account other factors such as age, class, and neo-colonialism, however, it tends to benefit women from social elites.

More radical feminist perspectives consider gender, technology, and power inextricably linked. An *eco-feminist* perspective, for example, sees technology as "deeply implicated in the masculine project of the domination and control of women and nature" (Association for Progressive Communication WNSP, 1997: para 11), whereas a *feminist Marxist* viewpoint posits that "technology from its origins reflects male power as well as capitalist domination" (para. 12). In contrast to the *women in technology* perspective, those who see technology and gender as socially constructed call for a redefinition of 'technical work' in de-gendered terms, and for a re-evaluation of normatively feminine work as skilled and technical, with appropriate pay and social status (Association for Progressive Communication WNSP, 1997: para. 13).

THE INTERNET AS A GENDERED DISCOURSE ENVIRONMENT

Although much of the literature on gender and the Internet still takes the *women in technology* perspective, a growing body of literature on gendered online harassment, disruptive communications (for example, Internet trolls)[3] and sexist spam shows that increased women's access to technologies does not guarantee a democratic online environment (Baker, 2001; Herring, Job-Sluder, Scheckler, & Barab, 2003; Lee, 1996). Susan Herring's (1999) analysis of an internet relay chat (IRC) and an academic electronic mailing list demonstrates a 'rhetoric of harassment' at play, wherein "even in environments where it is not possible to determine if a participant is biologically female or male, gender dualism may continue to operate" (152). Herring (1999) provides examples of how an 'oppositional and adversarial style' works to silence less adversarial participants in an environment "characterized by a high incidence of flaming[4] and verbal aggression" (152) and dominated by a male-gendered "civil libertarian ideological bent ... that advocates individual freedom of expression and condemns all forms of regulation as censorship" (163).

Beyond Herring's somewhat simplistic male-female framing, it must be noted that the enactment of normatively masculine perspectives or values is not necessarily limited to men. Challenging this dynamic requires more than making sure that women's voices are heard. It must also include an analysis of how normatively feminine ways of thinking become devalued and silenced, and the presentation of alternatives to challenge such dynamics. Herring's (1999) findings in particular are echoed in a growing body of analysis about and within Indymedia, to which this chapter owes a great deal.

GENDER DEBATES IN INDYMEDIA

IMC activists seeking gender equity in the network have been analyzing and discussing gender issues on Indymedia's gender-related electronic mailing lists, which include IMC-women,[5] IMC-women-tech,[6] CMI-mulheres,[7] IMC-antipatriarchy[8] and IMC-queer.[9] In addition to these internal discussion spaces, the open publishing features of IMC websites have also been used to publicly debate gender issues within Indymedia (and related social movements). In the following we examine discussions on gender from these websites and electronic mailing lists, with a focus on the work and thoughts of volunteers participating in the

IMC-women and IMC-antipatriarchy electronic mailing lists. Although our analysis is limited to discussions in English, we hope to encourage researchers competent in the network's other languages to conduct similar analyses.

The IMC-Women List and the IMCWOMYN Proposal

IMC-women was established in the summer of 2001 by women active in the network in order to provide a 'safe space' for women to discuss "the depressing situation of patriarchal repression in society which unfortunately doesn't stop at the doorstep of leftist groups" (IMCWomynProposal, 2003). An electronic mailing list with nonpublic archives, and self-introduction and moderator approval required for subscription, IMC-women currently includes female IMC activists from the Americas, Europe, the Middle East, and Australia.

One internal discussion on the IMC-women list eventually led to a policy change for the network. Through a consensus building process, IMC-women participants developed a proposal to address some of their concerns, which was then put forward to the network as a whole, along with a summary of their debate (IMCWomynProposal, 2003). They proposed three questions to be added to the application process for establishing a new IMC, which would require the group to assess how their collective reflects "the diversity of the local community" (IMCWomynProposal, 2003). There was consensus on the IMC-women list that the move was an important first step and would encourage already established IMC collectives to open a dialogue on these issues if they had not already done so.

The proposal generated a fair amount of controversy in local IMCs and online discussion spaces but was widely supported. Although some questioned whether sexism exists within the network, others listed specific incidences, such as sexist behavior at IMC meetings and at conferences where Indymedia groups participated, and 'pitbull' or 'macho-affirmation behavior' in IMC discussions both online and off. After some debate, the additions proposed by IMC-women became an official component of the application process for establishing a new IMC.

The IMC-ANTIPATRIARCHY List

With the IMC-women electronic mailing list restricted to women, members of IMC-women-tech in August 2002 decided to establish IMC-antipatriarchy, where both women and men could talk about gender issues unrelated to technology. Although the IMC-antipatriarchy list has been inactive for long periods, the archive shows that discussions on gender are usually sparked by specific incidences within local collectives. The discussions generally start with complaints and/or requests and offers of help that elicit both practical suggestions and the retelling of personal experiences, at times getting quite heated.

For example, the first archived discussion on the list involves the behavior of an individual who had reportedly joined a work meeting of an IMC collective after participating in online discussions on sexism and patriarchy in the collective.[10] Members of the collective concerned, both female and male, claim that he raised the issue of sexism and gender inequities and then proceeded to make derogatory comments towards the women present and refused to speak with them, in effect silencing them while attempting to speak on their behalf (burke, 2002; Strole, 2002). Another poster takes up the cause of the individual in question (warcry, 2002). Regardless of what happened 'objectively,' the issue of who gets to speak and to 'speak for' whom, in what manner, and for how long is a recurring concern in Indymedia gender debates. It also reveals the complexity of 'discussing gender' in a subculture that values critique and dissent.

'LEFTIST TECHIES' SURVEY

In November 2001, a member of the Indymedia Germany collective known by her handle[11] Blue, posted the results of a survey on gender she had sent to the mailing lists of approximately 60 IMC collectives (Blue, 2002). Blue conducted this survey in English, and asked participants a series of questions about sexism and patriarchal structures in their groups. She received responses from people in IMC collectives in Europe, North America, and Australia. In "Leftist Techies and Patriarchy," her introduction to the survey, Blue reflects:

> Discussions about patriarchal structures are always substantial. I mean that in two ways. First on the level of the group: people yell at each other, groups split, friendships break apart. Second on the individual level: the gender antagonism hits us personally. It is our fellow activists, friends and lovers, who hold up patriarchy.... So the fight against patriarchy intrudes into our private life. That makes the discussion so difficult. (Blue, 2002)

For this reason, she notes, many people hesitate to label problematic behavior a gender issue or 'patriarchal behavior,' but would rather chalk it up to 'individual dynamics' (Blue, 2002: para. 11).

This survey was met with both praise and critique in IMC discussions. Several respondents pointed out that the survey was framed using binary and essentialist notions of gender, neglected other factors known to affect Internet use (such as ethnicity, colonial experience, rural-urban differences, education, age, etc.), and failed to consider the local context—for example, the level of sexism in each IMC's surrounding culture. Some questioned the underlying assumption that getting more women into tech work is an end in itself. There was also some concern about the data collection method, including the questionnaire's focus on problems rather than possible good practices, and that over-reliance on English and 'open contribution' may have encouraged responses from relatively privileged people with an axe to grind. Nevertheless, the survey was welcomed by many and succeeded in raising the profile of gender issues especially related to tech work, prompting some IMCs to debate the gendered patterns of behavior in their collectives for the first time.

GENDERED PATTERNS

The Gendered Value of Work

A core concern in Blue's survey and the subsequent discussions was the fact that men dominate the technical work in Indymedia, as they do in mainstream cultures. This is in part because Indymedia relies on volunteer labor and hardware and server space donations. Especially in the setup phase of an IMC, people with system administration backgrounds, including experience in computer-network support and maintenance, play an important role. This is a professional area dominated by men in many cultures (Evan Henshaw Plath, personal communication, July 24, 2004; Blue 2001b: response from IMC Norway; Blue, personal communication, August 18, 2005).

Although female volunteers often find themselves as 'secretaries to the revolution' (Blue, 2001a: response from IMC St. Louis), a number of IMCs have women involved in technological work, and some activists feel this has a positive effect on the collective's gender culture. One IMC activist described the situation at a Latin American IMC:

> [W]e don't experience much of the sexism that's apparent in a lot of IMCs . . . and that's because . . . the person who holds that tech power in the IMC and the founding techy of the IMC is a woman and not one of the boys. (Evan Henshaw Plath, personal communication, July 24, 2004)

Blue also reports that she joined the Beirut IMC in its founding stages, providing the technical know-how to help get them up and running (Blue, 2003). She also provided all the technical training, which she believes altered perceptions about the gendered nature of tech work (Blue, personal communication, August 18, 2005). On the other hand, other volunteers feel that the fact that technological concerns about server administration, hardware procurement, and programming of the site's functions often dominate IMC meetings is in itself a gender issue, and wonder how the agenda-setting process could be improved.

Gender and the Consensus Process

The consensus process is ideally a nonhierarchical group decision-making process, and "with good self-facilitation and a good facilitator . . . everyone contributes to the meeting, without anyone taking control over it. People make constructive criticism, and try to incorporate concerns raised into their proposals" (Spalding, 2002: para.7). Yet the consensus process at Indymedia, as elsewhere, has been critiqued as time consuming, thereby excluding people with family commitments, working people, including women on double and triple shifts, and others with time constraints (Halleck, 2003: 14). Another key criticism of the process is its reliance on facilitation, because an incompetent facilitator can undermine equal participation and trust in the process.

Some question the consensus process altogether. In her master's thesis, Ballowe (2002), a member of the Washington DC IMC (or DC-IMC), discusses what she calls the 'antidemocratic' nature of consensus decision-making, in which groups can end up avoiding difficult decisions, in turn alienating members who then leave. In the end, "with fewer people participating, democracy is stifled" (Ballowe, 2002: 3). Ballowe (2002) argues that the unanimity required by consensus precludes alternative perspectives, because minorities are often intimidated by the dominant group, feel they cannot make their arguments convincingly, or don't want to cause conflict. Newcomers often do not understand or agree with the process, and thus have less power in the discussion. She also argues that assigned roles, such as facilitator and 'vibes watcher,' create "de facto hierarchies that undermine the process" (Ballowe, 2002: 34), and that although theoretically the facilitator must allow all a chance to speak, in practice more time is often given to those whose ideas the facilitator shares (Ballowe, 2002).

There is a gender aspect to this issue. Blue began taking a tally at meetings of the IMC-Germany collective after a male facilitator stopped her from talking by telling her that she was speaking too much. "I found that in general the women spoke a lot less than I myself would have thought. I knew of this phenomenon from theory . . . but I had never thought that my own perception would be as flawed" (Blue, personal communication, August 18, 2005). Similar accounts abound, including notes from a Washington DC-IMC meeting during which a woman "told the group that she had done a gender tally of who spoke at a general meeting . . . and the numbers were: 78 times that men spoke to 6 times that women spoke, even though there were roughly equal numbers of both at the meeting" (cited in Ballowe, 2002: 39). Men also reportedly dominate discussions on many Indymedia electronic mailing lists and internet relay chats (Blue, 2001b: response from IMC Norway; Herndon, 2003).

Meeting Dynamics

In a letter to the London-IMC general electronic mailing list, IMC activist Ionnek (2003) writes about her decision not to attend the collective's weekly meetings because she finds "the discussion structure deeply unsettling" (Ionnek, 2003: para. 6). She says the group's collective culture "raises feelings of not being respected" (para. 8) that stem from a "focus on talking rather than listening" (para. 9), and from a small-group organizing structure that the London-IMC has outgrown. Others point to the gender dimensions of such meeting dynamics. Notes from a Washington DC-IMC women's meeting, for example, refer to "the countless women who came to one general meeting then never came back, some of whom had vocalized their dislike of the male power dynamic at play" (cited in Ballowe, 2002: 39).

Men's behavior in meetings is the subject of a posting entitled "An open letter to other men in the movement: SHUT THE FUCK UP or, How to act better in meetings" (Spalding, 2002) which was posted to several IMCs' newswires and mailing lists. The writer, Dan Spalding (2002), identifies himself as a 'man of color' from the U.S. (para. 4), and provides suggestions for how men can be less dominating in IMC meetings. He argues that men tend to "reproduce patriarchy within the movement" through "domination, claiming authority, and belligerence" (para. 2). The result is that women (and nonaggressive men) often respond by withdrawing in exhaustion or frustration or, as another activist puts it, "some women are just too bored with educating men—they shut up in the meetings and go ahead with their projects within the IMC framework" (Blue, 2001b: response from IMC U.K.). Spalding (2002) maintains that "everyone who can't (or won't) compete on these terms—talking long, loud, first and often—get drowned out" (para. 11), so that those who speak the loudest and most often "get to make decisions, take credit for the work everyone does, and come out feeling more inspired and confident" (para. 13).

EDITING POLICIES: THE TENSION
BETWEEN CENSORSHIP AND HATEFUL POSTINGS

Indymedia has had to rethink its policy of open publishing in the face of a slew of hateful, sexist and racist postings on sites throughout the network (Kidd, 2004). Individual IMCs have adopted a range of editorial policies, including the requirement that postings must have some connection to social justice issues, as in the Quebec IMC (Langlois, 2004: para. 20), or the decision not to remove postings at all, but allow the feedback process to help counter problematic postings, as reflected in the Seattle IMC's policy (Langlois, 2004: para. 19). Some editorial policies contain specific restrictions on content that is racist, sexist, homophobic, violent or encouraging of violence, or potentially libelous. Yet, as Langlois (2004) points out, whether or not a particular posting can be labeled any of these terms is often a difficult and subtle question. Some argue that the purpose of Indymedia is to provide a space for discussions triggered by such postings, whereas others doubt that leaving such posts on the site as they are furthers Indymedia's stated goals and purpose.

A Rhetoric of Harassment

Gendered hierarchies often develop between discussants in an online public forum, discouraging substantive debate. One such example is the public discussion that followed the article, "Activist Scenes Are No Safe Space for Women," posted to the Melbourne IMCs' newswire (Nopper, 2005). The writer describes what occurs when female activists experience physical or emotional abuse from activist men (not necessarily referring to IMC per se), arguing that activist groups often shun women who try to address the abuse publicly, putting "more emphasis on helping men stay in activist circles than supporting women through their recoveries" (Nopper, 2005: para. 15). The second person to leave a comment on this article suggests (based on a single example) that women who encounter abuse usually have "a form of mental illness" (JD, 2005). This 'flame' succeeds at inciting a hot debate, yet worthy of note here is the way in which, despite the article's focus, this discussion avoids the issue of safety in activist spaces, taking up instead the character of those victimized within such spaces. References to the male victimizer rhetorically turn the responsibility for problematic male behavior back to women, as with one respondent who writes: "It's a fact—Men are pigs. Accept it, deal with it and move on with your life. Your mum was supposed to tell you all this" (Moss, 2005). This rhetorical move reframes the abuse as either invisible or inevitable and puts the onus to change on the victims rather than abusers.

Lack of Diversity, Lack of Time and Energy

At many IMCs in white majority cultures, the problem is less direct sexism, but difficulty expanding the volunteer base beyond a core group of white, mostly male, internet-educated activists. In some IMCs, awareness is low on the issue and means to address it. In others, time and resources may be lacking to do the necessary outreach and facilitation. The permanent 'protest mode' and precariousness of many IMCs exacerbates "power differences between women and men, techies and non-techies, and sites in the northern hemisphere and the south" (Kidd, 2003: 2). In a situation where much time is spent reacting to crises, people who try to raise gender, race, or class concerns often hear the tired argument that these will be discussed "*after* the revolution" (McClintock, 1997). This old debate over priorities between feminists and male-dominated leftist social movements is summed up by graffiti in the women's bathroom of a space used for IMC meetings in Austria: "Which shall I abolish first? Patriarchy or global capital?" The answer would have to be: "both at once."

MOVING FORWARD

Beyond Women vs. Men

Discussions on gender often fall into the essentialist trap of defining women and men as discreet groups characterized by shared traits assumed to fall exclusively to their gender. One female activist admits that in group discussions of gender, "many times I find the analyses offered too simplistic (male=x, female=y). I think that oppression is much more insidious than we realise [sic], and both the oppressor and the oppressed have internalized their roles" (Blue, 2001a: response from IMC Victoria). Another activist notes:

> [S]exism, although it is clearly a power relation, goes both ways. Men stick to their expert roles and boys networks because it is good for them, women stick to their roles as well—partly because it seems easier, partly because we like being women and sticking to our forms of communication. Sometimes we make it easy for men to stay in power. (Blue, 2001b: response from IMC U.K.)

Yet this activist also describes how at times she has gotten drawn into normatively masculine behavior patterns herself. "I think I have discriminated against women as well—as against the quieter men. It happens so easily—there are all these men going on about exciting things, and you get trapped in the power game, become complicit" (Blue, 2001b: response from IMC-U.K.). To achieve more equitable relationships beyond simplistic women vs. men categories, we must challenge normative thinking or risk allowing conventional binaries (feminine/masculine, professional class/working class, white/nonwhite, etc.) to restrict people to the behavior considered the 'norm' for their groups.

Acknowledging Existing Hierarchies

The strong disapproval of hierarchies in Indymedia culture makes it difficult to get people to reflect on them. However, considering how pervasively gender is used to construct hierarchies worldwide, it would be absurd to assume that any space would be free of them. In an early debate on this issue in the women's movement, Freeman (1972) famously argued that 'structurelessness' easily "becomes a smoke screen for the strong or lucky to establish unquestioned hegemony over others" (Freeman, 1972: 152). The rhetoric of 'independence,' then, hides more than it reveals. 'Independence' from socially oppressing norms, the market, the state, or internalized hierarchies is what IMCs agree to strive towards, but it is dangerous to assume this goal has been realized. In fact, feminists observed early on that an unwillingness to acknowledge existing power structures in a group allows those who hold power (however informally) to ignore the corresponding responsibilities of that power (Freeman, 1972).

Creating Safe Spaces

Many of the suggestions from within Indymedia for how to reach out in solidarity to others and combat destructive hierarchies within the network involve the creation of a comfortable and safe environment in the physical sites where Indymedia work gets done. Some also suggest conceptualizing Indymedia less as a website and its requisite technology and more as a set of social relationships, working out the meeting process as a group and then sticking to it, and developing a zero tolerance policy for marginalization and harassment and a transparent process for dealing with it (Sue, 2003).

A discussion on the IMC-antipatriarchy list addressed one man's concern about the lack of women in his collective's early stage of development (Ganesh Mukti, 2003). Responses suggest that attention to gender is necessary from the start, because it may be difficult to change behavioral dynamics *after* an IMC develops a normative culture. One response describes a meeting for a possible Okinawa IMC, where child care for meetings, internet access, safety, the use of radio and video as more familiar technologies, and tech training were all considered as part of an affirmative gender policy (anna, 2003). Another IMC-antipatriarchy member suggests:

> [L]ook into what kinds of events and actions they are doing, and go cover them! ... Both you and the women's group(s) benefit – you by meeting more women who are activated ... and potentially join the collective ... and they benefit from the coverage you provide. (sara, 2003: para. 3)

A respondent to Blue's survey took another approach, describing her discomfort with "prescribed gender discussions, which often start with a sexist incident, continue with the exclusion of the culprit and all too often end with men talking about women (instead of talking about themselves) and the victim being silenced" (Blue, 2001b: response from IMC U.K.). She recommends "constructive female conspiracies" in which women can "strengthen each other's backs, as men usually do routinely. Simple stuff, taking each other seriously, hyping each other's ideas, referring to each other in discussions, supporting each other's projects" (Blue, 2001b: response from IMC U.K.).

Improving Meetings

In order to make meetings more inclusive and welcoming, Spalding (2002) maintains that "it's obviously not the job of the people most trampled on by patriarchal behavior to always be calling it out. That's where we [men] come in. We are, at least at first, given the most respect when we call out bad behavior" (para. 23). He suggests constructive ways to do this, including not being too personal, making an effort to approach people individually, calling for regular meetings where people can check in regarding how they feel about meetings and working groups, as well as regular attempts at skill sharing to ensure that everyone in the group develops skills and confidence. He stresses that attentive and fair facilitation at meetings is key to encouraging those less confident in public.

Rethinking Consensus

Consensus building is central to Indymedia. The core members included it in the Principles of Unity because they considered it an effective and highly democratic practice. As the discussions we analyzed reveal, this assumption needs to be reconsidered, as the process is only 'democratic' under certain conditions. Participants in these gender debates point out that for consensus to work, attention must be paid to implementing it properly, including training facilitators, following procedures and guidelines, and giving attention to people and topics that are absent. Some suggest that IMCs should develop alternative models for when the consensus process is no longer working, or even abandon consensus making altogether (Ballowe, 2002). At the very least, consensus building should be seen as a means to achieve nonhierarchical relations rather than an end in itself.

Re-thinking Gender and Work

If technology is normatively masculine, as some feminist scholars have maintained (Rakow, 1988; Taylor & Bernstein Miller, 1994), the issue is how to revalue and recode the gendered norms of work and behavior. For example, if technological training is usually conducted by men, having a female trainer may send "a psychological message to other women" and increase their confidence (Blue, personal communication, August 18, 2005).[12] The implicit goal is to recode technical work not as masculine but as degendered or multigendered. Another tool would be regular discussions on gender and work in which, as a participant in the IMC women-tech list puts it, discussion participants must remain "open to looking at the existence of patriarchy in their own behavior, and be open to personal growth. No one comes into these settings as perfect beings, or untouched by the system" (Sue, 2002: Extra Notes).

FROM ANTICENSORSHIP
TO COMMUNICATION COMMONS

Indymedia discussions on gender suggest that the fierce noninterference stance of early IMCs may be incompatible with progressive and inclusive communication. It is rather an extreme liberalist position (connected to the U.S.–style 'freedom of the press' ideology) privileging normatively masculine behavior, and as such has a common root with the economic neoliberalism that Indymedia struggles against. In a world where power is distributed unequally, open publishing can end up giving more power and privilege to those who already wield it.

Open publishing is an important tool for participatory communication, for breaking down the producer/consumer binary and enabling people to 'be the media.' However, it has become clear that if Indymedia is to be inclusive and participatory, something more is required than simply removing barriers. The issue is to rethink Indymedia as a communication commons (Kidd, 2003), which is by no means a passive open space that is everybody's to use but nobody's responsibility (Kluitenberg, 2003). A functioning commons is well designed, with communally defined terms of use, rights, and responsibilities, sanctions for noncompliance, arbitration, and systems for collective-choice arrangements (Ostrom, 1991). IMCs have begun to define more clearly who their communication space should be created by and for, and how to best facilitate that, in the process rethinking their moderating/editing policies, facilitation, and outreach strategies. An approach some IMCs have taken is 'distributive justice,' for example in the form of policies and concerted efforts to facilitate, support, and prioritize participation by specific marginalized groups and individual voices. This is resource intensive, but arguably a way in which IMCs can both preserve a democratic degree of openness and live up to their promise of social justice.

THE JOURNEY AHEAD

Through their Principles of Unity, IMCs share with feminism conceptions of power as *power-with* rather than *power-over* and a strong commitment to challenging hierarchies and encouraging expression by those not usually heard. However, the debates in the IMC-women and other electronic mailing lists make clear that there is still a lot of work to be done. The Indymedia network's introspection on gender and hierarchies is ongoing, and although it is contentious, there is growing awareness that sexism must be addressed and gender norms challenged both within the network and without.

Feminist analysis makes clear that the current systems of unfettered and exploitative commerce and ineffective and conflict-oriented politics are sustained through the development and maintenance of gendered hierarchies. To deconstruct conceptions of normative gender is thus to deprive the current systems of inequity of a key component of their sustenance. If Indymedia is to live up to its promise of developing alternatives to the status quo, issues of gender and hierarchy will have to move from the periphery to the center of debate. Debates on gender and hierarchy are not optional, but an indispensable tool for movements towards more just and environmentally sane societies.

NOTES

1. The authors would like to acknowledge contributions to this chapter by Adilson Cabral, Sally McLaren, and IMC activists Blue and Ionnek.
2. Although the network's Principles of Unity have not been formally ratified, they are often referred to by IMC participants as the common principles upon which the network is based. There is an ongoing debate regarding whether or not to adopt the Principles of Unity as 'official' within the IMC network.
3. People who post inflammatory messages to online forums, electronic mailing lists, or the like with the express (and malicious and/or playful) purpose of disrupting the discussion and upsetting its participants.
4. In online discussions, flaming refers to the posting of comments designed to insult and 'inflame' rather than advance discussion.
5. http://lists.indymedia.org/mailman/listinfo/imc-women. Archive available only to members.
6. http://lists.indymedia.org/mailman/listinfo/imc-women-tech, retrieved February 11, 2007.
7. http://lists.indymedia.org/mailman/listinfo/cmi-mulheres, retrieved February 11, 2007.
8. http://lists.indymedia.org/mailman/listinfo/antipatriarchy, retrieved February 11, 2007.
9. http://lists.indymedia.org/mailman/listinfo/imc-queer, retrieved February 11, 2007.
10. This discussion appeared simultaneously on multiple lists and appears limited to members of the collective.
11. An Internet pseudonym.
12. Not all female activists share the assumption that he who controls the technology controls the power. Some feel that the gendered nature of tech work also limits male 'techies.' As one activist argues, "it's as if I would be forced to do all the typing because I type fast—no thanks" (Blue 2001b: response from IMC UK).

REFERENCES

anna (2003, October 24). [antipatriarchy] Re: Women in developing countries. Posting to IMC-antipatriarchy mailing list. Retrieved December 12, 2006, from http://mail.indymedia.org/antipatriarchy/2003-October/000045.html

Alexander, M. J., & Mohanty, C. T. (1997). Introduction: Genealogies, legacies, movements. In M. J. Alexander & C. Talpade Mohanty (Eds.), *Feminist genealogies, colonial legacies, democratic futures* (pp. xiii-xlii). New York: Routledge.

Association for Progressive Communication WNSP (1997). *Gender and information and communication technology: Towards an analytical framework.* Retrieved April 12, 2005, from http://www.apcwomen.org/work/research/analytical-framework.html

Baker, P. (2001, October) Moral panic and alternative identity construction in Usenet. *Journal of Computer-Mediated Communication,* 7(1) Retrieved June 25, 2005, from http://www.ascusc.org/jcmc/vol7/issue1/baker.html

Ballowe, M. (2002). *A critique of consensus process: Theory, practice and implications.* Unpublished masters thesis, St. Mary's University, Washington, DC.

Blue (Ed.). (2001a, November 18). Answers concerning gender issues from Northamerica [sic]. *Indymedia Deutschland.* Retrieved December 12, 2006, from http://web.archive.org/web/20030630094053/de.indymedia.org/2001/11/11129.shtml

Blue (Ed.). (2001b, November 18) Answers concerning gender issues from Europe. *Indymedia Deutschland.* Retrieved December 12, 2006, from http://web.archive.org/web/20030729233838/de.indymedia.org/2001/11/11124.shtml

Blue (2002, January 17). Leftist techies and patriarchy. *Indymedia Deutschland.* Retrieved August 8, 2005, from http://de.indymedia.org/2002/01/13720.shtml

Blue (2003, October 23). [antipatriarchy] Re: Women in developing countries. Posting to IMC-antipatriarchy mailing list. Retrieved December 12, 2006, from http://mail.indymedia.org/antipatriarchy/2003-October/000044.html

Brooten, L. (2004). The power of public reporting: The Independent Media Center's challenge to the corporate media machine. In L. Artz & Y. R. Kamalipour (Eds.), *Bring 'em on! Media and power in the Iraq war* (pp. 239-254). Lanham, MD: Rowman & Littlefield.

burke, m. (2002, August 5). [antipatriarchy] Re: [imc-nyc-process] Re: [imc-women] [antipatriarchy] My week.... Posting to IMC-patriarchy mailing list. Retrieved December 15, 2006, from http://archives.lists.indymedia.org/antipatriarchy/2002-August/000002.html

Cottingham, J. (1989). Isis: A decade of international networking. In R. R. Rush & D. Allen (Eds.), *Communications at the crossroads: The gender gap connection* (pp. 238-250). Norwood, NJ: Ablex.

Crafton Smith, M. (1989). Women's movement media and cultural politics. In P. J. Creedon (Ed.), *Women in mass communication: Challenging gender values* (pp. 278-298). Newbury Park, CA: Sage.

Enloe, C. (2000). *Maneuvers: The international politics of militarizing women's lives.* Berkeley: University of California Press.

Freeman, J. (1972). The tyranny of structurelessness. *Berkeley Journal of Sociology,* 17, 151-164.

Ganesh, M. (2003, October 23). [antipatriarchy] Women in developing countries. Retrieved December 12, 2006, from http://mail.indymedia.org/antipatriarchy/2003-October/000041.html

Halleck, D. (2003). Indymedia: Building an international activist Internet network. *Media Development, XLX*(4), 11-14. WACC: London.

Herndon, S. (2003). *Indymedia.* Paper presented at the OURMedia III Conference, Barranquilla, Colombia. Retrieved March 13, 2004, from http://www.ourmedia net.org/om2003/om2003.papers_eng.html

Herring, S.C. (1999). The rhetorical dynamics of gender harassment on-line. *The Information Society*, *15*, 151-167.

Herring, S., Job-Sluder, K., Scheckler, R., & Barab, S. (2003). *Searching for safety online: Managing 'trolling' in a feminist forum.* Retrieved June 25, 2005, from http://www.slis.Indiana.edu/CSI/WP/WP02-03B.html

IMCWomynProposal (2003). Retrieved July 7, 2004, from http://docs.indymedia.org/view/Global/ImcWomynProposal#4_Discussion

Indygender Researchers (2005). Hierarchy and gender: A case study of Indymedia. Retrieved January 10, 2006, from http://docs.indymedia.org/view/Main/Indygender Researchers

Indymedia Documentation Project (2000). Draft principles of unity (Ver. 2000). Retrieved November 14, 2003, from http://docs.indymedia.org/view/global/principlesofunity

Indymedia Documentation Project (2002). Draft of NIMC membership criteria. Retrieved November 14, 2003, from http://docs.indymedia.org/view/Global/Membership Criteria

Indymedia Documentation Project (2004). Guidelines for researchers. Retrieved January 10, 2007, from https://docs.indymedia.org/view/Local/ImcUkResearcherGuidelines.

Ionnek (2003, October 7). Love & rage 4 wed meetings! Posting to IMC-London mailing list. Retrieved August 12, 2005, from http://archives.lists.indymedia.org/imc-london/2003-October/000673.html

JD (2005, February 6) IImmmm. Comment posted on *Melbourne Indymedia* in response to Nopper (2005). Retrieved December 14, 2006, from http://melbourne.indymedia.org/news/2005/02/87132_comment.php#88420

Kidd D. (2003). The Independent Media Center: A new model. *Media Development, XLX*(4), 7-10.

Kidd D. (2004). From carnival to commons: The Global IMC network. In E. Yuen, G. Katsiaficas, & D. Burton-Rose, D. (Eds.), *Confronting capitalism: Dispatches from a global movement* (pp. 330-340). New York: Soft Skull Press.

Kluitenberg, E. (2003). Constructing the digital commons: A venture into hybridization. *De Balie.* Retrieved September 10, 2005, from http://www.debalie.nl/artikel.jsp?articleid=12648

Langlois, A. (2004). How open is open? The praxis of open publishing. *Open Journal Archives.* Retrieved August 4, 2005, from http://openj.touchbasic.com:8088/journal/archives/00000004.htm

Lee, G.B. (1996) Addressing anonymous messages in cyberspace. *Journal of Computer-Mediated Communication, 2*(1). Retrieved June 25, 2005, from http://www. ascusc.org/jcmc/vol2/issue1

Lorde, A. (1984). Age, race, class and sex: Women redefining difference. In A. Lorde (Ed.), *Sister outsider: Essays and speeches* (pp. 114-123). Freedom, CA: Crossing Press.

Lotz, A. (2003). Communicating third-wave feminism and new social movements: Challenges for the next century of feminist endeavor. *Women & Language, 26*(1), 2-9.

McClintock, A. (1997). No longer in a future heaven: Gender, race, and nationalism. In A. McClintock, A. Mufti, & E. Shohat (Eds.), *Dangerous liaisons: Gender, nation & postcolonial perspectives* (pp. 89-112). Minneapolis: University of Minnesota Press.

Mohanty Talpade, C. (1991). Under western eyes: Feminist scholarship and colonial discourses. In C. Mohanty Talpade, A. Russo, & L. Torres (Eds.), *Third world women and the politics of feminism* (pp. 51-80). Bloomington: Indiana University Press.

Moss, R. (2005, February 8). It's a fact. Comment posted on *Melbourne Indymedia* in response to Nopper (2005). Retrieved December 14, 2006, from http://melbourne.indy media.org/news/2005/02/87132_comment.php#88420

Nopper, T. K. (2005, February 4). Activist scenes are no safe space for women. Newswire posting to *Melbourne Indymedia*. Retrieved March 7, 2005, from http://melbourne.indy-media.org/news/2005/02/87132_comment.php#88420

Ostrom, E. (1991). *Governing the commons: The evolution of institutions for collective action.* Cambridge: Cambridge University Press.

Rakow, L. F. (1988). Gendered technology, gendered practice. *Critical Studies in Mass Communication, 5*, 57-70.

Riaño Alcalá, P. (Ed.). (1994). *Women in grassroots communications: Furthering social change.* London: Sage.

Sara (2003, October 23). [antipatriarchy] Women in developing countries. Posting to IMC-antipatriarchy mailing list. Retrieved December 12, 2006, from http://mail.indy-media.org/antipatriarchy/2003-October/000043.html

Smith, D. E. (1990). *Texts, facts, and femininity: Exploring the relations of ruling.* New York: Routledge.

Spalding, D. (2002, December 14). An open letter to other men in the movement. Newswire posting to *IMC-DC.* Retrieved December 14, 2006, from http://web. archive.org/web/20030615093541/http://internal.indymedia.org/front.php3?article_i d=779&group=webcast

Sreberny-Mohammadi, A. (1996). Women communication globally: Mediating interna-tional feminism. In D. Allen, R.R. Rush, & S.J. Kaufman (Eds.), *Women transforming com-munications: Global intersections* (pp. 233-242). Thousand Oaks, CA: Sage.

Strole, J. (2002, August 3). [antipatriarchy] My week …Posting to IMC-patriarchy mailing list. Retrieved December 15, 2006, from http://archives.lists.indymedia.org/antipatri-archy/2002-August/000000.html

Sue (2002, July 25). [imc-women-tech]: Re: antipatriarchy list. Posting to IMC-women-tech mailing list. Retrieved December 12, 2006, from http://archives.lists.indy media.org/imc-women-tech/2002-July/000039.html

Sue (2003, October 23). [antipatriarchy] Women in developing countries. Posting to IMC-antipatriarchy mailing list. Original posting not archived. Quoted in Sara (2003). Retrieved December 12, 2006, from http://mail.indymedia.org/antipatriarchy/2003-October/000043.html

Taylor, A., & Bernstein Miller, J. (1994). *Conflict and gender.* Cresskill, NJ: Hampton Press.

warcry (2002, August 4). [antipatriarchy] Re: [imc-women] My week … . Posting to IMC-patriarchy mailing list. Retrieved December 15, 2006, from http://archives.lists.indy-media.org/antipatriarchy/2002-August/000001.html

Werden, F. (1996). The Founding of WINGS (Women's International News Gathering Service). In D. Allen, R.R. Rush, & S. J. Kaufman (Eds.), *Women transforming communica-tions: Global intersections* (pp. 218-225). Thousand Oaks, CA: Sage.

CRYPTO-HIERARCHY AND ITS DISCONTENTS
Indymedia U. K.

Janet Jones & Royston Martin

It was a widespread notion in the 1990s that internet technology was a force in globalisation, creating borderless worlds and borderless communities, borderless organisations and borderless politics. There is a truth in that generalisation. But what is equally true, is that as one set of borders, one set of social structures is taken down, another set of borders is erected. (Carey, 2005: 453)

Social justice movements were among the first to recognize the Internet's potential for democratic communication and nonhierarchical decision making. In theory the internet offered a platform to fulfill an idealized, democratic public sphere through a system of open, equal and fluid interconnectivity, without restriction; one both affordable and global. It was seen as a means of fostering a model communicative space independent of economic systems and the state, well placed to act as a Habermasian Salon helping to restore forums of rational, critical debate and remedy what is commonly referred to as the 'communicative deficit' in society.

Subsequent critiques of how this works in practice have been mixed. Salter is cautiously optimistic, concluding that, empowered by the Internet, voices normally marginalized in mainstream media are able to participate on their own terms in the production of networks "for communicating information and points of view in a largely non-colonized space" (Salter, 2003: 164-165).

James Carey argues that amid the promise of this new technology, users and critics fail to see how changes in systems of production and dissemination can just as easily create new borders as break down old ones. Technology in and of itself, he affirms, is not necessarily liberating (Carey, 2005: 443).

In our observational study of Indymedia U.K. we wanted to explore the extent to which the Internet's potential to aid democratic, nonhierarchical decision making worked in practice. We examined the demands placed upon it by a group of media activists committed to an ideology of consensus, using open-source software to further its cause. We spent eight months investigating the communication practices and editorial decision making at Indymedia U.K., one of the largest international 'net social movements' whose mission it is to change the nature of news through open publishing, relying on a structural system of networked consensus.

Many studies have celebrated the potential of on-line, open publishing to revitalize news gathering and consumption along democratic lines. (Jankowski & Jansen, 2003; Mitra & Watts, 2002; Platon & Deuze, 2003; Salter, 2003, 2005; among many others.) In 2004, Jamie King published a controversial article on-line entitled, *Openness and Its Discontents*. In it he highlights how on-line, consensual decision making can create an unwieldy set of problems for any web-based organization that prides itself on its openness, and its nonhierarchical nature. King suggests that open-source publishing groups such as Indymedia leave themselves vulnerable to what he has termed 'crypto-hierarchies.' He defines these as the natural by-products of Internet organizations that have an "avowed absence of decision-making bodies and points of centralisation" and that can "too easily segue into a concealment of control per se" (King, 2004).

Building on these notions of accountability and invisible hierarchy, we investigate the extent to which Indymedia U.K.'s technological dependency affects its ability to enable the consensual decision making process it aspires to. Over the summer of 2004 we were invited by one member of the inner Indymedia U.K. circle to conduct on-line research into its user/contributor base. The invitation was then debated through IMC U.K. process, the main communication channel. We continued to monitor proceedings on the IMC U.K. process pages on the Internet into December 2006. We kept a diary of all the on-line discussions that ensued in an attempt to document the decision-making process and looked for evidence to support or refute King's description of the minority exercising 'soft control' over the majority.

We conclude from this study that the reliance on technological elites does effectively channel and centralize power in the hands of a few. Ironically, the very 'openness' of the decision making process allowed us to monitor this limitation. We also observed that there is a healthy degree of reflexivity within the group that recognizes this problem and seeks ways of addressing it.

We set our findings in the context of Habermas's theories on how flows of influence may be organized so as to allow the most extensive democratization possible (the ideal public sphere) but also how communication is often subverted by systematic imperatives. This study suggests manifest causal links between the technological elite and the power base of Indymedia U.K., suggesting that Habermas's ideal public sphere, where a social space is generated by communicative action *protected* from systematic imperatives by separation, is not easily facilitated through this form of Internet publishing (Habermas, 1987, 1989, 1996).

INTERNET UTOPIAS

This chapter is part of what has been called the second generation of Internet studies attempting to re-theorize the workings of the world wide web. Now that the Internet is maturing into its adolescence, we ask just how sustainable the micromanagement of open access, consensus-based democratic sites, such as Indymedia, are in relation to their reliance on computer aided information protocols.

The Internet has been largely successful in facilitating virtual political and alternative journalistic communities that provide for new forms of social capital in our society. Some theorists, however, have sounded cautionary notes. For example, Castells (2000) suggested that it was important to critically engage with the social ramifications of the Internet's technological underpinnings. He suggested that "larger questions remain regarding whether the Internet can facilitate this process of escaping technocratic modes of decision-making . . . or will the digital age be marked by a new form of class inequality, distinguished by the 'interacting' and the 'interacted'?" (Castells, 2000: 402)

Mitra and Watts argue in their article, "Theorising Cyberspace: The Idea of Voice Applied to the Internet Discourse", that this new century has witnessed the emergence of two distinct publics—one in real life and the other in the virtual reality of cyberspace (2002). They discuss 'the locus of discursive power' on the Internet, which they term 'voice', and they present a cautiously optimistic evaluation of the potential of cyberspace to liberate marginal voices, "with the potential to flatten hierarchies of power on the Internet" (Mitra & Watts, 2002: 494). They envisage a public sphere created whereby a speaker's persuasive power does not come from status or territory or the de facto power that the speaker brings to the forum and where communal voices can now be heard without pressures from real-life marginalizing forces.

> These characteristics of the Internet therefore have the potential of altering some of the traditional structures of speaking power where the marginal entities can now find a 'place at the table' and be able to challenge dominant voices. . . . It is not as if the problems relating to discursive and vocal power have suddenly been wiped away, but the new technology offers the chance to examine how 'marginal' people and nations can attempt to correct some of the biases that have been inherent in the traditional structures of speaking power. (Mitra and Watts, 2002: 489)

The authors include a disclaimer, warning that this form of egalitarianism cannot be taken for granted because the Internet is not necessarily free of specific structures of power.

In Lee Salter's analysis of new social movements and the Internet, he highlights the tensions that exist between democratic forms of use and forms of use concerned with the pursuit of economic profitability and efficiency (2005). He suggests that because radical media projects commonly don't divide operational functions between managerial and editorial, production relations tend to be cooperative, with a minimal division of labor between roles, and this in turn fosters an internal democracy and the rejection of formal hierarchies (Salter, 2005: 158, 234).

He suggests that if Net social relations can be removed from instrumental relations of efficiency, what he calls the 'pathological effect of technological structures' (i.e., a clean separation between the Habermasian life and systems worlds) then the Web can be successful in fostering radical public spheres, and that IMCs are a significant and relatively successful examples of this. Salter does, however, acknowledge that it is a mistake to interpret them as fully autonomous or liberated spaces given that they must function within what Habermas terms the systems world, subject to "dominant, colonizing forms of use" (Salter, 2005: 263).

TECHNOLOGY AGNOSTIC— NEITHER ENABLING NOR EMPOWERING

As our research developed, we recognized that the use of Open Source Software was regarded from its beginnings by many developers as a pragmatic methodology with no built-in guarantee of egalitarianism or freedom from specific structures of power. Yet, many previous studies in this area have side-stepped this issue, either downplaying the role of technology or celebrating it as empowering and liberating.

Indymedia may be opposed to hierarchies, but the system to which it owes its existence, the Internet, is largely dependent upon them. In illustration, by turning a critical eye toward Indymedia's technology we can analyze the publishing structures created by differing software applications and their political implications.

> The member must first go through the relevant decision making process before being issued with a community agent certificate to act on behalf of the community. This certificate is then passed to its parent community where it is checked to ensure that access rights for this resource have indeed been delegated to the sub community. The parent community then issues its community agent certificate and passes it onto its parent where the checks are repeated in turn until the owning community of the resource is reached and access is granted. (Feeney, Lewis, & Wade, 2004: 6)

GLOBAL INDYMEDIA AND INDYMEDIA U.K.

Indymedia today is a much hybridized and rarified version of the original form that branched out of the global Social Justice Movement of the 1990s. The movement, characterized in particular by anti–World Trade Organization protests, was somewhat of a hybrid itself, attempting as it did to form a coalition of interests to integrate the social justice concerns of many previous activist groups.

> The IMC Network has grown very rapidly from the downtown Seattle shop front in the midst of the anti-WTO mobilizations. As the wave of protests against corporate globalization grew, so did the network, as centres joined on their own, or with the boost of international support teams in hot spots such as Chiapas, Palestine and Iraq. (Kidd, 2003: 3)

In particular, Kidd suggests that Indymedia's success in providing near instant multimedia online reportage of violent clashes with police marked a major development in the history of news making and guaranteed the group's rapid development (Kidd, 2003). Like many networks that have spread rhizomically, so Indymedia has mutated. In the process each collective and user is at once endowed with a perception of the mission, and bound together by several key principles, among them a tacit commitment to a nonhierarchical structure based on consensus decision making and open publishing.

Open publishing is used by other Internet based entities such as Slashdot and Wikipedia. For Indymedia, though, open publishing means, at its best, that the process of creating news is transparent to the readers. They can contribute a story and see it instantly appear in the pool of stories publicly available. Ideally, readers can see editorial decisions being made by others. They can see how to get involved and help create content. If they can think of a better way for the software to help shape that process, they can copy the software because it is free and change it and start their own site. If they want to redistribute the news, they can, preferably on an open publishing site. It's a prime example of what Deuze defines as an open journalistic culture with a concentration of public connectivity (Deuze, 2003).

Although local Indymedia groups are asked to agree with the organization's Global Principles of Unity this document itself remains a work in progress that different groups interpret to suit their own regional interests. For example, part of the Indymedia U.K. mission statement dovetails neatly into the Global position, such as its commitment to nonhierarchical structures.[1]

In and of itself, Indymedia is not strictly a social movement; rather it seeks to be the gateway to the Internet through which the global social justice movements travels as it campaigns, informs itself, and grows through open publishing activities. It can be seen as the largest, global, public, democratic media news network.

Although no more than an infant next to the mainstream global media brands, Indymedia, as of this writing, has more than 130 sites in around 60 countries. As one Indymedia U.K. activist wrote in May 2005, the size of the organization is creating some new challenges.

> What is a network? The Indymedia Centre Network has grown substantially over the past five years, from its roots in Seattle spreading out to span hundreds of different media centres and thousands of volunteers.

> And now, five years down the road, are we seeing the time when Indymedia is approaching the limit of it's growing phase, and moving instead into some kind of 'plateau' phase, where the exponential growth of a fresh idea is replaced by the sustainability needed to survive? (GarconDuMonde http://docs.Indymedia.org/view/Global/NetWorkOld)

RESEARCH ACTIVITY

Survival will depend on how successful each collective is in reinventing itself as the organization matures. It is easy to see how Indymedia's open-publishing project might fail under pressures of scale and the splintering of the counter public. IMC sites have become targets for interventions by political opponents, often from the fascist right, seeking opportunities to disrupt what they regard as the IMCs' countercultural potential. As a defence, collectives have had to become increasingly sophisticated in the way that they selectively hide postings on their central news column. They use 'ad hoc' teams (whose function was previously to develop and maintain the IMCs open publishing system) to politically censor contributions (King, 2004). These censors have special password privileges and the ability to take off line anything they consider might be in breach of Indymedia's editorial guidelines.

Over eight months between 2004 and 2005, our research brought us into contact with Indymedia U.K. editorial activists through meetings, open e-mail 'chat' and through monitoring one of the central planks of Indymedia U.K.'s decision-making, IMC process. We attempted to analyze how transparent or opaque Indymedia's open editorial policy was and whether it could be externally validated.

Our first encounter with the editorial guidelines[2] came during the summer of 2004 as a result of an invitation by one of Indymedia's main activists to conduct research into on-line political activism and democracy through the newswire looking at Indymedia's user, reader, and reporter base.

It is important to make clear that we were ultimately unsuccessful in carrying out our original research brief. We drafted a joint proposal with our 'proposer' from the U.K. Kollective (Short for U.K.–United Kollectives of Britain) that was subsequently debated through IMC process. Our research plan was posted in early summer, 2004; however, it was apparent that there was a reluctance to debate the proposal at the outset. A second posting, a few weeks later, drew in three specific commentators who were all openly negative. They criticized our proposal on the basis that we were 'outsiders' and that we needed to work for the collective before they could 'trust' us with access to their user base.

It was made clear that as paid academics anything posted on our behalf would breach the 'hierarchical' and 'advertising' sections of their editorial code. We were told that, "Universities are by nature hierarchical." We fell foul of the 'advertising' code, possibly due to the fact that our university would be mentioned on the proposed questionnaire. We were also accused of having a potentially unacceptable level of institutional bias. It was suggested that any questionnaire we attempted to launch would be immediately 'hidden' on these grounds.

It struck us at the time that the published codes were nebulous enough to be open to a multitude of interpretations, and we were interested in what other readings might surface in what we hoped would be a constructive debate. It was at this early stage of the debate that we were sent the following message repeatedly through the IRC session (July 22, 2004).

> We're advising you that it is highly unlikely to be considered in what you would probably term as 'favourable' circumstances.

We were told later by our internal Indymedia proposer that we had been 'blocked.' We did not know by whom or why. At this point in time we had encountered a balance of negative and positive responses from the Kollective. One positive public posting read, "Some grounded research might hold a mirror to our current PROJECT rather than the phatasays (*sic*) I see so many people going round and round and round and round in there (*sic*) own heads" (June 23, 2004). Another public posting read, "I feel that we should grant a bit of latitude to a research team that seems sympathetic and sensitive and hasn't actually tried to Spam us or something" (June 23, 2004, Imc-uk-process). We had also privately received support through e-mail from others not engaged in the open debate, although the most vocal and persistent comments were from the dissenters mentioned earlier. Our Indymedia 'proposer,' still supported our proposal and offered this public comment, "It seems to me that three people inside IMC-U.K. want to stop process and debate on the subject of political apathy and the Internet, (our research proposal) probably one of the most important issues of our times" (Imc-uk-process, 9 August, 2004).

A further attempt was made to engage the Kollective in open debate, although we were warned again that we had been blocked. The process of decision making that led to the block had not been at all transparent to us as 'outsiders'; it did not appear to be overtly consensus based, as we could not identify decision making bodies or individuals, yet, it was clear that someone with a significant level of authority had influenced the outcome. We were eventually informed that the 'blocker' was one of Indymedia U.K.'s founders who 'rarely speaks.' Our 'proposer' in private correspondence told us, "I thought we could get through, but I can not square up to one of its founders. . . . I also read through the lines that he has weighed the personal political positions with Indymedia's position as a network and he has balanced at this particular moment in time against this project." In most organizations, this kind of decision making is common, as power is vested in a few senior figures as a matter of course and expediency; however, it seemed contrary to the ethos of collective decision making. In his article ("Openness and its Discontents") King describes figures with special authority as 'supernodes.'

> In the social movement, decision making often devolves to a surprisingly small number of individuals and groups who make a lot of the running in deciding what happens, where and when. Though they never officially speak for others, much unofficial doctrine, nonetheless, emanates from them. Within political networks, such groups and individuals can be seen as 'supernodes' not only routing more than their fair share of traffic, but actively determining the 'content' that traverses them. Such supernodes do not (necessarily) constitute themselves out of a malicious will-to-power: rather, power defaults to them through personal qualities like energy, commitment and charisma. (King, 2004)

If King is right and social position is key to decision making within the U.K. Kollective, then our experience should not be an isolated one. Our initial encounter over the summer of 2004 inspired a continued interest in the outcome of further debates posted on IMC process to see if any particular pattern emerged. We archived the Internet exchanges and monitored the agenda items, interventions, and (where possible) the outcome to the debates.

TACIT POWER AND SUPERNODES

We were told that the central decision-making arena was 'IMC Process', where our own proposal had first been introduced. The items posted for discussion on IMC process varied greatly.[3] There were 80 subscribers on the IMC Process list in June 2004, and this number had not changed substantially by May, 2005. Of these, around half contributed at least once to the discussions over the eight months we were monitoring. Fifty percent contributed on a rare basis, 20% contributed on an occasional basis, 6% on a semiregular basis, and 4% on a consistent basis. It is feasible that these final two categories contain within them what King refers to as 'supernodes' (those who have the time, knowledge, and commitment to engage on a regular basis with debate). However, our first encounter with Indymedia over the summer suggested that we could not rule out the significance of silent partners within the decision-making fold.

It was clear that IMC process tries to accommodate a variety of voices within a consensual decision-making environment, and there is a good level of transparency achieved through this open debating process. But certain aspects of this debate did stand out as problematic.

Technology is fundamentally at the heart of Indymedia's power structures. Those with the knowledge of technical operations and those who have the passwords to control server operations are central to all activities. One striking illustration of this came via a vociferous complaint from the Cyprus Indymedia Collective after the U.K. 'techies' had acted autocratically and changed a number of key settings that affected Cyprus quite profoundly.

> You did this without communicating with anyone among us, without warning, without permission. . . . It's no wonder that we keep discovering that at the very core of imc there is something so rotten it's unspeakable. Over and over, we keep finding that there are individuals entrusted with access to and power to influence the most sensitive technical operations of Indymedia. . . . . who decides that a person like you should be entrusted with so much, and have the power to disrupt and poison relations among us? (September 26, 2004 Imc-Cyprus)

There are very few password holders, and these people have to be well versed in computer code and Internet languages in order to do their jobs effectively. Their 'elite' status is acquired through their superior knowledge of code and their longevity within the collective. Another example of the central role these people play was evidenced when the U.K. Kollective needed to purchase a replacement server after the U. S. server, on which Indymedia U.K. relied, was seized by the U. S. administration (October 7, 2004, http://www.Indymedia.org /en/2004/10/111999.shtml).[4]

At this time there were a considerable number of technically worded e-mails floating through the system. Finally a member of the 'techie' group after a long period of debate admitted:

> Generally the way that IMC servers tend to get run is that people doing the sysadmin on them seem to be the ones who make the decisions about what goes on them in terms of software and sites. Are we happy for decisions like this around the new box to be sorted out by the techies or do we want some other kind of process to be used? (November 24, 2004, Imc-uk-process)

Our attention was focused on the extent to which the 'sysadmin' represents an important power base at Indymedia, and the study was naturally limited to what we could observe from the 'open access' channels. There was an indication that the problem of too few 'techies' led to control in the hands of a minority of hardworking members. This, in turn, had the potential to lead to problems and tensions within the Kollective. For example, it is clear that Indymedia U.K. (different from its sister operations in North America) has a strong central core, and many regional centers are dependent on this core for rackspace, technical expertise, and finance.

> The coordination, maintenance and further development of the hardware and software infrastructure that underpins Indymedia U.K. is in the hands of a very few people in London. (December 19, 2004, Imc-uk-process)

In November 2004 the Oxford collective chose to discuss possible 'improvements' to this structure, concerned that too much power was relinquished to the center. Their disquiet was made public on line and started a key debate on the nature of federalism and power. One solution Oxford proposed was:

> Each U.K. collective should operate a server ... that is essentially independent of the database. . . . The practice of running a U.K. collective should cease. This would free up U.K. contributors to return to work at their local collective. The U.K. site (new) would become an aggregation of features from local collectives ... local collectives would be relied upon to do their own editing. There would be no U.K. newswire anymore. (December 15, 2004, Imc-uk-process)

and

> Currently there is a de facto imc 'elite' who work on national sites and the global site, who are not necessarily finding time to contribute to their local imc's. . . . These changes would be empowering to local reporters, and would reduce the extent to which the U.K. is seen to be hierarchically organized (December 11, 2004, Imc-uk-process)

Here is evidence of a healthy degree of reflexivity enabled by open Internet discourse. If the discussion were to mature and be resolved nonhierarchically, it would potentially disprove King's thesis. However, this debate remained frustratingly unresolved on the open access channels. One of the 'supernodes,' identified earlier by our quantitative discourse study, made this comment.

> The term 'elite,' by human beings conditioned to live in a hierarchical/patriarchical society (that'd be us!) is sometimes indiscriminately/unreflectively used to describe those who do things and get on with it ... but of course it might be a real issue, leading to some central questions. . . . So if anyone feels excluded in anyway, please let myself or one of the other list admins know. (December 15, 2004, Imc-uk-process)

The challenge issued at the end of this last posting 'to let us know' certainly has the tone of a hierarchical structure at work. Other centralizing voices quickly came forward at this point, leaving Oxford on the defensive:

> What Oxford is proposing is to find ways of 'improving' the U.K. network, not scrapping it … and I understand that some proposals may be radical and 'emotionally difficult' to consider (especially for people who have been involved in the U.K. site from the beginning). (December 21, 2004, Imc-uk-process)

This in turn led to a wider discussion of the nature of a 'collective within a collective', and the word 'status' was debated in relation to the regions and the centre.

> Isn't this (Indymedia) about freely associating with each other and engaging where you want, with whom you want, and when you want? (December 21, 2004, Imc-uk-process)

Reply:

> I think that's certainly one of the things it's meant to be about. But in practice, informal structures form automatically (and unavoidably) in any group situation. That's not a bad thing in itself; but it's important to see these informal structures, and understand them. *And as it happens the informal structures within Indymedia tend to be quite opaque.* (December 21, 2004, Imc-uk-process)

What seemed to be the final word on the matter was issued by the same London-based, 'supernode' who had declared our original research project defunct.

> Although I can understand that the U.K. network is not the most perfect—I don't really see it being hierarchical as it is the same people working on both levels in the main. . . . I think … if we dissolve U.K. I doubt many small collectives would survive or ones in the pipeline even start. (December 21, 2004, Imc-uk-process)

That appeared to represent the final open exchange—resolved to the status quo.

CENSORSHIP

At the core of Indymedia's adoption of open publishing is a frustration with and a distrust of what it calls the 'corporate media', which it argues blocks or ignores significant items of news because of its own inherent capitalistic profit motive. In doing so, Indymedia would like to emphasize important organizational distinc-

tions between 'corporate' and the self-defined 'democratic' journalism it
embraces. 'Corporate' or traditional journalism, it maintains, is largely determined by the forces of commercialism, the use of hierarchies, centrally controlled one-way communication, and entrenched editorial attitudes relating to
concepts of impartiality, balance, and news priorities that largely prohibit the
expression of opinion.

Indymedia lays claim to an alternative news agenda airing a different set of
political voices, those often considered deviant in the mainstream. Yet, as mentioned earlier, the editorial guidelines impose a strict regime of censorship
around certain stories that are considered offensive to its philosophically progressive nature, such as racist, homophobic, fascist, and sexist postings.

Censorship of illegal posts is a sensitive issue within the collective. "In many
IMC collectives, the editing vs. free speech dichotomy is argued as hotly as abor-
tion is debated by members of congregations and Congress" (Whitney, 2005).
The problem with autonomy, as identified by many contributions to the debate
on the federal structure, is that the censorship (or hiding) of illegal posts is done
centrally, and therefore regional collectives are disempowered editorially; they
are not enabled to decide for themselves what postings need to be 'cleaned.'
Arguably, the list cleaners or 'admins' in London act very much like the silent,
invisible hand of the 'corporate' news editor. One vocal dissenter from the Bristol
branch of the IMC launched an attack on the working practices of the central
'admins.'

> What laughable lengths you appear prepared to go to—to censor stories you
> don't approve of with neither discussion nor explanation. (September 27,
> 2004, Imc-uk-process)

This comment reflects an important aspect associated with the act of censorship.
How do you build accountability and openness into the hiding process? There is
a natural tension between protecting Indymedia U.K. from legal suits and
upholding the philosophy of openness. One significant debate focused around a
proposed change to current editorial policy. The proposal was that the list cleaners use a 'watermark,' which would leave a vague imprint where a hidden story
was originally launched, less conspicuous than the present policy, which uses
black text on a black background. Both systems would act to leave a trace of the
editorial decision to kill the story, but the former, the new proposal, would be
more subtle. The main difference would be that only 'admins' would be allowed
to read the cleaned copy in the new system to protect Indymedia from legal
threats. A dissenter to this change remarked:

> If our intention is that only admins should be allowed to read the stuff, then
> why not just password protect it, and forget about the legalese/black-on-
> black/solid watermark nonsense? Answer, because we're committed to Open

Posting. . . . I'm against the hiding thing altogether, as it happens; I think it's intellectually dishonest. I go along with it in the spirit of compromise—because it's the best practical approximation to openness that I know of. (February 1, 2005, Imc-uk-process)

One watermark proposer argued:

Accessibility is not about making the rubbis-sorry, the hidden posts ;-) easier to smel-sorry to read. :-p ... In my opinion making hidden posts harder to read is a form of respecting and appreciating the work that the very dedicated 'hiders' do. Remember that it is a very ungrateful task and one which also makes the site "more accessible", yes, and less frustrating for people who do not have much time ... and given that we are giving those (hidden) posts web space even though we ALL do not approve of them, at least let's provide that web space with a difference. (February 2, 2005, Imc-uk-process)

This was another form of self-reflexive debate, internally vetting and criticizing transparency in editorial decision making, as yet unresolved. What motivates the 'discontents' is a reaction against any process (no matter how well-meaning) that centrally controls the content on the site. At the time, there is no obvious resolution to the problems discussed. There is no organized 'appeal' procedure against hidden posts, and this leaves the system open to the criticism of unfair practice.

Among several similar disputes posted between 2004-2005, the following case is symptomatic of the problems facing Indymedia U.K. An article appeared and was immediately 'cleaned,' contravening its rigid advertising policy because it mentioned where readers might purchase a particular book that exposed a 'right wing conspiracy.' The censored individual wrote:

So who hid it? The BNP, The world Bank, NATO ... or was it Mr. Smith's mate that hid it—another anonymous player of 'pass the password' ... lying/ditching editorial guidelines to cover his tracks. (April 3, 2005, Imc-uk-process)

The row that ensued involved vitriol, libelous statements, and ended with the call for the censored individual's expulsion. Despite the hot air, nothing was resolved; editorially, it was business as usual.

PRAXIS

The ideal of creating a media source that would be totally inclusive has had to endure tremendous tests. Open publishing, the purest form of the idea, has become, in some instances, *Indymedia*'s greatest liability. (Beckerman, 2003)

The reality of running an Indymedia site is a daily grind of filtering the 'sea of noise' that inevitably accompanies open source news outlets. This forces a form of structure to be imposed at the back end of the editorial process rather than the front end. Tensions naturally arise in the process of back-end editing.

> Some of us encourage more 'art' on the newswire, others are hiding poems. Some of us hide every corporate repost, others argue for keeping some of them. One person's 'disruptive' is another person's inspiration. As a result, the threshold in what is seen as unacceptable is quite high. (Indymedia documentation Project: https://docs.Indymedia.org/view/Local/UkEditorial Guidelines)

Imposing structure at the back end is very time consuming and fraught with difficulty, forcing collectives worldwide to seek sweeping methods of filtering stories to keep wires clean and relevant.

Currently there are a variety of models in place that attempt to deal with this problem. These range from the establishment of 'validation committees,' who are charged with reading every post before promotion to the main central column, to a range of filters or rating systems with built-in editorial criteria not dissimilar to the classic Galtung and Ruge industrial model (Local Relevance, Fairness, Quality of Prose, Factuality, Novelty, and Other) (Jay, 2003).

All these interventionist policies sit uncomfortably with the philosophy of open publishing. Despite the potential of open publishing to liberate marginal voices and flatten hierarchies, each collective is being forced to learn to negotiate its role as mediator.

> On a wider scale, we all agree that the newswire is the backbone of Indymedia. But then there are different interpretations: some of us want to see the open newswire as a running commentary on the website, fast and chaotic, like a messy free radio station. Others want a newswire that features straightforward Indymedia news from the streets. (Indymedia documentation Project: https://docs.Indymedia.org/view/Local/UkEditorialGuidelines)

What exactly gets promoted depends on those volunteers who participate in the process. This again makes the organization dependent on a small group of specialists who need to construct hierarchies of information and cellular knowledge systems to keep the organization running smoothly, keeping Indymedia's systems free from hacking or hijacking and simultaneously producing a site that is readable, user-friendly, and significant to the majority of users.

Thus, the technological and philosophical base underpinning open-publishing systems simultaneously promotes both an inclusive and exclusive operating system. While initially encouraging free, ubiquitous, horizontal interactions it also triggers an equal and opposite limiting reaction imposed through the necessity of coherent, legal publishing. This brings with it the risk that long-time facilitators might form an inner circle, with a culture of understanding what works best (or quickest or most strategically). As Douglas Morris identifies in *Globalization and Media Democracy* (2003) it raises a key organizational issue defined in Roberto Michel's (1962) Iron Law of Oligarchy, which proposes that organizers, who arise out of a desire for a group to be effective, may develop eventually into an elite cultivating professional interests inside the movement. As we have observed, these tend to be a few active and centralized individuals who can exercise real power through the provision of the necessary password privileges.

CONCLUSIONS

Despite the potential of the Internet to facilitate consensual decision making at Indymedia U.K., there is inevitably an aspirational element to the notion of open publishing that buckles under the constraints of its operating base.

Ideally, what defines Indymedia's relationship with its users is its decentralized organizational structure, aimed at empowering individuals through the autonomy and interactivity of open publishing. However, practical and technological restraints mean that there are significant limits to this open-access editorial policy.

All new social justice movements that have embraced the Internet as central to their organizational structures are potentially vulnerable to the emergence of technologically based hierarchies. This is what Kidd and others have referred to as 'growing pains,' the problems and difficulties inherent in "creating and sustaining a more democratic communications model in an increasingly enclosed corporate media environment" (Kidd, 2003: 3).

It would be simplistic to suggest that only social justice movements on the Internet are vulnerable to the counter-elite pressures noted here. Chris Atton conducted an analysis of the journalistic sources used in a local U.K. activist newspaper, *SchNEWS*. He concluded that "the U.K. experience suggests that the primary definers in the radical community press remain as an elite, as hierarchically structured as those for the mainstream media" (Atton & Wickenden, 2005: 350).

Atton describes these dominant sources as a 'counter-elite' and suggests that the deployment of these sources is just as reliant on expertise, authoritativeness, and legitimacy as are mainstream corporate press' sourcing routines. He suggests that the primary reason for this was most likely to be "low capital funding, poorly-paid or voluntary staff and organizational pressures" all of which are structural reasons that work to prevent access to a wide range of sources and impede the aspirational goal of rewriting the rules of corporate-based journalism. These limits, he suggests, "might lead to a structural determinism as powerful and predictable as that of the mainstream media. To ignore these limits and their outcomes is to idealize alternative media as 'free spaces,' mysteriously liberated from the everyday, structural considerations of the practice of journalism" (Atton & Wickenden, 2003: 351).

Indymedia U.K. recognizes that it must continue to recruit activists who are willing to put in the unpaid work on a daily basis, as they are fighting against the problems of dispersed political energies. With a small activist base straining under the pressure of too much work, it is not surprising that editorial power is vested in the hands of a few, confirming King's notion of 'supernodes.' In the U.K., at least, few have mastered the language of computer programmers, a skill which appears increasingly essential to maintain a voice in the Indymedia U.K. debate, if not the editorial process itself. Indeed it could be argued that if the group is to continue to publicize itself by calling on would-be contributors to *be the media*, then it may need to encourage a wider understanding of its technological foundations.

As Hill (2003) and Feeney, Lewis and Wade (2004) have suggested, perhaps one answer lies with the development and adoption of more open content management systems. This will at least minimize the danger of Indymedia U.K.'s technocrats becoming little more than gatekeepers acting (perhaps unwittingly, perhaps knowingly) as opaque censors inadvertently working against the spirit of the global social justice movement.

Robert McChesney, author of *Rich Media, Poor Democracy*, has said that Indymedia "need(s) to make tough editorial decisions, and that's not something to be despondent about. The problem is not that you have to make decisions. The important thing is that you make them on principles that are transparent" (McChesney, cited by Beckerman, 2003). This is not the first time social justice movements have had to deal with difficult questions about the way in which they are structured. In her article, "The Tyranny of Structurelessness," written about her involvement in the organization of the 1960s women's liberation movement, Jo Freeman attacks the problems of 'structurelessness.' The noble aim to create the leaderless organizational form of the movement (what she termed a natural reaction against an overstructured, hierarchical society) became an intrinsic and unquestioned part of the women's liberation ideology without a realization of its limitations. She concluded that, "if the movement is to grow beyond these elementary stages of development, it will have to disabuse itself of some of the prejudices about organization and structure ... to reject them out of hand is to deny ourselves the necessary tools to further development" (Freeman, 1970).

It is doubtful that any news-based organization can operate without structure and clear decision making channels. Indymedia is of course aware of such problems, yet, as we observed here, in its attempt to be nonhierarchical it is still challenged by the test of transparency.

Accountability can only come via a recognized group of editors who do not exercise 'silent' privileges, only 'transparent' privileges. In this way, the organization can balance the need for the necessary infrastructure, keeping it safe and secure from outside interference, and yet remain open to the consensual decision making systems that lie at the heart of the organization.

The analysis of technologically routed power systems is critical to long-term success. Alongside public service broadcasters, the BBC, for example, and commercial personal view providers such as My Space and You Tube, Indymedia is now one of many systems to offer de facto online status to contributors. And, like all the newer social internet brands, it needs accountability at its heart if it is to maintain credibility among a core of contributors willing to provide the 'critical mass of content' necessary for the system to survive. Software solutions to enable transparent consensual decision making are being constantly upgraded. One such pioneering group is Crabgrass, a loose collective of computer programmers (among them some of Indymedia's key personnel) attempting to improve the source code and software available to social justice groups in order to better facilitate democratic decision making.[5]

It is not surprising then, that technology, the midwife at Indymedia's birth, may at once be its curse and potential cure as it seeks to grow into something more than a once useful nerdy kid on the virtual block. Indymedia's call in 1999 was to 'be the media.' It appears anyone now can be the media.

When Indymedia started in 1999, nobody knew of blogs, people couldn't just go and publish on the web, the active software was cutting edge and so was open publishing (November, 1, 2006 Imc-uk-process).

We can all now publish and 'be the media' with limited computer knowledge and computer access. Indymedia increasingly has to ask how it can differentiate itself and its content from the huge mass of independent information and content providers working on the Net.

NOTES

1. All IMC's recognize the importance of process to social change and are committed to the development of non-hierarchical and anti-authoritarian relationships, from interpersonal relationships to group dynamic and therefore shall organize themselves collectively and be committed to the principle of consensus decision making and the development of direct, participatory democratic process that is transparent to its membership. (From the Principles of Unity Statement {draft}) http://docs.*Indymedia*.org/view/Global/PrinciplesOfUnity retrieved February 11, 2007.
2. The published guidelines instruct 'wire-cleaners' to hide posts that are repeated; non-news (comment or opinion); discriminatory, sexist, racist, etc; inaccurate or misleading; advertising; hierarchical; disruptive or reposts (copied and pasted from other sites).

   The word audience is not used in this context because the philosophy of Indymedia suggests that the connotation of the word audience is too passive. Their Outreach document instead defines three levels of IMC use: (1) Read only users (2) Read and comment (3) Active reporter/admin. http://docs.*Indymedia*.org/view/Local/ImcUk OutreachStaticPage retrieved February 11, 2007.
3. Agenda items discussed on-line during our research period included such things as the purchase of a new server; the addition of the word 'homophobia' to the list of unacceptable postings; the possible expulsion of certain international and local collectives

not seen to be in-line with the central organizational ethos; the coverage of the London European Social Forum; fundraising; Indymedia's legal status; redesigning the outreach web page; negotiating hidden posts; and federalization.

4. On 7 October 2004, hard drives from two Indymedia servers were seized from the London office of a U.S.–owned web hosting company, Rackspace, at the request of the U.S. Justice Department, apparently in collaboration with Italian and Swiss authorities (for more information see Indymedia.org October 17, 2004).

5. Our primary focus is to facilitate directly democratic decision making for groups and networks. This means easy tools for polling, voting and achieving consensus. Since different situations call for different tools, we plan to support up-down polls, rate-many-polls, vote-for-one, ranked voting, formal consensus, informal consensus, and different forms of modified consensus (http://cats.revolt.org/cats-vii/crabgrass/one-pager/ retrieved February 11, 2007).

REFERENCES

Atton, C., & Wickenden, E. (2005). Sourcing routines and representation in alternative journalism: A case study approach. *Journalism Studies, 6*(3), 347-359.

Beckerman, G. (2003, September/October). Emerging alternatives: Edging away from anarchy. Inside the *Indymedia* collective, passion vs. pragmatism, *Columbia Journalism Review, 5.* Retrieved January 8, 2006, from http://www.cjr.org/issues/2003/5/anarchy-beckerman.asp

Carey, J.W. (2005). Historical pragmatism and the Internet. *New Media & Society, 4*(4), 443-455.

Castells, M. (2000). *The rise of the network society* (2nd ed.). London: Blackwell.

Deuze, M. (2003). The Web and its journalism: Considering the consequences of different types of newsmedia online. *New Media and Society, 18*(2), 203-230.

Feeney, K. C., Lewis, D., & Wade, D. P. (2004). *Policy based management for internet communities.* In Fifth IEEE International Workshop on Policies for Distributed Systems and Networks (POLICY'04) 06 07-06 (2004). Retrieved September 1, 2006, from http://www.m-zones.org/deliverables/d234_2/papers/1-03-tcd-forpolicy04-v5.pdf

Freeman, J. (1970). The tyranny of structurelessness. *The second wave, 2*(1). Retrieved September 2, 2006, from http://www.jofreeman.com/joreen/tyranny.htm

Habermas, J. (1987). *The theory of communicative action: The critique of functionalist reason.* Cambridge: Polity Press.

Habermas, J. (1989). *The structural transformation of the public sphere.* London: Polity Press.

Habermas, J. (1996). *Between facts and norms.* London: Polity Press.

Hill. B. M. (2003). *Software, politics and indymedia.* Retrieved October 12, 2004, from http://mako.yukidoke.org/writing/mute-*Indymedia*_software.html

Jankowski, N., &, Jansen, M. (2003). *Indymedia.* Exploration of an Alternative Internet-based Source of Movement News. Paper presented at the Digital News, Social Change and Globalisation Conference, Hong Kong Baptist University, Hong Kong, December 12, 2003.

Jay, D. O. (2003). Three proposals for open publishing. Retrieved January 5, 2006, from http://dru.ca/imc/open_pub.html

Kidd, D. (2003). The independent media center: A new model. *Media Development, 4*, 7-11. Retrieved October 12, 2004, from http://www.wacc.org.uk/wacc/publications/media _development

King, J. (2004). The packet gang (Part One): Openness and its discontents. Retrieved October 12, 2004, from http://www.Discordia.us/scoop/story/2004/2/18/153734/296

Mitra, A., & Watts, E. (2002). Theorising cyberspace: The idea of voice applied to the Internet discourse. *New Media & Society, 4*(4), 499-498.

Morris, D. (2004). Globalization and media democracy: The case of Indymedia. In D. Schuler & P. Day (Eds.), *Shaping the network society. The new role of civil society in cyber space* (pp. 325-352). Cambridge, MA: MIT Press.

Platon, S., & Deuze, M. (2003). Indymedia journalism: A radical way of making selecting and sharing news? *Journalism, 4*(3), 336-355.

Salter, L. (2003). Democracy, new social movements and the Internet. In M. McCaughey & M. Ayers (Eds.), *Cyberactivism: Online activism in theory and practice* (pp. 117-144). London: Routledge.

Salter, L. (2005). Colonization tendencies in the development of the world wide web. *New Media and Society, 7*(3), 291-309.

Whitney, J. (2005). *What's the matter with Indymedia?* Retrieved July 28, 2005, from http://www.alternet.org/module

SECTION IV
Our Media and the State

INTRODUCTION TO SECTION IV

John Downing

The connecting thread in the three chapters in this section is their reflection on the potential for democratic and social justice–oriented mass communication in state-permitted and/or state-funded media systems. The Chilean case study addresses the experience of these media under a very strong state, namely a U.S.–backed military dictatorship, and subsequently in the dictatorship's aftermath. The Mexican case study addresses the particular experience of indigenous people's movements and state-run media, both before and since the 1994 Zapatista uprising in the southern state of Chiapas. The Wales case study—as distinct from 'the Welsh case,' because language was not its pivot—addresses the potential for the public's voices to be heard within the context of a public service broadcasting institution in a liberal democracy—a state-form sharply different both from the extreme authoritarianism of the Chilean dictatorship and from the top-down heavy-handedness that still characterizes the Mexican state.

All three chapters therefore address the uncertain middle ground of social justice movement media, one that resembles neither the crisp binary categories of Leninist media (the workers' and farmers' state vs. the capitalist state), nor the plague-on-the-state! position of classical anarchist media. (Nor, I might add, the binarism of the 1984 version of my own Radical Media.) Although they do not reference the case studies of media-state relations edited by Morris and Waisbord (2001), which present powerful empirical arguments for disaggregating the concept of the State and acknowledging its variable characteristics in different nations and zones, their analyses lie very much within and contribute further to that line of reasoning. Nor do they reference anthropologist James Scott's dissection of what he terms "the immense political terrain that lies between quiescence and revolt" (Scott, 1990: 199), meaning the everyday low-intensity contestation of established power. Nonetheless the feel in these case studies for the texture of that contestation is akin in a number of ways to his.

In what follows, I will particularly focus on what these case studies illuminate about state power, and then about political change, as they affect social justice movement media. To begin, the conventional image of a violent military dictatorship such as Augusto Pinochet's in Chile is often of a situation where politics screeches to a halt. In very important ways public political activity does get stifled, but there are sometimes unexpected cracks and chinks in the carapace of power. In her chapter, Bresnahan identifies several such, notably the role of the Catholic hierarchy in Chile and the dictatorship's concern to be perceived in Washington, DC as staying within the confines of respect for law, however profound its contempt for legal and human rights in many key regards. Thus the Church's sponsorship of the magazine Análisis provided it with a protective covering from 1977 up to the state of emergency in force over 1984-85. From 1986 onwards, Análisis was printed in Germany by a German labor union, which, under Chilean law, meant that it was no longer a Chilean publication and was thus immune from censorship. Perhaps if it had been printed in Paraguay the outcome would have changed, but the German Federal Republic was a key regime in the 'Christian West' that the thugs in charge of Chile vociferously proclaimed they represented.

The importance of the Catholic Vicariat's stance is illustrated by the contrast with Argentina, where active complicity with the hideous crimes of the military junta there over 1976-83 was the stock in trade of the Catholic hierarchy and contributed to the long silence on the junta's crimes after its fall. It is exemplified even more sharply still by Guatemala's genocide of Mayans over a 40-year period, from the U.S.–backed coup of 1954 through the end of the 1990s. For the first twenty years the Guatemalan Catholic hierarchy was silent, and even when it began reluctantly to address the situation, Pentecostalist and Evangelical church leaders continued to endorse the genocide in the name of religion. Fear was pandemic, infinitely more entrenched even than during the civil wars then in force in neighboring Nicaragua and El Salvador.

Thus even draconic state power can be seen to be relational—relational to powerful institutions within the nation, and relational to powerful states from which an authoritarian regime seeks tolerance, if not full credence. This relational dimension may open up spaces that can be seized upon by movement media activists. Conversely, in the absence of those counterweights, as in Argentina and Guatemala where neither religious leaders nor leading Western governments spoke out, the prospect for social justice media is extremely bleak.

The Mexican case study concerns indigenous peoples' radio stations, though the stations themselves, despite being run mostly by indigenous broadcasters, were owned by the Mexican government. Rural Mexicans are typically much poorer still than urban Mexicans, and indigenous rural Mexicans, numbering some 10% of the population, are generally the poorest of all. Rural Mexico has a considerable history of untrammeled landowner power, and also a history of revolts against it. The marginalization of most indigenous peoples is massive. Thus on the face of it, the radio stations should have served as simply a loudspeaker for the powers that be.

Yet surprisingly often this was not the case, as Castells-Talens demonstrates in Chapter 8. For him, the Mexican case illustrates par excellence the way in which in practice "the stations negotiate [government policies] ... creating a hazy and malleable space." The numerous details he supplies of how this operates in practice are highly informative, and the emphasis he places on the high levels of community participation in these stations is very encouraging. Some community members were even unaware that the State was the sponsor of these stations. A high level of open meetings to discuss community issues, and funding toward the end of the 1990s to enable participation in a national advisory council for these stations, co-existed with a general failure to develop in two other areas, namely a community correspondent program and training of volunteer radio production units.

He stresses how varying agencies of the State, at different times, engaged in evidently different ways with these stations. One example was how during the tense height of the Zapatista movement in the mid-1990s, political police observers would come to check on the stations, but always in a rather off-hand and casual manner, not breathing down the editors' necks or issuing dictates to them. A different example was how after the Zapatista uprising some very highly placed politicians announced themselves as advocates of these stations, but not out of any sincere commitment to a pluricultural Mexico, rather because they saw a multicultural and intercultural emphasis as a way of drawing the Zapatistas' sting. 'Culture' appeared much safer to them than power.

Thus, as one radio activist is cited in the first full-length English-language account of these stations (Vargas, 1995: 242), indigenous peoples' "music, stories and traditional knowledge" are acceptable, but not "their reality." Despite this, Castells-Talens notes how in Yucatán stations, in Mexico's far south, there came to emerge in the second half of the 1990s numerous signals of subtle and not-so-subtle emphasis on Mayan themes, as opposed to the Mexican Federal State's traditional orthodoxy defining the country as a mestizo (euro-indigenous) nation. This needs to be put in the context of Mexico's television channels, whose immensely popular telenovelas are populated almost exclusively by White Mexicans, with darker skins reserved for domestics. In other words, the racial mythology of Mexico as a postracist mestizo nation is typically blanked out on television—but only in favor of whiteness, not of indigenous groups. The Mayan themes in Yucatán indigenous radio stations had to be hesitant, while whiteness on national TV could be pervasive.

J. Kidd's elaboration of Capture Wales in Chapter 10, a digital story-telling case study, comes out of a sharply different historical and political context. The Welsh were invaded by the English nearly 1,100 years ago and finally subjugated some three centuries later in 1282, the first of the 'internal colonies,' to be followed by Scotland (1707) and Ireland (1800). At present, although the Welsh language has had a significant renaissance and is still the mother-tongue of many in the rural northern part of the country, and although recently Wales was granted its own Assembly, the dominance of English culture as well as the English language is stable. Wales' political self-assertion is therefore a linguistic and cultural issue for some citizens, but more of a regional than a strictly national or indigenous issue for a majority (the independence movement is tiny, unlike in Scotland).

A highly influential component of English culture in Wales since the mid-1920s has been the BBC. This is an institution born principally as an elite cultural leader rather than as a democratic cultural forum, an institution ultimately on the side of the power structure, as its founder noted in his memoir when writing about the role of BBC radio news as the sole source of independent national information during the historic nine-day nationwide strike of 1926. And yet as Kidd notes, there has predictably been a history of attempts by activist radio and television producers to push the BBC in the direction of enabling everyday voices to be heard. These attempts reflected the BBC's stated mission, but more rarely its actual practice.

The activists' objectives were not those of political revolutionaries, even though the latter might have been supportive of them. What drove the activists was rather the conviction that the voices of everyday life were sparkier, wittier, and more vivid than the sage grave tones of professional broadcasters, educators, and politicians; their insights more acute; their visions sharper. They shared a common intellectual space, whether or not they answered to them, with Mikhail Bakhtin (1984) and his celebration of the carnivalesque, and with sociolinguist William Labov's (1972) epiphany that African American English speech was not only just as rich in nuance and expression as professionals' speech, but often more so. We might similarly conclude that despite the commercial media distortions in both sport and reality TV, the residual appeal of each lies in the sense that the ending is not yet known, and also that both television genres feature us, our lives, our warts, our wit, our skills.

Kidd frames adoption by the august BBC as a potential problem, a form of corralling rather than amplifying such voices (their 'containment'). This perhaps overstates the political rather than cultural undesirability among BBC officials of opening up the airwaves in the ways she describes. The voices projects she outlines that the BBC has permitted over the years did not have anything like the ominous resonance of black radio stations for the racist Thatcher Administration, which in 1985 suddenly canceled the review of 200 community radio license applications, just in case such 'insurgent' stations took hold! The details of Kidd's study, then, strongly support the culturalist explanation of why the BBC has supported but not energetically underwritten these projects. (They are also very helpful in providing specifics for media activists planning similar work.)

One more word is in order regarding the Capture Wales project and similar story-telling endeavors. Kidd nicely describes and underscores the many long-term empowerment consequences of participation in Capture Wales. Her analysis is very reminiscent of Clemencia Rodríguez' commentary on the impact of participation in a community video project by women in a poor Bogotá barrio (Rodríguez, 2001). Both cases explode the false parallelism between the modes of media impact research appropriate to conventional mass media audiences and to alternative media users—a parallelism that typically appears to justify dismissing small-scale media use as ephemeral and trivial.

The other major focus of these three studies is on political change. In Chile we see shifts from democracy to military dictatorship, to renewed state of emergency, to the end of dictatorship but a very quiescent democracy, and most recently a somewhat reinvigorated democracy. In Mexico, the shift was between pre- and post-1994 (the Zapatista uprising). In Wales, the political change is less at the level of the state, and insurgency, as the unceasing influence of pressure on the BBC to compete with commercial rivals in a newly multichannel media ecology and to cease to rely for support on its historic status within the British polity.

In each case, the unitary conception of the state receives another kick. Not only is the contemporary state, even in a harsh military dictatorship, an internally contradictory structure in certain significant ways, but it also changes over time. This is no mere conceptual quibble. Insofar as these understandings of the state are correct, social justice movements need to incorporate them into their media practice and strategies. One size does not fit all. . . .

REFERENCE

Bakhtin, M. (1984). *Rabelais and his world.* Bloomington: Indiana University Press.

Downing, J. D. (1984). *Radical media: The political organization of alternative communication.* Boston: South End Press.

Labov, W. (1972). *Language in the inner city.* Philadelphia: University of Pennsylvania Press.

Morris, N., & Waisbord, S. (Eds.). (2001). *Media and globalization: Why the state matters.* Lanham, MD: Rowman & Littlefield.

Rodríguez, C. (2001). *Fissures in the mediascape: An international study of citizens' media.* Cresskill, NJ: Hampton Press.

Scott, J. (1990). *Domination and the arts of resistance: Hidden transcripts.* New Haven, CT: Yale University Press.

Vargas, L. (1995). *Social uses and participatory practices: The use of radio by indigenous minorities in Mexico.* Boulder, CO: Westview Press.

WHEN OUR MEDIA BELONG TO THE STATE
Policy And Negotiation In Indigenous-Language Radio In Mexico

11

Antoni Castells-Talens

A radio system in Mexico poses a challenge to the concept of alternative media. Throughout the country, 25 radio stations promote grassroots participation, offer noncommercial programming, and foster minority languages. The project's theoretical foundations rest on the work of community media scholars.[1] Indigenous audiences have accepted the stations as their own, granting them an elevated symbolic value (Ramos Rodríguez, 2005). In sum, the everyday operation of these stations exemplifies a democratic use of the media.[2]

The 25 stations, however, belong to the State. The Mexican government, through its branch of indigenous affairs, controls the stations' budgets, appoints their managers, delineates the goals of the project, and decides when and where to install new stations. Official ownership presents a contradiction to the stations' operation as community media. Is it possible for alternative media to belong to the State?

It is tempting to answer to the question negatively based on what seems a fundamental violation of generally accepted characteristics of alternative media. The ownership of the network and the guidelines for its objectives are set in a reality that is out of reach (physically, culturally, and politically) of indigenous listeners. Additionally, as Vargas (1995) points out, Mexican bureaucratic institutions have "a structural bias toward keeping indigenous people in a disadvantaged position" (241).

The answer, however, is much more problematic. As Dervin and Huesca suggest (1997), the development of Latin American alternative media research has been hindered by the use of binary oppositions (such as media for domination versus media for liberation). In that respect, Clemencia Rodríguez's (2001) work is particularly useful. Rather than using the term 'alternative media' (which reinforces a binary model), Rodríguez favors 'citizens' media,' conceiving citizenship not as a legal or inherent characteristic, but as a practice of empowerment in everyday life.

The significance of this concept for indigenous-language radio in Mexico rests in that the fixed identity of radio as a State-owned medium is transgressed by stations and by listeners alike. Not that ownership and control are irrelevant (they are not), but the appropriation of the airwaves by indigenous communities has become crucial to understand how these stations operate. Citizens' media, Rodríguez argues, contest "social codes, legitimized identities, and institutionalized social relations" (20). In Mexico, State ownership can be treated as a constraint to the freedom of action of the broadcasts. In many stations, in fact, it is hard to see State ownership as anything more than a constraint, a limitation to the project. Because the symbolic line of ownership has blurred, though, the State has symbolically 'lost' many stations.

Another theoretical basis that can help frame this problem is Riggins' (1992) models of the State's multicultural media strategies. A policy that promotes the development of community media vertically, especially in the case of ethnic minorities, could respond to the State's attempt to integrate, monitor, assimilate, divide, neutralize, or limit the power of indigenous groups (Riggins, 1992).[3] In Mexico, the genuineness of a community-oriented media discourse has been contradicted by top-down, unilateral practices that will be explored further in this chapter.

In the case of indigenous-language radio stations, the explicit policy (the set of actions that the government says it is implementing) often differs from the implicit policies (the set of actions that the government implements or that the stations actually develop). The contradictions between formulation and implementation of policy have created, and still create, conflict in the stations.

The tensions that emanate from the direct intervention of the State, however, do not necessarily invalidate the radio project. Rather than accept all the governmental policies, whether they be implicit or explicit, the stations negotiate them on an everyday basis, creating a hazy and malleable space. This chapter analyzes this space and the negotiation that takes place in it. This space, moreover, includes more social actors than just the government. An intricate web of agents at the federal, state, and local levels intervene in setting a course of action for the broadcasts and operation of the stations (see Figure 11.1). The complexity of this space explains the inconsistency of some governmental policies and how traditionally antagonized forces—the State and indigenous peoples—use it to interact on an everyday basis.

Although, as seen in Figure 11.1, the forces of civil society are key to an understanding of indigenist radio (Castells-Talens, 2004), this chapter focuses primarily on a relationship that has been given much less attention, that of citizens'

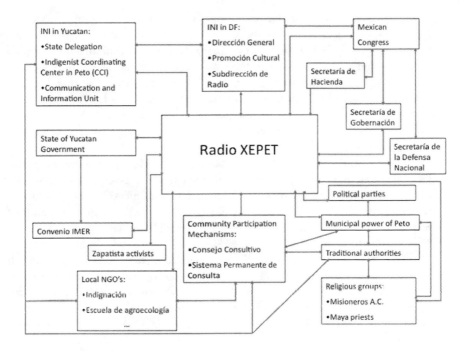

FIGURE 11.1. Social agents involved in the negotiation of indigenist radio policy.

media and the State. The final section of this chapter brings back the role of civil society into the negotiation of the policy.

The findings of this chapter are the result of twelve years of research. The data were gathered through documentary analysis of public records and other documents, direct observation of the daily practices of several radio stations,[4] and in-depth interviews with government officials, radio workers, and other social actors.

BACKGROUND

In Mexico, 10-13 million people belong to one of the approximately 60 native peoples. According to official statistics, 80% of indigenous towns have high levels of marginality (Comisión Nacional para el Desarrollo de los Pueblos Indígenas, 2005). Throughout the country's history, official nationalism has attempted to eliminate these cultures as part of its drive to assimilate indigenous populations into the dominant society. To this end, the State has used an array of methods that range from primary education to film, from architecture to mural painting.

The most recent assimilative attempt, which dates back from the Mexican Revolution and became one of the key policies and theoretical justifications of state formation, is *indigenism*. Since its early days, indigenism aimed at 'hispanicizing' the indigenous populations through several mechanisms, including education and the use of the mass media, but it was not until 1979 that Mexico's Instituto Nacional Indigenista, or National Indigenist Institute (INI), the branch of the government in charge of indigenous affairs, began the consistent use of indigenous languages in the media for development purposes and to integrate native populations into mainstream society.

During that year, a radio station began its broadcasts in three indigenous languages and in Spanish in the mountainous state of Guerrero, an area with low agricultural production that lacked adequate communications, electric power, industries that could generate employment, community infrastructure, and medical services (Secretaría de Agricultura y Recursos Hidráulicos, 1977: 2-3).

At the time, the population—85% of whom were Nahuatl, Mixtec, or Tlapanec, with 55% not knowing Spanish—had a higher mortality rate than the national or state average. About half the children of school age did not attend school. Of those who attended, 80% did not finish primary school. Of those who finished primary school, 1% had the means to continue studying. Seventy-five percent of the population was illiterate (Secretaría de Agricultura y Recursos Hidráulicos, 1977: 2-3).

Within a decade, INI started up other stations throughout Mexico, forming a radio network that broadcast in indigenous languages. In many stations, the community acceptance of the project translated into impassioned participation in the programming. Additionally, the government affiliation sometimes remained a little-known fact. An audience study in one station's area of coverage showed that over 90% of the respondents did not know that the government owned the station, a fact attributed to the trust and credibility that the station had built among its listeners (Cornejo Portugal, 1998: 47).

In spite of their proximity to indigenous communities, however, the stations have been inevitably accompanied by the adjective *indigenist* (as opposed to *indigenous*), as a reminder that they belonged to the government's National Indigenist Institute, not to the indigenous communities. The relationship between stations and the government varied from station to station, but it was usually not exempt from tension.

The relationship between the Mexican State and indigenous peoples changed for good in 1994. On January 1, the mostly indigenous guerrillas of the Ejército Zapatista de Liberación Nacional, or Zapatista Army of National Liberation (EZLN), erupted in several towns of the state of Chiapas. During the uprising, the Zapatista rebels occupied a local indigenist radio station for a few hours. From then on, the State's communication policy became more restrictive. Censorship and self-censorship increased in the stations' programming. Devices were placed on the transmitters to kill the signal in case of necessity. In some stations, fear became common among staff members. Meanwhile, the Zapatistas demanded the transfer of the stations to the indigenous communities.

In February 1996, the government and the guerrillas met and signed a series of documents that came to be known as the Agreements of San Andrés. In the Agreements, the federal government committed itself to "recommend to the respective national institutions that the 17 INI radio stations be handed over to the indigenous communities in their respective regions, along with the transference of licenses, infrastructure and resources, whenever the indigenous communities so request it" (Anzaldo Meneses, 1998: 293). The agreements were never implemented, as the government accused the guerrillas of refusing to keep the negotiation open and the guerrillas accused the government of overturning an arrangement that had been settled.

The mid and late 1990s witnessed an increase in the number of radio stations. Between 1994 and 1999, the network grew from 11 to 20 stations. Additionally, four low-power FM stations began their broadcasts from boarding centers for children of low-income families. The children conducted the shows.

In 2003, INI disappeared, and most of its functions, including the management of the radio network, were transferred to a new office, the Comisión Nacional para el Desarrollo de los Pueblos Indígenas or National Commission for the Development of Indigenous Peoples (CDI). The project has continued under the same premises. Radio is used as a tool of horizontal participation and noncommercial programming, but the structure of the network continues as vertical as it has been for over two decades.

GRASSROOTS PARTICIPATION

Indigenist radio in Mexico, as much of the work of grassroots communication in Latin America, followed the philosophical footsteps of Mario Kaplun, one of the leading theorists of democratic communication in the 1970s. Kaplun (1985) divided what he called *people's media* in two types: dominant and participatory (73). Although people's communication is participatory by definition because the audience actively engages in the programs, when Kaplun referred to a participatory philosophy of the media, he attributed a meaning related to direct democratic practices. Instead of media *for* the people, Kaplun argued that participatory communication involved media *by* the people, or at least, *with* the people (74).

According to this participatory philosophy, therefore, content alone does not necessarily imply a participatory medium. Participatory communication challenges the sender-receiver opposition between communicators and the community. People's media practitioners work, instead, as facilitators or organizers of communication (Kaplun, 1985: 76-77). Kaplun's conception of popular communication, like that of other scholars and activists, emanated in part from the pedagogic theories of Paulo Freire (23).

The practice of these ideas, generally traced back to the late 1940s with experiences of radio stations in Colombia and Bolivia (see, e.g., Geerts & Van Oeyen, 2001; Gumucio-Dagrón, 2001), developed throughout the second half of the 20th century and peaked in the 1970s and 1980s (Alfaro Moreno, 2002). The end of the Cold War and the intensification of globalization eroded many of the principles on which people's *radio popular* rested. For instance, Alfaro Moreno (2002) attributes the fall of the class-struggle content of popular communication to the downfall of world socialism. As a consequence, social actors ceased perceiving themselves as antagonistic or opposed. The dominant economic model contributed to a new perception of social change, as its discourse claimed social integration and avoided radical opposition (Alfaro Moreno, 2002). Similarly, Camacho (2001) noted that the new logic of capitalism set forward the idea of popular communication as a synonym of mediocrity because of its characteristics as anti-technological, anti-professional, anti-urban, and anti-mass audience.

In Mexico, however, the participatory discourse has endured to this date among indigenist radio practitioners and policymakers. By using a participatory discourse, the State has contributed to the acceptance of grassroots philosophies, but some researchers have pointed out that this discourse is far from sincere. In a study of indigenist radio, Vargas (1995) concluded that the government had a structural bias toward keeping indigenous peoples in disadvantaged positions. Although most of the staff in the radio system is indigenous, managerial positions have often been occupied by non-indigenous officials. Additionally, INI was accused of presenting a romanticized view of indigenous peoples, a view that prevents social change. The social space within stations itself, it has been argued, duplicates the racism of Mexican society (Vargas, 1995).

Even critics admit, nevertheless, that it was impossible for the government to have complete control of the stations because its power was not monolithic, nor efficient enough to achieve total control. Stations could actually contribute to an awakening of indigenous consciousness through their indigenous staff (241-242). In fact, the stations fostered participation through mechanisms inspired by the experiences of Latin American community radio.

Individual listener participation has been high since the first days of these stations. The high numbers of listeners who visit, call, or e-mail the stations have a direct impact on the programming. The music that community members request, the poems they write, the announcements they make, and the songs they compose and sing all make it to the programming of indigenist stations. Most stations have made an effort to get to know who the listeners are and what they want. Audience research has always been welcome by the stations (see, e.g., Cornejo Portugal, 1998).

However, the impact of listeners on decisions beyond their individual participation in programs is most obvious in the organized mechanisms of participation. In the early 1990s, the stations decided that participation needed to extend beyond individual visits and letters to announcers. To the extent that was possible, organized participation was encouraged through open meetings to discuss community concerns, a community advisory council to help shape the direction of the station, voluntary community correspondents, and the establishment of radio production units, equipped by the stations, but operated by trained volunteers.

Over the years, the advisory council had experienced a slump. In many stations, participation had decreased. Some possible reasons included lack of resources: A one to two-day meeting of the advisory council meant for many a one to two-day period without working—and, therefore, without an income. "People will not stop eating to come to the station," said a station's manager in Yucatan. Another possible explanation for the problems of the council was the lack of response by some advisors, who were sent to represent their organization (e.g., a peasant's association), but had little interest in radio programming.

The situation called for a new approach to participation. If until 1997 councils had relied solely on representatives of local NGOs, now listeners too were invited to participate directly in the shaping of the station's programming. The new project created a permanent advisory system, which started to operate in January 1998. One of the main differences between this decision body and the old council was that the new organization, made up of permanent members, managed a budget, granted by INI, that could reach US $3,000, a considerable amount of cash that gave the new council a certain degree of autonomy from the stations and from INI. The budget helped organize meetings to determine what programs were the most (and least) popular, what topics should be included in the programming, and what kind of music the stations should broadcast.

Whereas the council was arguably one of the success stories of fostering participation, the network of correspondents was often one of the failures. Most radio stations never developed a strong system of community correspondents. In the state of Yucatan, for example, most of the little information received from correspondents came from INI offices throughout the state, not from volunteer-journalists in other towns. Finally, the system of *cabinas* (independent production units installed by stations but operated by community volunteers), which seemed to have started on the right foot in the early 1990s, progressively lost its momentum.

These experiences have shown that participatory policies in Mexico have been, without any doubt, contradictory. Grassroots participation is encouraged from the very top, which may explain why some participatory mechanisms have failed. The question of whether a medium can be truly participatory when it belongs to the State was addressed in the mid-1990s by a station worker in Guerrero who expressed that "the station encourages the people to participate through their music, stories, and traditional knowledge, but when they want to talk about their reality, the station stops them" (Vargas, 1995: 242).

Simultaneously, though, indigenous-language stations are valued even by their critics. In spite of the Zapatista aversion toward indigenism, the events of 1994 hint a certain degree of respect—no matter how questionable—toward the work of the radio stations. In the Chiapas insurrection, the EZLN occupied

XEVFS, the INI radio station in Las Margaritas, and an official station that did not belong to the INI network in Ocosingo, but to the state government. When the Zapatistas left the stations, they trashed the facilities of the Ocosingo station. The installations of XEVFS were left intact.

NONINDIGENIST STATE AGENTS

Besides the structural connection of the radio network with INI/CDI's offices in Mexico City, several federal institutions play an influential role in the policy of the stations. The extent of agency of these federal institutions varies from station to station, but the actors involved do not differ greatly. The Secretaría de Hacienda (Ministry of Treasury), the military (especially since 1994), the Secretaría de Gobernación (Ministry of Interior Affairs), and hostile legislators are the main actors who have participated—either directly or indirectly—in the negotiation of indigenist radio policy.

During the 1990s, fourteen stations were installed, but no new professional positions were approved for the radio project. By 1999, the same number of jobs had to satisfy three times as many stations as in 1990. Indigenist officials usually blame the Ministry of Treasury for the policy. The budget for new positions, the argument goes, must be approved by the Secretaría de Hacienda, but the neoliberal policies of the federal government do not allow for the creation of new jobs. As a consequence, an equal number of radio positions has to cover more and more radio stations. Government officials claim that they are forced to lay off people at older radio stations so they can hire the staff of the newer stations.

In less than 10 years, Radio XEPET's staff was reduced almost in half. The manager of the station recalled:

> In 1990 we had a first [personnel] cut, which is not a real cut because the positions are still there [in the INI radio system]; it was more like a reassignment of jobs. It must have been in 92 or 93, I can't remember … three people from the radio left. There were 21 of us then. It went down to 18. Later, in 96, there was another one, and 15 were left. In 98 there's a new cut, but this time 5 people left, so from 15, only 10 of us were left (Víctor Canto Ramírez, personal communication, July 10, 2002)

The consequences for the medium have been severe. The station has cut back on production of drama content and on visits to the communities. When I first visited Radio XEPET in 1993, the station workers traveled to small villages with frequency. A decade later, the trips were rare, unless to cover a particular event. XEPET's manager explained how else the decrease of professional staff had an impact on the operation of the station:

> [The cuts] have affected the quality. One cannot make big productions. We
> do not have radio novelas nor a lot of production. They [the staff] all have to
> stay in the broadcasting booth (Victor Canto, personal communication, June
> 22, 2000)

One of the solutions to the lack of staff had been to rely on volunteers. The volunteers served as announcers in music shows, so they were closer to free labor than they were to a participation mechanism. Most volunteers had a solely instrumental role, in which they went to the station, played and announced music, and left. Additionally, volunteers tended to speak Spanish, even though XEPET encouraged them to use Maya, whereas paid staff were required to speak Maya, unless it was indispensable to use Spanish (e.g., when interviewing a non-Mayan guest).

Budget freezes and austerity policies are ultimately decided by legislators. Therefore, the Mexican Congress also has an effect on the policy. Luis Pazos, president of the Budget Commission of the Mexican Congress at the time of the research and a federal representative of the ruling Partido Acción Nacional, National Action Party (PAN), has positioned himself against any policy that strengthens a multicultural state. He does not represent the official position of Congress nor the position of PAN toward indigenism or indigenous peoples, but according to some indigenist officials his views may be shared by a larger group of legislators who prefer not to be perceived as holding uniformist conceptions of the State. Until recently, these conceptions were the official policy of the Mexican State and considered part of the mainstream, but today, after constitutional reforms that recognized the value of indigenous cultures, they tend to be viewed as extremist. Pazos himself subscribes to the idea of a silent majority of legislators who support multicultural legislation only "to disarm leftist groups in Chiapas" because a central claim of the Zapatistas is the lack of State sensitivity to multiculturalism (Luis Pazos, personal communication, June 27, 2002), but who agree that multiculturalism is a mistake for the Mexican State:

> Neither PRI nor PAN wanted [the constitutional reforms to recognize
> indigenous rights and cultures]. [The reforms] came out as a consensus to
> de-activate the radicals in Chiapas. (Luis Pazos, personal communication,
> June 27, 2002)

Luis Pazos' opinions can contribute to understanding a different conception of the Mexican State, a conception that may be more widespread than publicly admitted. Additionally, his views are significant, as he served as the president of the Budget Commission of the Chamber of Representatives. As a former candidate for governor of the state of Veracruz,[5] he claims that he has been in touch with indigenous realities and that indigenous peoples do not aspire to maintain their own culture, as the explicit discourse of indigenism—and the State—now advocates, but to assimilation. About the indigenous claims for indigenous-language radio, Pazos claimed that the demand did not exist:

> These are not demands by indigenous people, but manipulations by political groups. What they [indigenous peoples] want is water, roads, and schooling. I have never heard any indigenous person ask for a radio station. It is not an indigenous demand. It is [a demand] of politicians who are using indigenous people as a flag with political goals. (Luis Pazos, personal communication, June 27, 2002)

Another federal agency that participates in the implicit policy of the Mexican State is the Secretaría de Gobernación (SEGOB), or Ministry of Interior Affairs. When in the early to mid 1990s, INI's headquarters adopted measures claiming they would protect the stations and their staff from guerrilla supporters, the feeling of control and censorship inside the stations intensified.

Shortly after the uprising, I met with some station managers who thought that the station's telephones were being bugged and that the SEGOB was monitoring their conversations.

The INI subdirector of radio during that troubled period denied any external involvement in the indigenist response to the Zapatista threat:

- *Question:* What was the policy of SEGOB toward the stations? Did you have visits or did you have...?
- *Answer:* No.
- *Question:* Telephone calls?...
- *Answer:* No, no, no, no. No, we didn't have any type of calls. I'll tell you that these things are managed in a very interesting way. At the state level they are managed in a different way. At the central level there was no intervention from Gobernación, nothing regarding communication, nothing regarding radio. Not even: "record this for me to see what they are saying." No, not at all. Nor: "Oh, translate this for me because, what if they say something that ...?" No, not at all, not at all. We did not have that sort of things. (Citlali Ruiz, personal communication, June 26, 2002).

A former state delegate of INI in Mérida, the capital city of Yucatan, said that he did not recall any pressure from SEGOB, either, except for a ban on broadcasting programs that could benefit one party. This ban followed the strict guidelines of the Instituto Federal Electoral, Electoral Federal Institute (IFE), to guarantee impartiality in the media. "*Gobernación* was always aware, but I never had a signal or restriction from their part" (Caballero Barrón, personal communication, July 4, 2002).

However, the Centro de Investigación y Seguridad Nacional (CISEN), Mexico's intelligence service, may have showed an interest in the activities of the station:

> I know that [SEGOB] was attentive to what was happening at the station. And, very frequently, I received the visit of a character who ... with whom later we even became friends because I saw him everywhere. And that was the character that CISEN had commissioned to oversee INI's things and our trips to communities or with unknown people. And, anyway, I already. . . . We knew each other well and I used to warn him about what we were going to do or not going to do. I do not know whether they had equipment to monitor us or not. I do not know. What I can tell you is that when we went on the air clandestinely [with the low-power stations at shelters], they never monitored us and no radio broadcasts were stopped by any cause. (Caballero Barrón, personal communication, July 4, 2002)

A similar version of the story in Peto, the Maya town of Radio XEPET, also suggests governmental monitoring:

> *Question:* After 1994, were there other changes in policy, at the local or state levels? From SEGOB? From the military?
>
> *Answer:* Well, here there really wasn't any. . . . Maybe the presence of *Gobernación* increased a little. They would ask us for something specific, in relation to a story, to a comment. They were listening to the radio and they came to ask us from where we received the information. And we would send them the data, and that's it. But there was never a bigger problem with the state government, nor with the army. There was nothing here that affected the activities [of XEPET].
>
> *Question:* Had this thing with *Gobernación* happened before 94?
>
> *Answer:* That I can remember, it hadn't. But since then and until now [2002], occasionally, they come visit to ask us things. There have been events that I suppose they have to cover. They are sent to cover them and, even if the events are not related to the station or to INI, they come to the station to ask for information about where they are going to be, at what time, what for, because they know that here we have this information. And lately the contact is reduced to this. But there have been moments in which they have asked us to clarify information that we have aired, without any reprisal. (Víctor Canto Ramírez, personal communication, July 10, 2002)

This type of pressure is not exclusive to the Yucatan. The former station manager of Radio XECTZ, in Cuetzalan, Puebla, recalls similar episodes with the judiciary police:[6]

In Cuetzalan, the officers of the judiciary police arrived to ask whether we needed something, whether the station was secure, whether we had a security guard or not, whether we had a night watchman. . . . At times it was uncomfortable, but well, you realize that it is a job that they are supposed to do. And well, let them do it. No, it's alright. It does not interfere with the station; it does not interfere with the station. It's simply a routine that they have to carry out, and they do it and that's it. But pressure, in the sense of "don't do this," "do that" there never was. (Angel Díez Mendoza, personal communication, June 26, 2002)

The 1994 Zapatista uprising catapulted indigenous peoples and issues to the forefront of the national security debate in Mexico. Endemic poverty[7] has been treated as the variable that most directly affects Mexican national security (Benítez Manaut, 2000). The State, consequently, has addressed the problems of indigenous peoples also as a matter of national security:

From a governmental point of view, the appearance of an armed movement, per se, must be assumed as a problem of national security. It, therefore, must be neutralized and contained by the means that the State has for this type of situation: the employment of the army, intelligence systems, social policies to try to take the fish out of the water, and other mechanisms, so this type of movements do not raise sympathies. (Benítez Manaut, 2000: 6)

The preceding text would not draw any more attention than any other intelligence or military report if it were not because it was published by INI and co-edited by Melba Pría, general director of INI at the time of publication, and because it was followed by the following commentary:

When a guerrilla movement amasses a considerable amount of support among the population and advocates socially acceptable demands, such as the EZLN did, it cannot be stopped with coercive, military, or repressive measures. (Benítez Manaut, 2000: 6)

According to the author, Mexico has produced at least two interpretations of national security to deal with the indigenous peoples: an excluding, coercive interpretation in which "cancer is eliminated with military chemotherapy" and a political and social interpretation (7).

The first reading advocates the use of force. The second reading favors social policies. The approach of the later includes a democratic and participatory component with actions to:

- Combat poverty;
- Establish solid justice systems;

- Democratize indigenous communities while respecting traditional forms and means of organization;
- Strengthen indigenous cultures, values, and traditions; and
- Develop a strategy to make indigenous micro-economies viable to break the culture of paternalistic assistance (Benítez Manaut, 2000: 7).

Whereas the Mexican State has used both approaches to national security in dealing with indigenous peoples, INI's official rhetoric tended to follow the social view. In any case, INI explicitly accepted the connection between indigenous affairs and national security.

In the mid and late 1990s, after the uprising, military roadblocks were common in some strategic parts of Mexico. As a part of the Law of Arms and Explosives, the military were granted the power to search vehicles. Often, they also self-assigned the role of doormen and asked questions about the destiny and origin of the drivers or the motives behind their trip.

In Yucatan, the armed forces chose to place one of the roadblocks in the 10-mile road between the Maya towns of Tzucacab and Peto, a road that at the time only led to Peto, the site of Radio XEPET. Whether Peto had some unknown military strategic importance escapes most inhabitants, but a common interpretation is that the military had the roadblock because of the radio station.

On at least one occasion, a military officer entered the station: "He asked permission to enter and see the station, he visited the offices, he visited everything, and then he left," said a station worker. In fact, a few months after the 1994 Chiapas uprising, the army placed a military camp in the outskirts of Peto. It looked provisional at first, but it turned out to be one of the twelve training camps of conventional units that the Army and the Air Force have throughout Mexico, and the only one installed in the Yucatan Peninsula (Secretaría de la Defensa Nacional, 2003).

THE ROLE OF INDIGENIST ACTORS

The role of indigenism best exemplifies the negotiation of policy. On the one hand, it has promoted a discourse of indigenous liberation. On the other hand, it has occasionally made clear to the indigenous-language stations that the network is and will remain under federal control.

Thus, in 1993, months before the Zapatista uprising, INI defined the objectives of the radio system as "contributing to the free development of indigenous peoples of Mexico through radio communication actions that involve community participation and that respond to [the community's] needs and expectations to consolidate the plural and diverse nature of our nationality" (XEPET, 1993).

Radio, therefore, aimed at the 'free development' of indigenous people, a rather blurred term that offered a wide range of interpretations, from a paternalistic view of development to an openly self-determinationist statement, but that differed from the traditional assimilative language used by the Mexican State just a decade earlier.

Two years later, a manual on indigenous rights, published in 1995, that INI distributed for free throughout Mexico's indigenous regions interprets the constitutional text of 1992 through pictures describing everyday situations involving land disputes, media access, education in indigenous languages, traditional authorities, environmental issues, or legal rights over natural resources.

The vague constitutional sentence "the law shall protect and promote [indigenous] cultural development" thus took practical meanings. In one of the drawings in the booklet, as two police officers hold an indigenous man, an armed soldier says: "We are going to accuse you of being a drug dealer for transporting peyote [narcotic plant used by some indigenous groups for religious purposes]" (see Figure 11.2). INI's interpretation of the Constitution read: "Civilian and military authorities must respect and enforce the respect for indigenous religious offerings and pilgrimages" (Instituto Nacional Indigenista, 1995: 22). The drawing illustrated how the police and the army should not act, with the purpose of educating indigenous readers about their constitutional rights in case of an illegal detention.

FIGURE 11.2. Indigenist interpretation of the constitutional protection of religious ceremonies.

Four pages later, a police officer and an armed soldier take away an indigenous man as a second soldier pushes a woman. The soldier who is arresting the indigenous man says: "He is a warlock! And he is using forbidden herbs." The indigenous people who are witnessing the scene reply: "He is the one who has always healed our people" (see Figure 11.3). Again, INI interpreted the constitutional segment in its own words: "It is necessary that traditional medicine be preserved. It is up to the indigenous people to identify their health practitioners. The State may support them through projects to promote and guarantee the free implementation of their healing practices" (Instituto Nacional Indigenista, 1995: 26).

As with the previous example, by showing the armed forces performing an illegal arrest, they are portrayed as the violators of the law. Again, the booklet's purpose is to teach indigenous individuals about how their constitutional rights cannot—on paper—be violated by the authorities, and specifically by the army (one of the main opponents of the Zapatista rebels).

Although this case shows that INI's discourse disapproved of the State's abuse of authority, at least two dramatic events show suspiciously authoritarian-looking practices that contradict that discourse. The first instance took place in Nacajuca, Tabasco, with Radio XENAC, the second station installed by INI, which allegedly became heavily involved with party politics. As a result of political struggles and after receiving accusations of using the airwaves to support the

FIGURE 11.3. Indigenist interpretation of the constitutional protection of traditional medicine.

official party's campaigns, INI took the station off the air in 1990. Indigenist officials still claim that the station was becoming a tool of propaganda of the then
ruling party.

As mentioned earlier, whether the closing of the station responded to political manipulations or to an attempt to silence dissenting voices, the governmental
action sent a signal that the ultimate power to operate an indigenist station
emanates from Mexico City.

Another instance of possible censorship occurred shortly after the EZLN
uprising of 1994. The National Indigenist Institute installed devices on the stations' transmitters that allowed killing the signal at a distance with a remote control. The measure was criticized, but the 1994 director of indigenist radio justified it:

> It got started for several reasons: One, to protect the stations' staff and to
> protect the radio station itself. This as in the sense that if there were any vio-
> lent takeovers of the stations or something like that, one could (on the dis-
> cretion of the manager, or I think it rather was on the discretion of the dele-
> gate) turn it off from somewhere else. I think the remote control, I can't
> remember if the delegation has it, or the coordinator of the CCI,[8] or the
> manager of the station. If they saw that things were very, very, very hot, at
> their discretion, they could get the signal off the air. And yes, it was very
> criticized. It really was very criticized. (Citlali Ruiz, personal communica-
> tion, June 26, 2002)

This official denied any involvement from higher instances and assumed all
responsibility for INI. She also implied that because INI was in possession of the
remote control, the device constituted less an example of censorship than an
attempt to protect the stations:

> It was very criticized. It was something that was not understood. But these
> are the reasons they gave me and these are the reasons I gave, especially
> since the remote control was not in the hands of anyone outside INI. If they
> had told me, this secret is going to be in the hands of Secretary X, who from
> a helicopter is going to. . . . Then maybe yes, it could have been interpreted
> as censorship. But if it was in the hands of INI people, of the same INI peo-
> ple, of the state delegations, or the local INI offices, or ... Then it was all
> different. These are the reasons they gave me and these are the reasons I
> gave. And yes, it was criticized. (Citlali Ruiz, personal communication, June
> 26, 2002)

It is plausible, though unlikely, that INI was covering its back from possible
attacks from other governmental institutions by showing that the stations were
under its authority and that, therefore, the rebels could not infiltrate them.
However, these measures show that INI had a large degree of responsibility in
promoting a sense of control.

The Negotiation of the Policy

Taking advantage of the distance that separates the stations from Mexico City and protected by a combination of physical space and linguistic and cultural barriers that not even the State can overcome, indigenous radio staff and members of the local communities often manage to include dissent in their message. Other times, the very explicit governmental policy is used to circumvent difficult issues.

In the mid-1990s, while the conflict in Chiapas lived its most tense episodes, one indigenist station in Chiapas received communiqués from Mexico City to broadcast the anti-insurgent messages of the Secretario de Gobernación (Minister of Interior). The station followed directions, translated them into the indigenous languages of its audience, and aired them during its news programs. In the name of fair and balanced information, however, the station staff also translated and aired the communiqués of the EZLN guerrillas. Aware of the lack of innocence of both actions, the manager of that station acknowledges being on both sides at the same time.

The Maya-language stations of the Yucatan Peninsula provide another example of the subtleties used to bypass State power. An analysis of the iconographic self-representation of these stations illustrates how the tools of Mexican nationalism are used to foster—and arguably, even to create—a Mayan nationalistic discourse. Like in other parts of Mexico, pre-Hispanic iconography has been used to create a myth in which indigenous peoples' past is glorified, while in the present they are victims of State repression. In the late eighteenth and the beginning of the nineteenth centuries, the concept of 'lost cities' of the Maya justified the need to be 'discovered' (Castañeda, 1996: 108). Artifacts, ancient gods, and pyramids in the jungle become synonyms of the Maya. Throughout the Americas, archeology contributes to the dehistorization of indigenous peoples, their cultures "reassigned to a departed age" (Pratt, 1992: 134). Mural paintings, company and governmental logos, music, architecture, and literature are but a few of the means by which Mexican nationalism broke the link between indigenous past and indigenous present.

For some years, the radio stations in the Yucatan Peninsula have been using the same tools and iconography to re-establish this link between past and present and to imagine a discursively coherent Maya people, much in the same way Mexicans imagine a discursively coherent Mexican, *mestizo* (mixed-blooded) people. The past of the Maya is now present in the representation of the stations' logos, mural paintings, and programming to promote a Maya, not Mexican, identity. Pre-hispanic design abounds in the stations. In the Maya states of Yucatan and Quintana Roo, the stations' logos are inspired on conch motives, perceived as pre-Hispanic tools of communication. Radio XEPET's auditorium is named after a legendary Maya rebel hero, Jacinto Canek. The Caste War[9] is also present. In 1997, the station decided to tie the celebration of its fifteenth anniversary to the violent event. The poster that announced the festivities read: "1997: 150 years from the claim for Maya identity. XEPET: 15 years broadcasting Maya identity," an implicit reference to 1982, the year of the inauguration of the station, and 1847, the year the Caste War erupted.

The reference to the Caste War continued in the opening remarks of the celebration, when XEPET's manager began his speech to a live radio audience saying: "There is no armed movement in Yucatan, but the demand that originated the Caste War is a demand that continues to be current." In that same speech, the station's manager justified that the idea of including the commemoration of the Caste War is "that the station be a space where the Maya people demonstrates that it's a living people, working, struggling; that the Maya are not just archeological artifacts. The radio works for the dignity and the freedom of the Maya people."

The Caste War also forms the central image of a magnificent mural painting that welcomes visitors to Radio XENKA, in the state of Quintana Roo (see Figure 11.4). Like some of Diego Rivera's great murals, the station's painting portrays a sequence of events, from pre-Conquest times to the present, only the mural in Radio XENKA has been painted in the 21st century and the present is exemplified by a Maya, not a Mexican, face.

The concept of negotiation usually implies reaching an agreement. In the case of indigenist radio policy, how the agreement is reached (when it is) depends on each actor involved and on contextual conditions. An actor can have different types of leverage in different aspects of the negotiation and the leverage can also change at different times. Thus, for example, the local indigenist centers have power on administrative decisions, but this power diminishes greatly when making programming and everyday decisions or designing the station's internal policy.

The mechanisms used in the negotiation also differ. Social actors use money, coercive measures, and probably favors that assure a smooth operation of the stations to influence negotiations. Stations have an array of arguments to use in their everyday negotiations. When dealing with local actors, dependence on Mexico City is often used as a mode of protection. If a local politician seeks biased cover-

FIGURE 11.4. Caste War mural in Radio XENKA.

age during an election, stations can fall back on the federal electoral laws or on the stations' goals as established by the INI (or the CDI, after 2003). In both Mexico City and in some stations, the often-loathed dependence on Mexico City is also seen as a way to protect the interests of the station from local landowners or politicians. When dealing with federal agents, the opposite might be done. In this case, the mandate to include local participation or the claim of local political pressures can be used as a defense mechanism not to implement an inconvenient federal policy.

DISCUSSION

Riggins (1992) described the debate over the *dual role* of ethnic minority media as an argument in which these media are seen as either tools of cultural resistance or tools of assimilation (276). Although the role of the government varies depending on its commitment to multiculturalism, the State uses its power to intervene if the message is perceived as subversive. This study's findings confirm that the State reacts with any means necessary when it perceives a threat from the media.

Policy, however, is defined in everyday actions, not just in extreme cases (such as when a radio station is closed or when censorship shows its most overt shapes). Joseph and Nugent (1994) identify a permanent tension between Mexican grassroots society and the processes of state formation, and propose that this tension manifests itself on quotidian life and on the dynamics of state engagements in everyday society. Indigenous-language radio is precisely one of these instances.

The explicit indigenist radio policy tends to be vague, much more centered on philosophical goals, such as participation and development of indigenous cultures, than on concrete measures to implement these goals. Although radio producers have often complained about the lack of definition of explicit policy, this impreciseness has helped maintain an open space of implicit quotidian negotiation. Everyday indigenist radio policy is simultaneously flexible, malleable, and diffuse. It is flexible because the State, which defines the explicit policies, does not expect every rule to be followed and leaves some room open for dissent, even if just symbolic. It is malleable because the stations know that the rules can be shaped to fit their own needs. It is diffuse because the actors involved in the negotiation are not all located in one space (they operate at the local, state, and federal levels), and the agency of each actor is not always obvious. It is also diffuse because indigenist headquarters cannot maintain strict control over all its actors.

In this process, it is hard to identify a single weight that upsets the balance of the negotiation. True, the ultimate power of closing down the station rests on the State, but many more agents determine policy. Indigenist stations have to accept some imposed decisions, but at the same time they know that they can break and bend the rules.

The theoretical implications of this negotiation in the context of the relationship between citizens' media and the State raise several issues. The stations may have been meant to serve as tools of State formation by following the strategies suggested by Riggins (1992) and attempting to integrate, monitor, assimilate, divide, neutralize, or limit the power of indigenous peoples.

However, they also fostered some sort of indigenous nationalism by creating a space of indigenous self-expression. The apparent contradiction between simultaneously contributing to state formation and to an indigenous nationalism is well known within the system. When I put a station manager in Chiapas in the unfair position of having to choose sides and asked him whether his station was a tool of government propaganda or a guerrilla station, he answered: "We are both."

Perhaps one of the main theoretical conclusions of this study is the application to policy analysis of Riggins' (1992) claims that "the long-term effect of ethnic minority media is neither total assimilation nor total cultural preservation but some moderate degree of preservation that represents a compromise between the two extremes" (276). As for policy, this translates into a space of negotiation in which traditionally antagonized forces—the State and indigenous cultures—both exert influence on the stations. While dealing with State pressures and with indigenous needs and wants, the stations 'knead' a local space, their own local space. In this space, they do not aggravate the State (and therefore guarantee their survival) while at the same time they address the information and communication needs of their local audiences, knowing that frequently these information and communication needs are clearly in the realm of dissent.

In the case of Mexico, the original question, *Is it possible for citizens' media to belong to the State?*, poses a double challenge. First, treating ownership as a defining characteristic of citizens' media undermines the contribution of indigenist radio to the opening of a mediascape for native peoples. Second, equating a restrictive State intervention with the implementation of a unilateral policy oversimplifies the process of negotiation and leaves little room for citizens' use of the media. Citizens' media may not belong to the State, but Mexico's indigenist stations suggest that citizens can, to some extent, make a democratic use of state-owned media.

NOTES

1. One of the founding documents of the system cites the works of Mario Kaplun, Xavier Albó, Paulo Freire, Emile McAnany, Armand Mattelart, and Antonio Pasquali.
2. Some parts of this article are excerpts from the unpublished doctoral dissertation, *The Negotiation of Indigenist Radio Policy in Mexico* (University of Florida, 2004).
3. Riggins (1992) proposes five models to explain the State's multicultural media strategies towards ethnic minorities.

4. The bulk of the field research was conducted in Mexico City and Radio XEPET, in Yucatan, but I also visited indigenist stations in the states of Campeche, Chiapas, Guerrero, Puebla, and Quintana Roo.
5. The state of Veracruz is home to a dozen indigenous language groups that account for over 10% of the total population.
6. It is not uncommon for an average Mexican citizen to associate the judiciary police with corruption, extortion, and impunity.
7. Extreme poverty and indigenous peoples are almost synonyms, because in Mexico the rural poor are poorer than the urban poor, and among the rural communities, indigenous communities are the poorest (Benítez Manaut, 2000).
8. The CCI are the Centros Coordinadores Indigenistas, Indigenist Coordinating Centers, local indigenist offices operated independently from the stations.
9 The Caste War, a violent Maya rebellion of the nineteenth century, is often qualified as one the most successful and most generalized indigenous uprisings in the Americas.

REFERENCES

Alfaro Moreno, R. M. (2002). Culturas populares y comunicación participativa: En la ruta de las redefiniciones [Popular cultures and participatory communication: In the route of redefinitions]. *The Communication Initiative.* Retrieved January 17, 2004, from http://www.comminit.com/la/lasth/sld-116.html

Anzaldo Meneses, J. (1998). *Nunca Más Un México sin nosotros* [Never again a Mexico without us]. Mexico City: Ce-Acatl.

Benítez Manaut, R. (2000). La cuestión indígena y la seguridad nacional [The indigenous question and national security]. In C. Henríquez & M. Pría (Eds.), *Regiones indígenas Tradicionales. Un enfoque geopolítico para la seguridad nacional* [Traditional indigenous regions. A geopolitical approach for national security] (pp. 5-8). Mexico City: Instituto Nacional Indigenista.

Camacho, C. A. (2001). *Investigar lo popular hoy ¿Qué es?: Miradas ciudadanas desde las radios populares* [What does it mean to research popular [media] today?: Citizens' gazes from people's radio stations]. PCLA-Pensamento Comunicacional Latino Americano. Retrieved October 29, 2003, from http://www.metodista.br/unesco/PCLA/revista8/projetos%208-1.htm

Castañeda, Q. E. (1996). *In the museum of Maya culture: Touring Chichén Itzá.* Minneapolis: University Of Minnesota.

Castells-Talens, A. (2004). *The negotiation of indigenist radio policy in Mexico.* Unpublished doctoral dissertation, University of Florida, Gainesville, Florida.

Comisión Nacional para el Desarrollo de los Pueblos Indígenas. (2005). *Indicadores socioeconómicos de los pueblos indígenas: Los números* [Socioeconomic indicators of the indigenous peoples: Figures]. Retrieved September 7, 2005, from http://www.cdi.gob.mx/index.php?id_seccion=399

Cornejo Portugal, I. (1998). *Estudio sobre la recepción de la audiencia de la radiodifusora cultural indigenista "La Voz de los Mayas" (XEPET)* [Audience-reception study of cultural indigenist radio "The voice of the Maya" (XEPET), Peto, Yucatan]. Unpublished work, Peto, Yucatán.

Dervin, B., & Huesca, R. (1997). Reaching for the communicating in participatory communication. A meta-theoretical analysis. *The Journal of International Communication, 4*(2), 46-74.

Geerts, A., & van Oeyen, V. (2001). *La radio popular frente al nuevo siglo: Estudio de vigencia e incidencia* [People's radio before the new century: A study of its validity and incidence]. Quito, Ecuador: ALER.

Gumucio-Dagrón, A. (2001). *Making waves: Stories of participatory communication for social change.* New York: The Rockefeller Foundation.

Instituto Nacional Indigenista. (1995). Derechos indígenas: Los pueblos indígenas en la constitución Mexicana [Indigenous rights: Indigenous peoples in the Mexican constitution]. Mexico City: Instituto Nacional Indigenista.

Joseph, G. M., & Nugent, D. (Eds.). (1994). *Everyday forms of state formation: Revolution and the negotiation of rule in modern Mexico.* Durham, NC: Duke University.

Kaplun, M. (1985). *El comunicador popular* [The people's communicator] (2nd ed.). Buenos Aires, Argentina: Lumen-Humanitas.

Pratt, M. L. (1992). *Imperial eyes: Studies in travel writing and transculturation.* London: Routledge.

Ramos Rodríguez, J. M. (2005). *Ecos de "La Voz de la Montaña": La radio como factor de cohesión y fortalecimiento cultural de los pueblos indígenas* [Echoes of "The voice of the mountain": Radio as a factor of cohesion and cultural strengthening of indigenous peoples]. Unpublished doctoral dissertation, Universidad Nacional Autónoma de México: Mexico City.

Riggins, S. H. (1992). *Ethnic minority media: An international perspective.* Newbury Park, CA: Sage.

Rodríguez, C. (2001). *Fissures in the mediascape: An international study of citizen's media.* Cresskill, NJ: Hampton Press.

Secretaría de Agricultura y Recursos Hidráulicos-Comisión del Río Balsas. (1977). *Anteproyecto para la instalación de una radio difusora En Tlapa, Gro* [Pre-Project to install a radio station in Tlapa, Guerrero]. Mexico.

Secretaría de la Defensa Nacional. (2003). El Adiestramiento en el Ejército Y Fuerza Aérea Mexicanos: Adiestramiento de unidades convencionales [Training in the Mexican Army and Air Force: Training of conventional units]. Retrieved September 27, 2003, from http://www.sedena.gob.mx/ejto/adiestra/adto_1n.html

Vargas, L. (1995). *Social uses and radio practices: The use of participatory radio by ethnic minorities in Mexico.* Boulder, CO: Westview.

XEPET. (1993). *Objetivos de XEPET.* Peto, Yucatan, Mexico.

RECLAIMING THE PUBLIC SPHERE IN CHILE UNDER DICTATORSHIP AND NEOLIBERAL DEMOCRACY

Rosalind Bresnahan

This chapter examines three key sectors of alternative media in Chile—print, radio, and video—from 1973 to 2006. This unusually long-term view encompasses two radically different political-economic environments—the 17-year dictatorship of General Augusto Pinochet and the 16-year 'transition to democracy'[1] under the leadership of the center-left political coalition known as the *Concertación*. It describes the impressive growth of alternative media in the hostile environment of the dictatorship, their collapse during the seemingly more favorable conditions of the early transition to democracy, and their partial recovery since the political watershed of Pinochet's 1998 arrest in London. The selected examples included in this discussion are part of a broader study of Chilean alternative media during this period of profound political and economic change. This chapter draws on some of the more than 100 personal interviews conducted by the author in Chile with professional journalists and media producers, grassroots media activists, and media policy makers.

This case study offers empirical support for the arguments of Sreberny-Mohammadi and Mohammadi (1994) and Downing (1984, 2001) who assert the centrality of alternative media in the development of mass movements confronting repressive regimes and criticize insufficient attention to the media-movement nexus in both the communication and social movement literature. This study of the Chilean experience contributes to filling this gap by analyzing how alternative media served to inform, cohere, amplify, mobilize, and empower the developing mass movement against the Pinochet dictatorship.

Downing (2001: 23) further contends that the media-movement relationship is one of "dialectical and indeed acute interdependence." Downing avoids the "superficially easy" analysis that alternative media rise and fall mechanically in tandem with the number of "bodies in the streets," noting they both predate and postdate movement upsurges and respond to historically specific circumstances (1984: 356-357). He also argues that networks of organized grassroots activist groups "provide key communicative linkages between radical alternative media and social movements" (2001: 33). The Chilean case demonstrates the complexity of the media-movement interaction, as well as the impact on it of political economic factors such as domestic and international institutional and financial support. The importance of grassroots activist networks in media production, distribution, and reception is another salient characteristic of the Chilean experience.

C. Rodríguez (2001) argues that although grassroots 'citizens" media are often ephemeral, like "bubbles in the swamp," they manifest an underlying social ferment and should not be dismissed as insignificant merely because their direct contribution to the ultimate goal of democracy is not readily apparent. Her point is particularly applicable to what Chileans call 'micromedia,' such as leaflets or small circulation newsletters, whose importance in this case was collective and cumulative, despite the short life and limited circulation of many individual efforts.

The Chilean case also supports key contentions by theorists of media democratization and critics of neoliberalism. O'Neil (1998) and Bennett (1998) have argued that media democratization should be a priority during political transitions from authoritarianism. They and other theorists contend that media democratization requires public policies that promote and sustain diversity and decentralization, including support for a wide array of what Jakubowicz (1995: 132) terms a noncommercial 'civic' media sector and what C. Rodríguez (2001: 20) describes as "citizens media" (Garnham, 1994; Keane, 1991; Waisbord, 1998). Critics of neoliberalism argue that strictly market-based media systems stifle critical voices and contribute to a "hollowing out of democracy" (McChesney, 1999: 112). This chapter takes issue with the contentions of two prominent Chilean scholars and policymakers, Tironi and Sunkel (1993, 2000), who argue that alternative media were marginal during the dictatorship and that their disappearance represents a desirable market-based modernization of Chilean media. Instead, it argues that the dramatic decline of alternative media in Chile during the transition phase was not the natural result of a successful social movement no longer needing them but to a significant extent reflects the Concertación's choice to adopt neoliberal and other media policies that effectively weakened potential critics rather than strengthened the democratic public sphere.

BACKGROUND: CHILEAN POLITICS
AND MEDIA 1970-1973

On September 11, 1973, the democratically elected government of Chile was overthrown in a violent military coup led by General Augusto Pinochet. Three years earlier Salvador Allende had been elected president as the candidate of the broad-based Unidad Popular (UP) electoral coalition that advocated democratic socialism and an increased state role in the economy. Prior to the coup, Chile's multiparty system and hotly contested elections were paralleled by a vigorous mass media representing the full range of national political opinion. Most commercial media were identified with the right, but party-owned daily newspapers and radio stations gave the UP a significant media presence. The country's four television channels were split between UP supporters and opponents.[2] As Chile became increasingly polarized, the media became a key terrain of the intensifying social conflict. The political right's commercial mass media openly advocated military intervention, and the UP's party-based press and radio were reinforced by militant grassroots media, especially among workers in Santiago's industrial zones.[3]

THE PINOCHET DICTATORSHIP 1973-1990

Political Repression and Neoliberal Economic Shock

The military coup of 1973 went far beyond removing the Allende government. It constituted a full-scale assault on civil society and the public sphere. The junta dissolved Congress, outlawed the political parties of the UP, labor unions, and other organizations that could offer potential resistance,[4] and prohibited all independent forms of public expression. The media associated with the UP were closed and their facilities were destroyed or confiscated. The remaining media were subject to strict controls. Although restrictions varied over time, they ranged from broad prohibitions of 'unpatriotic propaganda' and any information or opinion that would "defame, libel, or slander the President, government ministers, members of Congress, superior court judges, and the commanders in chief of the armed forces" to very specific regulation of content, such as forbidding the words 'Allende' and 'torture,' prohibiting reporting about the detention and whereabouts of specific individuals, and banning magazine cover stories featuring protest actions. For extended periods of time, the government imposed prior censorship of content, and new media could not be created without government authorization. An array of decrees and regulations granted authorities the power to confiscate publications deemed in violation of the law, to temporarily suspend publications and broadcasts, and to prosecute journalists and editors (for chronologies, see Baltra, 1988; Consejo Metropolitano, 1988). Extralegal consequences included the risk of torture, disappearance, or murder—human rights abuses for which the regime became infamous internationally.[5] During the dictatorship, at least 50 journalists, photographers, filmmakers, and other media and communication workers 'disappeared' or were murdered (see Carmona, 1998).[6]

The junta's determination to remake Chilean society extended to the economic realm. The regime adopted a radical neoliberal model and imposed 'shock therapy' that combined free markets and privatization of state enterprises with drastic reduction and privatization of social services. Among the outcomes were massive unemployment, hunger, homelessness, and increasing income inequality.[7] In 1983, an economic crisis transformed the political situation by generating mass protests.[8] This sudden social eruption reflected not only the immediate economic circumstances, but a decade of less visible, often clandestine, organizing and the emergence of new grassroots organizations.

Building the Democratic Movement

In order to construct a social movement capable of ending the dictatorship, the prodemocracy forces had to overcome both political and geographic divisions. Politically, this required bridging deep divisions within the left and finding common ground for the left and Christian Democrats, who had opposed Allende and initially supported the coup.[9] Creating a national movement was also complicated by Chile's unusual geography in which vast deserts in the north and rugged mountains and forests in the south separate population centers.

Alternative media helped surmount these political and geographic obstacles. Alternative media's evolving role will be considered during two broad periods of the dictatorship—the first decade during which open opposition within Chile was almost impossible[10] and the period of mass action dating from the eruption of protests in 1983 until Pinochet's defeat in the 1988 plebiscite on continued military rule.[11] In the decade before mass protests began, media took the lead in opening up social space for the expression of dissent and in disseminating a new political discourse centered on support for democratic and human rights that facilitated an alliance of the center and the left. After the mass movement erupted in Santiago, alternative media helped it expand nationwide. Not only did the opposition media provide a vital communication infrastructure for the movement, they also took advantage of the expanded political space they were helping to create to become even more visible and audacious. In a dynamic familiar from such experiences as the Sandinista struggle in Nicaragua, Solidarity in Poland, and the Iranian revolution, the increasing reach and sophistication of Chilean alternative media were both stimulus for, and the product of, an ascendant social movement.[12]

The Politics of Repression

Political calculations affected the military's response to the prodemocracy media. Some alternative media had ties to the Catholic or other churches with which the regime did not want a direct confrontation. Other media producers had international connections that offered them some protection. The military authorized or tolerated some media whose potential it underestimated. Its actions were also influenced by the need to win majority support in the 1988 plebiscite. Severe repression tended to solidify the uneasy Christian Democrat-Socialist opposition alliance that would evolve into the Concertación. In response to the 1983 protests, the regime briefly tested a policy of *apertura* or opening in which it hoped some limited concessions, including authorizing new opposition media, would improve relations with the Christian Democrats and split the prodemocracy movement. When this policy was unsuccessful, repression increased, culminating in the 1984 state of siege and closure of opposition media. The junta's dilemma was that although severe repression curtailed protest in the short run, it also jeopardized future support in the plebiscite. Once a significant alternative media sector had developed and obtained a mass following, media closures and arrests of journalists alienated those who had tolerated the regime's repression of militant street protesters. The movement also made press freedom part of its democratic program and mobilized public support for media and journalists under attack.

THE DEVELOPMENT OF ALTERNATIVE MEDIA

From Micromedia to Magazines

Given the impossibility of open protest in the immediate aftermath of the coup, leaflets and newsletters that were produced in small quantities and distributed clandestinely demonstrated the survival of the banned organizations of the left and allowed them to denounce the repression and call for resistance. New groups that formed in response to the junta's use of disappearance and torture used newsletters to publicize these practices that were hidden and denied by the regime. These publications, and the social networks through which they circulated, were crucial to making human rights an axis of opposition activity. Producing micromedia, as newsletters and leaflets are known in Chile, was a principal activity of student groups, labor organizations, Christian base communities, and community groups in *poblaciones* (poor urban neighborhoods) that gradually reorganized after 1975. By 1977, opposition newsletters reached an estimated 100,000 readers in Santiago alone (Dorfman, 1983: 209), each copy typically passed along to ten different people (A.N.C.H.A., 1979: 3). Although generally produced by artisan techniques and of low quality, they advanced the process of constructing an opposition movement

by opening up 'new discursive spaces' reflecting grassroots responses to the griev-
ances of different social sectors (Munizaga, 1981: 64-65).

Professional quality magazines by openly identified producers that could
offer more in-depth reporting than the micromedia and that were directed at a
national public represented a qualitative advance in reclaiming expressive spaces.
The first two appeared in 1976 and 1977,[13] using different strategies in response
to legal requirements for government authorization and prior censorship. APSI,
an acronym for Agencia de Prensa de Servicios Internacionales (Press Agency for
International Services) obtained approval in 1976 by proposing to limit its content to international news. The following year *Análisis,* launching without
approval and refusing to submit to censorship, relied on a vague *patrocinio* or
sponsorship of a Catholic Church agency to shield it from reprisals. Its editor
believes that the regime underestimated the magazine's potential and did not
want to stir conflict with the church over a publication it considered insignificant
(J. Cárdenas, personal interview, August 30, 2000). Similarly, the government did
not recognize the critical potential of APSI, which legally reported such stories as
international protests against the junta, the successes of social movements against
other Latin American dictatorships, and stories about assassinations carried out
by the junta's agents abroad.

At a time when the opposition was embryonic, fragmented, and localized,
the earliest magazines helped constitute a national movement and a new, democratic voice. Breaking with the pre-coup predominance of party-based publications of the left, the magazines were intentionally pluralist in their personnel and
content, an important step in promoting dialogue and overcoming divisions
among opponents of the regime. APSI's editor stressed that a new democratic
discourse "requires a communication space to express itself and develop." APSI
was to be "not only the voice of the voiceless. It was its own voice to call together, link, and foster agreement" among the prodemocratic forces in society
(Contreras, 1983: 143-144).

Although subscriptions and circulation via social organizations had been sufficient to establish the magazines, expanding their influence required increasing
circulation from hundreds to tens of thousands. Open sales in kiosks began in
1980,[14] providing the needed leap in circulation. For example, *Análisis* jumped
from 2,500-3,500 copies per issue to 10,000-15,000 (Cárdenas, personal interview,
August 30, 2000). The magazines also circulated within the international exile
community and received both financial and political support from abroad.

The magazines founded after mass protests began responded to the more
favorable conditions with even more daring content. *Cauce,* authorized during the
apertura, saw its mission as 'direct confrontation' with the regime through denun-
ciation of corruption and abuses of power, including well-documented exposés of
financial dealings of the Pinochet family (Richards, 1985: 18-19). The older magazines also challenged the dictatorship more boldly. For example, APSI cover
stories included, "This Is How They Torture in Chile," "Who Disappeared and
How," "Those Executed by the Regime," and *Análisis* covers proclaimed "Chile

Wants Democracy," and "He [Pinochet] Must Go!" Circulation surged. APSI reached 25,000 (J. Rodríguez, 2001), *Análisis* 30,000 (Richards, 1985: 4), and *Cauce* set the record for a single issue with over 98,000 copies sold (Segovia, 1990: 87). Furthermore, the magazines' influence extended beyond purchasers. Issues and photocopied articles were passed from one reader to another, public readings took place in some *poblaciones*, and magazine content entered the national political conversation through word of mouth and radio reports.

In addition to continually testing the boundaries of what the government would tolerate, the magazines also 'complied' with some restrictions in ways that subverted their intent. For example, when photos were temporarily prohibited, *Análisis* created images formed entirely by letters (Reyes Matta, 1985: 15), and when APSI was denied permission to cover national stories, it once printed blank pages with the word 'Censored' and in another issue, excerpts from *Alice in Wonderland* (J. Rodríguez, 2001). They contested censorship in court, and after 1983 used the jailing of their editors to foment political challenges to the regime. Social movements responded by organizing protests and incorporating defense of press freedom into their agendas.

When the magazines were closed for seven months during the state of siege in 1984-1985 and for four months after an assassination attempt on Pinochet in 1986, they relied on their ties to social movements for alternative means of distribution. APSI produced a lengthy typewritten weekly newsletter titled SIC for Servicio Informativo Confidencial that was distributed to prodemocracy organizations which, in turn, circulated it among their members (S. Marras, personal interview, Sept. 9, 1998).[15] *Análisis* also produced a shorter clandestine version distributed by fax to people who reproduced it. In 1986, *Análisis* responded to its closure in an even more creative way by utilizing international solidarity networks. Proofs were smuggled out of Chile to Germany by Lufthansa pilots and given to the German Graphic Workers Union, who produced approximately 4,000 copies every two weeks for *Análisis* subscribers. Once printed in Germany, under Chilean law it became a German magazine, and was not subject to the Chilean prohibition. According to director Juan Pablo Cárdenas, "The print quality was much better…. It caused a great impact and the government looked ridiculous. So they decided it was better to let us publish in Chile where they could charge us in court" (personal interview, August 30, 2000).[16]

Radio

Radio played a crucial role in opening space for dissent in the early years of the dictatorship and in disseminating a discourse of respect for human rights and concern for the poor that helped create a unifying framework for the democratic movement. The station that played the most significant role in that period was the Catholic Church's Radio Chilena. This affiliation not only shielded it from repression,[17] but also ensured that its message reached a public, many of whom had opposed Allende and were hostile to the traditional left. An important defensive strategy was to broadcast the Cardinal's weekly sermons, which raised issues of human rights and poverty, and to use them as the basis for commentary during the week. The station identified itself as "the voice of the voiceless" that reported "from the point of view of justice not politics" (S. Conejeros, personal interview, August 29, 2000).

The protests of 1983 galvanized the Christian Democrat station Radio Cooperativa, which became the most consistent and widely respected radio source for nonofficial news when stations throughout the country restransmitted its programs. Its ability to instantaneously transmit news of events in Santiago to even the most remote areas of Chile helped create "a new collective feeling" (Ossandón, 1983: 5) of social agency and the protests quickly became a national phenomenon. Temporary closures by the junta only served to increase Cooperativa's credibility and influence. However, the station rejected the label of 'opposition.' Rather it affirmed its commitment to full and truthful reporting in which "all the political interests and all the social interests have the ability to express themselves" (Lasagni, Edwards, & Bonnefoy, 1985: 90).

In 1987, as the democratic movement prepared for the 1988 plebiscite, the Methodist Church's Radio Umbral initiated the most dramatic expansion of radio's activist role. The station revolutionized programming by daring to play music by executed and exiled artists closely identified with the Unidad Popular, which had not been aired since the coup. Its audience mushroomed, and the enthusiastic response stimulated further experimentation with new forms of participatory relationships between the station and its public. The station aired live interviews with human rights advocates and former political prisoners and created a network of grassroots reporters based in the *poblaciones* who called in news, often allowing Umbral to scoop other stations. It also broadcast alerts, such as calls for lawyers to respond to raids in *poblaciones* by security forces. Umbral made it possible for women political prisoners to become program producers by broadcasting tapes the women made clandestinely in jail. The station became so popular that some of its programs were number one in their time slot. Furthermore, Umbral's cultural resistance was not limited to its programming. It organized the first outdoor concert by opposition musicians and continued to sponsor cultural events attended by as many as 25,000 people, which also served as fund-raisers (personal interviews, P. Enriquez, August 15, 2000; M. Ordenes, Sept. 11, 2002).[18]

Video

During the last decade of the dictatorship, independent video producers challenged the military's use of television "to institutionalize forgetting, reinterpret history and erase the collective memory of the people of Chile" (Góngora, 1988: 155). The production and dissemination of authentic images of repression, poverty, and resistance were a key component of the struggle to create a political alternative, and video provided a particularly effective means of sharing the experiences of activists from different regions of the country who would ordinarily have been unaware of each other's activities.

The well-known theater group ICTUS pioneered the use of video in 1980 with funding from a Dutch foundation. At that time, video technology was new to Chile and unfamiliar to the majority of *población* residents who were the programs' target audience. The screenings were usually held in the neighborhood church and, in this period before the protests, the ICTUS team frequently had to go door to door persuading residents to take the risk of attending (B. Quintenal de Salas, personal interview, July 24, 1998). In contrast, the protests inspired the formation of the other two principal video production groups, Proceso and Teleanálisis, an outgrowth of *Análisis* magazine, and they found a public hungry for alternative images. Although these three groups were not the only video producers, they were the most significant, not only for the consistency of their production but for the participatory reception they promoted and the national distribution systems they created based on ties to social organizations. Video screenings were followed by discussions with the audience, facilitated by representatives from the production group or the sponsoring organization. Discussion objectives included consciousness-raising and involvement in the democratic struggle. Audience feedback influenced future video production. For example, in response to comments that the videos were too focused on repression, Proceso shifted to programs dealing with successful examples of organization and protest (H. Mondaca, personal interview, August 6, 1998). Just as the videos became a valuable organizing tool for prodemocracy organizations, the expansion of the movement increased the possibilities for video distribution. ICTUS created a network of video libraries housed in churches or other grassroots organizations with 15 centers in Santiago and 33 more in 20 other cities (ICTUS, n.d.). Proceso sent 200 copies of each program to grassroots organizations and requested that each organization make five more copies. Teleanálisis's tapes were distributed to 350 subscribing organizations. Because the producers refused to submit the tapes for censorship, they bore the disclaimer "Showing in Chile prohibited" although "in reality, we encouraged everyone to pirate them" (A. Góngora, personal interview, August 10, 2000). Despite the relatively small audiences for each showing, over time individual programs reached as many as 100,000 viewers (Sahli, 1987: 23).

Political space expanded considerably during the plebiscite when previously prohibited actions such as mass demonstrations were legalized, although repression continued to occur. Although full consideration of the role of media during the plebiscite is beyond the scope of this chapter, it should be noted that two opposition daily newspapers[19] increased the presence of alternative media and that the democratic movement gained access to television for the first time. Both sides had equal time for nightly political spots and the effectiveness of the ads for the Campaign for the No contributed significantly to its victory. Many of those who produced the television campaign came from the alternative media sector (see *La Campaña del No*, 1989).

During this period alternative media made a significant collective contribution to reclaiming the public sphere for civil society. They helped develop and circulate the democratic discourse that unified the democratic movement. Their reporting of human rights abuses deprived the regime of legitimacy. The direct voice they offered to opposition forces allowed them to win adherents and counter the regime's misrepresentations of their program and actions. Eventually, they forced even the proregime mass media to broaden their own coverage to avoid losing credibility. Ultimately, they constituted a powerful legacy of social struggle poised to actively contribute to the process of reconstructing Chilean democracy.

THE TRANSITION TO DEMOCRACY

The restoration of democracy was not only the result of the political victories of the opposition in the plebiscite and the 1989 election but of private, elite negotiations between Concertación leaders and the military. This negotiated transition was based on the Concertación's commitment to retain a neoliberal economic model and honor the military's self-granted amnesty for human rights abuses. Although much of the prodemocracy movement deferred to Concertación leadership, this agreement placed the incoming government at odds with its most activist sectors which saw an ongoing need for social movements to demand prosecution of human rights abuses, to press for the rapid advancement of labor, women's, and indigenous rights, and to combat extreme income inequality and environmental degradation. The contradiction between these grassroots demands and the Concertación's determination not to antagonize the military and powerful domestic and transnational economic interests led the government to view independent social mobilization as an obstacle to its ability to control the pace and direction of the transition. Similarly, alternative media that could critique the new government's limited political and economic agenda were seen more as potential adversaries than as a vital democratic resource to be nourished.[20]

While gradually eliminating authoritarian restrictions on free expression, Concertación media policy emphasized free operation of market forces. The resulting advertising-based, highly concentrated, and largely unregulated media system placed socially critical media at a severe economic disadvantage in a highly politicized media market and constituted a serious impediment to the maintenance of an open and vigorous public sphere. Other adverse public policies and the cooptation or demobilization of social movements compounded the disadvantage for alternative media by eroding their social base.[21]

After a brief upsurge of new participatory initiatives, the alternative media sector virtually collapsed at both the national and community levels. Most alternative media disappeared during the first few years of the transition, and by mid-1998 none of the independent media that had fought the dictatorship remained.[22] However, the startling arrest of Pinochet in London[23] in the fall of that year transformed the political climate and triggered a new wave of activism and independent media initiatives that have struggled to survive in a largely unfavorable political, economic and regulatory environment.

THE DISAPPEARANCE OF ALTERNATIVE MEDIA

The Demise of Dictatorship-era Opposition Media

Eugenio Tironi, a leading Concertación media policymaker, articulated the government's neoliberal argument that a purely market-based media system is democratic because, as profit-seeking businesses, commercial media must satisfy the needs of advertisers who, in turn, respond to audience preferences (cited in Otano, 1991: 19). However, he revealingly linked this celebration of markets as democratic agents to the Concertación's intention that the media no longer serve "as promoters of political change but as agents that contribute to the stability of the system" by "creating a basic consensus around pluralist democracy and an open market economy" (Tironi & Sunkel, 1993: 216, 242). He approvingly noted that media such as the opposition magazines "have little chance of survival" (cited in Otano, 1991: 19).

This prediction of market hostility to alternative media proved correct. However, Tironi's argument that this phenomenon was a democratic reflection of consumer preferences is especially flawed in the Chilean context, where conservative corporate advertisers have traditionally avoided media identified with the left, regardless of their popularity. Moreover, the government, itself a major advertiser, could have used its economic resources to compensate for the anti-left bias of commercial advertisers, but instead favored what had been the pro-Pinochet commercial media. Finally, some decline in use of alternative media reflected disillusionment with the Concertación and feelings of political impotence by former activists. What Tironi portrayed positively as free consumer choice is better interpreted as the deliberately induced decline of active citizenship.

The fate of Radio Umbral clearly refuted the neoliberal assertion of advertisers as responsive democratic agents. Despite the station having one of the largest audiences in Santiago, commercial advertisers avoided it. So did government agencies. Even during elections, the station received almost no Concertación campaign ads (M. Ordenes, personal interview, September 11, 2002). In 1993, the Methodist church sold the station when it could no longer afford to subsidize it.

The Concertación's role in the demise of alternative magazines appears to have gone beyond mere failure to provide advertising support. Juan Pablo Cárdenas of *Análisis* has repeatedly charged that the first Concertación administration intervened to prevent the Dutch government from making a substantial grant to *Análisis* and the other opposition magazines to support them as they adjusted to the new political and commercial environment after 1990.[24] In the case of *Análisis*, the government went even further. Investors close to the president acquired an ownership share in the magazine, fired Cárdenas, changed the editorial direction, and ultimately closed it (J. Cárdenas, personal interview, August 30, 2000). Although there was no such concerted effort against any of the other magazines, and their editors have not echoed Cárdenas' allegations of blocked international funding, there is considerable bitterness over the impact of government policy. According to Rafael Otano, a former editor of APSI, it was clear that "there would be no payment for services rendered, not even a special consideration for the media that had contributed significantly to the recovery of democracy" (2000: 44). Furthermore, he noted that the political and economic timidity of the Concertación indirectly affected the magazines by creating a political environment of resignation that he described as "politics in the refrigerator" (48).

One after another, the magazines closed, and by July 1998 the last of the opposition media, the daily newspaper *La Epoca,* succumbed to financial stress, after years of limping from crisis to crisis. Despite failure to reach its full potential, the paper's death was widely viewed in Chile as a crisis of the public sphere, which left the right-wing *El Mercurio*-Copesa[25] duopoly's control of the daily press unchallenged with the exception of the government paper *La Nación*.[26]

New Community Media

Just as existing alternative media faltered during the early years of the transition, this period also proved to be unfavorable for sustaining new grassroots initiatives. In the initial euphoria of the democratic victory, activists saw community radio and video as a means "to express themselves, raise their voices, and become protagonists of their own history in actions and in words, thereby reaching higher levels of human dignity" (ANARAP, 1992: 68). These aspirations inspired an upsurge of new media projects. However, most were unable to overcome the combination of indifferent or hostile government policies and diminished political activism.

Community Radio

Especially in some militant *poblaciones*, radio activists sought to follow the example of Radio Umbral as a grassroots voice and mobilizer within their own neighborhoods. In January of 1990, the National Organization of Grassroots Radio Stations (Agrupación Nacional de Radio Popular,[27] ANARAP) was founded to promote community radio stations run by "unions, community groups, ethnic groups, youth, women, cultural centers, NGOs, and all entities that seek to democratize radio for the benefit of average people" (ANARAP, 1992: 69).

The first new community station began clandestine transmissions in a Santiago *población* in April 1990, and within a year 38 stations were on the air.

Although their status was undefined in Chilean law, the political right and commercial stations accused the activist radio stations of being dangerous and illegal. To end the controversy, the government promised the stations that it would quickly pass legislation legalizing them if they voluntarily ceased broadcasting. ANARAP agreed, and in July 1991 the stations fell silent. However, legalization was delayed more than two years whereas a measure criminalizing unauthorized broadcasts passed almost immediately. Moreover, what the new law authorized was low-power, rather than community radio, and it favored more affluent applicants such as churches or local governments over true grassroots groups. The few ANARAP groups that had not dissolved during the long delay found it difficult to muster the resources to apply or were unsuccessful in seeking the single license available for each *comuna*.[28] Although ultimately over 400 licenses nationwide have been issued under the new law, activist community radio never recovered its initial momentum (see Yañez & Aguilera, 2000). Some activist stations, both licensed and unlicensed, have succeeded in *poblaciones* where political mobilization remains high.

Video

The community radio movement was paralleled by a profusion of community video production groups, primarily young people in the *poblaciones*. Although video was not dependent on legislation as was radio, public policy did have an adverse impact in terms of funding and distribution.

Videos dealt with community issues such as human rights, youth unemployment, and drug addiction. The videos were shown using the *pantalla grande* or *pantallazo* (big screen), which is an outdoor screening in a public place, such as a plaza or street corner, projecting the image on a sheet or wall. Although the producers valued the interactivity of the *pantallazo*, they also experienced frustration at the limited exposure available in relation to the work required to produce the programs (personal interviews, J. Bertín, July 27, 1998; C. Gómez, July 29, 1998; A. Leal, August 17, 1998). An annual video festival sponsored by the National Network of Community Video Producers only partially filled the need for a wider audience.

Creative attempts to provide broader distribution channels via cable television were unsuccessful because the Concertación intentionally failed to require public access when establishing cable television policies. As a result, *VTR Cableexpress*, one of the two major cable companies, was able to renege on its agreement with the environmental NGO Canelo de Nos to offer an 'ecological, citizen and cultural' channel featuring independent and community video (H. Dinamarca, personal interview, August 6, 1998). Similarly, the other major cable operator, Metropolis Intercom, was able to shut down a community channel in the *comuna* of Ñuñoa for showing a program on human rights (C. Messina, personal interview, August 17, 1998).

Lack of public financial support also undermined the community video movement. The national annual arts grants competition did not provide a separate category for grassroots, nonprofessional groups, and only a few local governments made funding available.

The frustrations involved in production and distribution would not have been as serious an impediment in a different political environment. The video network's national assembly in January 2000 concluded that decreased community video production reflected the low level of social and community activism, which, in turn, reflected the loss of optimism after ten years of political transition (J. Bertín, personal interview, September 6, 2000).

NEW ALTERNATIVE MASS MEDIA

AM Radio

In the early years of the transition, AM radio proved an exception to the inability of new alternative media to sustain themselves. Three new radio stations, each fortified by its affiliation with an existing institution linked to social movements, offset the loss of Radio Umbral. These new stations grew out of organized civil society and, in turn, not only supported the organizations that gave birth to them but bolstered social activism in general.

With initial funding from Denmark, Radio Tierra was launched in 1991 as Latin America's first feminist station by the women's NGO La Morada, active in women's issues since 1983. Replacing its feminist designation with the less controversial 'station for women,' Radio Tierra has broadened its identity to 'human rights radio' and 'the voice of civil society' and offers airtime to a variety of activist organizations. So does Radio Canelo, which was inaugurated in 1994 by the environmental NGO Canelo de Nos, under the direction of a former Radio Umbral host. The station features socially conscious music and environmental and human rights programming. Radio Nuevo Mundo became the unofficial station of the Communist Party, which was never compensated for the dictatorship's confiscation of its ten radio stations. Although not formally party-owned, Nuevo Mundo is directed and staffed by party members. The station emphasizes news and political discussion in its programming.

Lacking major advertisers, all three stations rely on low salaries for permanent staff and unpaid volunteer work. Even so, none of them can afford to broadcast all day and must resort to leasing approximately half of their air time to other, primarily religious, broadcasters as a way of financing their own programming (personal interviews, H. Barahona, August 25, 2000; M. Mesa, August 4, 1998; M. Ordenes, September 11, 2002). Nuevo Mundo has advanced the most in developing a listener-support system. It receives monthly contributions from about 1,000 listener-members, as well as funds raised by local clubs of listeners.

The station also organizes fundraisers such as cultural events with donated performances and sells tapes of popular educational and cultural programs.

Magazines

If the demise of *La Epoca* in mid-1998 marked the nadir of the alternative press, the unexpected arrest of Pinochet in London in September of that year redefined the politically possible and energized media and human rights activism. Almost immediately two new publications appeared, the satiric paper, *The Clinic,* and the political-cultural monthly, *Rocinante.* Since then, media diversity has been enriched by the appearance of additional critical voices.[29] *The Clinic,* named for the London medical clinic where Pinochet was detained, is an iconoclastic biweekly paper that perfectly captured the historical moment. Its founder, Patricio Fernandez, considers the detention of Pinochet a landmark event that "removed a terrible shadow from the minds of the Chilean people" and made them realize that "you don't have to go around on your knees" (personal interview, September 6, 2000). *The Clinic* attracted an enthusiastic readership, especially among young people, with its blunt and sarcastic language, irreverence toward political leaders, skewering of hypocrisy, open discussion of sexuality, and indignation at the failure to prosecute human rights abuses and the persistent social inequality of the neoliberal economy. It relies on volunteer contributions and inexpensive black-and-white newsprint[30] to minimize production costs, and sells for 200 pesos or about 40 U.S. cents. Its small paid staff continues to be supplemented by many unpaid collaborators. Its paid circulation grew from an initial 10,000 to 40,000 by 2000. However, it faces the same economic obstacle that confronts all progressive media in Chile—a lack of advertising. Fernandez noted the challenge of attracting advertisers in a "country where above all the right and its businessmen are very fascist and exceedingly conservative. . . . Even if placing an ad is greatly to their advantage, they are capable of never doing it because of ideology" (personal interview, September 6, 2000).

Rocinante pursued a different economic strategy. As a large-format, political-cultural monthly magazine, aimed at a well-educated and more affluent public, it charged a relatively high price to reduce the need for advertising (F. Zerán, personal interview, August 28, 2000). In the inaugural issue in November 1998, director Faride Zerán[31] described the magazine's philosophy as "freedom of expression, recreated in a critical journalism . . . that subscribes unrestrictedly to democracy. That is, in *Rocinante* there is no journalism of the transition, if that is understood as unlimited euphemisms and fear of debate."

In October 2003, these and other alternative media created the Association of Independent Media in order to sell advertising collectively in an effort to improve their financial stability. This initiative was not sufficient to save *Rocinante,* which closed in October 2005. In an open letter to then-President Lagos, the editorial board criticized "the indifference of your administration to the lack of pluralism that afflicts our society, leaving to the laws of an ideological and non-transparent market the fate of media that expand horizons of tolerance, diversity, and democracy" especially because the state, which "concentrates a great quantity of resources for advertising, reinforce this lack of pluralism due to the almost exclusive investment of these resources in large communication conglomerates and monopolies" ("Carta Abierta," 2005: 2).

Internet-only Newspapers

Although the new alternative magazines reclaimed important expressive space for critical ideas, the daily press continued to be dominated by the papers of the right-wing *El Mercurio*-Copesa duopoly. A creative response to the high cost of starting a new print daily was the creation of independent, left-leaning, on-line newspapers with no print editions. The first was *El Mostrador,* which was initially financed by a small group of investors who hoped it would become self-financing after a year (F. Joannón, personal interview, August 28, 2000). It made a major impact when it scooped the print dailies during the dramatic legal procedures to strip Pinochet of his legal immunity in 2000. However, advertisers did not respond to its high hit rate and affluent readership,[32] and it was forced to implement a subscription system. Only subscribers can access the complete content, although about half remains available to all users. In September of 2000, *El Mostrador* was followed by *Primera Línea*, a project of former *Análisis* editor Juan Pablo Cárdenas. Well-financed by the public-private corporation that owns the official daily *La Nación*, it fell victim to political considerations. Although he had been promised journalistic autonomy, Cárdenas was replaced as editor after several months due to government pressure (personal communication, September 25, 2001), and eventually the paper itself was replaced by an on-line edition of *La Nación* in January of 2003. In their final statement, the *Primera Línea* journalists decried the destruction of critical journalism by "the cruelty of the market" and "political indifference." (*"Otro adios a un medio,"* 2003). An internet-only revival of the pre-coup pro-UP *Clarín,* based in Spain, added another voice to on-line independent journalism in 2005.[33]

Although internet-only papers do not reach a mass public as a print daily could, they nonetheless have opened up daily space for critical voices. The alternative content they inject into the public sphere affects the broader news environment and circulates via word of mouth to a broader public than their on-line readership.

CONCLUSION

The Chilean case reinforces the argument that alternative media contribute significantly to the development of mass social movements in authoritarian contexts. In Chile, with great courage and creativity, mass and grassroots alternative media reclaimed the public sphere for critical social voices. What the Chilean case makes especially clear is the dynamic of mutual empowerment between media and other sectors of the democratic movement. As the earliest form of public opposition, alternative media encouraged other forms of organized resistance. The growth of a mass movement then expanded the possibilities for media action, which in turn fueled the mass movement. And the cycle continued. The Chilean case suggests that the longer the struggle against a repressive regime and the greater the initial political, geographic, and organizational fragmentation of the future mass movement, the more crucial is the development of an alternative communication infrastructure and the counter public sphere it makes possible.

The Chilean experience also demonstrates the limitations of neoliberal democratization, which restored electoral democracy but debilitated the democratic process by impoverishing the public sphere. Forced by Concertación policy into a purely market environment, existing alternative mass media foundered economically having to confront simultaneously the loss of domestic and international subsidies and the adverse impact of politically based decisions of potential commercial and state advertisers. Likewise, promising new community-based media were undermined by unfavorable public policies. More broadly, Concertación policy eroded the alternative media's social base in organized mass movements as supporters of the Concertación parties deferred to its limited agenda, and many of those who desired deeper and more rapid change became discouraged and demobilized. Nonetheless, committed activists continue to press for progress on human rights, economic justice, and other social issues. In their efforts to transcend the narrow boundaries of the Concertación's neoliberal vision of Chile's future, alternative media struggle to sustain and expand critical expressive space. However, despite persistent and innovative efforts to overcome political and economic obstacles, reclaiming the public sphere remains an unfinished democratic challenge.

NOTES

1. The transition refers to the gradual elimination of undemocratic institutions established by the authoritarian constitution of 1980, such as appointed senators (former presidents such as Pinochet becoming senators for life) and a Congressional electoral system that assures overrepresentation of the right. By the end of 2006, only the electoral system remained in effect and several proposals to replace it were under consideration.
2. Initially, television licenses were limited to universities, which were financed by a combination of government support and advertising. In 1969, a state channel was created. There were no commercial channels until 1990.
3. See Mattelart (1980) for critical analysis of UP media policies and detailed discussion of grassroots media.

4. Greatly restricted political activity was later permitted under the Constitution of
   1980. Weak labor unions were also legalized. Proregime political organizations were
   allowed, but formal political parties were not permitted until the 1988 plebiscite,
   although the UP parties remained banned.
5. Two government commissions were established to investigate human rights abuses. In
   1991, the National Truth and Reconciliation Commission documented 2,095 execu-
   tions and 1,102 disappearances during the dictatorship. In 2004, the National
   Commission on Political Imprisonment and Torture documented 28,459 cases of
   political imprisonment, of whom 94% were tortured. The actual numbers may be
   higher. Some cases were never reported, and others lacked sufficient documentation
   to be included in the official totals. According to the Catholic Church's human rights
   office, the *Vicaría de la Solidaridad*, in the period between 1973 and 1975 there were
   42,486 political detentions. The political imprisonment figures do not include those
   arrested during public demonstrations and charged in court. According to the Chilean
   Human Rights Commission, during the protests of 1984, there were 28,548 detentions.
6. In some cases, this repression was due at least as much to their political activities as to
   their professional work.
7. For detailed discussion of the economic consequences of neoliberalism, see Collins
   and Lear (1995).
8. The protests involved monthly coordinated actions throughout the country and were
   characterized by violent confrontations between security forces and residents, especially youth, in the *poblaciones* of Santiago and other urban centers until they were
   ended by a state of siege in November 1984. See de la Maza & Garcés (1985) for a
   detailed account.
9. Traditionally, the UP parties and the Christian Democrats each represented about
   one third of the electorate. The Christian Democrats went into opposition when the
   intention of the military to retain long-term power became clear.
10 During this time, campaigns organized abroad by Chilean exiles and international solidarity organizations were the primary form of open opposition to the regime.
11. The plebiscite was mandated by the constitution of 1980 and allowed only a yes or no
   vote on another eight-year term for Pinochet. It was intended to provide a veneer of
   legitimacy for the regime, and before the emergence of the mass movement approval
   seemed inevitable. Pinochet's defeat in the plebiscite triggered the competitive election of 1989 which was won by the Concertación candidate. The Concertación has
   won every presidential election during the transition.
12. For detailed discussion of media in these movements, see Cabezas (1984) for
   Nicaragua, Sreberny-Mohammadi and Mohammadi (1994) for Iran, and Downing
   (1984) and Jakubowicz (1995) for Poland.
13. Eventually the opposition magazine sector included *Hoy, Cauce, Fortín Mapocho*, two
   cultural magazines *La Bicicleta, Pluma y Pincel*, and two Catholic magazines, *Mensaje* and
   Solidaridad. With the exception of the pre-existing *Mensaje*, all the magazines began
   publishing between 1976 and 1984.
14. The Constitution of 1980 accorded de facto legalization to all existing publications,
   thereby allowing even magazines such as *Análisis*, which had never been authorized, to
   begin open sales.
15. Other organizations, such as the Colegio de Periodistas or the Association of
   Professional Journalists, also produced newsletters that were circulated through the
   grassroots channels of the democratic movement.

16. Charges of violating internal security laws and other restrictions on the press were brought against the magazine at least 30 times and Cárdenas was jailed seven times. In 1987, Cárdenas was sentenced to three years of night-time house arrest for defaming Pinochet in five articles published in 1986. The Supreme Court reduced the sentence to 541 days. In addition to legal intimidation, his house was set on fire twice and his family lived under constant threat. Journalists at the other opposition magazines suffered similar harassment.

17. Although the regime was unwilling to attack the church as an institution, individual priests and other religious personnel were targeted, and these cases received particular attention from the Cardinal and the station.

18. For more detailed discussion of radio, including clandestine and short wave radio, see Bresnahan (2002).

19. *Fortin Mapocho* magazine was transformed into a militant tabloid, and a new paper, *La Epoca*, was modeled on Spain's *El País*.

20. For detailed discussion of the Concertación's neoliberal media policies and the contrast between its market-based concept of democratization and a public sphere model, see Bresnahan (2003).

21. For a revealing case study of how the Concertación achieved social demobilization, see Paley (2001).

22. The Communist Party had resumed weekly publication of its former daily *El Siglo*, and *Punto Final*, the magazine of the disbanded armed resistance group the Movement of the Revolutionary Left (MIR), was revived by its former editor. However, these openly Marxist publications, which still publish, could not fill the void created by the disappearance of the politically independent magazines and newspapers.

23. Pinochet was arrested in England pursuant to an extradition request by Spain which intended to prosecute him for human rights abuses under international law granting jurisdiction to any country to try crimes against humanity. Chile vigorously opposed the Spanish request, arguing that it violated Chilean sovereignty. After a lengthy process of decisions and appeals in England, the British authorized extradition. However, Britain then released Pinochet to Chile on humanitarian grounds for medical reasons. Chilean human rights groups then filed suit demanding that he be stripped of his immunity as Senator for Life to stand trial in Chile. In a landmark decision, in 2000 the Chilean Supreme Court did strip his immunity but later suspended the legal process against him for health reasons. Pinochet was stripped of his immunity in several additional human rights cases and, at the time of his death in December 2006, was under house arrest and facing prosecution. He was also being investigated for financial crimes related to secret bank accounts in the United States.

24. The government denies his charges.

25. Both the *El Mercurio* and Copesa chains actively supported the dictatorship. The *El Mercurio* chain owns three national newspapers and 18 regional dailies. Copesa owns three national papers, one free daily, and several magazines and radio stations.

26. Although *La Nación* is only partially owned by the state, it is considered the official government newspaper. Subsequently, conservative investors established *El Metropolitano* to compete with the *El Mercurio*-Copesa duopoly, but it failed after several years. Several free dailies are distributed at transit stops, but they are not serious journalistic enterprises. Recently, Copesa purchased the pro-Concertación magazine *Siete + 7* and transformed it into the daily paper, *Diario Siete*, which offers progressive viewpoints but is nonetheless controlled by its conservative parent.

27. In Spanish, 'popular' has a strong class connotation, referring to working people or those with low or modest incomes. To avoid confusion with its English usage, I will use "grassroots" as the closest English equivalent.
28. In cities, a *comuna* is similar to a borough. Santiago has 32 *comunas*, each with its own mayor. In rural areas, a *comuna* would be similar to a county.
29. Among new progressive publications are *El Periodista, La Firme,* and a Chilean edition of *Le Monde Diplomatique.* A journalist-owned biweekly, *Plan B,* survived less than two years.
30. The front page now appears in color.
31. Faride Zerán is Director of the Institute of Communication and the Image at the University of Chile, which includes the School of Journalism, and a member of the board of National Television. During the dictatorship, she was involved with the cultural magazine *Pluma y Pincel.* She also contributed to the cultural supplement of *La Epoca.*
32. Computer ownership and internet access tend to be concentrated among higher income groups. In 2000, *El Mostrador* claimed an average of 60,000 hits a day.
33. The publishers include the Salvador Allende Foundation of Spain, headed by Spanish human rights lawyer Joan Garcés, a former advisor to Allende who represented the families of the disappeared in the Spanish case seeking Pinochet's extradition from England. The Spanish group wanted to revive *Clarín* as a print daily and hoped to fund it with compensation from the Chilean government for the newspaper's assets confiscated by the military after the coup. However, the Chilean government recognized a competing group of claimants, who had no interest in resuming publication, as the legitimate owners and paid them $10 million. The Spanish group sued the Chilean government in the commercial claims court of the World Bank and sought over $500 million for lost earnings since 1973. In April 2008 the court recognized the Spanish group as the rightful owners but awarded them only $10 million plus interest. As of November 2008, the Spanish group had filed an appeal for reconsideration of the monetary award. Full details of the case are available in Spanish at www. elclarin.cl.

REFERENCES

ANARAP. (1992). Proyecto radiofónico presentado por la ANARAP a la Subsecretaría de Telecomunicaciones [Radio broadcasting project presented by the ANARAP to the Telecommunications Subsecretariat]. In *La radio popular en Chile* [Popular radio in Chile] (pp. 66-69). Santiago: Ediciones Sonoradio Producciones.

A.N.C.H.A. (1979). *The legal press and the development of the clandestine press.* No. 47 (Special ed.). Paris: Author.

Baltra, L. (1988). *Atentados a la libertad de información y a los medios de comunicación en Chile 1973-1987* [Violations against the media and freedom of information in Chile 1973-1987]. Santiago: CENECA.

Bennett, W. L. (1998). The media and democratic development: The social basis of political communication. In P. O'Neil (Ed.), *Communicating democracy: The media and political transition* (pp. 195-207). Boulder, CO: Lynne Rienner.

Bresnahan, R. (2002). Radio and the democratic movement in Chile 1973-1990: Independent and grass roots voices during the Pinochet dictatorship. *Journal of Radio Studies, 9*(1), 161-181.

Bresnahan, R. (2003). The media and the neoliberal transition in Chile: Democratic promise unfulfilled. *Latin American Perspectives, 30*(6), 39-68.

Cabezas, O. (1984). La voz del pueblo es la voz de las pintas [The people's voice is the voice of graffiti]. In *La insurrección de las paredes* [The walls' insurrection] (pp. 21-27). Managua: Editorial Nueva Nicaragua.

Carmona, E. (Ed.). (1998). *Morir es la noticia* [To die is the news]. Santiago: J & C Productores Gráficos.

"Carta abierta al Presidente Ricardo Lagos" [Open letter to president Ricardo Lagos]. (2005, October). *Rocinante*, 2.

Collins, J., & Lear, J. (1995). *Chile's free market miracle: A second look.* Oakland, CA: The Institute for Food and Development Policy.

Consejo Metropolitano, Colegio de Periodistas de Chile. (1988). *La dictadura contra los periodistas chilenos* [Dictatorship against Chilean journalists]. Santiago: Author.

Contreras, M. (1983). Las revistas alternativas: Expresiones democráticas en medio de los autoritarismos, éxitos, y fracasos [Alternative magazines: Democratic expressions in authoritarian regimes. Successes and failures]. In F. Reyes Matta (Ed.), *Comunicación alternativa y búsquedas democráticas* [Alternative communication and democratic search] (pp. 141- 154). Santiago: ILET.

de la Maza, G., & Garcés, M. (1985). *La explosión de las mayorías: Protesta nacional 1983-1984* [The explosion of the majorities: National protest 1983-1984]. Santiago: ECO.

Dorfman, A. (1983). The invisible Chile: Three years of cultural resistance. In A. Mattelart & S. Siegelaub (Eds.), *Communication and class struggle 2. Liberation, socialism* (pp. 207-210). New York: International General.

Downing, J. (1984). *Radical media: The political experience of alternative communication.* Boston: South End Press.

Downing, J. D. H. with Ford, T. V., Gil, G., & Stein, L. (2001). *Radical media: Rebellious communication and social movements.* London: Sage.

Garnham, N. (1994). The media and the public sphere. In C. Calhoun (Ed.), *Habermas and the public sphere* (pp. 359-376). Cambridge, MA: MIT Press.

Góngora, A. (1988). Videos alternativas: Las imágenes de un país invisible [Alternative video: Images of an invisible country]. *Mensaje, 37*(368), 155-159.

ICTUS. (n.d.). *Distribución de videos* [Video distribution]. Santiago: Author.

Jakubowicz, K. (1995). Poland. In D. Paletz, K. Jakubowicz, & P. Novosel (Eds.), *Glasnost and after: Media and change in Central and Eastern Europe* (pp. 129-148). Cresskill, NJ: Hampton Press.

Keane, J. (1991). *The media and democracy.* London: Polity Press.

La campaña del NO vista por sus creadores [The NO campaign seen by its creators]. (1989). Santiago: Ediciones Malquiades.

Lasagni, M., Edwards, P., & Bonnefoy, J. (1985). *La radio en Chile: Historia, modelos, perspectivas* [Radio in Chile: History, models, and perspectivas]. Santiago: CENECA.

Mattelart, A. (1980). *Mass media, ideologies and the revolutionary movement.* Brighton, Sussex: Harvester.

McChesney, R. (1999). *Rich media, poor democracy: Communication politics in dubious times.* Urbana and Chicago: University of Illinois Press.

Munizaga, G. (1981). *Prensa sindical y universitaria* [Labor and student press]. Santiago: CENECA.

O'Neil, P. (Ed.). (1998). *Communicating democracy: The media and political transitions.* Boulder, CO: Lynne Rienner.

Ossandón, F. (1983). *Chile: Hay ruido de cacerolas en el escenario de las comunicaciones* [Chile: There is the noise of pots and pans in the communication scenario]. Lima: Centro de Estudios sobre Cultural Transnacional.

Otano, R. (1991). Jaque al pluralismo: La venta de *La Epoca* [Checkmate to pluralism: The sale of *Epoca*]. *APSI, 14*(401), 15-19.

Otano, R. (2000). Seis revistas, dos diarios y ningún funeral [Six magazines, two dailies and no funeral]. *Comunicación y medios, 12*(12), 42-51.

"Otro adiós de un medio" [Another goodbye to a medium]. (2003). *Primera Línea,* January 30. Retrieved May 19, 2003, from www.primeralinea.cl/p4_plinea/site/200301/pags/ 20030130153417.html

Paley, J. (2001). *Marketing democracy: Power and social movements in post-dictatorship Chile.* Berkeley and Los Angeles: University of California Press.

Reyes Matta, F. (1985). Periodismo independiente alternativo en Chile: Aportes en la reconstrucción democrática [Alternative and independent journalism in Chile: Contributions to democratic reconstruction]. In F. Reyes Matta & J. Richards (Eds.), *Periodismo Independiente: Mito O Realidad?* [Independent journalism: Myth or reality?] (pp. 12-38). Santiago: ILET.

Richards, J. (1985). *Periodismo independiente, bajo el autoritarismo en Chile: 1976-1984. Entrevistas con los directores* [Independent journalism under dictatorship in Chile: 1976-1984. Interviews with directors]. Santiago: ILET.

Rodríguez, C. (2001). *Fissures in the mediascape: An international study of citizens' media.* Cresskill, NJ: Hampton Press.

Rodríguez, J. (2001). APSI o las mil formas de combatir la censura de Pinochet [APSI or the thousand ways to combat Pinochet's censorship]. *Primera Línea* (August 24). Retrieved August 24, 2001, from http://www.primeralinea.cl/p4_plinea/ site/20010824/pags/19800101144415.html

Sahli, J. (1987, November 23). Existe una explosión de video [There is a video explosion]. *Ictus Informa.*

Segovia, E. (1990). *La historia secreta de "Cauce": Gloria, pasión y muerte de una revista de oposición* [The secret history of *Cauce*: Glory, passion and death of an opposition magazine]. Santiago: Pehuén Editores.

Sreberny-Mohammadi, A., & Mohammadi, A. (1994). *Small media, big revolution: Communication, culture, and the Iranian revolution.* Minneapolis: University of Minnesota Press.

Tironi, E., & Sunkel, G. (1993). Modernización de las comunicaciones y democratización de la política [Communication modernization and political democratization]. *Estudios Públicos, 52,* 215-246.

Tironi, E., & Sunkel, G. (2000). The modernization of communications: The media in the transition to democracy in Chile. In R. Gunther & R. Mughan (Eds.), *Democracy and the media: A comparative perspective* (pp. 165-194). Cambridge & New York: Cambridge University Press.

Waisbord, S. (1998). The unfinished project of media democratization in Argentina. In P. O'Neil (Ed.), *Communicating democracy: The media and political transitions* (pp. 41-62). Boulder, CO: Lynne Rienner.

Yañez, L., & Aguilera, O. (2000). *Radios comunitarias y de mínima cobertura: Diagnóstico del estado de situación en las radios comunitarias Chilenas* [Community and low-power radio: Diagnostic of the Chilean community radio stations]. Santiago: ECO.

CAPTURE WALES DIGITAL STORYTELLING
Community Media
Meets the BBC

13

Jenny Kidd

Digital Stories are short multimedia films of an often intensely personal nature that, since the 1990s, have been created around the globe. Digital Storytelling originated in the United States as an alternative media form taught in community workshops. The nature of the workshop set-up, the individual's use of biographical materials, and the software employed allow complete control of representation to remain in the hands of the storyteller and those stories produced as a result to be used in any way the maker deems appropriate. Often used as a form of therapy, workshop participants learn not only how to use the technology, but also a lot about their notions of self and ability.

The *Capture Wales* Digital Storytelling team was put together in 2001 with a remit to connect the British Broadcasting Corporation (BBC) more closely with communities, increase media literacy, and create content for an archive of the 'real' Wales. Since that time, workshops have been held throughout Wales with members of the public, creating films with nonlinear editing software for display on the web (www.bbc.co.uk/capturewales) and on television.

This chapter aims to introduce, contextualize, and analyze the *Capture Wales* initiative, detailing the history behind its inception and briefly outlining findings about participants gleaned from a three-year piece of empirical work carried out from Cardiff University. From the study, I am able to draw conclusions about the actuality of using such a form within an organization where public service is in competition with commercial viability.

It is inevitable that questions will be asked about the place of forms arising around an ethos of media democratization within public service broadcasters like the BBC. A look at the history of the Corporation highlights that periodically, projects encouraging and utilizing input from 'the public' have been commissioned, and that increasingly, they have allowed members of that public to take control of the technologies and thus their representation (such as *Open Door* and *Video Nation*).[1] None have done so, however, to the extent that *Capture Wales* has. Workshop participants provide the script, images, and voice for the story, but crucially maintain responsibility for editing the finished product as well.

But why would such a form be incorporated into the workings of an organization like the BBC? Is it indicative of the more cynical sounding process of containment (Fiske, 1989)? Does a project such as this represent the democratization of a corporation that since its inception has been accused of paternalism and elitism? Or does it demonstrate a Welsh public pushing at the boundaries of its 'role' as noncontributory sponsor of the Corporation (in all but money)?

Digital Storytelling exists at the most active end of the media spectrum, but has its roots in oral cultures; the employment of narrative to impart knowledge, assert power, and entertain. As a part of what has been called the 'restorification' of our culture (Lambert, 2002: xviii), the form allows individuals to express themselves through narrative in a similar way to those who have discovered genealogy, personal autobiography, and the Internet as means for placing order and significance upon events in their lives. This new form finds its virtual home in the information age and utilizes high-end professional software and hardware in the making of personal stories.

A BRIEF HISTORY OF DIGITAL STORYTELLING

The Internet has facilitated the origination of story not simply from one central point, but from a multitude of sources as many-to-many communication on an unprecedented scale. The intangibility of stories told in hypertext, on blogs, and through Digital Storytelling enables their 'recital' to a possible global audience and their authoring to be carried out by anyone with the means and the motivation. More so than in other narrative environments, in theory at least, we are able to impact upon stories told, and indeed tell our own (Murray, 1999). As a part of this shift, we have seen a growth in the telling of personal stories both to those within our geographical proximity and to those separated by time, space, and traditional barriers to entry in the mass media—specifically access to tools and resources. Digital Storytelling as a multimedia form in itself has emerged as a mechanism for telling personal narratives in a bid to explore or cement our humanity (the link between humanity and storytelling is made with great frequency in both popular and academic debate).[2]

The term 'Digital Storytelling' as an overarching banner for this work was first coined by Dana Atchley in the 1990s to describe "the art of using computers to create media-rich stories, and the Internet to share them" (Atchley, in *Story*, 1999). Atchley saw the benefit of combining personal stories, our archived lives (photos, home movies), and the tools being developed by software manufacturers in a bid to communicate or translate our experiences. His own experimentation culminated in *Next Exit*, a multimedia performance piece that inspired individuals to want to 'make' their own stories. The result was the origination of a series of workshops facilitated by Joe Lambert and later the Center for Digital Storytelling (CDS) in Berkeley, California.[3] The outcome of Atchley's work was thought to be the building of global communities of 'common concern' (Atchley, n.d.). However, as the scope and size of the 'movement' has intensified, the above definition has been subject to expansion. Practitioners of Digital Story now use a number of other avenues for story dissemination, including museum spaces and television sets (if the storyteller's wish is to display the work at all).

Joe Lambert says of the work of CDS, "we can use media, ironically, to overcome the more troublesome residual effects of our consumer media culture … we want to talk back, not on the terms of the governors of media empires, but on our own terms" (Lambert, 2002: xix). In so doing, Lambert asserts the importance of 'power' to any discussion of storytelling; defining function and influencing form from its very origins. In this new form, however (in theory), anyone can wield the power to tell narrative. The craft belongs not only with certified 'creative people' but with 'any people.' This is indicative of Nora Paul's 'taxonomy of terms' for Digital Storytelling, which emphasizes the development of active over passive usage models for information technologies:

> Digital storytelling [in general] has created a paradigm shift from traditional *storytelling* controlled by the content developer, to *storymaking* in which the user is actively involved with the content. (Paul, 2003: 15)

The capacity for living story through computers and the agency they facilitate is potentially life altering, especially in terms of the increasing frequency and intensity of arguments for a resultant democratization of the media. No longer should we need to depend on Sven Birkerts' "premise behind the textual interchange" (Birkerts, 1994: 163) whereby a 'wise,' established writer imparts something to the reader. We see the storyteller's power exerted not only at the production end to the value chain (Paterson, 2002: 137), but also, in the case of stories made in the U.S. workshop model, over any desired distribution and circulation. This philosophy rests behind the continuing work of the Center for Digital Storytelling and the work of Daniel Meadows, the individual who united Digital Storytelling and the BBC in the U.K. (starting in Wales).

Whether this level of control can be maintained when stories are facilitated by mainstream media institutions, however, is questionable and will be discussed after a brief look at previous BBC attempts to voice the stories of 'real' people.

EXTRAORDINARY PEOPLE BRING THE 'ORDINARY' TO THE BBC

The BBC has worked with communities and individuals to create 'real' content using 'ordinary' people since the 1930s. Above and beyond its mission to inform, educate, and entertain, the Corporation has sought to connect with the public through documenting the audience and giving them a voice, creating content and championing a means for increased confidence in the BBC, and providing mechanisms for feedback. For the BBC historically, there has been evident an ongoing concern with inclusion:[4]

> In all sorts of ways the early BBC stations sought to establish an interactive relationship with their audiences, a relationship in which the broadcasters did not set themselves up as superior to their listeners but treated them as equals and acknowledged that they were accountable to them. The stations tried to become integral parts of the local community, working with the civic authorities, with local cultural organisations, businesses, universities and schools, churches, hospitals and so forth. They were open to their publics. . . . The early stations worked at what we might now call community services: that is, they interacted with and became part of their local culture. (Scannell, 1993: 29)

However, our current broadcasting ecology brings new and intensely threatening catalysts to change. Spectrum scarcity no longer dictates services, digital technologies are being touted by some as the death knell for public service broadcasting, and discussions rage on the subject of national identity and 'Britishness.' This scenario is inevitably encouraging the BBC to position (or reposition?) itself as a truly democratic, responsive media Corporation working in conjunction with license payers to create content, exchange knowledge, share experience, and truly represent the people. At a time when audience share perhaps pales into insignificance in favor of 'reach,' community projects of the kind described below are invaluable to the future of the BBC.

It is notable, however, that these projects have often been the brainchildren of specific individuals, not simply the culture of the Corporation at a particular time. It is perhaps doubtful whether the philosophy of interaction at this level would ever have arisen, or have been seen as desirable, without them. The most notable examples of this type of interaction have been attributable to the exceptional nature of the few individuals who have taken it upon themselves to work with the public, in whichever format they deemed most appropriate (and coincided with the prevalent technological modes of the time).

Olive Shapley was one such example, a self-confessed liberal who spent time in the 1930s recording for broadcast on BBC radio the needs and desires of 'ordinary' people. In her autobiography, *Broadcasting A Life*, Shapley eloquently describes how, as a child, she felt caged not only by her God (being raised in a strict Unitarian family), but by her sex. Feeling that her means for expression was hindered by limitations imposed upon her from outside of her control, she became enthralled by what would later become known as the 'documentary style,' portraying lives and stories that were previously excluded; "As is probably clear, I was fascinated by the nuts and bolts of other people's jobs and lives" (Shapley, 1996: 53). It became clear to Shapley that the best stories were currently going unheard, as she says of her one time landlady:

> Her jokes seemed to me so much better, so much funnier, than the jokes the scriptwriters wrote, and her point of view on almost anything was worth having. She was certainly one of my inspirations for the experiments I was to make at putting real live people on radio. (Shapley, 1996: 36)

Given space to 'experiment' while working for the BBC in Manchester, Shapley made use of a mobile recording van and portable recording equipment in order to tape members of the public. In her autobiography, Shapley says "In a humble way, I think we were making broadcasting history" (Shapley, 1996: 50).

Previous to the recordings of Olive Shapley, the BBC had been accused of attempting to dictate culture, 'giving' it to 'the people,' and letting them have no part in the creative process. Shapley's work marked the beginning of a shift toward representing the 'real' audience and telling their stories, which was reawoken in the 1950s with *The Radio Ballads*.

The Radio Ballads consisted of eight stories to song commissioned by the BBC and created and produced by Ewan MacColl, Charles Parker, and Peggy Seeger between 1957 and 1964. The ballads were a collection of "sound pictures, impressions in fragmentary interlays, of song and speech and music and chanted chorus" (McCormick, 1999). They were not bound by the same editorial restrictions as other radio output, and with the use of original recordings of members of the public, retained a personal feel. This made the project risky—both in terms of audience reception and reception by others at the BBC. The producers, aware of the possible controversial nature of the project they were embarking on, felt it necessary to publish an introduction in the *Radio Times* before the first broadcast stating that "we took liberties with conventions you may cherish" (Aston, n.d.: 5). They were aware not only of the radical nature in terms of format and content, but that what they were doing could change the very nature of the radio experience.

It was initially intended that those recordings of 'real' people made during research would later be replaced by the voices of actors, but, as the first was put together, *The Ballad of John Axon,* the timing, words, and cadence of those who had been interviewed were impossible to manufacture. They had taken on a quality that could not be recreated—authenticity. Significantly, the result was that the Ballads would not be retold, but would remain in the voices of those who had lived, worked, and interacted with the subject, John Axon.

The Ballad of John Axon was aired on 2 July 1958 and began; "We present, the ballad of John Axon, the real life story of a railway man, told by the men who knew him, worked with him, and set into song by Ewan MacColl" (*The Ballad of John Axon*). The emphasis, it can be seen, was on the 'real.'

However, in the changing broadcast environment of the 1950s and 1960s, the BBC were facing competition from the commercial broadcaster ITV and, in part due to the rising expense of *The Radio Ballads* project, it was called to a close. There had also been controversy surrounding the last broadcast ballad, *The Travelling People,* which had been reacted to with venom by some within the BBC for its portrayal of 'outcasts,' angry and unsettling. It appeared that, as the producers had feared, some at the BBC were not ready for the voice of the people if this meant the voice of *all* the people. Charles Parker bit back, referring to the decision makers at the BBC as 'bland bastards' (McCormick, 1999). It seemed that "There was no longer a place in radio for the sponsoring of innovative art forms for a minority audience" (McCormick, 1999).

The most recent precursor to the work of *Capture Wales* was the *Video Nation* project of the 1990s (broadcast between 1994 and 1999). *Video Nation* was conceptualized by Mandy Rose and Chris Mohr (from the BBC Community Programmes Unit) as a project that would provide "an anthropology of Britain in the Nineties seen through the eyes of the people themselves," a "fusion between *Video Diaries* and *Mass-Observation*" (Rose, 2000: 174). It was also, rather self-consciously perhaps, a means for the BBC to counter accusations that their demographic representation of the British public was far from realistic; "The BBC needed to find new ways of reflecting the wide range of views, attitudes and lifestyles that were out there and the *Video Nation* project was one way of doing that" (Rose, 2000: 177).

During a period of research for the series, the team took camcorders to film prospective contributors and asked them why they wanted to take part. Rather revealingly, "Again and again they said that they felt misrepresented or unrepresented on TV" (Rose, 2000: 181). The extent of this underrepresentation they could not have predicted:

> We were surprised however and then nonplussed by just how many people said that they felt their lifestyle or community was not currently reflected. Gays, single mothers—sure, but also Christians, and Pagans, and housewives in Cheshire and bikers and bankers—everyone seemed to feel it. At first I wondered whether it was a symptom of what Robert Hughes has called the 'culture of complaint.' But seeing the material that people have recorded, I have come to realize that they were articulating something very significant

about the gap between television representation and lived experience. (Rose, 2000: 181)

The contributors to *Video Nation* were entirely responsible for the filming of their subject, and although not actually editing the finished 'shorts,' maintained ultimate responsibility for their content. They were given a right of veto, and nothing was to be broadcast without the seal of approval of the filmmaker. Even more so then than in the works of Olive Shapley and those behind *The Radio Ballads*, the BBC was passing responsibility for representation to (some of) the license payers—a more democratic, satisfactory and, it seems, popular way of producing media. *Video Nation* shorts, aired nationally on BBC2, received much acclaim within the press and to this day maintain a healthy web presence and a place within the public consciousness.

Thus, although those projects above coincided with and utilized relatively new technological developments, the level to which they gave voice and control to 'real' people was often attributable to the individuals who were behind their inception, or (as is the case for *The Radio Ballads*), the result of their interventions during the life of the project. They do however indicate an ongoing desire within the BBC to work with communities in the creation of content. They also highlight the difficulties of working for a corporation such as the BBC within what was an increasingly commercial media spectrum. Interestingly, even the most high profile of these projects created very little quantitative impact on the overall output of the BBC (hours-wise they were certainly not creating a wealth of content to air). Consequently, and conversely, they could therefore be considered to be very *small* steps in terms of democratizing the media. For those people who were involved in the creation of this content, however, both the members of the public and those working at the BBC, being involved with the project was perhaps of great personal significance. With this thought in mind, an analysis of the BBC's involvement with Digital Storytelling has been carried out with a view to establishing the mindset behind its inception and the ways in which participating has impacted upon members of the public. From a research base at Cardiff University, Wales, the author has been able to administer surveys, interview participants and BBC employees, observe workshops around the country, and carry out ethnographic work within the BBC itself. A total of 116 workshop participants were questioned about their experiences with *Capture Wales*, often as much as three years after the making of their story. It was the intention that this piece of doctoral research would both provide a narrative of the project, and begin to understand and locate measures for its impact.

DIGITAL STORYTELLING AND THE BBC

The *Capture Wales* Digital Storytelling project was initiated when Daniel Meadows, Lecturer in Photography and New Media at Cardiff University, on introduction by Professor Ian Hargreaves to BBC Wales, became the uniting force between the form and the Corporation. Since that time, monthly five-day workshops have been held throughout Wales.

Meadows' enthusiasm for the form and hopes for the medium come across not only in his writings, stories, and interviews, but also through *Capture Wales* workshops. He is of the belief that Digital Storytelling represents a nonretractable shift away from the traditional audience as a homogenous whole to be 'done to' by a media organization. Through the individual, personal process of Digital Storytelling "a story might be told unlike any that ever was told" (Meadows, n.d.).

Digital Stories in the *Capture Wales* model adhere to a strict form in terms of length and copyright restrictions; stories are roughly 250 words and 2 to 3 minutes long. These restrictions are imposed due to the technicalities of showing stories on the web, and in order to preserve what Meadows calls the 'multimedia sonnet' nature of the form (Meadows, 2004). Ten participants per workshop take part in scripting and storytelling sessions, capture images, learn how to use software, including Adobe Photoshop and Premiere, record a voiceover, and compile a finished film ahead of a screening on the final day that is attended by participants, their friends and families.

The workshop process (in the *Capture Wales* model) involves a number of stages of story development over a period of time approximating one month. Firstly, a public presentation is held in order to gather members of the community who are interested in taking part in a workshop. At this time, they are introduced to the form, the team of professionals who facilitate the workshops, and the ethos behind the 'movement'—that this is a technology whose application could alter the balance of media power as it is perceived (for the most part) by participants before the workshop.

Attendees are encouraged to submit a story idea to the *Capture Wales* team, and a decision is made on the suitability of applicants for the project. This is done through a number of means, and perhaps sits uncomfortably with the idea that 'everybody has a story to tell' (the *Capture Wales* tagline) and should be able to tell it through democratic and nonexclusive means. The practicalities of running (costly) workshops on the road, however, mean that only ten participants can take part in a workshop at any one time, and so, if a workshop is oversubscribed, judgements have to be made. When this is the case, I have witnessed a journalistic sense of balance being respected; thus, decisions are made based on diversity of the individual applicants, and even on their diversity of story ideas. For the most part, however, the process is what the Project Producer calls 'unscientific' (Lewis, 2003).

Whether by accident or by design, workshop participants are, on the whole, representative of the population of Wales. More so than in any other archive produced within the mainstream media, real 'Welsh' people of all ages are getting their opportunity to speak.[5] They are, however, only 'Welsh' insofar as they are united by their geographic location and the banner '*Capture Wales.*' They are not solely Welsh and English-speaking Welsh people (stories can be made in both languages). Non–U.K. and English-born residents are also well represented, with ethnic minorities making up a disproportionately high percentage of participants. This is good news in a media system where legitimacy is too often equated with official 'white,' and often male, voices.

The hope is that alongside previously unvoiced segments of the population, individuals will attend who have access to possible means for providing Digital Storytelling experiences to others. It is thus no accident that 30% of participants have come to Digital Storytelling through community and arts organizations, and 6% through educational institutions. This is hugely important to the long-term sustainability of the medium in Wales and a priority for the team.

Once a selection has been made, the ten participants begin the workshop process with a gathering where they are introduced to each other and can ask questions about the process they are to undergo. The first full day of the *Capture Wales* workshop is spent in a 'story circle' set up. This involves the participants and the team members engaging in a number of activities designed to loosen boundaries, free up the authentic voice of the storyteller, and boost confidence in storytelling ability. As facilitator Gilly Adams says, this is a vastly important aspect of the workshop that is "very much a process of sharing" (Adams, 2003). It is hoped that over the course of the day, through game playing and the creation of short, often ridiculous stories and scenarios, "we are able to get over some of the things, the cultural stuff that people bring into the room with them, which begins 'I can't write, I got two out of ten for this at school and I don't want to be made to feel that you are about to give me two out of ten'" (Adams, 2003). Thus, an informal leveling process is carried out that involves not only the participants, but all members of the BBC team (observation of the process is looked upon unfavorably and so all in the room are encouraged to take part). Here, the emphasis is not on the writing of stories—often there are people in the room who find this challenging or uncomfortable—but on their telling. By the end of the day, all participants will have aired their story idea to the rest of the participants, and through a 'group conference' approach to feedback (Kamler, 2001), the group is able to critique, and in some instances co-edit the final story idea. Work can then begin on scripting.

There is thus a full day devoted to story technique and exploration, a luxury that is not afforded in the U.S. workshop model, which is limited to three days. The day is commented upon in much of the feedback received as being the most rewarding and enjoyable aspect of the workshop.

The next day is given over to 'Image Capture' and involves each participant in turn bringing in images, artifacts, and any film they intend to use in his/her final story for digitization.

The following week a three-day production workshop begins. The first day includes participants' inauguration to the Apple Mac machines that will house their stories for the remainder of the workshop. A Photoshop tutorial lasting one hour is enough to give the necessary skills to participants in order to size images, carry out some simple image manipulation, and learn the crucial skills of file management. *Capture Wales* workshops are frequently peppered with people who have never before used computers and to whom they represent great challenges (for example, one participant who could only make sense of the technique for using a mouse as 'finger-on, finger-off'). This first day is also the time for record-ing voiceovers to accompany the visual elements they have gathered.

During the second production day, participants complete a Premiere tutorial (one hour) which teaches enough skill to enable the assemblage of a 'rough cut' of the film by the end of the day. They also have a further Photoshop tutorial (one hour) so that titles can be prepared.

The final day of the workshop involves the metamorphosis of the 'rough cut' into a story that can be shown at the final screening, which takes place in the afternoon. These screenings are, in the experience of the researcher, invariably emotionally charged events.

Following the workshop process, participants receive a copy of their story on CD (with all its various elements), and on VHS/DVD. They do not (more's the pity) receive an Apple Mac computer and the software to enable an ongoing relationship with the medium. If they want this kind of a relationship, they will have to seek it out themselves. For the most part however, this is not the case.

Alternative media forms are notoriously underresearched from a user per-spective (as acknowledged by Couldry, 2000a, and Downing, 2001), and, when research is carried out, the results can be disheartening. When looking at the uses made of *Capture Wales* stories and ongoing use of the technology, there is evi-dence of reluctance, or inability, of participants to go on and reproduce the expe-rience in the 'real' world (that is, outside of the workshop environment). This is in part due to lack of access to the tools of production, and for some, is attribut-able to a feeling that they are privileged, a lucky few (as indeed they might be) who have received a one-time opportunity to tell a story that fulfils some kind of therapeutic or cathartic function:[6]

> Telling my story felt as though I had lifted a heavy burden from my back. The slate was clean and I could move on. That period of my life now had a line drawn under it.

> In a way I won't go into detail over, it has helped to lay a personal ghost.

> I feel I have left something which will still be here for others to see long after I'm gone.

> I will always be grateful to BBC Wales for the opportunity to lose my inhibi-tions about my poor English and spelling and get on with telling a story.

For these and other reasons, it is often indicated that the workshop process is of ongoing significance to the participant (79% thought the experience would have a lasting effect on them). Although not representative of the impact of telling a story for all participants, there are individual instances where the making of the story *has* been a life-changing experience.

Frequently, this is because of changing work practices as a result of taking part, including three workshop participants who have gone on to get jobs with the BBC. In one instance, the storyteller, a community artist without the desire or necessary educational background to work for the BBC, now works full time on the *Capture Wales* team as a workshop facilitator. In his own words, one can't 'get more lasting than that.' Others have gone on to use Digital Storytelling within their current work practice; examples including an arts development officer for a local council who provides Digital Storytelling opportunities for local residents, disability and mental health charities, and at least two instances of teachers going on to use the work in their institutions.

However, there are also instances where, for much more personal reasons, the making of the story has empowered individuals. It has greatly helped some to increase their confidence, and as a result of this, enabled positive change. One participant professed that "Without a doubt it [making the story] has changed my life. I went out and got myself a grant and set up my own project" in a bid to aid voluntary organizations to promote themselves through multimedia. An elderly couple who anticipated that the technology would be their 'Achilles heel' during the workshop, as computers were new to them, have been able to remain in e-mail contact throughout her six month visit to China, a triumph they feel is attributable to the workshop process. Another participant felt the impact of making her story ricochet through her family. For her, the 'emotional gain' was huge, but also, her husband, who had not played his guitar since a family bereavement (the subject of the story), wrote and played a song for the story's soundtrack. Since that time he has set up a recording studio and continues to play.

For some, then, the empowering potential of the medium is achieved, even if their relationships with the mainstream media remain unchanged. This individual empowerment is, according to the research, more common than empowerment of whole groups or institutions working for social or political change. The ways in which stories are catalogued on the project website tend to reflect this and remain fairly neutral: challenge, community, family, memory, and passion. There is no specific area collating stories relating to the more contentious topics of nation, myth, or language, for example, even though there are certainly stories that would fall under those headings.[7]

Respondents generally talk of their involvement with Digital Storytelling not in terms of an ongoing relationship, but as a 'thing' or an 'it,' one story that has been brought to light through *Capture Wales*. It is perhaps of no great surprise then that given the chance to tell one story, and only one, the opportunity is often taken to communicate a story that will not only 'self-medicate' but also help others in similar situations come to rational and rewarding decisions about their future:

I feel that if my story gives just one victim, man or woman, the courage and incentive to get out of a similar situation and turn their lives around too, then my story will not have been made in vain.

If my story can help anyone to come to terms with their depression, then it has been well worthwhile.

I hope this film will give people like me the inspiration to kick the habit.

I wanted to tell this story in the hope that it might inspire people and make them realize that life is there for the taking.

The focus of my story is not looking back reminiscing, but look forward. . . . I can't change my past, but I can let it have a positive effect on my own and my children's future.

Couldry recognizes the nature of this type of social process as rare, often a one-off interaction, but asserts that this "does not mean that it is insignificant" (Couldry, 2000b: 275). He does, however, assert that those members of the public who are involved tend to remain 'ordinary' people—that is, 'nonmedia'—who operate 'outside the media world' (Couldry, 2000b: 281). This is certainly the case for those stories made through *Capture Wales*. Although control over production remains in the storyteller's hands, the distribution and circulation of stories is the responsibility of the BBC. In this sense, it is debatable to what extent these stories have penetrated the media in actuality. The *Capture Wales* team have endured a struggle over the course of the project to find a home within the BBC's network output (on BBC1 or BBC2 nationally) that has yet to be resolved. Stories currently reside on the BBC website, are aired on BBC Wales' digital channel BBC 2W, and are occasionally shown on the regional news broadcast *Wales Today*. More recently, stories have been aired nationwide as part of *Your Stories*, an interactive 'red button' option from BBCi, but remain without a network slot available to all. It appears there is a reluctance to give stories network time for a number of reasons; the ferocity of competition for network 'space,' the attitude of some toward the 'quality' and content of the pieces, and an overriding attitude that positions online or interactive services as the natural home for content made in participation with the public (or 'user-generated content'). It thus remains the case that viewing is dependent on access to resources that are unavailable to much of the license-paying Welsh (and U.K.) public.[8]

CONCLUSIONS

The works of alternative media theorists (Atton, 2002; Downing, 1988, 2001; Rodríguez, 2001) allow us a framework for thinking about Digital Storytelling as an activity or form both inside and outside the BBC. Digital Storytelling does challenge the hegemonic norm that producing and consuming are polarized activities that can be only singularly identified with, in the same way that alternative or radical works of literature do. However, the involvement of the BBC appears to complicate the scenario and, through the work of John Fiske, could be seen to be a sinister act of containment—taking charge of an activity that has arisen outside of the media 'norm' in order to control its application. Conversely, it appears to be the case that the BBC has increasingly sought to incorporate the voices, opinions, and faces of the 'real' people who, through direct payment for public service or indirect funding of commercial media, have supported those very services that (for the most part) have sought to exclude them.[9] However, the BBC operates within an environment where the temptation appears to be for those very media that are heralded for their democratic potential to be used as a repository for those voices. These kinds of projects can thus become victims of the very regimes within which they were finally able to germinate.[10]

The reality is that our media system, designed to work with the freedoms and desires of the public in mind, has given way to one whereby power is very much out of the hands of that public (McChesney & Nichols, 2002). All that are offered by the media system are feeble attempts at gratification (Downing, 2001). The coming of new Internet and multimedia technologies was heralded as the dawn of a more democratic media where control would be dispersed and the public could be 'empowered' (Jordan, 1999; Murray, 1999; Paul, 2003). This is however a grossly simplified scenario and one that is not supported by the findings of the research into *Capture Wales*.

The research shows that those members of the public chosen to take part in the project *are* furthering their skills in a number of ways. However, by and large their long-term ability to make and distribute media is hampered by the perennial problem of access. Making one digital story as part of *Capture Wales* does not make a person a media producer and distributor in his/her own right until he/she has the means and the desire to go forth and make media independently. As Tambini says in *New Media and Society*, "As long as access to the new media is restricted ... it will be impossible to realize their democratic potential" (Tambini, 1999: 306). Building this type of democratic scenario for Digital Storytelling in Wales realistically requires continued interest and investment from the BBC in the name of public service until sustainable relationships can be built with partners who can provide that access (for example educational establishments, local council initiatives, and arts organizations).

Although partnerships are historically rare for a Corporation like the BBC, they are invaluable for projects that hope to engage the public in a long-term relationship of knowledge exchange. They would imply a commitment on behalf of the BBC to the form and the ethos and a realistic proposition in terms of training the public how to create and distribute media in a democratic way. The *Capture Wales* team is currently in the process of setting up such partnerships, having successfully aided the origination of Digital Storytelling projects in

Caerphilly (with the local council) and Wrexham (Yale College), but within a post-Hutton BBC, nowhere is there a safehouse.[11, 12] Until such time as ongoing partnerships are put in place, the BBC will be creating only 'content,' which it then offers up for very limited audience appreciation. Time, however, is a luxury seldom afforded to such experimentation within an organization that has been forced to operate in a media system that demands instant success (as is exemplified by the demise of the English Regions Digital Storytelling project in Spring 2005).[13]

Digital Storytelling will continue to have to fight its corner within the BBC. *Capture Wales* exemplifies the mainstream media acknowledging the possibilities for agency that the new media open up at the same time as they stifle that very agency by allowing its results limited air time and putting stories in a 'user generated content' catch all.

NOTES

1. Both initiatives of the BBC Community Programmes Unit in the 1990s
2. See Finnegan (1997), Fulford (1999), Murray (1999), Ong (1982), Sloane (2000) for examples.
3. Visit the work of Dana Winslow Atchley III at http://www.nextexit.com (retrieved February 11, 2007).
4. This maxim still exists at the heart of the BBC's Corporate mission (see www.bbc.co.uk), or the current BBC Charter Agreement, Department of National Heritage, 1996 (retrieved February 11, 2007).
5. Osmond (1995) and Cameron (1999) both agree that historically, representations of the Welsh within the media have been either stereotypical or entirely absent.
6. Nearly 50% of respondents answered that they had not used the technology since the workshop due to its cost or a lack of access, time, or confidence.
7. One reason why these would be seen as inappropriate is that stories would then fall into stereotypes of 'Welsh' concern, something that the project's director and creative director (Daniel Meadows) are keen to avoid.
8. In September 2006, figures show that 52% of Welsh households had access to the Internet (National Statistics, 2006). On digital television, the potential audience is much higher, with penetration in Wales at 80% by the close of 2005 (OFCOM, 2005). During the data collection period, however, the stories on digital television made little measurable impact in terms of audience figures.
9. See for example the conclusions reached in Allan (2004) and in the work of Article 19 (www.article19.org), retrieved February 11, 2007.
10. Such as the 'Girls, Girls, Girls' Channel 4 project in the 1990s, which had to change its approach midway in order to satisfy the channel's changing climate and priorities. See Tony Dowmunt's discussion 'Dear Camera … Video Diaries, Subjectivity and Media Power' at www.ourmedianet.org/general/papers.html.
11. *Capture Wales'* current community partners have their work displayed at http://www.bbc.co.uk/wales/digitalstorytelling/sites/sirgar/ (retrieved August 26, 2005).

12. The Hutton Inquiry into BBC news reporting in 2003 and the subsequent resignations of key personnel (not least director general Greg Dyke who was a known supporter of the Digital Storytelling project and of attempts to connect the BBC more closely with communities).

13. The English Regions *Telling Lives* project ran between 2002 and 2005 but suffered pressure from within the BBC to run themed workshops, involve themselves in internal competition to secure content on Network television, and to adhere to certain notions of 'quality.' It was commented on in interviews with BBC personnel that the 'risk-taking' culture of BBC Wales made a different level of commitment to the form possible. The English Regions stories can still be seen at http://www.bbc.co.uk/ tellinglives (retrieved February 11, 2007).

REFERENCES

Adams, G. (2003, November). Part 1–The story. Presentation to the International Digital Storytelling Conference. Cardiff: BBC Wales.

Allan, S. (2004). *News culture* (2nd ed.). Maidenhead: Open University Press.

Aston, L. (n.d.). *The radio ballads* [leaflet]. London: Topic Records.

Atchley, D. (n.d.). What is digital storytelling? Retrieved December 12, 2006, from http://www.nextexit.com/dap/dapframeset.html.

Atton, C. (2002). *Alternative media*. London: Sage.

Birkerts, S. (1994). *The Gutenberg elegies: The fate of reading in an electronic age*. Boston: Faber & Faber.

Cameron, K (Ed.). (1999). *National identity*. Exeter: Intellect.

Couldry, N. (2000a). *The place of media power*. London: Routledge.

Couldry, N. (2000b). Media organisations and non-media people. In J. Curran (Ed.), *Media organisations in society* (pp. 273-288). London: Arnold.

Department of National Heritage. (1996). Charter and agreement. Retrieved February 11, 2007, from http://www.bbc.co.uk/info/policies/charter/.

Downing, J. D. H. (1988). The alternative public realm: The organization of the 1980s anti-nuclear press in Germany and Britain. *Media, Culture and Society, 10*(2), 163-181.

Downing, J. D. H., with Ford, T. V., Gil, G., & Stein, L. (2001). *Radical media: Rebellious communication and social movements*. London: Sage.

Finnegan, R. (1997). Storying the self: Personal narratives and identity. In H. McKay (Ed.), *Consumption and everyday life* (pp. 65-112). London: Sage.

Fiske, J. (1989). *Understanding popular culture*. London & New York: Routledge.

Fulford, R. (1999). *The triumph of narrative: Storytelling in the age of mass culture*. New York: Broadway Books.

Jordan, T. (1999). *Cyberpower: The culture and politics of cyberspace and the internet*. New York & London: Routledge.

Kamler, B. (2001). *Relocating the personal: A critical writing pedagogy*. Albany: State University of New York Press.

Lambert, J. (2002). *Digital storytelling: Capturing lives, creating community*. Berkeley, CA: Digital Diner Press.

Lewis, K. (2003, December 16). Interview with author. BBC Wales, U. K.

McChesney, R. W, & Nichols, J. (2002). *Our media, not theirs: The democratic struggle against corporate media.* New York: Seven Stories.

McCormick, F. (1999) *The radio ballads:* A personal overview of the series. Retrieved June 19, 2002, from www.mustrad.org.uk/reviews/rad_bal.htm.

Meadows, D. (n.d.). What is digital storytelling? Retrieved December 12, 2006, from http://www.photobus.co.uk/dstory_pages/what_dstory.html.

Meadows, D. (2004, May 27). Interview with author. Cardiff University, Australia.

Murray, J. (1999). *Hamlet on the holodeck: The future of narrative in cyberspace* (2nd ed.). Cambridge: MIT Press.

National Statistics. (2006). First release: Internet access, households and individuals. Retrieved September 29, 2006, from http://www.statistics.gov.uk/pdfdir/inta0806.pdf

OFCOM. (2005). Digital progress report. Retrieved September 29, 2006, from http://www.ofcom.org.uk/research/tv/reports/dtv/dtu_2005_q4/

Ong, W. J. (1982/2002). *Orality and literacy: The technology of the word.* London: Routledge.

Osmond, J. (1995). *Welsh Europeans.* Wales: Seren.

Paterson, R. (2002). Television: A framework for analysing contemporary television. In A. Briggs & P. Cobley (Eds.), *The media: An introduction* (pp. 135-147). Essex: Pearson Education.

Paul, N. (2003). *Elements of digital storytelling: A taxonomy of terms and a lot of questions.* Paper presented to the II A20 COST Conference, Towards New Media Paradigms: Content, Producers, Organizations and Audiences, Pamplona, June 27–28.

Rodríguez, C. (2001). *Fissures in the mediascape: An international study of citizen's media.* Cresskill, NJ: Hampton Press.

Rose, M. (2000). Through the eyes of the *Video Nation.* In J. Izod, R. Kilborn, & M. Hibber (Eds.), *From Grierson to the docu-soap: Breaking the boundaries* (pp. 173-184). Luton: University of Luton Press.

Scannel, P. (1993). The origins of BBC regional policy. In S. Harvey & K. Robins (Eds.), *The regions, the nations and the BBC* (pp. 27-37). London: Mandarin.

Shapley, O. (1996). *Broadcasting a life: The autobiography of Olive Shapley in association with Christina Hart.* London: Scarlet Press.

Sloane, S. (2000). *Digital fictions: Storytelling in a material world.* Norwood, NJ: Ablex.

Story, D. (1999). Question and answer with Dana Atchley. Emotional branding through digital storytelling. Retrieved June 12, 2002, from http://webreview.com/1999/06_25/strategists/06_25_99_10.shtml.

Tambini, D. (1999). New media and democracy. *New Media and Society, 1*(3), 305-329.

ABOUT THE AUTHORS

Christopher Anderson is completing his Communications PhD research at Columbia University's Graduate School of Journalism. His dissertation examines current journalistic practices in Philadelphia, Pennsylvania, along with the knowledge claims embedded within those practices. With Michael Schudson he has published "News Production and Organizations: Professionalism, Objectivity, and Truth Seeking," in the *Handbook of Journalism Studies*, as well as additional chapters in a number of academic collections. Prior to graduate school he worked as a reporter/editor in all stages of the news production process with New York City Indymedia and *The New York Indypendent*, a local biweekly newspaper. He holds a BA in Political Science from Indiana University and an MA and MPhil from Columbia.

Tanja E. Bosch is a former Fulbright scholar who completed her Masters in Communication and Development Studies at Ohio University, focusing on community radio in the Caribbean. Her PhD, also at Ohio, was entitled: "Radio, Community and Identity in South Africa: A Rhizomatic Study of Bush Radio in Cape Town." The dissertation won the BEA Kenneth Harwood Outstanding Dissertation Award for 2003. She has worked on community radio projects with UNESCO, and with radio stations in South Africa, Jamaica, Trinidad and Barbados. She held the position of station manager at Bush Radio in Cape Town, Africa's oldest community radio station, upon return to South Africa. She is currently a lecturer at the Centre for Film and Media Studies at the University of Cape Town.

Rosalind Bresnahan (PhD, Temple University) is a Coordinating Editor of the journal *Latin American Perspectives* and in 2003 edited a two-part issue on the contradictions of neoliberal democratization in Chile. She lived in Chile from 1968 to 1972, a period that included the first two years of the Allende government. Since 1998, she has conducted research in Chile, interviewing media producers, distributors and policy makers, especially those active in the struggle to end the Pinochet dictatorship. She has published articles on Chilean media, presented her research at conferences in the United States, Europe and Latin America, and is writing a book on the role of alternative and grassroots media in the struggle for democracy in Chile from 1973-1990. She is retired from the Department of Communication Studies at California State University, San Bernardino.

Lisa Brooten (PhD, Ohio University) is an Associate Professor at Southern Illinois University Carbondale, College of Mass Communication and Media Arts, and a member of the advisory board of the college's Global Media Research Center. Her research interests include globalization and media; alternative, community and indigenous media; social movements; gender and militarization; human rights; and interpretive/critical research methods. Her research interrogates the ways in which gender, ethnicity, and patterns of discourse are used to perpetuate divisive media practices and content, and the work being done to counteract these trends. Her regional area of expertise is Southeast Asia, and she has recently completed research under a Fulbright grant in Thailand and the Philippines to develop a comparative case study of media reform and democratization efforts in these countries with similar efforts in Burma/Myanmar and the United States.

Antoni Castells-Talens (PhD, University of Florida) is a researcher at the Universidad Veracruzana, in Mexico. For the past fifteen years, Castells-Talens has been researching indigenous-language media in Latin America. He has presented his research at international conferences and has published several articles. Besides his academic work, Castells-Talens has reported for two daily newspapers: *Avui* (Barcelona) and *Diario de Yucatán* (Mérida). His interest in alternative and citizens' media transcends the academic field. He has directed a short, *Tu K'aaxal Ha'* (2001), and a documentary, *Ramon* (2003), which received the Best Documentary Award during the 2004 Cinerama Film Festival. Castells-Talens is a member of OURMedia, a global network of academics, activists, practitioners and experts on citizens' media.

Nick Couldry is Professor of Media and Communications at Goldsmiths College, University of London. He is the author or editor of seven books, including most recently *Listening Beyond the Echoes: Media, Ethics and Agency in an Uncertain World* (Paradigm Books, 2006) and (with Sonia Livingstone and Tim Markham) *Media Consumption and Public Engagement: Beyond the Presumption of Attention* (Palgrave Macmillan, 2007).

John Downing is author of *Radical Media* (1984, South End Press; 2nd substantially revised edition 2001, Sage Publications), and a number of chapters and articles addressed to alternative media and social movement issues. He also researches and writes on issues of racism, ethnicity and media (with Charles

Husband, *Representing 'Race': Racisms, Ethnicities and Media*, Sage Publications, 2005). He is English by birth and formal education, but has worked in the United States since 1980. Since 2004 he has served as founding director of Southern Illinois University's Global Media Research Center, where he is also involved in some comparative research initiatives on the Nigerian video and film industry ("Nollywood"), and on advertising billboards and 'race.'

Frédéric Dubois is a media activist and independent journalist. He wrote his Master's thesis on "Autonomous Media and the Internet" at the University of Quebec in Montreal (UQÀM). He has spent many years 'off the beaten track' living, traveling and writing in Africa, the Americas, Europe and India. He has taken part in several media projects such as CMAQ (Indymedia Quebec) and is co-editor of *Autonomous Media: Activating Resistance and Dissent*. The latest book he edited is called *EXTRACTION! Comix Reportage* (Cumulus Press, 2007).

Kerrie Foxwell is a lecturer at Griffith University Gold Coast. She was the senior researcher on the Australian Community Radio Audience Research Project (2004-2006). She is interested in critical discussions of community, culture and citizenship. Her research seeks pragmatic avenues to support and encourage community awareness and participation in policy making and the public sphere.

Susan Forde is a Senior Lecturer at Griffith University in Brisbane. She was one of three Chief Investigators (with Dr. Ewart and Associate Professor Meadows) on the qualitative study of Australian community radio audiences from which the chapter in this book is drawn. She conducted the first study of Australia's independent press sector from 1996-1999, surveying journalists and editors from a range of alternative and independent publications around the nation. She has been widely published in national and international journals on issues surrounding community and independent media, and media policy. Before moving into academia in 1998, She worked as a journalist with independent press organizations and indigenous newspapers in Queensland.

Jacqui Ewart has worked as an academic for twelve years and is now a Senior Lecturer at Griffith University. Her research interests focus on community media audiences and journalistic practices and culture. She has published more than 30 journal papers and is co-author of a book on professional writing. She worked as a journalist in community and regional media and in media relations roles for a decade, as well as working as a trainer for regional newspapers in Australia. Dr. Ewart has a PhD and a Masters in journalism and media studies and with her colleagues is working on research projects that involve community radio and community newspapers. She is currently co-editing a book on Islam and the Australian News Media to be published through Melbourne University Press in 2009.

Gabriele Hadl is a media researcher and activist. A former post-doctoral research fellow at the University of Tokyo Interfaculty Initiative in Information Studies, she is an Assistant Professor at Kwansei Gakuin University and coordinates the international Civil Society Media Policy Research Consortium (http://homepage.mac.com/ellenycx/CSMPolicy/). She participated in the WSIS (World Summit on Information Society) and is active in the OURMedia network, the CRIS campaign, IAMCR (International Association of Media and Communication Research) and the Japan Council for Citizens, Community and Alternative Media (J-CAM). Born in Austria, her parents' home movies eclipsed television in her childhood home, beginning a lifelong involvement in do-it-yourself cultural production, most recently Buy Nothing Day Japan (for which she created the Zenta Claus icon) and Indymedia Jp. She is greatly indebted to her late mentor, the media literacy educator and communication rights advocate Midori Suzuki.

Janet Jones spent fifteen years as a broadcast journalist producing BBC news and current affairs in London on strands such as *Panorama, The Money Programme* and *Newsnight*. She began a full time academic career in 2000 and is currently a Principal Lecturer at the University of the West of England. Her main research interests cover the reception of factual discourses in contemporary global television, the role of journalists in mediating democracy, and the study of the internet and the public sphere. Current work focuses on the role of new social movements and open source journalism in changing the way news is produced and consumed. Recent articles have appeared in *New Media and Society* and *Journal of Media Practice*. Her co-edited collections include, *Big Brother International, Media, Critics and Publics* (Wallflower Press/Columbia University Press, 2004) and *Understanding Peacock: The Genesis and Influence of the Peacock Report on UK Broadcasting Policy 1950-2004* (Palgrave, 2009). Her co-authored book, *Journalism Online*, will be published by Sage in 2010.

Dorothy Kidd began her career as a community video producer and media activist in Toronto in the early 1970s, and then worked at Vancouver Cooperative Radio, Wawatay Native Communications, and the Inuit Broadcasting Corporation in Canada. She now teaches in the Department of Media Studies at the University of San Francisco, and volunteers with Media Alliance and Labortech, among others. Her writing on the communications commons, and its relevance for understanding community radio and the global Independent Media Center Network (IMC) has circulated widely. Her larger research agenda concerns the role of grassroots media and social justice movements in social and political change, and includes fieldwork in the United States, South Korea, India, northern aboriginal Canada, and Latin America.

Jenny Kidd is Lecturer at City University London, in the Department of Cultural Policy and Management. In 2005, she completed PhD research at the

School of Journalism, Media and Cultural Studies, Cardiff University, taking a detailed case study approach to BBC Wales' Digital Storytelling initiative, *Capture Wales*. Her research interests include the culture industries, audiences and various forms of digital storytelling. Before commencing her doctoral research, Jenny worked on a community media project in the London boroughs of Camden and Newham under the banner of dktv (a different kind of television).

Andrea Langlois has a Masters in media studies from Concordia University in Montreal and is the co-editor of *Autonomous Media: Activating Resistance and Dissent* (Cumulus Press, 2006). Driven by a need to understand why autonomous media are imperative to social movements, her research has focused on deconstructing the relationship between social movements and mass, alternative, and autonomous media. As an activist, Andrea is involved in feminist and queer movements as well as the struggle for food sovereignty, and she has participated in autonomous media projects ranging from culture jamming to Indymedia, to community and pirate radio.

Kanchan K. Malik is an Assistant Professor in Communication at the University of Hyderabad (UoH), India. With a dual Master's degree in Economics and in Mass Communication, she worked as a professional journalist with *The Economic Times* for two years before settling for a career in academics. Her doctoral work at UoH (2000-2005) examined the politics of community radio in India. She has published research papers based on her empirical work that systematically engages with the processes of media interventions by non-governmental organizations for empowerment at the grassroots level. Her areas of scholastic interest include community media, communication research methods, print journalism, and gender and media. Her book (with Vinod Pavarala) published by Sage (2007) is titled *Other Voices: The Struggle for Community Radio in India*.

Royston Martin is a journalist and filmmaker with research interests in the digital media. He has reported on international conflicts including the Gulf War, and the collapse of former Yugoslavia. From 1994 until 1997 he lived and worked in Italy where he co-produced several short films including investigative documentaries into the prison lives of former Red Brigade members and the death of Pier Paolo Passolini. He is now a senior consultant at the Thomson Reuters Foundation and his book *Digital Culture Understanding New Media* was published by Oxford University Press.

Chido Erica Felicity Matewa is the current Director of Africa Women Filmmakers Trust. She holds a BA General Degree from the University of Zimbabwe, a diploma in Film Production and Directing from Kenya Institute of Mass Communication, a Masters in Education and the Mass Media, Msc. in Educational Research and PhD (University of Manchester-United Kingdom), which focused on the media and the empowerment of Communities for Social Change.

Michael Meadows started as a journalist in community media before moving into mainstream newspapers and television in the late 1970s. He worked in print and broadcast media for ten years before moving into journalism education. He has published two books and around 100 journal articles and book chapters in his areas of research interests spanning the media representation of Indigenous people, through journalism practices, to community media history and production. He is Associate Professor of Journalism at Griffith University in Brisbane.

Vinod Pavarala is currently a Professor of Communication and Dean of the Sarojini Naidu School of Performing Arts, Fine Arts and Communication, University of Hyderbad, India. He holds a PhD from the University of Pittsburgh and has taught previously at the University of Pittsburgh, Virginia Tech, Blacksburg, as well as at the Indian Institute of Technology in Mumbai. He was visiting fellow at the Shelby Cullom Davis Center for Historical Studies, Princeton University in 1998-1999. His areas of interest include communication and social change, community media, and popular culture. He has been a leading campaigner for community radio in India and is the founding member of the Community Radio Forum of India. His forthcoming book (with Kanchan K. Malik) is titled *Other Voices: The Struggle for Community Radio in India.*

Ellie Rennie is a Research Fellow at the Institute for Social Research, Swinburne University of Technology (Australia), working in the areas of media policy and community communication. In mid-2008 she commenced work on a three-year project, The Reinvention of Indigenous Media: Innovation, Expansion and Social Development, funded by the Australian Research Council. Her second book, *Life of SYN: A Story of the Digital Generation*, is due for release in 2009. *Community Media: A Global Introduction* was published in 2006 (Rowman & Littlefield). Ellie is involved in a number of academic and community associations, including the International Association of Media Communication Research, Open Spectrum Australia, OURMedia/NuestrosMedios and the Wesley College Institute for Innovation in Education.

Clemencia Rodríguez is Associate Professor in the Department of Communication, University of Oklahoma. Since 1984 she has researched citizens' media in different international contexts including Nicaragua, Colombia, Spain, Chile, and among Latino communities in the United States. Clemencia's publications on citizens' media include *Fissures in the Mediascape: An International Study of Citizens' Media* (2001); The Bishop and His Star: Citizens' Communication in Southern Chile (in Couldry and Curran (eds.) *Contesting Media Power. Alternative Media in a Networked World*, 2003); Citizens' Media and the Voice of the Angel/Poet (in *Media International Australia*, 2002); Civil Society and Citizens' Media: Peace Architects for the New Millennium (in Wilkins (ed.) *Redeveloping Communication for Social Change: Theory, Practice, Power*, 2002) and *Contando Historias, Tejiendo Identidades*. In 2001, together with Dr. Nick Couldry (Goldsmith

College) and Dr. John Downing (Southern Illinois University), Clemencia founded OURMedia/NuestrosMedios (www.ourmedianetwork.org), a global network of citizens' media activists, artists, advocates, and academics.

Juan Salazar is a Chilean anthropologist and videomaker living in Sydney, Australia since 1998. He holds a PhD in Communications from the University of Western Sydney where he is a lecturer in media studies and a researcher at the Centre for Cultural Research (CCR). He has worked extensively in a wide range of cross-disciplinary research projects including consultancies for government and international non-governmental organizations. He has written several journal articles and book chapters on media anthropology and more recently indigenous media in Latin America and is involved with several transnational advocacy groups such as OURMedia network and CLACPI, the Coordinadora Latinoamericana de Comunicación de los Pueblos Indígenas. He has produced and directed several documentaries, experimental films and video installations exhibited internationally.

David Skinner is an Associate Professor in the Communication Program at York University in Toronto, Ontario. He is co-author of *Mass Communication in Canada* (6th ed., 2008), and he has published a number of articles and book chapters on media history, media reform, and alternative media in Canada. He has also been active in the media democracy movement in Canada.

Laura Stein is an Associate Professor in the Radio-Television-Film Department at the University of Texas at Austin. She writes about communication law and policy, political communication, and alternative and public media. Her writing has appeared in numerous journals and books, including *Media, Culture & Society, The Communication Review, New Media & Society, Javnost/The Public, The Handbook of New Media, Community Media in the Information Age,* and *Radical Media.* Her first book, titled *Speech Rights in America: The First Amendment, Democracy and the Media,* explores the failure of neoliberal democratic theory and the courts to protect speech rights in US media. Dr. Stein began her career in the management, production, and distribution of alternative media, working with both *Paper Tiger Television* and *Deep Dish TV.*

Scott Uzelman is a Postdoctoral Fellow in the Department of Sociology at Queen's University where he is researching struggles to preserve or create commons in a context of intensifying capitalist enclosure. He has been involved in the media democracy movement for several years as a researcher with NewsWatch Canada at Simon Fraser University and as a founding member of the Vancouver Chapter of the Campaign for Press and Broadcasting Freedom. In 2002 he completed a MA thesis at SFU on participatory research he conducted with fellow media activists in establishing and developing the Vancouver Independent Media Centre.

AUTHOR INDEX

SUBJECT INDEX

LaVergne, TN USA
22 July 2010
190384LV00001B/82/P